AGRICULTURAL DEVELOPMENT AND
TENANCY DISPUTES IN JAPAN, 1870-1940

RICHARD J. SMETHURST

Agricultural Development and Tenancy Disputes in Japan,
1870 – 1940

PRINCETON UNIVERSITY PRESS

In memory of the Wiener sisters,
Helen Smethurst and
Amelia Blumenfeld

TABLE OF CONTENTS

vii

CONTENTS

PREFACE

LIKE most of us who first studied Japanese history in the 1950s and 1960s, I learned that the peasantry paid a heavy price as Japan modernized. We were taught that the Meiji government in the nineteenth century financed the creation of its military and industrial machine by the only means possible, an exploitative land tax, and that in the process Japanese peasants fell more and more deeply into debt even as the nation grew in wealth and power. By the 1920s and 1930s when Japan moved toward a vicious and ultimately disastrous war, the peasantry had fallen so deeply into tenancy, debt, and poverty that they rose up against their oppressors, the landlords. When poor farmers failed in this effort, they, simple, benighted men, fell prey to the nostrums of young army officers and the radical right, and thus played a role, albeit a passive one, in the road to World War II.

Even as I wrote my doctoral dissertation and then revised it for publication as *A Social Basis for Prewar Japanese Militarism*, I began to have doubts about this interpretation of the countryside. If rural people were suffering to the extent that we learned they were, why did more farm than city boys pass the army's conscription physical examination? How could one explain that a higher percentage of 20-year-olds in rural Iwate, one of Japan's poorest prefectures, passed their physicals in 1934–1935, years of "famine" in its region, than in Tokyo or the nation as a whole? But it was my experiences in the spring of 1969 that finally led me to attempt a reinterpretation of Japan's modern agricultural experience.

In May and June of that year, I interviewed fourteen former members of the Imperial Military Reserve Association, all of whom had supported themselves before World War II through tenant farming, and found them to be men who did

ix

not seem benighted or passive or easily manipulated or bitter at all. What I found instead were men, who, even in their sixties and seventies, worked hard, had positive ideas about their ability to control their own destinies and advance their own and their families' ambitions, and who looked back to the "poverty-stricken" 1930s with nostalgia. One of them, the late Fukada Hiroshi of Ōkamada Village in Yamanashi Prefecture, owned in 1969 a farm on which he raised 2,500 pigs. Fukada's family in the 1870s had been landless, but by the 1930s, when he took over the headship, it had become an owner tenant household; a few years before he died and left his farm to his son, Fukada had traveled to the American midwest and Europe to study foreign farming techniques. Unless I were to believe that the poor, benighted tenant farmers of the prewar era had, by some magical process, turned into the prosperous, enlightened entrepreneurs of 1969, which I did not, I found myself compelled to look more deeply into the modern development of the Japanese countryside. What I have found, as the reader shall see, is that the prewar Japanese tenant farmer had both a better standard of living and a greater sense that he could control his own life than most interpretations of rural society allow. In other words, I challenge the standard explanations advanced by both Japanese and Western students of the countryside.

Although I am, of course, responsible for whatever errors of fact or interpretation appear in this book, I want to thank the many people who have helped me in researching and writing my study of prewar Japanese rural society. To begin with, I am indebted to the works and assistance of two scholars with whose views to different degrees I do not concur. I have spent many hours reading the books and articles of Nakamura Masanori and Nishida Yoshiaki. Nakamura read and commented critically on a paper in which in 1980 I first wrote down my ideas about agricultural development and tenant farmer disputes. Nishida reacted to both that paper and this book's introduction; of the latter, he commented that although he did not agree with my interpretation, I had presented his views accurately. I also want to express my thanks to Professor Inoue Kiyoshi and the other members of his seminar on early Shōwa history at Kyoto University's Institute of Humanistic Studies. When I was enrolled in the seminar in 1974-1975, I benefited especially from the help of Professors Inoue and Matsuo Takayoshi.

I want to thank those organizations which have supported me financially during my many years of research and writing. I am indebted to the United States Educational Commission in Japan and the Japan Foundation respectively for the aid they provided me while I had a Fulbright research fellowship in 1974-1975 and a Japan Foundation research grant in the spring of 1984. I am also indebted to the Joint Committee on Japanese Studies of the American Council of Learned Societies and the Social Science Research Council, which supported me twice, in 1977-1978 and 1983-1984, and to the University of Pittsburgh's University Center for International Studies and Japan Iron and Steel Federation and Mitsubishi endowment funds, which provided me with small but timely grants of money over the decade in which this project was coming slowly to fruition.

A number of scholars have read and commented critically (often quite critically) on my work as it advanced from note cards to manuscript to book. I particularly want to thank Keith Brown, Michael Donnelly, William Hauser, Lillian Li, Hugh Patrick, Thomas Rawski, Julius Rubin, Stephen Vlastos, Ann Waswo, Jerome Wells, Kozo Yamamura, and Yasukichi Yasuba; I shall find it difficult to repay my colleague Robert Doherty, who read the manuscript at a time when I thought it needed one more revision and told me the time had come to send it off to a publisher. I am grateful to Russell Hannula, who assisted me in my statistical analysis. The staffs of a number of libraries also have given me extraordinary service. I want to thank especially those librarians who have helped me at the Harvard-Yenching Library, Hoover Institution East Asian Library, the Asian Division of the Li-

brary of Congress, the National Diet Library, and the Local
History Room of the Yamanashi Prefectural Library, and
among their staffs, Emiko Moffitt and Iida Ban'ya.

Finally, I want to thank those people to whom I have special debts of gratitude: my wife, Mae Smethurst, encourager
and critic; Bernard Knox of the Center for Hellenic Studies,
where I first began to write this book in 1980; my mentors
in Japan, Kamikawa Rikuzō and Morioka Kiyomi; my guide
to rural Yamanashi, Hattori Harunori; and my pig farmer
friend, the late Fukada Hiroshi.

AGRICULTURAL DEVELOPMENT AND
TENANCY DISPUTES IN JAPAN, 1870-1940

INTRODUCTION

JAPAN'S rural economy expanded dramatically between 1868, when that nation's modern government came to power, and the late 1930s, when World War II erupted. Between 1879-1880, the first years for which we have national data, and 1935-1939, real value of agricultural production[1] per farm worker increased by 3.3 times at an average growth rate of 2.1 percent per year. Between 1886-1888 and 1937-1939, real wages for agricultural day laborers, who made up the very poorest stratum of rural society, doubled, a growth rate of 1.3 percent per year.[2] Farm workers' wages grew two times (or more) faster in Japan than they had in England during a comparable period of industrial growth, 1781-1851.[3]

Both the government and the farmers themselves played a

[1] Real value of agricultural production equals cash income and value of crops consumed at home, adjusted by the rural consumer price index.

[2] *Chōki keizai tōkei*, Vol. 8, pp. 135-136; Vol. 9, pp. 146-147, 220-221; Kazushi Ohkawa and Miyohei Shinohara, eds., with Larry Meissner, *Patterns of Japanese Economic Development* (New Haven, 1979), pp. 293-295, 388. The beginning years for the calculations are chosen because of the availability of data.

[3] Peter H. Lindert and Jeffrey G. Williamson write in "English Workers' Living Standards during the Industrial Revolution: A New Look," *The Economic History Review*, Second Series, 36 (1983), p. 13, that real wages for farm workers rose 64 percent, at an annual growth rate of 0.7 percent, between 1781 and 1851. I write "or more" in the text because the question of whether English workers' wages increased during the Industrial Revolution is a controversial one, and some scholars think wages actually declined. See E. J. Hobsbawm, "The British Standard of Living, 1790-1850," *The Economic History Review*, Second Series, 10 (1957) and "The Standard of Living during the Industrial Revolution: A Discussion," *ibid.*, 16 (1963) for the declination position. See R. M. Hartwell, "The Rising Standard of Living in England, 1800-1850," *ibid.*, 13 (1961), and ed., *The Causes of the Industrial Revolution* (London, 1967), for advocacy of rising wages and standard of living.

role in this growth. The new Meiji government in the 1870s established orderly political, financial, educational, and technical institutions; encouraged literacy, agricultural research, experimentation, and entrepreneurship; and otherwise created a framework within which farm productivity could grow. Cultivators themselves, some of whom lived in regions with long histories of agricultural innovation and growth, committed themselves to the improvement of cultivating techniques and the enlargement of profits. This in turn allowed them to accumulate and invest capital and accordingly innovate and profit even more.

The exploration of new methods to increase productivity, in which officials and landlords took the lead in the nineteenth century, became an important concern of tenant farmers in the twentieth. Because of these efforts at expanding production, tenants by the 1920s had larger incomes and thus more capital, used more advanced farming techniques, were better educated and more cosmopolitan, and managed their farms more economically than ever before. These newly literate cultivators had become small businessmen who produced crops to take advantage of the expanding domestic need for food and foreign demand for raw silk and who no longer farmed simply to subsist. They made economic choices about what to plant by balancing the profits and dangers of cultivating more speculative crops like cocoons against the smaller returns but greater security of producing less risky foodstuffs like wheat, barley, and oats (*mugi*). Since the average farm household tilled 20-25 fields (and thus could be owner farmer, tenant farmer, and even landlord at the same time) and also had the opportunity for work outside of agriculture, the cultivator could organize a balanced portfolio of security, risk, and secondary work. In other words, the tenant farmer of the 1920s and 1930s made rational decisions in managing his farm and was no longer a prisoner to the dictates of custom, environment, and landlord authority. He was a farmer who managed his farm for profit, not a peasant who reacted to the initiatives of others.

4

When landlord-tenant disputes arose in the years between the two world wars after a half century of rural economic growth, tenants joined in, therefore, not to stave off poverty, as one might expect of peasants, but as small-scale entrepreneurs to increase profits and to better business conditions. Tenants joined together to negotiate collectively with their landlords, used various techniques such as the threat of non-cultivation of the landlord's land to pressure him to make concessions, and eschewed violence. Since almost all disputes (97 percent) ended in compromise or landlord defeat, the tenants gained reduced rents, more secure land tenure, better contract terms, and increased political power. The tenant movement allowed, as did chemical fertilizer, new seed types, better cultivating techniques, and written account books, tenants to rationalize farm management and increase profits even more. Moreover, it appears that tenants strove to better themselves economically and politically through the disputes while still recognizing their landlord's social predominance. We can interpret the disputes, therefore, as the tenants' pragmatic and reformist efforts to increase their economic and political opportunities rather than as radical attempts to overturn the customary rural order.

This explanation of the growth of tenant income and rationality both before and during the tenant movement era is not among the orthodox ones. Japanese scholars, who have written prolifically on both landlord-tenant relations and disputes, forward two basic lines of interpretation, both of which differ from mine. The first of these, the "pauperization-revolution" approach, can be traced to the work of Hirano Yoshitarō and Yamada Moritarō in the 1930s, and has as its current champion Nakamura Masanori. The second, the "middle farming" or "commercial production tenant farming" interpretation, was first advanced by Kurihara Hakujū during World War II, and has as its present advocate Nishida Yoshiaki, and in the west Ann Waswo.[4] Before de-

---

[4] Yamada Moritarō, *Nihon shihonshugi bunseki* (Tokyo, 1934); *Nihon nōgyō*

veloping my interpretation further, I would like to introduce in greater detail these two modes of analyzing agricultural change and landlord-tenant relations in the modern era.[5]

---

seisanryoku kōzō (reprinted, Tokyo, 1960); Hirano Yoshitarō, *Nihon shihonshugi shakai no kikō* (Tokyo, 1934); Nakamura Masanori, *Kindai Nihon jinushiseishi kenkyū* (Tokyo, 1979); for an English language version, drawn partly from Nakamura, see Mikiso Hane, *Peasants, Rebels, and Outcastes: The Underside of Modern Japan* (New York, 1982); Kurihara Hakujū, *Nihon nōgyō no kiso kōzō* (Tokyo, 1948); Nishida Yoshiaki, "Nōmin undō no hatten to jinushisei," *Iwanami kōza Nihon rekishi* (Tokyo, 1975), Vol. 18, pp. 141-181; Ann Waswo, "The Transformation of Rural Society, 1900-1950," *Cambridge History of Japan*, Vol. 6, *The Twentieth Century* (Cambridge, forthcoming). In this article, Waswo explicitly aligns herself with Nishida and the "revisionist" school.

[5] As some readers of my introduction will realize, the differences of interpretation which I describe here are part of a much larger controversy, the "debate over the nature of Japanese capitalism" (*Nihon shihonshugi ronsō*). As early as the formative years of the Japan Communist Party in the 1920s, two groups of Marxist economists, the *kōzaha* (Seminar faction) and the *rōnōha* (Farmer Labor faction), began a controversy which continued into the postwar era over the nature of Japan's economic development. On the one hand, the *kōzaha*, led by Hirano Yoshitarō, Yamada Moritarō, and others, argued that holdovers from Japan's feudal past prevented it from achieving a bourgeois revolution and warped its capitalist development so that a two-stage bourgeois-proletarian revolution would be necessary before the desired socialist era could be ushered in. To them, and especially to Yamada, who wrote extensively on agriculture, high rents, tenant subservience to landlords, and tenant farmer poverty remained because Japan had not escaped its feudal past. The *rōnōha*, on the other hand, guided by Yamakawa Hitoshi, Ōuchi Hyōe et al., wrote that the Meiji Restoration and its aftermath brought about a true bourgeois revolution; Japan's capitalist development, to them, was not unlike that of the advanced Western nations, and Japan need achieve only a proletarian revolution to enter the socialist era. To the *rōnōha*, high rents and restrictive landlord-tenant relations could be explained by the nature of Japanese capitalism, especially by the inability of the slowly expanding industrial sector to absorb excess agricultural labor fast enough. I have not framed my introduction in terms of this longstanding debate for two reasons. First, I concentrate on the ideas of two contemporary scholars, Nakamura Masanori and Nishida Yoshiaki, and, since World War II, the *kōzaha-rōnōha* differences have blurred. Second, given the length of even this note, I fear that a full-blown treatment of the debate would carry me far off my subject: agricultural development and tenancy disputes.

INTEPRETATIONS OF THE SOCIAL IMPACT
OF AGRICULTURAL DEVELOPMENT

Yamada argued in his book, *An Analysis of Japanese Capitalism*, published in 1934, that "middle farmers," that is small-holders who cultivated crops for the market and thus managed their farms as petty entrepreneurs to maximize profits, did not appear in Japan because inordinately high rents prevented farm households from accumulating any excess income above that needed to subsist. Modern Japanese rural society was founded on a base of "militaristic, half slave Japanese capitalism," farmers paid rents far in excess of European and American ones, and this led to "pauperization" (*hinkyūka*) and left no room for petty commercial cultivation.[6] The group of scholars who wrote *A Detailed Summary of the Land Reform*, a postwar analysis of the American occupation's land reform published in 1951, tied Yamada's conclusions to the tenant movement of the 1920s. To them, the rural poverty created by exploitative rents impelled "poor peasants to resist the landlord system"; their resistance took the form of unionization and acrimonious disputation. The movement was an angry, revolutionary attempt to sweep away an inequitable system.[7]

Few current students of landlords and tenant disputes accept "pauperization-revolution theory" without some reservations, but Nakamura Masanori comes very close. Although he agrees with Kurihara Hakujū that "to view tenant disputes as rising from the depths (*donzoko*) of poverty caused by the burden of high rents is an oversimplification,"

[6] Yamada, *Nihon shihonshugi bunseki*, pp. 186-188, 215. Yamada draws conclusions about rents in Japan, Europe, and the United States which his data do not support. To show that Japanese rents are higher than those in England, Scotland, Ireland, Germany, Italy, France, and the United States, he compares rents per unit of land. Since the average Japanese farm is much smaller, but much more productive per unit of land, recalculations based on rents per farm show rent in the various countries to be more or less the same.

[7] Nōchi kaikaku kiroku iinkai, *Nōchi kaikaku temmatsu gaiyō* (Tokyo, 1951), p. 59. Yamada himself was the principal author of this volume.

7

Nakamura goes on, as Kase Kazuyoshi has pointed out, to take a position not unlike that of Yamada and the authors of the land reform volume.[8]

Nakamura writes that, although the growth of rural capitalism in the Meiji period led to higher average incomes in the countryside, it also brought greater inequality in their distribution.[9] Landlords who through exploitative rents had crop surpluses to sell profited from increased market activity, but owner farmers who were required to pay high taxes, tenant farmers who were required to pay high rents, and owner tenant farmers who were required to pay both, suffered. Existing close to or at the margin of subsistence, owners, owner tenants, and tenants in bad years lived and planted by borrowing from landlords and merchant usurers. Many of the debtors, especially during the Matsukata Deflation of the 1880s, defaulted on these loans, lost the land they offered as security, and fell more and more deeply into debt and tenancy—or, worst of all, out of tenancy altogether and into the landless farm labor stratum. By the end of the nineteenth century, not only had tenancy increased dramatically, by over a million *chō* of land between 1873 and 1912 (20 percent of Japan's farmland), but also a new class of "parasitical landlord" (*kisei jinushi*), which did not farm itself, viewed its land as a capitalistic investment, and thus lived by exploiting the labor of its tenants, had arisen.[10]

In the 1920s, both rural poverty and the growing gap between the living standards of well-to-do landlords and impoverished tenants, together with exogenous influences like the Russian Revolution, Rice Riots of 1918, fledgling social-

---

[8] Nakamura, *Jinushiseishi kenkyū*, p. 227. Kase Kazuyoshi, review essay of Nakamura, *Rekishigaku kenkyū*, 486 (1980), pp. 59-67, 73.

[9] Nakamura, *Jinushiseishi kenkyū*, Chapter Three; Ōuchi Tsutomu, *Nōgyōshi* (Tokyo, 1965), p. 85.

[10] Nakamura, *Jinushiseishi kenkyū*, Chapters One and Two; *Rōdōsha to nōmin* (Tokyo, 1976), p. 45. Although there has been no debate among Japanese scholars over whether or not "parasitical landlords" existed, there has been a lively debate over when they first became the norm.

ist and communist movements, and urban strikes and labor organizers, created among Japanese tenant farmers what Nakamura calls a "rural proletarian mentality."[11] "Semi-feudal high rents," as Nakamura quotes Yamada sympathetically, "did not allow the accumulation of a profit and also cut into the farmer's necessary wages," that is, into that part of the household's budget which was allocated as "wages."[12] Tenant farmers had little room to develop commercial attitudes or seek profits because their balance sheets consistently indicated losses when one added in unpaid wages. Thus, during years of bad harvests and low crop prices, and often during good years as well, Japanese tenants behaved as Karl Kautsky said peasants in general did—they practiced "self-exploitation" (*jiko sakushu*). Because of low "wages," tenants invested less in current inputs like commercial fertilizers, worked longer hours to compensate for the concomitant lost productivity, and practiced frugality in food, clothing, and entertainment.[13] Accordingly, Nakamura strongly criticizes revisionist scholars like Nishida Yoshiaki of the "commercial tenant farming school," because Nakamura believes they do not include "wages" when calculating statistics to demonstrate that market-minded tenant owner and tenant farmers made profits.[14]

When tenant farmers in the 1920s discovered that they were not being paid wages commensurate with their production, Nakamura continues, they increasingly joined with urban laborers and radical intellectuals to challenge their landlords, and more generally to fight the repressive "landlord-capitalist-militarist-civil-bureaucratic-authoritarian emperor system." It was the tenant farmers' realization that they were "wage earners," their development of a "rural proletarian mentality," which is central to Nakamura's interpre-

---

[11] Nakamura, *Jinushiseishi kenkyū*, p. 244.

[12] *Ibid.*, p. 243.

[13] *Ibid.*, pp. 263-264; Ōuchi Tsutomu, *Nihon ni okeru nōminsō no bunkai* (Tokyo, 1969), p. 4.

[14] Nakamura, *Jinushiseishi kenkyū*, p. 246.

tation of the rise of the tenant farmers' movement in the 1920s.[15]

In the end, Nakamura writes, the tenant farmers' rebellion failed. The government, as the core of the "authoritarian emperor system," came to the aid of the landlords and used "premodern incentives" like rewards and punishments to crush the tenant movement.[16] Landlords relied on the police with their truncheons and infamous *Peace Preservation Law*, and the court system which allowed confiscation of the tenants' crops and other property; they also used the government to detach some tenants from the movement by establishing systems to mediate disputes and to underwrite low-interest loans to allow more well-to-do tenants to buy land. Under this two-pronged attack, Nakamura concludes (and I disagree with him both on the nature and the efficacy of the attack), the tenants' revolutionary assault on the landlords and the emperor system crumbled.[17]

But the tenant movement failed for another reason, according to Nakamura, and this he admits clearly with regret. Japanese tenants faced two ways in terms of social and economic class; they were both petit bourgeois and proletarian. To make this point, Nakamura quotes Ōyama Hatsutarō, a tenant union organizer from Tottori Prefecture whom he greatly admires. Ōyama wrote that "farmers have a two-sided character. As laborers with low levels of living, they can become socialists; as small landowners who produce for the market, they can become anti-socialists."[18] Nakamura thinks that in the early years of the movement tenant farmers followed their proletarian, socialist inclinations and fought their landlords tooth and nail, but when the government began to apply the "candy and the whip" in the late 1920s, the anti-socialist, petit bourgeois defensive side of their character

---

[15] *Ibid.*, pp. 244-246, 249; "Nisshin sengo keieiron," *Hitotsubashi ronsō*, 64-11 (1970), pp. 138-160.

[16] Nakamura, *Rōdōsha to nōmin*, p. 64.

[17] Nakamura, *Jinushiseishi kenkyū*, pp. 247, 253-257, 298-309.

[18] *Ibid.*, p. 234; *Rōdōsha to nōmin*, pp. 244-246.

won out and tenants chose harmony and compromise over confrontation.[19] As Nakamura wrote in an analysis of the effect of one piece of this candy, the *Tenant Dispute Mediation Law* of 1924, under the influence of the terms of this law, "tenants who had gambled their lives to fight the landlords in disputes now sought harmonious solutions based on the spirit of mutuality and compromise. In the end, tenants abandoned their resolve to cut themselves off from their customary authority and won nothing but partial victories from their landlords."[20] A promising revolution was ended by the tenant farmers' class vacillation as well as by the government's "skillful conflict management."[21]

As will become increasingly clear as I develop my arguments, I think that there are serious flaws in the "pauperization-revolution" approach to the rise and fall of the Japanese tenant movement. The view that the poor farmers got poorer as Japanese capitalism developed, even in the Meiji period, is much less certain than Yamada and Nakamura would have us believe. Regional and temporal analyses of the relationship between poverty and disputation do not demonstrate the expected correlations; as Nishida Yoshiaki points out, if Nakamura is correct, why was there not an upsurge of disputation during the depression?[22] Data on rural borrowing show that farm indebtedness expanded in good times and contracted in bad, a finding not in keeping with "pauperization" theory. Agriculture and Home Ministry records show little police or court intervention on the side of

[19] Nakamura, *Jinushiseishi kenkyū*, pp. 232-234, 247; Nakamura uses the metaphor the "candy and the whip," the Japanese equivalent of the English "carrot and stick," in describing the tactics used by the Homma household, a major landlord in northern Japan, in dealing with its tenants. *Rōdōsha to nōmin*, p. 69.

[20] Nakamura, *Jinushiseishi kenkyū*, pp. 301-302.

[21] Waswo uses the expression "skillful conflict management" in describing how the government dealt with tenant disputes in the late 1920s. Waswo, "The Transformation of Rural Society," p. 64.

[22] Nishida, "Shōnō keiei no hatten to kosaku sōgi," *Tochi seido shigaku*, 38 (1968), p. 25.

landlords, and may even indicate that the court system aided the tenants, not the landlords. Using this kind of evidence, I propose that owner tenant and tenant farmers, whose living standards clearly improved in the twentieth century, viewed tenant disputes primarily as efficacious reformist efforts to lower rents and better conditions of tenancy, and only secondarily as a means of seeking an abstract goal like "equity" or destroying an inequitable land tenure system. They certainly did not see the disputes' aim as the elimination of the private ownership of land![23] But before expanding my view of Japan's modern agricultural development and tenant farmer movement, we must also look at the ideas propounded by the scholars of the revisionist, "commercial production tenant farming" school, with whose point of view mine shows considerable affinity.

In the 1940s, the late Kurihara Hakujū pointed out two trends which challenged the validity of Yamada's "pauperization-revolution" concept of the tenant movement and led to the development of the "commercial production tenant farming" school. First, admitting that in the late nineteenth century there was a gradual polarization of landholdings between expanding landlords and increasingly landless tenants, he found that after the Russo-Japanese War this movement slowed. Kurihara discovered that from 1910 to 1940 there was a steady rise in the percentage of owner tenant farmers, those farmers who tilled both fields they owned and fields they rented, and, at the same time, a gradual decline in the size of holdings and number of large landlords; his statistics also show that from 1920 on there was a reduction in the number of pure tenant farmers as well. The percentage of arable land cultivated by tenant farmers neared its peak at the end of the first decade of the twentieth century, and in spite

[23] For use of the term "equity" as a tenant movement goal, see Waswo, "In Search of Equity: Japanese Tenant Unions in the 1920s," in Tetsuo Najita and J. Victor Koschmann, *Conflict in Modern Japanese History: The Neglected Tradition* (Princeton, 1982), pp. 366-411.

12

of slight subsequent fluctuations did not increase significantly after that time.[24]

Second, and even more important, Kurihara found trends away from both tiny farms and large estates, and toward middle-sized farms beginning in the early twentieth century. He pointed out that from 1908 through 1939, the number of farms between 0.5 and 2 *chō* (farms outside Hokkaidō averaged 0.9 *chō* in this period) increased by 307,000 while the number of farms under 0.5 *chō* and over 2 *chō* decreased by 163,000 and 96,000, respectively; after 1930, the number of 0.5 to 1 *chō* farms also began to shrink, and the number of 1-2 *chō* farms grew even more rapidly than before. Moreover, Kurihara found that these movements away from large estates and toward middle-sized farms took place with only slight variations in regions of the country as disparate in degree of market intrusion and scale of cultivation as Kinki, one of the most highly commercial areas near Kyoto and Osaka in the west, and Tōhoku, the least commercialized area in the east. Kurihara called the 1908-1940 period in which the trends toward both an extension of tenancy and of large and small farms were halted or reversed as the era of "the trend toward the standardization of the petty farmer" (*shōnō hyōjunka keikō*).[25]

In essays on tenant disputes in Okayama and Kagawa prefectures, respectively, published in 1961 in *A History of the Japanese Farmers' Movement*, a monumental enterprise in col-

[24] Kurihara, *Nihon nōgyō no kiso kōzō*, pp. 81-85; *Gendai Nihon nōgyōron* (Tokyo, 1951), pp. 32-34.

[25] Kurihara, *Kiso kōzō*, pp. 3-7, 27-28; *Wagakuni ni okeru antei nōkasō no kenkyū* (Tokyo, 1942). Ōuchi Tsutomu, faced with this trend away from polarization of area cultivated, reaches two conclusions. The first, as we shall discuss below, is that imperialism reversed the trend toward the differentiation of rural classes. The second is that since farm size was relatively uniform among farm households, area of land cultivated must not be a good determinant of class distinctions. *Nōgyōshi*, p. 66. In other words, Ōuchi, faced with evidence that challenges the theory that capitalism ipso facto leads to class distinctions, rejects the evidence, not the theory.

lective scholarship, Kurihara connected his concept of the growth of petty or middle farming with the tenant movement.[26] Kurihara began by writing, as we have seen, that "to view tenant disputes as rising from the depths of poverty caused by the burden of high rents is an oversimplification."[27] "If the tenant class had been only poverty-stricken, disputes would not have occurred. . . . Rather, as tenant farmers' productive power increased and a commercial economy developed, tenants experienced some of the 'charms of farm management,' and for the first time had the power to fight the landlords."[28] In other words, the trend toward middle-sized farms and away from tenancy allowed tenants and owner tenants to become small-scale commercial farmers, and this gave them both the economic independence and the desire to challenge their landlords.

In his analysis of the tenant movement in Kōjō Village in Okayama, Kurihara added that the leaders of the local union tended to be "middle farmers," the upper tenants and tenant owners who profited most from producing for the market; thus, the Kōjō union sought positive, material goals (*monotori shugi*) and gave overthrowing the landlord system, because it was an unrealistic goal, a low priority. Kurihara concluded his discussion of the petit bourgeois nature of the Kōjō tenant movement in the 1920s by apologizing for the villagers. "Even though the nature of the Kōjō movement was petit bourgeois, it did not cast shame on the village; it was a progressive, advanced movement in its heyday."[29] Kurihara expresses here a sentiment one finds throughout the literature on the Japanese countryside, that somehow it is more praiseworthy to be proletarian than bourgeois!

In spite of his convincing revision of the "poverty-revolution" school, Kurihara and, following him, scholars like Kimbara Samon find it difficult to reject completely poverty

[26] Nōmin undōshi kenkyūkai, *Nihon nōmin undōshi* (Tokyo, 1961, reprinted 1977).

[27] *Ibid.*, p. 515. [28] *Ibid.*, p. 750.

[29] *Ibid.*, p. 572.

14

as a cause of tenant disputes in the 1920s.[30] Thus, Kurihara
in his analysis of tenant disputes in Kagawa wrote that "the
basic cause of the outbreak of tenant disputes in the Taishō
era was the growth of the tenant household's productive
power, and especially the development of wheat and barley
production, which gave the household a little power, and the
fear of possible future poverty because of the increasing commercialization of the farm economy. The sharp drop in the
price of farm products during the 1921 recession struck an
unprecedented blow at the commercially developed farm
households."[31] Although regional differences may have led
to the materialism of Kōjō and what seems to be something
akin to a theory of rising expectations for Kagawa, what one
also sees here, I think, is the difficulty many Japanese scholars meet when faced with data which indicate that rural Japan
may not have been quite as poor as they thought. Kurihara
and Kimbara seem to find it difficult to downgrade, much
less eliminate, poverty as a cause of disputes.

Nishida Yoshiaki, in a remarkable series of articles beginning in 1967, has bolstered and carried further Kurihara's
"petty farmer standardization line," although Nishida calls it
the "commercial production tenant farming" approach.[32]

[30] Kimbara Samon, "Taishō demokurashii jōkyōka no nōmin kumiai
undō no kōzō," *Nihon rekishi*, 210, 211.

[31] Kurihara, in *Nihon nōmin undōshi*, p. 748.

[32] "Kosaku sōgi no tenkai to jisakunō sōsetsu iji seisaku," *Hitotsubashi
ronsō*, 60-5 (1967), pp. 524-546; "Shōnō keiei no hatten to kosaku sōgi";
"Nōmin tōsō no tenkai to jinushisei no kōtai," *Rekishigaku kenkyū*, 343
(1968) pp. 1-16; "Reisainō kōsei to jinushiteki tochi shoyū," *Hitotsubashi
ronsō*, 63-5 (1970), pp. 89-105; "Yōsan seishi chitai ni okeru jinushi keiei no
kōzō," Chapter 3, Nagahara Keiji et al., *Nihon jinushisei no kōsei to dankai*
(Tokyo, 1972), pp. 219-318; "Nōchi kaikaku no rekishiteki seikaku," *Rekishigaku kenkyū*, special edition, 1973, pp. 159-174; "Nōmin undō no hatten
to jinushisei": "Shōwa kyōkōki ni okeru nōmin undō no tokushitsu," Tokyo daigaku shakai kagaku kenkyūjo, *Shōwa kyōkō*, Vol. 1 of *Fashizumuki
no kokka to shakai* (Tokyo, 1978); ed., *Shōwa kyōfuka no nōson shakai undō*
(Tokyo, 1978); "Jisakunō sōsetsu iji seisaku no rekishiteki seisaku," in Hayama Teisaku et al., *Dentōteki keizai shakai no rekishiteki tenkai*, Vol. 1 (Tokyo, 1983), pp. 257-283.

15

Drawing on both macroscopic national and regional data and microscopic analyses of several farm communities, especially Hanabusa in Yamanashi and Kanazuka in Niigata, Nishida demonstrates in various ways the growth of commercial farming among owner tenant, tenant owner, and upper tenant farmers between 1900 and 1940.[33] He writes that a majority of Japanese farmers were involved in profitable market activities by the 1920s, and that the "contradiction" (*mujun*, a ubiquitous word in Japanese historical writing) between this and the landlord system of land ownership with its high rents paid in kind led to owner tenant and upper tenant efforts to challenge the rural social and economic order through disputation.[34] Nishida shows increased marketing of rice and other crops by small-scale farmers.[35] He finds that the surplus grain that tenants maintained after payment of rent increased more rapidly than the rents themselves from one government tenancy survey to the next between 1908-1912, 1916-1920, and 1933-1935.[36] This trend, together with more widespread cultivation of relatively low rent, high income crops like mulberry and animal feed, led to the increased surpluses for marketing.[37] Nishida writes, following Ogura Sōichi, that although the compulsory rice inspection system instituted in most prefectures in the first two decades of the twentieth century benefited landlords and rice merchants in the short run, as virtually everyone who writes on the subject agrees, it also drew commercial tenants more deeply and advantageously into the market in the long run,

[33] Nishida points out that most students of landlords and the tenant movement do not take into account the importance of the transitional period between the rise of "parasitical landlords" in the nineteenth century and the landlord system's collapse in the late 1930s. He also finds more emphasis on the creation than on the collapse of the system. "Nōmin undō no hatten to jinushisei," p. 142.

[34] Nishida, "Nōchi kaikaku no rekishiteki seikaku," p. 160.

[35] Nishida, "Nōmin undō," pp. 144-146, 163-164, 179-180.

[36] Nishida, "Nōchi kaikaku no rekishiteki seikaku," p. 163.

[37] Nagahara, *Nihon jinushisei*, pp. 225-227.

as few scholars point out.[38] He also posits that in commercial areas where there was a high incidence of landlord-tenant conflict in the 1920s, like Kanazuka's Kita Kambara County, tenancy dropped sharply in the twentieth century.[39] And, finally, by analyzing the records of the H-household, a landlord-cultivator in Kanazuka, Nishida proposes that market-minded petty entrepreneurial farmers, to increase yields and thus surpluses to sell, rationalized their labor practices, spread more commercial, and especially more chemical, fertilizer, and used improved seed types.[40] Better farming methods led to increased profits and capital and to the growth of middle farming, and vice versa.

This sharp increase in commercial farming between 1905 and 1930 created two groups of tenant farmers, the owner tenants and upper tenant commercial farmers who tilled medium-sized farms (*shōhin seisan kosakunō*) and the subsistence farmers (*hammai kōnyū kosakunō*) who cultivated small ones.[41] Although there is some disagreement over the size of this commercial group, Nishida seems to view it as including a majority of the countryside. In his analysis of a prewar marketing survey taken in Yamagata Prefecture's Shōnai plain in 1935, Nishida finds that all the 2,594 tenant and owner tenant households sampled sold some rice, that 39 percent marketed twice as much or more than they consumed, and that 84 percent marketed more than they used at home. The remaining 16 percent, those who consumed more at home than they sold and who tilled small farms, made up Nishida's rural poor, the subsistence farmers.[42] Most of the rest fell into

---

[38] Nishida, "Nōmin undō," pp. 145-146, 155-156; Ogura Sōichi, "Niigata-ken beikoku keizaishi no isshaku," *Nihon nōgyō hattatsushi*, supplementary volume 2 (Tokyo, 1959), pp. 605-616.

[39] Nishida, "Shōnō keiei," p. 32.

[40] Nishida, "Reisainō kōsei to jinushiteki tochi shoyū," pp. 89-105.

[41] Nagahara, *Nihon jinushisei*, p. 315.

[42] Nishida, "Nōmin undō," pp. 165-166; Nishida's source, Tsumoyuki chihō nōrin keizai chōsasho, *Shōnai chihō beisaku nōson chōsa* (Tokyo, 1937),

the category of commercial production tenant farmer. In his analysis of Hanabusa, Nishida finds that 220 of 349 households (excluding 31 landlords and 34 non-farmers), 63 percent, those who tilled 5 *tan* of land or more, fell into his commercial category, with 71 households, 20 percent, in the poorer, subsistence class whose members cultivated 3 *tan* of land or less. (Fifty-eight households, 17 percent, tilled 3-5 *tan* and fell between the two groups.)[43] Therefore, it would seem that at the very least the 60-65 percent of farm households that fell into the 0.5-3 *chō* group of cultivators in Kurihara's national data represent Nishida's commercial tenants.[44]

When tenant disputes broke out in Kanazuka in 1922 and Hanabusa in 1930, both commercial and poor farmers participated, according to Nishida, but for different reasons. The upper tenants wanted lower rents as a step toward becoming owner farmers; i.e., they challenged the landlord system of land ownership. The poorer tenants hoped simply to lower rents a bit to relieve their poverty.[45] The better-educated, more enterprising commercial tenants provided the initiative and leadership in this joint effort to challenge their landlords.[46]

Nishida believes, as does Nakamura, that the tenant movement of the 1920s ended in failure and for more or less the same reasons. Government-landlord repression and skill at manipulating the tenants led upper tenants to abandon the movement once "minimal" demands for lower rents were met and systems were in place to allow compromised solutions in future disputes and the purchase of land with low

can be found in the library of Tokyo University's Social Science Research Institute.

[43] Nagahara, *Nihon jinushisei*, pp. 239-240.

[44] Ōuchi, *Nōminsō no bunkai*, pp. 168, 258.

[45] Nishida, "Nōmin undō," pp. 174-175; Nagahara, *Nihon jinushisei*, pp. 168, 251.

[46] Nagahara, *Nihon jinushisei*, p. 268; Nishida, "Nōchi kaikaku no rekishiteki seikaku," p. 160.

interest loans. In other words, they drew back from their challenge to the landlord system. Poor tenants, desperately afraid that they might lose their right to till the landlord's land altogether if they continued the struggle alone, also withdrew from the movement.[47] The basic difference between Nishida's and Nakamura's views of disputes is over the morphology of the tenant farmer class and movement. Although Nishida sees two classes, one more well-to-do and the other poorer, abandoning the disputes, Nakamura sees only one *poor* group, albeit with petit bourgeois and proletarian faces.[48]

Critique of the Standard Interpretations of the Social Impact of Agricultural Development

Although I find Nishida's analysis of twentieth-century agricultural development and tenant dispute causation convincing, I have several areas of disagreement which need to be pointed out. Although he has made a thorough and compelling critique of Nakamura and the "pauperization-revolution" approach to the tenant movement, one which Nakamura has tried but I think failed to refute, Nishida, like Kurihara before him, stops short of carrying his middle-farmer-commercialization analysis to what seems to me its logical conclusions.[49] To begin with, Nishida sees the tenant movement of the 1920s as a failure because at the end of the decade the landlord system still stood—or was reintegrated (*saihensei*), to use Nishida's term.[50] If one interprets the tenant movement as I do, as a gradualist, reformist effort to lower rents and better conditions of tenancy, that is, as a Bernsteinian evolutionary, not a Kautskian revolutionary,

[47] Nagahara, *Nihon jinushisei*, pp. 251-252, 264-265, 273, 317.

[48] Nishida, "Nōchi kaikaku no rekishiteki seikaku," p. 160; Nakamura, *Jinushiseishi kenkyū*, pp. 233-236.

[49] Nakamura uses long sections of his Chapters Three and Four in *Jinushiseishi kenkyū* in attempts to refute Nishida's arguments.

[50] Nagahara, *Nihon jinushisei*, pp. 269-270, 272.

movement, then it was a clearcut success. By the end of the 1920s, tenant farmers had lower rents and more freedom from landlord domination than ever before in history; by the end of the 1930s, the landlord system was in disarray. Nishida's analysis demonstrates the validity of this evolutionary interpretation, but he refrains from drawing this conclusion. What makes his comments about failure and reintegration particularly difficult to comprehend is that he goes on to write that from the middle of the 1930s until the end of World War II the landlord system collapsed so that by 1945 tenants had even greater freedom than in 1930.[51]

Second, I cannot concur with Nishida's view and, for that matter, the generally accepted view among scholars of Japanese tenant disputes, that a combination of landlord-government coercion and manipulation weakened the tenant movement in the late 1920s.[52] Not only do I believe that the tenants' evolutionary movement continued unabated in the 1930s, but also I think that its success in that decade can be attributed to the national government's forbearance and even aid. Japan's national and local governments invested over ten trillion yen in emergency relief, much of it for rural areas, between 1929 and 1936; these expenditures were 70 percent greater than the funds spent on the military in the same eight years.[53] The much maligned mediation system permitted

[51] *Ibid.*, pp. 314-318.

[52] *Ibid.*, pp. 251-252, 264. Waswo presents a concise description of government efforts at coercion and reform from above in "In Search of Equity," pp. 406-411. She argues that government policies prevented tenant unions from achieving their goal, equity, in the 1920s. If one sees the tenants' goal as incremental change rather than equity, then the government's efforts at reform through systems to create owner farmers and encourage mediation can be interpreted as advancing, not hindering, the tenants' cause. If one sees the national and regional officials of tenant unions as outsiders whom actual tenants often mistrusted, then government repression aimed at non-tenant leaders (Waswo's Yamasaki Toyosada, for example, was a non-tenant tenant union activist) did not necessarily hurt the tenants' reformist movement.

[53] Takafusa Nakamura, translated by Robert A. Feldman, *Economic Growth in Prewar Japan* (New Haven, 1983), pp. 237-238.

tenant farmers to continue to seek and receive reduced rents; it allowed them consistently to block the landlords' efforts at repossessing their own land to use it as they wanted. The failure of the police and the courts to intervene very often in support of the landlords allowed tenants frequently to violate their landlord's rights of private property and pay no penalty.

Third, Nishida writes about his poor subsistence farmers as if they lived at the very margin of existence. If landlords evicted these poor tenants, they and their families would have had no other resources. Even in the best of times, they, to supplement their meager livelihoods, had to send daughters out to work in silk and cotton mills or sons to factories in the city.[54] I certainly agree that there was poverty in pre-war rural Japan, but I also think that its extent and depth have been exaggerated. Poverty, after all, is relative. In the Tokugawa period bad harvests caused people to starve to death by the hundreds or even thousands; this one might want to call a "Dickensian state of poverty."[55] In the twentieth century, however, even during so-called "famines" like the one in Tōhoku during the early 1930s, people did not actually starve to death; rather, they ate other grains or, worse yet, radishes and sweet potatoes instead of rice. Members of the bottom stratum of rural society in the 1920s and 1930s were without doubt poor, but in their poverty they lived better than their late Tokugawa, early Meiji ancestors, and probably also better than a large percentage of the parents and grandparents of their commercial middle farmer neighbors. In fact, they had higher standards of living partly because of an opportunity they had which their predecessors did not: the factory. That they sent their children to work in cotton mills and silk filatures should not be interpreted as

[54] Nagahara, *Nihon jinushisei*, pp. 236, 275.

[55] I have borrowed this phrase from Roger W. Bowen, *Rebellion and Democracy in Meiji Japan: A Study of Commoners in the Popular Rights Movement* (Berkeley, 1980), p. 104. He uses it to describe conditions in the Chichibu region of eastern Japan during the Matsukata Deflation of the 1880s.

moves taken out of desperation; rather, we should realize that tenants perceived of these jobs as opportunities, as new and welcome ways of climbing further out of poverty.[56]

Finally, I disagree with Nishida's view that the major dilemma of modern Japanese agriculture is the continued existence even today of family farming on small farms. As Nishida writes in his study of Hanabusa, "the village's upper limit of farm size was about 1.5 *chō* (3.75 acres), and we can find no evidence for the development of farm management on a larger scale. This kind of narrow productive base, the tiny farm system (*reisai nōkōsei*), did not permit the birth of large-scale capitalist farm management, but formed the base which led to parasitical landlordism. When the landlord system was challenged in the 1920s, small-scale farming was not changed at all."[57] Nishida develops this idea in his study of Kanazuka. "Although tenant disputes lasted for a long time, in the end the union broke up and the tenants' energy was

[56] Nishida writes, on p. 171 of "Nōmin undō," that poor farmers were forced by poverty to send their daughters out to work for low wages in silk filatures and cotton mills, but he admits, on page 237 of Nagahara, that these jobs had not been available before the growth of capitalism and that they did provide secondary income for tenant households. Nakamura, in a long section in *Nōmin to rōdōsha*, pp. 81ff, describing the hardships endured by female silk filature workers, found himself forced to rationalize the answers given him by ten interview respondents who did not find work in the filatures particularly unpleasant. These Niigata women told him things like "poor people naturally went out to work in order to help their families. We did so happily" or "we overjoyed our fathers by working hard." Nakamura thinks that these women did not describe how unpleasant their experiences were because (1) they had beautified their dark experiences to make them bearable, (2) the bad memories had faded, (3) they did not realize how bad their experience had been because everyone had suffered equally in the filatures, and (4), as he admits reluctantly, life in the filatures may not have been as harsh in some periods as in others and these Niigata women may have worked in the mills in relatively comfortable times (p. 84).

[57] Nagahara, *Nihon jinushisei*, p. 271. Most scholars of Japanese agriculture share Nishida's views about small farms. See, for example, Asakura Kōkichi and Tobata Seiichi, *Nōgyō kin'yūron* (Tokyo, 1949), p. 17, and Hoshino Atsushi, *Nihon nōgyō hatten no ronri* (Tokyo, 1960), p. 27.

dissipated. Political authority and landlord pressure crushed the tenants. The breakup and the pressure led in the final analysis to the maintenance of fragmented, tiny farms even after the land reform established owner farms and interrupted what had been the main direction of Japanese agriculture, the dissolution of landlord ownership of land and the conversion of rent into capital."[58]

On the one hand, Nishida seems to believe that small, fragmented farms are inefficient. What he overlooks here, as Eduard Bernstein's revisionist Marxists pointed out almost three-quarters of a century ago, is that the benefits lost by sacrificing economies of scale may be more than compensated by the advantages of incentive.[59] As China's recent experience with the "contract responsibility system" shows, a farmer tilling a small farm from which he and his family can keep or market everything above what they owe the landlord or the state will probably produce more than a wage worker employed on a corporation's or even the state's larger farm, tractors and combines notwithstanding. Similarly, R. Albert Berry and William R. Cline, in a study of agriculture in various parts of the world, and Penelope Francks, in a study of Japanese agriculture, have concluded that large farms are less productive and economical than smaller ones.[60]

On the other hand, the maintenance of the "tiny farm system" interrupted what Nishida calls the "main direction of Japanese agriculture," or, in Ōuchi Tsutomu's words, as quoted by Nishida, "the tide of history." "The land reform," Ōuchi writes, "by eliminating landlords, democratized the farm village to a certain extent. . . . But the reform did not

---

[58] Nishida, "Shōnō keiei," p. 39.

[59] Peter Gay, *The Dilemma of Democratic Socialism: Eduard Bernstein's Challenge to Marx* (New York, 1952), pp. 203-204; Ōuchi, *Nōminsō no bunkai*, pp. 3-4; Ōuchi, *Nōgyōshi*, p. 84.

[60] Albert Keidel, "Incentive Farming," *China Business Review* (Nov./Dec. 1983), pp. 12-14; R. Albert Berry and William R. Cline, *Agrarian Structure and Productivity in Developing Countries* (Baltimore, 1979); Penelope Francks, *Technology and Agricultural Development in Pre-war Japan* (New Haven, 1984), pp. 64, 88-89, 199, 262.

free Japanese agriculture from the small farm form of agriculture. . . . This reform was thus an empty effort which
ran against *the tide of history*" (italics mine).[61] What does
Nishida mean by tiny farms interrupting "the main direction
of Japanese agriculture" or Ōuchi mean by small farms running "against the tide of history"? To understand this, and
also to appreciate one reason why Nishida places so much
emphasis on poverty, we must briefly introduce one of the
basic concepts of virtually every Japanese scholar who studies landlord-tenant relations: the concept of the "differentiation of the rural classes" (*nōminsō bunkai*).[62] To comprehend
why Nishida places such emphasis on the failure of the tenant movement when his evidence seems to indicate otherwise, we must also introduce another basic principle of Japanese scholarship: the labor theory of value.

Ōuchi Tsutomu, in a book entirely devoted to the subject,
gives what he calls the orthodox definition of the first of
these two principles, the concept of the "differentiation of
the rural classes," and I would like to translate from it at
length:

> The small-scale farmer, who possesses his own land
> and other means of production and who operates his
> own farm using only his own household's labor, exists
> universally at the onset of capitalism. . . . As feudal so-
> ciety breaks up and capitalism develops, farmers are re-
> leased from the feudal status system . . . and are forced
> to operate according to the principles of commercial
> production.
>
> As many people since Marx's time have pointed out,
> these small-scale farmers cannot adjust to a market
> economy, are ensnared by capitalist commercialization,
> and are inevitably divided by competition into distinct

[61] Ōuchi, *Nōgyō mondai* (Tokyo, 1961), pp. 254-255.

[62] Kautsky, following Marx, argued for the "differentiation of the rural
classes"; Bernstein and his followers argued against it. Ōuchi, *Nōminsō no
bunkai*, pp. 2-3; Gay, *The Dilemma of Democratic Socialism*, pp. 202-214.

classes. One group rises and "bourgeoisifies" (*burujioka suru*) and another falls, loses its land and other means of production and "proletarianizes" (*puroretariaka suru*). Thus, farmers who originally were small holders are no longer farmers. (I.e., they are either capitalists who own all available arable land or landless farm workers.) Capitalism inevitably "divides all of society into two large opposing camps—two large, mutually exclusive and opposing classes—the bourgeoisie and the proletariat" (Marx, *Communist Manifesto*).[63] . . . Under capitalism, this differentiation of the rural classes ought to move ceaselessly toward the two extremes . . . and Japan is no exception.[64]

Revisionist critics of Marx from at least the time of Eduard Bernstein have written that the social and economic realities of capitalist society do not match the theory—German society, according to Bernstein, became less, not more, polarized as the nineteenth century progressed—but Marx's followers, who are particularly influential among scholars of the Japanese landlord system, have used various explanations to deflect these criticisms. All but the most orthodox recognize the evidential challenge to the theory: small owner farms still exist over a century (or more if one includes several hundred years of market growth before the modern period) after the onset of capitalism; Kurihara's evidence shows a reversal of the trend toward landlord-tenant differentiation in the twentieth century; polarization and tenancy declined most in the most commercial areas, etc.

In spite of this and other contrary evidence that scholars like Kurihara and Nishida have advanced which challenge the validity of the differentiation theory, they have not used

[63] The line from the *Communist Manifesto* is my translation of a Japanese translation of the original German made by Ōuchi Hyōe, the famous *rōnōha* economist and the father of Ōuchi Tsutomu, and Sakisaka Itsurō. *Kyōsantō sengen* (Tokyo, 1951), p. 40.

[64] Ōuchi, *Nōminsō no bunkai*, pp. 1-2, 247.

their findings to reject the theory. Rather, students of rural Japan forward various explanations to demonstrate why, in spite of the data, the theory is still valid. Scholars like Nakamura Masanori who most strongly emphasize a more or less steady movement toward differentiation tend to depreciate the significance of the contrary evidence. Nakamura argues that Kurihara's and Nishida's so-called middle or commercial tenants did not prosper at all, but were only slightly less poverty-stricken than the subsistence tenants; in fact, he believes that Nishida errs in writing of a rural middle class at all.[65] Accordingly, Nakamura asserts that the observed trend toward middle-sized farms took place not because tenants ran their farms more efficiently than in the past and prospered, but because landlords managed their estates badly and accordingly had to turn land over to tenants for cultivation. He adds to this that one should not overemphasize the importance of this national trend toward middle farming since at the same time in several regions of the country differentiation continued unabated.[66] In other words, Naka-

---

[65] Nakamura, *Jinushiseishi kenkyū*, pp. 233, 243.

[66] *Ibid.*, pp. 268-269. Nakamura's statistical evidence to support his assertion about continued differentiation is an increase between 1928 and 1935 in the number of farm households tilling 0.5 *chō* of land or less in four regions, Hokkaidō, Okinawa, Tōzan, and Tōhoku, of a total of eleven regions nationwide. On close analysis, however, Nakamura's data are not strong enough to bear the weight of his contention. Hokkaidō, which shows the only sharp increase in tiny farms, contains but 3-4 percent of the nation's farm households; Okinawa, which has the third clearest increase, contains about 1½ percent. Tōzan, which includes Nagano, Niigata, and Yamanashi prefectures, has 7-8 percent of the nation's farms, but only a 1.2 percent increase in number of half *chō* or smaller farms; since the total number of farm households increased by 2.9 percent over the same years, small households as a percentage of total households actually declined between 1928 and 1935. Thus, only the remaining district, Tōhoku in the north of the main island, a region with 10-11 percent of the nation's farm households, shows a clear and significant growth of small farms; farms of 0.5 *chō* or less increased by 8 percent, while the number of farm households increased by 6.3 percent. But in Tōhoku as well as in Tōzan and Okinawa, *large* households decreased in number at the same time. In Tōhoku, farms of 3 *chō* or larger

mura argues that in reality there is no significant trend toward middle farming and away from continued polarization between large landowners and small tenants. Nevertheless, even Nakamura has to admit that this kind of separation of the rural classes differs from Marx's view of a capitalist-proletarian division. Nakamura writes that in Japan "we see not 'polarized differentiation,' but rather the nationwide division of rural classes into overwhelming *superiority* of land *ownership* and overwhelming *inferiority* of tiny-scale (farm) *management*" (Nakamura's italics).[67]

Other believers in the differentiation of the rural classes select various explanations to sustain the continued validity of the theory. Ōuchi Tsutomu argues that the trends away from polarization in both Bernstein's Germany and twentieth-century Japan originated because both societies entered the "imperialist stage of capitalist development." In fact, Ōuchi writes that he is surprised to find that polarization continued in Japan in the 1890-1910 period (before Kurihara's trend set in) since this is contrary to "the trend toward middle farming which one expects under imperialism."[68]

Others have added that the process toward polarization does not advance in an invariably forward movement. As

---

decreased by 15.8 percent between 1928 and 1935, while middle-sized, 0.5-3 *chō* farms increased by 7.4 percent. Thus, in Tōhoku (and in Tōzan and on Okinawa) small farms increased at the expense of large, not middle, farms, vitiating Nakamura's point. Finally, since the number of workers per farm household either declined absolutely or increased more slowly than the growth of small farms in all the districts except Hokkaidō, area cultivated per farm *worker* increased even while area worked per farm *household* decreased. The best that one can say in support of Nakamura's contention is that the trend toward middle farming slowed or reversed itself weakly (except in Hokkaidō, a frontier region which for a variety of reasons is exceptional) in some regions between 1928 and 1935. What strikes me in Nakamura's data is the absence rather than the presence of a strong movement toward differentiation of rural classes, i.e., that there are not more foreclosures of mortgages, etc., during the depression.

[67] *Ibid.*, p. 136.

[68] Ōuchi, *Nōminsō no bunkai*, pp. 158, 249; *Nōgyōshi*, pp. 14-15.

27

Japan proceeds along the different steps of its relentless development from feudalism through capitalism to socialism (I use the present tense because the process is said still to continue), from the stage of "primitive capital accumulation" to "industrial capital" to "imperialism" to "monopoly capital," there are times of greater and lesser differentiation.[69] Nevertheless, the overall process, like Lenin's "two steps forward and one step backward," is in the direction of polarization.[70] Another group, recognizing that landlords and tenants still existed in the interwar Japanese countryside when capitalists and workers should already have begun to appear (one finds few wage workers in the Japanese countryside, at most 5-6 percent of the rural population in the 1920s, 1930s and 1950s), argues that Japan's surplus of tenants drove up rents and made it more profitable for landlords to rent to tenants than to hire farm workers.[71] The obvious weakness of this position is that a labor surplus (and Ron Napier argues convincingly that there was not one), which scholars like Minami Ryōshin say continued well into the post-World War II period, should not only drive up rents but also drive down wages for agricultural workers.[72] Thus, the excess of tenants could just as easily be an excess of farm laborers and should not hinder the differentiation into capitalists and proletarians at all.

Even others have created a surrogate proletariat by using the term "semi-proletarian" (*hanpuro*) to define those tenants with holdings under 0.5 *chō* who held side jobs or sent household members out to work in factories.[73] Since many

---

[69] I recognize that "imperialism" is not a separate stage, but a phenomenon which should appear during the "monopoly capital" phase of development.

[70] Ōuchi, *Nōminsō no bunkai*, pp. 6-7, 137-139.

[71] *Ibid.*, p. 159.

[72] Minami Ryōshin, *Nihon keizai no tenkanten* (Tokyo, 1970); Ron Napier, "The Transformation of the Japanese Labor Market, 1894-1937," Najita and Koschmann, *Conflict*, pp. 342-365.

[73] Ōuchi, *Nōminsō no bunkai*, p. 169.

landlords invested in capitalist industry, these scholars find here some of the expected polarization in the countryside. This position fits in with Nishida's view that differentiation in the 1920s was not only between the rural haute bourgeoisie, landlords and owner farmers, on the one hand, and tenant farmers, on the other. In addition, he finds differentiation between commercial tenants, the petit bourgeoisie or *puchiburu*, and subsistence tenants, the *hanpuro*. The former were becoming increasingly prosperous, while the latter remained close to the subsistence level. If the land reform had not frozen Japan's system of smallholding in place after World War II, the trend toward commercial tenant and subsistence tenant differentiation, Nishida writes, would eventually have led to the inevitable capitalist-proletarian differentiation.[74] These are only a few of the Japanese variations on Marx's and Kautsky's theme of the differentiation of the rural classes.

The basic points that I want to make here are three. First, the belief that differentiation between rural classes took place in modern Japan is not one that has been arrived at empirically. Although there is evidence to demonstrate that the development of a capitalist market economy led to increased tenancy and thus differentiation in the Meiji period, there is equally compelling evidence to show that this trend was reversed in the twentieth century. (Moreover, I shall argue that the increases in tenancy in the nineteenth century came about more because of land reclamation and the liberation of farmers from feudal semi-bondage on large estates than by capitalists' foreclosures.) The belief in the trend toward polarization is based on the acceptance of a mode of analysis which precedes the accumulation of evidence, and this seems to make it difficult to abandon. Kurihara and Nishida have gathered empirical data which to me help negate the validity of this concept; nevertheless, they have eschewed taking that final step.

[74] Nagahara, *Nihon jinushisei*, p. 315.

Second, the process of the differentiation of the rural classes is not an idiosyncratic or haphazard trend. Its followers believe that this process takes place in all human societies along more or less similar routes until complete polarization between capitalist and proletarian classes, and between large, capitalist-owned estates and landless agricultural workers, has occurred. Because of the relentlessness and inevitability of this trend, the continued existence of small farms is not only undesirable because they are allegedly inefficient, as Waswo points out, but also because they are an affront to theory—they run against "the tide of history." If Ōuchi is correct that "Japan is no exception" to the validity of differentiation theory, today's small, family-operated farms demonstrate that the agricultural sector in one of the world's most powerful economies is still backward.[75]

Third, and finally, if differentiation is inevitable and universal, penury is too. The existence of a capitalist society which has no indigent people contradicts the scientific laws of history, and this contradiction may have led Nishida to emphasize growing poverty in the face of his own evidence which points in a different direction. In fact, the more orthodox Nakamura seems to recognize this "flaw" in Nishida's argument. In a page and one-half long footnote criticizing Nishida's analysis of tenant disputes during the depression of the early 1930s, Nakamura writes that the "key to Nishida's approach, the category of commercial production tenant farmer, lacks scientific rigor."[76] Although Nakamura does not define "scientific rigor," it is not unlikely that he means

---

[75] Many non-Marxist, as well as Marxist, scholars argue that, given the advanced agricultural technology of the 1980s, Japan's farms, which average about one hectare in size, are too small to be efficient. I agree, but do not think that, because Japan lacks immense agro-business or collective farms of several hundred hectares or more, its agriculture is backward. What Japan needs are not great "economies of scale," but larger small farms. The optimum farm size is not the largest, but that which is determined by the area small numbers of workers who benefit directly from increased productivity and profits can till efficiently with the use of the new technology.

[76] Nakamura, *Jinushiseishi kenkyū*, footnote 18, pp. 295-296.

Nishida's revisionist findings fall outside the confines of the scientific laws of historical development as reflected in the concept of differentiation of the rural classes. And yet, Nishida clearly sees himself within these confines.

The second principle central to most students of Japanese landlord-tenant relations is that of the labor theory of value. According to this concept, "variable capital," i.e., the wages of a laborer, has a smaller exchange-value than does the object he produces—that is to say, the product the worker makes can be sold for more money than he receives in wages for making it. This difference, the "surplus value" of the object produced, falls into the hands of the capitalist who controls "constant capital," i.e., the raw materials, tools, and other means of production aside from the worker's labor. According to Marx and his orthodox followers like Kautsky, the capitalist inevitably tries to increase this surplus and accordingly his profits, while the worker struggles to keep more of it for himself. Because, on the one hand, capitalists control raw materials and tools, and, on the other hand, workers are many and can be easily fired and replaced, expropriated surplus value gradually increases and the two classes are increasingly differentiated until finally the workers fall so deeply into poverty that they face a subsistence crisis. The ensuing revolution ushers in an egalitarian, socialist era.[77]

Although tenants are not wage laborers and, moreover, as owners of tools, current inputs like fertilizers and seeds, and often small parcels of land are potential petit bourgeois entrepreneurs, many scholars of Japan's rural society see them as proletarian—or at least semi-proletarian. Nakamura, as we have seen, for example, considers the proletarian mentality of tenant farmers, their desire for a day's wages for a day's production, as the main cause of the disputes in the 1920s. Thus, in his critique of Nishida's failure to calculate tenants' wages, Nakamura makes calculations using Marx's cate-

---

[77] Karl Marx, *Capital* (New York, n.d.), pp. 239-241, 707, 836-837.

gories of "constant capital" and "variable capital."[78] Still, while Nakamura here as above seems to view Nishida as having fallen into heresy, Nishida perceives of himself as operating within the broad outlines of the orthodox Marxist tradition.[79] Thus, he judges the tenant movement of the 1920s a failure because it did not sweep away the landlord system; in the 1930s, landlords still "expropriated" large amounts of surplus value, albeit less than ever before. The gradual reduction of rents, augmentation of profits, and improvement of tenancy conditions which began in the 1920s and continued into World War II were not, because they were evolutionary, adequate proof to Nishida of the tenants' success. Nishida, who has demonstrated to me the validity for Japan of Bernstein's evolutionary mode of analysis, in the final analysis cannot break with the revolutionary tradition.[80]

PURPOSES OF THE BOOK

I intend in this book to break out of the tradition within which Nakamura and even Nishida write, and to make two "heterodox" points.[81] First, the growth of a market econ-

[78] Nakamura, *Jinushiseishi kenkyū*, pp. 246-247.

[79] Conversations with Nishida in Cambridge, Massachusetts, June 22-23, 1982, and in Tokyo, June 5, 1984.

[80] Nishida, "Nōchi kaikaku no rekishiteki seikaku," p. 163. Kurihara also uses the term "revolutionary movement" (*kakumei undō*) to describe the tenant movement. *Nihon nōmin undōshi*, p. 176.

[81] The economist Kozo Yamamura, at a seminar presentation at the University of Washington on January 27, 1984, asked me how what I have to say differs from what non-Marxist economic historians like James Nakamura, Yamada Saburō, Hayami Yūjirō, Yasuba Yasukichi, and he himself write. Although I have drawn deeply on the ideas of all the scholars listed above, there *are* differences between my work and theirs. To begin with, we do not all interpret Japan's modern agricultural development the same way. Second, as one pages through the writings of these and other similar economic historians, one finds almost no discussion of social conflict. (Yamamura himself, an admirably eclectic economist, is an obvious exception.) The tenant disputes of the interwar years are intimately tied to Japan's economic development, but those who study the latter rarely discuss its effect

omy between 1870 and 1940 brought Japanese farmers, rich and poor alike, great benefits, even in the nineteenth century; moreover, contrary to differentiation theory, the more commercial the area, the greater the rewards. Second, the tenant farmers' movement in the 1920s *and* the 1930s, especially in the commercial areas where farmers were better off, was both entrepreneurial and reformist in nature and highly successful.[82] I shall demonstrate that the gradual commerciali-

---

on the former. Third, these writers pay little attention to income distribution (albeit, more than to conflict). Although Arlon Tussing, Alan Gleason, Yamada, and Hayami see improving rural levels of living in the late Meiji and Taishō eras, unlike the Marxists, they do not treat systematically the question of the effect of capitalist development on rural income distribution. One of the main purposes of my book is to analyze and relate these two questions. Finally, perhaps because I am not an economist, I believe I view the questions of agricultural development and its resultant rural conflict from a different perspective than the economists do. I attempt, by treating the effects of non-economic influences like education, literacy, and cosmopolitanism as well as economic influences like the expanding market, to explain the tenant farmer's way of thinking about his farm, his landlords, and his world. Although it might seem a bit presumptuous to compare myself to Le Roy Ladurie and his *Annales* compatriots, what I am concerned with is what they would call the tenant farmer's *mentalité*.

[82] Nishida, as we have seen, and Waswo make part of both of these arguments. He writes that a trend toward increased incomes for middle farmers began about 1908 after decades of sharpening differentiation between the rural rich and poor. She asserts that "desperate poverty" did not pervade the countryside, and especially the more commercial areas, in the 1920s; nevertheless, she, like many other scholars, believes that the Meiji land tax, which had to be paid in money, created a system under which many landowners lost much of their land through foreclosures and their inability to pay their debts, and that this led to a sharp rise in tenancy, i.e., a rapid differentiation of rural classes, between 1868 and 1908. "The Transformation of Rural Society," pp. 4-5; *Japanese Landlords: The Decline of a Rural Elite* (Berkeley, 1977), pp. 102-103. Nishida writes that tenant farmers involved themselves in disputes in the 1920s because of their "commercial" attitudes, but he also believes that these attitudes faltered during the depression. Waswo states that tenants "engaged in a wide range of goal-oriented activities designed to improve their lives and livelihoods" in the disputes of the 1920s; nevertheless, she also argues that the tenant movement waned from the late 1920s, and that the disputes which did take place in the 1930s

zation of agriculture and, simultaneously, the steady spread of technology, more sophisticated farming, education, literacy, cosmopolitanism, and political opportunity created increasingly prosperous and well-informed owner tenant and tenant farmers who challenged their landlords in the prewar decades as they managed their farms, on the basis of careful calculations of profit and loss. Unlike James C. Scott's peasants, who chose safety over risk, these Japanese small businessmen/farmers balanced the two and expanded production of speculative crops like mulberry on some fields while growing surer but less profitable crops like wheat and rice on others.[83] They made decisions about participation in tenant disputes in much the same way.

Admittedly neither the efficacy of the growth of commercial farming nor the rational motivations for tenant disputation were universal. Without question many farmers suffered during the Matsukata Deflation of the early 1880s, the post-World War I recession of 1920-1922, and the world depression of 1930-1934; certainly some frustrated, poverty-stricken tenant farmers exploded in angry outbursts against their landlords in the 1920s and 1930s. After all, real motivations for human activity, both within groups and within individuals' psyches, are often more complex than those attributed to them by historians. Still, it is my contention that the extent and adverse effects of the nineteenth-century polarization of landlords and tenants, on which writers as diverse as Nakamura Masanori and Kenneth Pyle have commented, and of the twentieth-century economic crises have

---

were more likely to be caused by poverty, and were less militant and more defensive than the earlier ones. "The Transformation of Rural Society," pp. 48, 58; *Japanese Landlords*, pp. 128-134. And neither, as I, see the tenants' motivation in disputation as one more entrepreneurial technique: if they wanted to increase their profits, they used new farming methods, better tools, more fertilizer, *and* disputes to win lower rents and more freedom to farm as they wanted.

[83] James C. Scott, *The Moral Economy of the Peasant: Rebellion and Subsistence in Southeast Asia* (New Haven, 1976), pp. 5, 13-55.

been exaggerated.[84] Recognizing these occasional, temporary (and often severe) setbacks, different regional speeds of commercialization and development, and unequal distribution from farmer to farmer of the benefits of the market, I believe that living standards for most rural Japanese households improved more or less steadily throughout the modern period.

It is also my view that the differences in causation between the "offensive" disputes of the 1920s, which Kurihara, Nishida and, to a lesser extent, Waswo see as having been driven by commercially minded tenants, and the "defensive" disputes of the 1930s, in which poor tenants, according to Nakamura, Nishida, and Waswo, tried to defend their fragile tenure and livelihoods against the landlords' efforts at taking their land back, have been overstated.[85] Although one does find during the 1930-1934 depression an increase in the number of disputes caused by landlord efforts to evict tenants, i.e., disputes where tenants are forced to "defend" their land, not only did the landlords fail more often than they succeeded in getting their land back, but also tenant initiatives to lower rents and better conditions of tenancy, i.e., com-

---

[84] Kenneth B. Pyle, *The Making of Modern Japan* (Lexington, Massachusetts, 1978), pp. 115-116; Ronald P. Dore, "Land Reform and Japan's Economic Development—A Reactionary Thesis," in Teodor Shanin, *Peasants and Peasant Societies* (New York, 1971), p. 381; Penelope Francks, *Technology and Agricultural Development*, pp. 65-70. See Kozo Yamamura, "The Meiji Land Tax Reform and Its Effects," in *Japan in Transition from Tokugawa to Meiji*, edited by Marius B. Jansen and Gilbert Rozman (Princeton, 1986), pp. 382-399, on other western scholars who have adopted this view.

[85] Waswo, *Japanese Landlords*, pp. 127-134; Nishida, "Nōchi kaikaku no rekishiteki seikaku," pp. 160-162; Nakamura, *Jinushiseishi kenkyū*, pp. 269-279. I write "to a lesser extent, Waswo" because she argues that the commercially minded tenants, her "middling farmers" (*chūnō*), were those who tilled between 1 and 3 *chō*, not between 0.5 and 3 *chō*, farms. Thus, the *chūnō* made up 25.4 percent, not 58.8 percent of the nation's farm households in 1908, and 28.9 percent, not 64.2 percent in 1937. "The Transformation of Rural Society," p. 13a. Francks, on the other hand, defines her middle group as made up of those farmers who tilled 0.5 to 2 *chō*; they were 58.7 percent of Japan's farm households in 1937; *Technology and Agricultural Development*, pp. 87-90.

mercial, "offensive" efforts, still held the center of disputational gravity.[86]

Most studies of peasant uprisings stress the participants' reactions to outside stimuli, their frustrations, as the spark which sets off their explosion. Whether it be the differentiation school's pauperization caused by parasitical landlords' exploitative rents, or the rising expectation school's temporary economic setbacks following a period of improvement, or the moral economists' landlord abandonment of traditional ways of supplying economic, social, and psychic insurance, scholars argue that peasants rise up only when something has been done to them or taken away from them. After all, it does not make sense for people to rebel when life is improving. And yet, I argue for two reasons that Japanese tenant farmers did just that—that the tenants' participation in disputes can be traced not to landlord actions or inactions, or to bad harvests and recessions, but to the tenants' awareness of their increasing ability to control their own destinies, which in turn can be traced to their improved livelihoods, educations, and political opportunities. What are these two reasons?

First, if one views Japanese tenant disputes in the light of peasant uprisings in Russia, Viet Nam, or even mid-nineteenth-century Japan, the tenant disputes of the 1920s and 1930s were not rebellions at all. Tenants rarely marched on the landlord's house and never put it to the torch or its inhabitants to the pitchfork. Violent confrontations and attacks on landlords were almost unheard of; between 1925 and 1941, police charged ten of 1,300,000 tenant participants (allowing, which we have no reason to do, that the police arrested only tenants) with arson, thirteen with murder or attempted murder, and 3,061 with assault, theft, property

---

[86] Even Nishida, who emphasizes a shift in the nature of disputes from those concerned with rent in the west in the 1920s to those concerned with contract problems and the continuation of land tenure in the east in the 1930s, writes that rent-related disputes continued to occur all over Japan in the 1930s. "Nōchi kaikaku no rekishiteki seikaku," p. 161.

damage, disruption of public order, or use of threatening language.[87] Moreover, the police rarely intervened in disputes, as we shall see in Chapters Five and Six, indicating both that the government did not feel particularly threatened by the tenant movement, and the absence of violence to which to react. The police arrested more people during two months of the urban Rice Riots in August and September of 1918 than they did in sixteen years of the tenant movement.[88] Rather than fight, tenants formed unions to negotiate with landlords to gain lower rents and better terms of tenancy and to exert their political power within the community. Eighty-six and six-tenths percent of all tenant disputes between 1920 and 1941 were settled by compromise, 10.4 percent ended in tenant victory, and only 3 percent in landlord victory.[89] Ten-

---

[87] Naimushō keihōkyoku, *Shōwa 7, 10, 17 nenchū ni okeru shakai undō no jōkyō.*

[88] The police arrested 8,253 people during the Rice Riots. Inoue Kiyoshi, *Nihon no rekishi*, Vol. 3 (Tokyo, 1966), p. 138. Police brought 8,538 charges in 16 years of tenancy disputes, but since we know that often people were charged with multiple offenses at the time of a single arrest, the number of individuals actually charged was as much as 60 percent lower than the 8,538 total. See Chapter Five, footnote 51.

[89] Waswo, in writing of the disputes of the 1930s, states that "in most (compromise) cases, tenants were deprived in some measure of their livelihood." *Japanese Landlords*, p. 133. She reaches this conclusion because of her view that the desire for the continuation of tenancy contract, i.e., to avoid eviction, replaced the desire for lower rent as the primary cause of disputes from the 1920s to the 1930s. While, according to her, compromise over rent gives the tenant something, compromise over continuation of contract takes something away from him and harms his livelihood. In fact, as we shall see in more detail in Chapters Five and Six, Waswo's view is probably incorrect; for two reasons, most compromise settlements did not hurt tenants, but continued to benefit them in the 1930s. First, even when contract problems became the primary causes of disputes, they represented only 48 percent of all disputes; rent problems in the 1930s continued to cause almost as many, 43 percent. Second, the scale of rent disputes seems to have been much larger than that of contract disputes. In 1935, for example, twice as many disputes took place in Tōhoku, where contract problems made up 72 percent of all disputes, as in Kinki, where rent problems made up 76 percent; nevertheless, only 7,516 tenants participated in the Tōhoku disputes

---

ant farmers held seats on 27-32 percent of all village assemblies in Japan from 1925 until World War II, although landlords had dominated local politics before 1920.[90]

What this suggests to me is that the tenant farmer disputes should not be studied as peasant rebellions because Japan had no peasant rebellions in the twentieth century. The disputes were rather generally peaceful efforts by tenants to form unions to negotiate collectively with their landlords. The tenants, as American and Japanese labor unions have found in recent decades, used the leverage provided by their increasing scarcity, their growing incomes, universal manhood suffrage, union solidarity in the face of the landlords, and a menu of tactics which included negotiating, picketing (demonstrations near the landlord's house), strikes (non-cultivation of the landlords' fields), and, as a last resort, disruptions of village harmony to improve their position dramatically.[91] The causes of disputes were not immediate outside stimuli like landlord refusals to lower rents in the face of poverty in recession years like 1920-1922, but the tenants' newfound awareness that if they dealt with their landlords peacefully, but collectively and firmly, they could improve their livelihoods through negotiations and compromise. The disputes began in the 1920s and primarily in the most commercial areas in western Japan because that is when and where this awareness came first.

Second, Japanese tenant disputes in the 1920s and 1930s

---

compared to 49,104 in Kinki. Nōchi seido shiryō shūsei hensan iinkai, *Nōchi seido shiryō shūsei* (Tokyo, 1969), Vol. 2, pp. 286-287, 295-296, hereafter abbreviated as *NSSS. Kosaku nempō*, 1935. Although one must be wary of the dangers of falling into an ecological fallacy, these data seem to support the view that even in the 1930s many more tenants were involved in rent than contract disputes, and thus that compromise solutions deprived landlords far more often than tenants of part of their livelihoods.

[90] *Kosaku chōtei nempō*, 1925-1926; *Kosaku nempō*, 1927-1939; *Nōchi nempō*, 1940-1941; Nōrinshō nōmukyoku, *Shōwa hachinendo chōson kaigi sōsenkyo ni okeru kosakuningawa tōsen no gaikyō*, p. 21.

[91] My colleague Julius Rubin pointed out to me the similarity between the tenant disputes and the contemporary labor movement.

were not explosive peasant reactions to outside stimuli because most Japanese tenant farmers were not peasants. As farmers in modern Japan benefited from the growth of a rural market economy, the concomitant development of better agricultural technology, the government's educational, and in the twentieth century, political liberalization policies (in 1919 the tax requirement for voting was lowered to 3 yen in direct taxes, and in 1925, universal manhood suffrage was established), they developed increasingly positive attitudes about their ability to control their own lives and manage their farms entrepreneurially.

Definitions of the term "peasant" are many, but whether one uses Edward Norbeck's broad view that a peasant is a cultivator with a fixed way of life who cultivates to feed his own household and lives in a community sharply separated from the rest of society, or Eric Wolf's commercial view that "the peasant does not operate an enterprise in the economic sense; he runs a household, not a business concern," or William Roseberry's more carefully delineated definition that peasants are "persons who, owning or controlling land and resources, produce primarily agricultural crops for their own subsistence, a portion of which is appropriated, directly or indirectly, by representatives of a larger economic system," most Japanese tenant farmers were not peasants in 1920.[92] By the dispute era, Japanese farmers' increased education, cosmopolitanism, and political opportunities allowed them to break with a fixed way of life and mix with the larger society. They developed techniques to increase their surplus product so that the surplus was no longer marketed to purchase products merely to support their households at the subsistence level, but became the basis for the beginnings of "capitalist accumulation." Peasants, according to Roseberry,

[92] Edward Norbeck, "Common-Interest Associations in Japan," Robert Smith and Richard K. Beardsley, *Japanese Culture: Its Development and Characteristics* (Chicago, 1972), p. 82; Eric Wolf, *Peasants* (New York, 1966), p. 2; William Roseberry, "Rent, Differentiation, and the Development of Capitalism among Peasants," *American Anthropologist*, 78-1 (1976), p. 47.

are members of a "precapitalist mode of production" who are forced to operate in a "capitalist mode of production," and do so at a disadvantage.[93] But most Japanese farmers in the 1920s, especially outside the northeast, were rural members of the capitalist mode of production who were able to function positively and successfully within it, and thus were not peasants. To borrow Wolf's definition of a farmer, the Japanese farmer in the 1920s ran "a business enterprise, combining factors of production purchased in a market to obtain a profit by selling advantageously in a products market."[94] He approached tenant disputation in the same rational way, to lower the costs of production and increase profits and capital.

The transformation of the Japanese peasant of the Tokugawa era into the Japanese farmer of the 1920s and 1930s is tied, needless to say, to the growth of commercial agriculture in the modern period. Without the intrusion of the capitalist market into rural Japan between 1870 and 1920-1940, peasants would still be peasants. The growth of the market, together with the government's various educational, technical, and political programs, and the growing commitment among a widening circle of farmers to innovation and change, stimulated this transformation.[95] By the 1920s and 1930s, even tenant farmers had developed positive attitudes about farm management and techniques to improve their standards of living. They used tenant disputes as one such technique. Rather than view the disputes as peasant outbursts, therefore, we should see them as we do the actions of, say, local American teachers' unions in September; tenant disputes took place when, at contract renewal time, union members decided to negotiate for pay increases and better fringe benefits. Thus, although we do see during the depres-

---

[93] Roseberry, "Capitalism among Peasants," p. 47.

[94] Wolf, *Peasants*, p. 2.

[95] This transformation from peasant to farmer had begun in the more economically advanced parts of Japan even before the end of the Tokugawa era, but speeded up dramatically after the Meiji Restoration.

sion years an upsurge of "defensive" disputes, especially in the northeast, which was poorer, less commercial, and probably more widely inhabited by peasants, commercial, offensive disputes still held sway in most other places.

In order to test these hypotheses about commercialization, changing attitudes, and tenant disputes, I intend to analyze both national data and materials from one commercial district, Yamanashi Prefecture, located just to the west of Tokyo, and, within that region, Naka Koma County, Ōkamada Village, and Kubo Nakajima hamlet in the central Kōfu Basin. Because of its proximity to Yokohama, the major egress for raw silk to Europe and the United States, Yamanashi took up sericulture and thus commercial farming as early as the 1860s. By the late 1920s, when American demand for silk stockings reached its peak, cocoons had become the prefecture's most profitable crop and had changed the lives of its farmers dramatically.

But the commercial activity and new attitudes which silk engendered did not uniformly help and change Yamanashi. The central regions like Naka Koma in the agricultural basin around Kōfu, the administrative center, benefited most from their proximity to silk filatures, capital, railroads, and highways, and from good agricultural land, water supply, and drainage; the remote, cold, and hilly areas like Minami Tsuru County near Mt. Fuji, which had been the center of the premodern silk industry, declined because of their topography, climate, and distance from modern facilities, entrepreneurs, and markets. And yet it was in the flourishing "six villages of eastern Naka Koma," of which Ōkamada was one, and in other villages of the central basin that Yamanashi's most active tenant farmer unions won the greatest concessions from landlords; in poorer areas like Minami Tsuru, where farmers had the prefecture's lowest standards of living, little anti-landlord activity occurred. The regional, like the national, data indicate that relatively prosperous tenant cultivators with confident, businesslike approaches to farm management were more likely to involve themselves in anti-landlord activity than their poorer compeers. These improving standards of living and their concomitant positive, entrepreneurial attitudes seem to have played a greater role in producing tenant disputes both in the 1920s and 1930s than did "pauperization," "rural proletarian mentalities," or tenant farmer reactions to outside stimuli.

ONE

Agricultural Growth in
Modern Japan

THE Japanese countryside underwent a striking transformation between the formation of a modern government in 1868 and the outbreak of World War II. The governmental policies which created schools, universities, banks, constituent assemblies, corporations, factories, technical centers, new opportunities for social and economic mobility and a host of other accoutrements of the modern industrial society had their impact on the village as well. Villagers' levels of living, education, literacy, cosmopolitanism, and farming technology improved, and their attitudes about the degree to which they could control their own environments and livelihoods matured remarkably. By the decades between the two world wars, rural Japanese, in this modern milieu, had metamorphosed from peasants into farmers.

The basic evidence which demonstrates this development is data on the growth of agricultural production presented in Table 1-1. Value added per farm worker in current prices increased by nine and one-half times, a growth rate of 4.2 percent per year between 1879-1880 and the last prewar decade; real productivity per worker grew by three times, at an average rate of 2 percent per year. The enlargement of Japan's farm production and productivity in a half century was as great or greater than that in France, Sweden, Russia, Austria, Belgium, England, Italy, Switzerland, and Germany in comparable stages of industrial development.[1]

[1] Hayami Yūjirō and Yamada Saburō, "Agricultural Productivity at the Beginning of Industrialization," Ohkawa Kazushi et al., *Agricultural and Economic Growth: Japan's Experience* (Princeton and Tokyo, 1969-1970), p. 111;

TABLE 1-1
Growth of Agricultural Productivity, 1879–1940

Year	Farm Value of Agric Product	Current Inputs	Value Added	Agric Workers (in 1,000s)	Value Added (per worker)	Rural CPI	Index of Productivity (per worker)
	(in millions of yen)						
1879-80	507	146	361	15,588	23.2	34.9	100
1881-90	429	101	328	15,606	21.0	31.6	100
1891-00	715	160	555	15,718	35.3	36.9	144
1901-10	1,208	253	955	15,894	60.1	54.5	166
1911-20	2,647	551	2,096	15,038	139.4	85.5	245
1921-30	3,714	747	2,967	13,718	216.3	125.4	259
1931-40	3,820	809	3,011	13,721	219.5	109.2	302

Calculated from *Chōki keizai tōkei*, Vol. 8, pp. 135–136; Vol. 9, pp. 146–147, 183–184; Ohkawa and Shinohara, *Patterns of Japanese Economic Development*, pp. 293–295, 388.

What is especially noteworthy about this modern enlargement in productivity is that it came after several centuries of steady agricultural development.[2] Even if one takes issue, as many economic historians of Japanese agriculture do, with James Nakamura's view that the Tokugawa growth was so great that Japan's rice output per hectare in 1878-1882, produced using manure and grass as fertilizer, far exceeded Korea's and Taiwan's in 1960-1961, produced using chemical fertilizers, there are good grounds to reject the idea of premodern stagnation.[3] Kozo Yamamura and Susan Hanley calculate that rice production, including that brought about through the cultivation of newly reclaimed fields, expanded by at least one-quarter of a percent per year between 1645 and 1873.[4] They and other writers have traced the expansion of the cultivation of cash crops, either food to be sold in

Paul Bairoch, "Agriculture and the Industrial Revolution, 1700-1914," in Carlo M. Cipolla, ed., *The Fontana Economic History of Europe*, Vol. 3 (Glasgow, 1973), p. 484.

[2] Susan B. Hanley and Kozo Yamamura, *Economic and Demographic Change in Preindustrial Japan, 1600-1868* (Princeton, 1977), pp. 69-90; Thomas C. Smith, *The Agrarian Origins of Modern Japan* (Stanford, 1959); William B. Hauser, "Some Misconceptions about the Economic History of Tokugawa Japan," *The History Teacher*, 16-4 (1983), pp. 560-583.

[3] Nakamura presents his estimates in *Agricultural Production and the Economic Development of Japan 1873-1922* (Princeton, 1966), p. 92. No matter which of his three estimates of yields one uses, high (3.38 tons per hectare), middle (3.22), or low (3.04), his 1878-1882 estimates are considerably higher than actual reported yields in Taiwan (2.53) in 1960 and Korea (2.75) in 1961. For the views of scholars who think that Nakamura's estimates of yields for early and middle Meiji farmers are too high, see Hayami and Yamada, "Agricultural Productivity," pp. 107-108; Henry Rosovsky, "Rumbles in the Ricefields: Professor Nakamura vs. the Official Statistics," *Journal of Asian Studies*, 27-2 (1968), pp. 347-360; Ohkawa Kazushi, "Phases of Agricultural Development and Economic Growth," in Ohkawa, ed., *Agricultural and Economic Growth*, p. 8; Waswo, "The Transformation of Rural Society," pp. 34-36.

[4] Hanley and Yamamura, *Economic and Demographic Change*, pp. 70-74. Thus, rice output was 75 percent higher in 1873 than in 1645. By way of comparison, rice output doubled between 1874 and the 1930s. *Chōki keizai tōkei*, Vol. 9, pp. 166-168.

castle towns or raw materials to be fabricated in the developing rural and semi-urban "factories." These "proto-industries," moreover, provided secondary job opportunities for farmers.[5] The rapid growth in the 1870-1940 period, therefore, should not be viewed as a new trend, but as the broadening and deepening with systematic government encouragement of a process already begun several centuries earlier.

The legacy of Tokugawa farming to modern agricultural growth was not only one of expanding production. When the countryside entered the modern era, many of its farmers already cultivated crops for commercial markets, paid taxes, and, in some regions, rents set at fixed amounts (rather than percentages of yields), which often motivated cultivators to increase production since they themselves could sell the entire surplus, had an interest in technical innovation, and received pragmatic educations. And, more important, large numbers of rural Japanese, in spite of a trend toward economic polarization between rich and poor in the Tokugawa era, were ambitious; farmers were willing to work long hours and to experiment with new crops and techniques because they aspired to upward social mobility.[6] What led to the greater increases in productivity and the more extensive social change after 1868 was that Japan, instead of being

[5] Hanley and Yamamura, *Economic and Demographic Change*, pp. 79-90; Hayami Akira, "Can Stagnation Create Growth? A Comment," paper presented at Conference on Social Structure and Population in Ch'ing China and Tokugawa Japan held at Princeton University, May 14, 1982; Thomas C. Smith, "Farm Family By-employments in Preindustrial Japan," *The Journal of Economic History*, Vol. 29-4 (1969); Hauser, "Misconceptions of Tokugawa Japan."

[6] Yasuba Yasukichi, "Another Look at the Tokugawa Heritage with Special Reference to Social Conditions," Discussion Paper #104, The Center for Southeast Asian Studies, Kyoto University (February 1979), pp. 18-19. By way of contrast, see Ester Boserup, *The Conditions of Agricultural Growth* (Chicago, 1965), who gives examples of African and Asian subsistence agriculturalists who work short hours to produce their necessary food. The case of the yams cultivators of southern Nigeria is particularly instructive because they choose to suffer from malnutrition rather than do the extra work necessary to produce food for a more adequate diet, pp. 46-47.

ruled by several hundred semi-autonomous feudal domains with varying commitments to development, had a single government dedicated to making the nation strong and rich, a policy which helped make the countryside richer as well.

THE MEIJI REFORMS AND AGRICULTURAL DEVELOPMENT

The Meiji government, as is widely recognized, introduced a variety of programs which speeded economic growth and social change in rural Japan. It abolished seigneurial rule and the ruling warrior class's legal preeminence; established military conscription, universal compulsory education, systematic local and national government, a legal framework for modern forms of economic organization, banking and financial institutions, a new tax system, and a host of other new organs of society; and encouraged technical and entrepreneurial activities which stimulated economic growth.[7] But some of these reforms touched rural Japan more than others and must be treated at greater length.

The government's abrogation of feudal privilege and land-ownership ended the time-honored class structure which gave warriors legal precedence over peasants, artisans, and merchants, and ultimate control of land and its productive wealth. From the 1870s on, farmers had the same legal rights as former samurai; they could bring suit in the same courts, even against ex-warriors, attend the same schools, serve in the same army, and perform equally as many of the same tasks as their education and financial resources allowed.

Farmers also gained the freedom to own and alienate land. Under seigneurial rule, the various feudal lords owned all their domain's agricultural land and collected taxes on it. During the Tokugawa era, a kind of sub-ruling-class land-ownership evolved in which some well-to-do peasants gained "holdership" of land by foreclosing on defaulted

[7] The word "seigneurial" as an adjective descriptive of the Tokugawa system is borrowed from Stephen Vlastos, *Peasant Protests and Uprisings in Tokugawa Japan* (Berkeley, 1986).

loans to poorer peasants who had borrowed money, using their landholdings as security, or by creating new fields out of wasteland. However, in legal theory always, and in practice occasionally, peasants were forbidden to own this land. Thus, although the rich peasant/landholder rented his land to the poor peasant/tenant, he did so only with the lord's indulgence. This kind of unstable situation, in which the rulers could arbitrarily appropriate a peasant's landed wealth, made rational economic planning by farm households difficult. The new government changed all of this. It abolished seigneurial control of land, recognized the customary peasant holder as the rightful owner, gave him the authority to sell his land (and to buy more), and thus established the basis for the modern landlord system under which both landlords and tenants were normally local farmers. This reform not only recognized legally the village's different levels of landownership, which as Ronald Dore points out, encouraged innovation, but also gave the "new" owner, who now need not fear unreasonable confiscation of his land, a greater stake in expanding his yields and income. Although technological innovation to increase production had taken place under the Tokugawa, it became a way of life, almost a religion, in the Meiji era, and this was partly because farmers now had greater security of landownership.[8]

Having given peasants clear title to what had formerly been the lord's land, to exploit its productive wealth the new national leaders created a taxation system. The Meiji regime had heavy initial obligations: the capitalizing of factories, the importation of technology, the payment of stipends and bond interest to ex-samurai, the modernizing of the military, the suppression of rebellion, and the creation of schools, but only one sure source of revenue, agricultural land. In the 1870s, when the new mode of taxation was established, about 80 percent of Japan's work force farmed. It is no won-

[8] Ronald P. Dore, "Agricultural Improvement in Japan: 1870-1900," *Economic Development and Cultural Change*, 9 (1960), pp. 77-81; Francks, *Technology and Agricultural Development*, pp. 66-67.

der then that, in 1878-1882, 77 percent of Japan's tax revenues came from direct taxes on the agricultural sector.

Under feudal rule, taxes on agricultural production often had been capriciously and inefficiently assessed and collected. Peasants faced periodic fluctuations in their taxes. The lord's need for revenues could lead to arbitrary increases in the tax burden; his and his officials' haphazardness could lead to assessments and rates increasing more slowly than production. In the 1860s, taxes varied greatly from domain to domain; they were as high as 40 percent of yields in some fiefs, as low as 15 percent of yields in others.[9]

Officials of the new regime, committed as they were to a program of modernization, decided that a rational, orderly tax system was necessary and set out to create one. In 1873, the government began to calculate the value of all of the agricultural land in Japan and set an annual tax of 4 percent of the assessment—3 percent for national and 1 percent for local taxes—to be paid in currency. The Meiji government, which had muddled along, depending on the preexisting feudal arrangement for the first five or six years of its existence, found that by the late 1870s it had created the basis for a steady source of income.

One of the clichés of the historical literature on modern Japan is that the Meiji leaders industrialized and modernized their nation at the expense of the peasantry. The new land tax, according to this view, was a harsh burden for rural Japanese to bear, and their prosperity was sacrificed to pay the costs of modern weapons, machines, and institutions.[10] One cannot deny that farmers paid most of the nation's taxes

[9] Calculated from Yamamura, "Meiji Land Tax Reform," Tables 14.2 and 14.3.
[10] G. C. Allen, *A Short Economic History of Modern Japan* (London, 1972), p. 64; Harry T. Oshima, "Meiji Fiscal Policy and Economic Progress," William W. Lockwood, ed., *The State and Economic Enterprise in Japan* (Princeton, 1965), pp. 353-389; Ōuchi, *Nōgyōshi*, pp. 51-78; E. Herbert Norman, *Japan's Emergence as a Modern State: Political and Economic Problems of the Meiji Period* (New York, 1940), pp. 144-148.

until the mid-1890s—this was natural enough since farmers were most of the Japanese people—but the available evidence does not indicate that the tax burden on Japanese farmers was as high as in the pre-1868 feudal era or that they were unfairly exploited (i.e., more harshly than other segments of the population).

To begin with, Kozo Yamamura has shown in his study of the Meiji land tax that this reform, which brought fairly uniform taxes ranging from 24.06 percent of yields in Nagano to 28.97 percent of yields in Yamanashi and Yamaguchi, led to tax reductions of 10 percent or more from feudal levels in 14 of 39 prefectures, but increases of 10 percent or more in only 6.[11] Second, Sidney Crawcour estimates that the value of late Tokugawa feudal revenues, computed in yen on the basis of 1878-1880 rice prices, was 103 million yen per year. Kazushi Ohkawa and Miyohei Shinohara calculate that the Meiji government's annual national and local tax revenues in 1878-1880, both agricultural and non-agricultural combined, were 71.4 million yen. These figures indicate a decrease in the annual tax burden of 30.7 percent under the new regime from Tokugawa times. When we subtract the 25 percent land tax reduction of 1877, we still find that the Meiji government even in the mid-1870s had lowered agricultural taxes by 5-6 percent at the very least.[12]

Third, even if we were to accept Ōuchi Tsutomu's view that the Meiji peasants shouldered on the average the same tax burdens as they had under the old regime, relief was on its way.[13] In January 1877, even before the Meiji tax system was in operation everywhere, officials lowered the national and local tax rates from 3 percent and 1 percent to 2.5 percent and 0.5 percent of the assessed value of farm land. Ōuchi, who emphasizes the oppressiveness of a modern tax

[11] Yamamura, "Meiji Land Tax Reform," Tables 14.2 and 14.3.

[12] E. Sidney Crawcour, "The Tokugawa Heritage," Lockwood, *State and Economic Enterprise*, p. 29; Ohkawa and Shinohara, *Patterns of Japanese Economic Development*, p. 376.

[13] Ōuchi, *Nōgyōshi*, pp. 45-54.

system which was to him as heavy as the feudal one, over-looks what seems a logical conclusion to draw from this step. It represented a reduction of 25 percent both from the 4 percent Meiji and from the feudal tax. Fourth, agricultural taxes as a percentage of the farm household's agricultural income continued to fall steadily throughout the 1877 to World War II era. In 1883–1887, farmers paid in direct taxes on agriculture 20.2 percent of their value of production; by the turn of the century they paid only 11.2 percent, and by 1933–1937, only 7.1 percent.[14]

Finally, the percentage of total government tax revenues paid in direct taxes by the agricultural sector fell much more rapidly than did the percentage of the work force that farmed. In 1878–1882, 77.4 percent of the nation's workers were farmers, and they provided 77.1 percent of its tax revenues; by the turn of the century, 67.2 percent of the work force paid 41.6 percent of the taxes; and by World War I, 58.7 percent paid only 25.3 percent of the taxes.[15] Within only a few years of the establishment of the new tax system, farmers paid less, not more, than their share of taxes.

But the significance of the government's new method of assessing and collecting taxes was not only that it gradually eased the tax burden on rural Japanese. Because landowners paid their taxes in money, not in produce as in the feudal era, the inauguration of the tax system led to a more rapid intrusion of commerce into the countryside. Landowning farmers were compelled to market some of their crops to pay taxes to a single, central government's national tax system. This led to the integration of local markets, to the gradual

[14] Alan H. Gleason, "Economic Growth and Consumption in Japan," Lockwood, *State and Economic Enterprise*, p. 412; see James Nakamura, *Agricultural Production*, pp. 160–162, for an analysis of the falling rural tax burden.

[15] James Nakamura, *Agricultural Production*, p. 161; Ohkawa and Shinohara, *Patterns of Japanese Economic Development*, pp. 376–377; Robert E. Cole and Ken'ichi Tominaga, "Japan's Changing Occupational Structure and Its Significance," Hugh Patrick, ed., *Japanese Industrialization and Its Social Consequences* (Berkeley, 1976), p. 58.

establishment of interregional crop prices, and to the allocation of resources nationwide, which in turn allowed farmers
to gauge their returns more accurately and thus encouraged
them to invest time and money in new cultivating and managerial techniques.[16] Although, as we shall see, the rapid expansion of commercial farming under the impetus of the new
tax plan threatened some farmers' livelihoods in the short
run, on balance it benefited farmers more than it hurt them
because it provided the opportunity for the safe and orderly
accumulation of profits.

The government, having established the framework
within which farmers could enlarge their profits and capital
if they could increase their crop yields, set up organs to help
tillers improve their cultivating techniques and thus increase
these yields. As we shall see in detail in Chapter Three,
which treats the development of sericultural technology in
Yamanashi Prefecture in the modern era, landlords, owner
farmers, prefectural officials, industrial entrepreneurs, and
even tenant farmers all joined in this effort. The government
established research stations to develop new seed strains and
information networks to facilitate the transfer of technical
knowledge from more to less advanced regions; in fact, it
has been said that a primary cause of increases in agricultural
productivity during the Meiji era was the diffusion nationwide of the regional "best practices" during the late Tokugawa years.[17] Well-to-do farmers, with government encouragement, undertook costly and often risky experiments with
new crops, seed types, and techniques. Entrepreneurs sold
traditional organic fertilizers in larger and larger quantities in
the nineteenth century, and then modern industry developed
and marketed inorganic, chemical ones in the twentieth. And
owner tenant, tenant owner, and tenant farmers, at first under landlord compulsion, and later as they became more lit-

---

[16] Yamamura, "Meiji Land Tax Reform," pp. 391-392.
[17] Rosovsky, "Rumbles in the Rice Fields," p. 358.

erate and independent, of their own accord made efforts to improve techniques, yields, and profits.

Before the end of the Meiji era, virtually all rice growers used new seed varieties, transplanted rice by regular spacing, tested seed rice grains for fertility by floating them in salt-water solution, improved the timing of the rice-growing process to avoid green grains by harvesting early or cracked grains by harvesting late, spread fish and seed meal and soy bean cake fertilizers in increasing amounts, and used improved tools like new plow types and the rotary weeder. In the twentieth century, farmers, again with governmental help and encouragement, used increasingly the products of modern science and industry: seed hybrids developed in the laboratory and superphosphate of lime and ammonium sulphate fertilizers, insecticides, fungicides, light traps for rice stem borers, chloropicrin for fumigation, and power threshers and hullers produced in the factory.[18] These improvements, many simply tinkering with traditional techniques, together with land reclamation, increased double cropping, land and irrigation improvements, and the cultivation of new crops, which the government also encouraged, led to the rapid enlargement of real value of production per farm worker introduced in Table 1-1.

Possibly the most dramatic single development in modern Japanese agriculture before World War II was the increased use of fertilizer, and especially of commercial organic and then chemical fertilizer. Between the 1890s and the 1930s, rice production grew by 67 percent, seed productivity by 7 percent, and fertilizer use by 100 percent; over the same forty

---

[18] Isaburō Nagai, *Japonica Rice: Its Breeding and Culture* (Tokyo, 1959), pp. 658-659, 689, 710; Ōuchi, *Nōgyōshi*, p. 83. Soybean cake fertilizers were imported from Manchuria. For a description of improvements in agricultural methods in late-nineteenth- and early-twentieth-century Yamanashi, see Ninomiya Masato and Ishikawa Jinzō, *Meijiki ni okeru Yamanashi-ken nōgyō hattatsushi shiryōshū* (Kōfu, 1952), an eighty-four-page mimeographed pamphlet.

years, commercial fertilizer, which cost money but saved labor time, expanded from 13 percent to 49 percent of total fertilizer used.[19] From World War I to the mid-1930s, organic commercial fertilizer use grew by 28 percent, but chemical fertilizer use by 277 percent, from 43 percent to 69 percent of all purchased fertilizer.[20]

One reason that farmers used more commercial and chemical fertilizer was its greater potency. But another was that the price of commercial and chemical fertilizer fell steadily as manufacturers improved their production techniques and achieved greater economies of scale. Between 1912-1916 and 1932-1936, the real unit cost of the three primary chemical fertilizers fell by 25 percent, 44 percent, and 62 percent, of the three primary organic fertilizers by 13 percent, 30 percent, and 40 percent, while the real value of agricultural production per farm worker increased by 24 percent.[21] Nevertheless, as some readers may recognize, fertilizer use increased much more rapidly (100 percent) in the twentieth century than did rice production (67 percent), and because of the shift to the commercial and chemical types, farmers spent three-and-one-half times more real yen on fertilizer in the 1930s than at the turn of the century.[22] As Hayami and Yamada write, ". . . it is generally known that the dramatic rise in fertilizer input accompanied the decline in marginal physical productivity, especially after the 1920s, in spite of efforts made in seed improvement to overcome the trend toward decreasing returns."[23] And yet, because Hayami and Yamada, like most writers on Japanese agricultural develop-

---

[19] Hayami and Yamada compare the 100 percent increase in fertilizer use with a 41 percent growth of yields per *tan* of paddy field, Hayami and Yamada, "Agricultural Productivity," p. 114, rather than with the 67 percent growth of total yields. I have used the latter figure because farmers spread larger and larger amounts of fertilizer not only to increase yields, but also because reclamation allowed them to till additional land. *Chōki keizai tōkei*, Vol. 9, pp. 167-168.

[20] Nōrinshō nōmukyoku, *Hiryō yōran* (1936), pp. 20-21.

[21] *Ibid.*   [22] *Ibid.*, pp. 19-21.

[23] Hayami and Yamada, "Agricultural Productivity," p. 115.

ment, focus their attention on rice, which accounted for only half of the total value of farm production, and because they overlook the ability of commercial fertilizer to free labor for non-agricultural work, they paint an excessively bleak picture of fertilizer's diminishing returns.[24] The 67 percent and 100 percent figures indicate increases in *rice* production and fertilizer use. But farmers used much of their fertilizer for crops other than rice; in fact, they spread a very high percentage in mulberry and fruit orchards and on feed grain fields, and sericultural, fruit, livestock, poultry, and dairy outputs grew far more rapidly than did those for rice. Between 1893-1897 and 1933-1937, output for cocoons grew by 353 percent, for mandarin oranges by 443 percent, for Japanese pears by 269 percent, for cattle by 122 percent, for hens by 316 percent, for eggs by 937 percent, for grapes by 1,958 percent, for apples by 1,659 percent, for swine by 1,209 percent, and for milk by 1,777 percent.[25]

Farmers also increased their use of commercial fertilizer to replace labor. Over these forty years, the number of agricultural workers decreased by 12.2 percent.[26] Commercial fertilizer helped replace the work of these men and women and of many part-time farmers who bolstered their households' income by working elsewhere and sending or bringing home part of their wages. Thus, it is very likely that the slowing

[24] *Chōki keizai tōkei*, Vol. 9, pp. 146-147; in 1893-1897, rice made up 50.1 percent of the total value of production; in 1933-1937, it made up 50.2 percent. In between it fell to a low of 47.7 percent in 1913-1917 and rose to a high of 51.2 percent in 1903-1907.

[25] *Chōki keizai tōkei*, Vol. 9, pp. 171-181; Ōuchi, writing about the use of commercial fertilizers in the late Tokugawa period, states that farmers were more likely to use them on commercial crops than on rice. If the same were true in the modern period, it would help explain why rice yields expanded more slowly than commercial crop yields. It would also help to support my contention that modern (and some Tokugawa era) farmers managed their farms as small businessmen to increase profits rather than as peasants to maintain the security of their marginal farms. *Nōgyōshi*, p. 25.

[26] Ohkawa and Shinohara, *Patterns of Japanese Economic Development*, pp. 293-295.

of the expansion of rice yields in the 1920s reflects not only a "decline in marginal physical productivity" of rice, but also a conscious decision by farmers to diversify, to shift the weight of their fertilizer and labor inputs from rice to more profitable cash crops or to secondary jobs. The beginnings of the trend toward diversified planting, a more varied diet, and part-time farming which we normally associate with post-World War II Japan seems to have begun earlier in the twentieth century.

A striking aspect of these joint government/farmer efforts at increasing production by improving cultivating techniques is that they were carried out with little immediate disruption of the customary rural order. Unlike Mexico, where large-scale commercial farm operators bypassed the nation's small farmers by introducing modern techniques wholesale, Japanese agricultural development came about because the great majority of the nation's farmers improved their techniques by building piecemeal on traditional methods. Unlike the Mexican approach, which created two groups of farmers—one with a small number of entrepreneurs managing huge, capital intensive mechanized estates, and another with a large number of impoverished cultivators tilling small traditional farms—in Japan relatively small capital inputs on almost all farms led to large increases in productivity.[27] Japanese eating habits and planting patterns did not change much before World War I, and then changed only gradually; thus, Japanese farmers could continue doing more or less what they always had done, except that after 1868 they did it better and better. Improved methods of planting, new seeds, more and then more and better fertilizer, insecticides, weed killers, gasoline-powered threshers, and electric pumps, but all used in the same time-tested, labor-intensive way, brought about substantial gains. The Japanese by following this approach

[27] Bruce F. Johnston, "The Japanese 'Model' of Agricultural Development: Its Relevance to Developing Nations," Ohkawa, *Agricultural and Economic Growth*, pp. 86-90.

continue even today to have small farms, but, as some researchers have shown in recent years, small farms can produce higher yields per hectare than large ones. As Bruce F.
Johnston writes, there is a "tradition in Marxist thought of
glorifying bigness and exaggerating the economies of scale
in agriculture," but as Berry, Cline, and Francks demonstrate, small farms are often more productive.[28] Japan clearly
benefited from this piecemeal approach to agricultural development by avoiding the creation of large, inefficient farms
and the concomitant polarization of the countryside into rich
agricultural entrepreneurs or powerful state authority, on the
one hand, and weaker farm wage earners or collective farm
members, on the other.

An Analysis of the Impact of the Land Tax Reform of 1873

As we have seen in our earlier discussion of the "differentiation of the rural classes," many economic historians, while
acknowledging the increases in *average* productivity per farm
worker and the absence of a capitalist-rural wage-earner division in the countryside, write that the land-tax system and
its resultant commercialization of the village still begat polarization: increased differentiation between larger landlord
and smaller tenant farmer holdings. The twin Meiji-period
banes of fixed cash taxes and market transactions, these
scholars write, forced farmers, who previously had produced
all they needed to eat and live, to sell crops in order to raise
the cash necessary for paying their taxes. When crop prices
dropped sharply, as they did during the Matsukata Deflation
of the early 1880s, cultivators had to sell land or borrow
money, using land as security, to fulfill their tax obligations.
Buffeted by successive years of low income, they either sold

[28] *Ibid.*, pp. 59, 93; R. Albert Berry and William R. Cline, *Agrarian Structure and Productivity in Developing Countries*; Francks, *Technology and Agricultural Development*, pp. 64, 88-89, 199, 262.

off much of their land or failed to meet their mortgage payments and were foreclosed; either way, the cultivators lost their fields and became tenants on land which they had previously owned.[29]

The foundation to support this view is five-fold. First, the theoretical framework within which many Japanese economic historians work posits that the growth of a commercial market, i.e., of capitalism, always leads to polarization.[30] Second, local studies of two regions in eastern Japan show that the consumption gap between rich and poor farm households increased slightly during the mid-Meiji years. Third, Paul Mayet, a European adviser to the Japanese government, reported that during the Matsukata Deflation of the 1880s, "roughly one-eighth of the entire arable acreage in Japan was given over to creditors in the space of but three years."[31] Fourth, scattered rural data for the late Meiji years show that, although there was both upward and downward economic mobility within villages, the downward trend was stronger.[32] And fifth and most significant, the percentage of cultivated land under tenancy rose from 30.6 percent in 1872 to 45.4 percent in 1912, the last year of the Meiji era, an increase of 48 percent in forty years.[33] And yet, in spite of

[29] See Introduction, footnote 84. Ōuchi discusses the impact of the land tax on differentiation and concludes that its effect has been overstated. He states that differentiation began long before the land tax, progressed at different speeds in various regions in spite of a uniform tax system, and did not speed up after the new land tax was instituted. Thus, he concludes his discussion by writing that, although he agrees with the many writers who believe the taxation system led to increased concentration of land ownership, he thinks it only one of many contributing causes. *Nōminsō no bunkai*, pp. 24-29, 129. In other words, Pyle, Dore, Francks, and the Western scholars cited by Yamamura are more orthodox than the orthodox.

[30] This theme runs through Ōuchi's *Nōgyōshi* like a Wagnerian leitmotif. See, for example, pp. 23, 28, 30, 57, 62, 91, and 92.

[31] Paul Mayet, *Nihon nōmin no hihei oyobi sono kyūjisaku*, in Sakurai Takeo, *Meiji nōgyō ronshū* (Tokyo, 1955), p. 208, quoted in Nakamura Takafusa, *Economic Growth in Prewar Japan*, p. 57.

[32] Ōuchi, *Nōminsō no bunkai*, pp. 137-139.

[33] Nakamura Takafusa, *Economic Growth in Prewar Japan*, pp. 55-56.

this weighty evidence, there are equally compelling reasons to believe that Meiji polarization has been overstated—or even possibly that it hardly occurred at all.[34]

To begin with, the putative harmful effects of the tax system, which forced farmers to sell large amounts of their crops, and of price fluctuations, which caused them sometimes to sell at a loss, have been exaggerated. A typical owner, as late as the 1930s, when rural commercialization had reached its prewar peak, marketed only slightly more than half, and a typical tenant less than half his total production.[35] When prices of crops that farmers sold fell, so too did

[34] Although E. H. Norman's evidence is dated, I want to mention his work here because of its prominent place in recent debates over approaches to the study of modern Japan. Norman, in *Japan's Emergence as a Modern State*, pp. 144-148, discusses the "dispossession of the peasantry" during the era of the Matsukata Deflation, but his evidence does not seem adequate to support his contention that the peasantry was actually dispossessed. Norman finds that between 1883 and 1890, 47,281 *chō* were auctioned off or confiscated for tax arrears, that in Okayama Prefecture 699 persons were forced to sell their land between 1879 and 1883, that tenanted land increased by 776,851 *chō* between 1883 and 1892, and that the number of owner households decreased (13.4 percent) and the number of owner tenant (19.3 percent) and tenant (0.3 percent) households increased between 1883 and 1888. Only the last data seem to me significant indicators of spreading rural poverty, and even their importance must be interpreted with care. The area auctioned off or confiscated for tax arrears does not reach 1 percent of all arable land in the 1880s; the sum of 699 forced sales in Okayama, if each sale is of one plot of land, comes to about one-half of one hamlet in a prefecture which had over 2,000 hamlets; although tenanted land increased by 776,851 *chō* between 1883 and 1892, land under cultivation, using Norman's own data, increased by 1,665,298 *chō*. Thus, we have no reason to believe that all or even most of the increase in tenancy came about through forced sale or confiscation rather than reclamation. Even the sharp drop in owner farming and increase in owner tenant farming, which does show that the Matsukata Deflation had a deleterious short-term effect on the countryside, can be attributed in part to the decision of owner farmers to increase their area of cultivation by renting newly reclaimed land from landlord/reclaimers. This interpretation is reinforced by the minuscule increase in pure tenant households between 1883 and 1888; in fact, pure tenants as a percentage of total farm households actually fell during these years.

[35] I base my calculations below on the supposition that owner, owner

the costs of fertilizers, seeds, tools, clothing, and foodstuffs which they bought. Cultivators from long premodern experience with fluctuations in the size of harvests were more likely than non-farmers to plan in long-range terms; certainly few farmers would have viewed one or two years of high or low prices as the beginning of a trend. Thus, the 44 percent drop in the farm value of agricultural production between the inflation year of 1881 and the worst Matsukata Deflation year of 1884, for example, should not be viewed as a 44 percent drop in the living standards of farm households.[36] When one recalculates in real terms, using the rural consumer price index, considering that in the 1880s the average farmer marketed at the very most half of his produce, and using three-year averages to control for long-range planning, real income per farm worker fell only 9.2 percent from 1879-1881 to 1882-1884, during the worst depression before 1930 in Japan's modern history.[37] Unpleasant as a 9.2 percent reduction in income is, one has difficulty believing that it led to Roger Bowen's three-million bankruptcies (at least half of all farm households in Japan in the mid-1880s) or even to Mayet's foreclosures of one-eighth of Japan's farm land. Even Nakamura Takafusa, who writes that Mayet's "estimate is a bit exaggerated because in some cases land changed hands more than once," may have given the European's opinion more credence than is due.[38]

The strongest evidence in support of the differentiation ap-

---

tenant, and tenant farmers marketed half of their crops in the 1880s. In a survey of 27 villages from various regions of Japan, conducted in 1890, Saitō Bankichi found, however, that tenant farmers marketed only 20 percent, and owner farmers only 49 percent of their produce. One assumes that owner tenant farmers fell in between. Thus, the 9.2 percent reduction in real income per farm worker presented below probably overstates the effects of the Matsukata Deflation on household incomes. Ōuchi, *Nōgyōshi*, p. 59.

[36] *Chōki keizai tōkei*, Vol. 9, p. 146.

[37] *Ibid.*, Vol. 8, p. 135; Vol. 9, p. 146; Ohkawa and Shinohara, *Patterns of Japanese Economic Development*, p. 293.

[38] Bowen, *Rebellion and Democracy in Meiji Japan*, p. 104; Nakamura Takafusa, *Economic Growth in Prewar Japan*, p. 57.

proach is the 48 percent increase in tenancy. At the beginning of the Meiji era, farmers tilled about 1.4 million *chō* of tenanted arable land; at the end, they cultivated almost 80 percent more, about 2.5 million *chō*, an increase of 1,154,200 *chō* in just forty years. And yet, one must restrain oneself from jumping to the conclusion that the 48 percent increase in percentage of land and the 80 percent increase in the amount of land tilled by tenants demonstrate polarization between rich landlords and poor tenants caused by price fluctuations, bankruptcies, and foreclosures in a spreading capitalist economy. Why do I write this?

One widely accepted explanation for the dramatic increase in agricultural production during the first half-century of Japan's modern economic growth is the sharp increase in area of land under cultivation. Landlords and rural merchants in the late nineteenth and early twentieth centuries viewed farm land as a profitable investment and financed the reclamation of new fields. The developers then contracted with the laborers who constructed them or with other local farmers to till the newly built arable.[39] The entrepreneur/landlord received in rent from his new tenants a return on his investment in reclamation while the poorer laborer/tenant households gained the opportunity to cultivate more land—which they could do because of additional labor and new labor-saving farming techniques. Between 1874 and 1912, arable land in Japan increased from 4.6 to 5.6 million *chō*, an increase of 1,044,600 *chō*; area tilled per farm worker grew by 20 percent from 2.96 to 3.55 *tan*.[40] If one accepts James Nakamura's view that there was a large area of unreported farmland in early Meiji and thus his estimates of land under cultivation, 4,847,000 *chō* in 1873-1877 and 5,675,000 *chō* in 1908-1912, arable land grew by 828,000 *chō* and by 14 per-

[39] Nakamura Takafusa, *Economic Growth in Prewar Japan*, p. 55; Ōuchi, *Nōgyōshi*, pp. 103-104; Ōuchi points out that many large landlords in the Tokugawa era built their holdings through reclamation, pp. 28, 32.

[40] *Chōki keizai tōkei*, Vol. 9, pp. 218-219; Ohkawa and Shinohara, *Patterns of Japanese Economic Development*, pp. 293-294.

cent per farm worker in forty years.[41] What is striking about these data, as presented in Table 1-2, is that the increase in the area of land tilled by tenants comes to 91 percent (and for Nakamura's estimates, 76 percent) of the expansion in arable land. Although one hesitates to claim that all 91 percent or 76 percent of the increases in tenancy in the Meiji period came about through land reclamation, one can only conclude that a very large part must have—how many owner cultivators had the capital necessary to reclaim fields, after all? The 80 percent growth of tenant-farmed land demonstrates new opportunities for poor farm households to till larger farms at least as much as it indicates polarization brought about by the purportedly invidious effects of the new tax system and the market economy. Specific case stud-

TABLE 1-2
Land Under Cultivation
(in *chō*)

Year	Farm Workers	Land Under Cultivation	Tenant-[42] Farmed Land	Land Under Cultivation Nakamura	Tenant-[42] Farmed Land Nakamura
1874	15,496,000	4,594,400	1,405,900	4,847,000	1,483,200
1912	15,884,000	5,639,000	2,560,100	5,675,000	2,576,450
Increase		1,044,600 (91%)	1,154,200	828,000 (76%)	1,093,250

Calculated from *Chōki keizai tōkei*, Vol. 9, pp. 216-218; James I. Nakamura, *Agricultural Production and the Economic Development of Japan, 1873-1922* (Princeton, 1966), pp. 43, 48; Nakamura Takafusa, *Economic Growth in Prewar Japan* (New Haven, 1983), p. 56; Ohkawa and Shinohara, *Patterns of Japanese Economic Development*, pp. 293-294.

[41] James I. Nakamura, *Agricultural Production and the Economic Development of Japan* (Princeton, 1966), pp. 43, 48.
[42] I have calculated area of tenanted land under cultivation by multiplying the total area of land under cultivation by 30.6 percent and 45.4 percent, the percentages of tenant farmed land in 1873 and 1912, respectively.

ies like that of Yachimata in Chiba Prefecture underline this conclusion. The community did not exist in the Tokugawa period, but between 1869 and the 1920s, entrepreneurs financed the reclamation of all of the town's arable; at the end of this period in 1924, tenants cultivated 90.9 percent of the town's farmland, double the national average, and Yachimata housed seven of the 3,000 landlords nationwide who owned 50 *chō* or more of land. Clearly reclamation not foreclosure led to this dramatic differentiation of Yachimata's classes.[43]

Prefectural data, presented for 1883-1884 and 1912 in Table 1-3, also reinforce our interpretation that reclamation

TABLE 1-3

Area of Reclaimed Land and Newly Tenanted Land, 1883/1884-1912

Prefecture	Reclaimed Land	Newly Tenanted Land
Kumamoto	71,994.0 *chō*	18,596.1 *chō*
Kōchi	60,706.8	18,835.1
Yamaguchi	45,590.6	31,134.1
Fukushima	31,625.7	36,850.8
Tokyo	30,984.8	13,587.8
Nagano	27,580.9	27,553.3
Miyazaki	25,920.0	14,787.0
Tochigi	21,007.0	26,493.0
Niigata	19,821.6	21,637.4
Okayama	17,638.9	16,453.1
Yamagata	14,624.2	16,096.5
Oita	14,011.2	18,775.4
Aichi	13,910.6	19,015.1
Yamanashi	13,817.1	11,920.2
Shimane	13,705.3	10,838.9
Gifu	13,566.0	14,519.5
Chiba	11,831.6	24,647.7

[43] Suzuki Kunio, "Nōmin undō no hatten to jisakunō sōsetsu," *Tochi seido shigaku*, 85 (1979), pp. 18-19.

(TABLE 1-3 *cont.*)

Prefecture	Reclaimed Land	Newly Tenanted Land
Toyama	11,729.6	8,226.0
Kyoto	11,445.4	7,759.1
Nagasaki	10,888.7	8,397.4
Miyagi	7,905.0	29,918.0
Saga	6,738.4	7,496.0
Mie	6,347.3	14,845.6
Gumma	5,814.9	13,788.5
Hiroshima	5,106.9	13,909.7
Tottori	4,466.7	9,068.2
Akita	4,362.3	19,630.7
Fukui	3,782.2	6,596.7
Saitama	3,124.3	5,696.4
Shiga	3,020.2	8,365.4
Wakayama	1,265.8	4,509.9
Total	534,334.0 *chō*	499,948.6 *chō*

Calculated from Nōshōmushō sōmukyoku hōkokuka, *Nōshōmu tō-keihyō*, 1883 and 1912.[44]

played a major role in the increase in tenant-farmed land in the Meiji era. To begin with, we can see that, with the exception of Kumamoto, Kōchi, and Tokyo prefectures, in one column, and Miyagi, Chiba, and Akita prefectures, in the other, there is a fairly close correlation between the areas of land presented in the two categories; the larger the increase in tenancy, the greater the expansion of arable land. Second, although 12 of the 31 prefectures covered had excesses of reclaimed land over newly tenanted land, only nine had surpluses of newly tenanted land which more than doubled reclaimed land. Third, the total area of newly tenanted over

[44] These data are subject to Professor James Nakamura's criticism that the official statistics understate land under cultivation in the Meiji period. Since, however, his revisions affect reclaimed and newly tenanted land equally, the correlations still hold.

reclaimed land in the 19 prefectures where tenancy grew faster than new land totalled 119,528.6 *chō*, about 24 percent of all newly tenanted land; therefore, we can set the upper limit of the possible increase in tenancy through reclamation, based on the assumption that landlords and merchants reclaimed *all* new land, at 76 percent of all newly tenanted land. If one posits conservatively that these well-to-do entrepreneurs financed only *two-thirds* of all projects to create arable, then the percentage of new tenancy brought about through reclamation came to 50 percent.[45] One should not assume, however, that bankruptcy, forced sales, and foreclosures necessarily caused the other 50 percent.

Tenant-farmed land increased in extent for other reasons besides reclamation and bankruptcy, and this also benefited cultivators. Although Ōuchi Tsutomu, in laying out the orthodox view of the differentiation of the rural classes, posits that the countryside on the verge of capitalist development should be inhabited by owner farmers, he and most other students of the rural economy recognize that Japanese reality differed from theory. When capitalist farming began to develop in Japan, many farmers tilled land not as owner farmers, but as hereditary servants on large estates.[46] Because

---

[45] I think it is a very conservative estimate to posit that landlord and merchant entrepreneurs developed only two-thirds of the new arable land, and thus that only 50 percent of the newly tenanted land came about through reclamation. Between 1897 and 1902, the Hypothec Bank (*Kangin*) lent more than two million yen, 40 percent of its total agricultural lending, for land reclamation. Since *Kangin* did not make loans of less than 10,000 yen, equal to the price of 6-7 *chō* of average grade rice paddy at the time, we can be fairly sure that only the well-to-do could afford the relatively low interest rates that the Hypothec and other quasi-official banks had to offer. Thus, in the Meiji period, when most modern reclamation was done and before general interest rates fell to 10-11 percent or less, as they did in the 1920s and 1930s, it would appear that only landlords and merchants had the capital, or access to the capital, to reclaim land.

[46] Thomas C. Smith, *Agrarian Origins*, pp. 1-35; Ōuchi, *Nōgyōshi*, p. 27; Francks, *Technology and Agricultural Development*, p. 64; Furushima Toshio, *Kinsei Nihon nōgyō no kōzō*, pp. 238-272, in *Furushima Toshio chosakushū*, Vol. 3.

these hierarchically structured farms continued to exist, especially in Tōhoku in the northeast, even into the twentieth century, the growth of tenancy in some regions reflected their disintegration rather than the decline of owner farming. In fact, of the eight prefectures in Table 1-3 with the greatest increases in newly tenanted land between 1883-1884 and 1912, four, Fukushima, Miyagi, Tochigi, and Akita, are in Tōhoku; three of the other four northeastern prefectures are not included in the 1883-1884 data. The two prefectures with the largest differential of area of newly tenanted over reclaimed land in Table 1-3, Miyagi and Akita, are located in the northeast. Increases in tenancy, which were greater by far in Tōhoku than in any other region in Japan except Hokkaidō (where reclamation was greatest) between 1883-1884 and 1922 (29 percent nationally and 73 percent in Tōhoku), thus also reflected the transformation of semi-bonded servant/peasants into semi-independent tenant farmers.[47] Becoming a tenant for these farmers reflected a step up, not down, the economic and social ladder, and must be seen as one of the good, not bad, effects of the tax system and the growth of farming for the market.

Other farmers, especially after 1900, farmed tenanted land by choice. Frequently an owner or owner tenant farmer and even a small landlord tilled borrowed land not because of forced sale, foreclosure, or reclamation, but to augment his production and income. Either he was particularly energetic, or he had several able-bodied, unmarried sons at home, or new technology improved his labor productivity, or he hoped to take advantage of favorable crop prices, but, whatever the reason, he wanted to till a larger farm. Thus, he cultivated rented land not from poverty, but for prosperity.[48] It would seem that the growth of tenancy in the Meiji and early Taishō eras does not reflect differentiation and the pau-

[47] Ōuchi, *Nōgyōshi*, pp. 29-30; Nakamura Takafusa, *Economic Growth in Prewar Japan*, p. 56.

[48] Nakamura, *ibid.*, p. 58; Yanagida Kunio, *Nihon nōminshi* in *Teihon Yanagida Kunioshū*, Vol. 16 (Tokyo, 1962), p. 204.

perization of small-scale farmers as much as it reveals improved opportunities for the rural poor.

Another trend in pre-World War II modern Japan which underlines rising standards of living for all rural Japanese rather than increased differentiation between rich and poor is the improvement in per capita caloric consumption. The Japanese Welfare Ministry estimated in 1941 that the average 21-30-year-old male, in the prime of his working life, performing moderate labor, required 2,500 calories per day in food. The average Japanese male in this age group reached this level by 1888-1892 and had moved 600 calories beyond it by the 1920s; in fact, per capita caloric consumption for all Japanese increased by 39 percent between 1874-1877 and 1923-1927. This improvement in eating habits reflected itself in the larger body size of prewar Japanese compared to their nineteenth-century forbears. Army recruits were 2.3 percent taller in the 1930s than the 1880s; eight-, ten-, and twelve-year-old schoolchildren were 2.5 percent taller and 4.5 percent heavier in the 1930s than in the 1890s.[49] Since according to differentiation theory, far more people stood near the poor than the rich pole, and because no matter how rich one is there are physical limits on the amount of food one can consume, an average caloric intake which was 600 calories above the necessary must indicate that almost everyone in the 1920s ate adequately. Similarly, unless one envisages farm villages populated by landlord giants and tenant pygmies, increases in average height and weight must have reflected increased growth and thus improved eating habits for almost everyone.

Alan Gleason's estimates of increases per capita in disposable income also underline improving living standards for all

---

[49] Hayami and Yamada, "Agricultural Productivity," pp. 123-125. The authors point out that foreign observers like Helen Farnsworth, ignoring the relationship between body size and diet, often write that prewar Japanese had "threatening low" caloric intake or were "semi-starving." Hayami and Yamada disagree; since Japanese are shorter and lighter than Westerners, they need not eat as much to function efficiently.

rural Japanese. Rural real disposable income, according to him, more than tripled between 1883-1887 and 1933-1937, and fell sharply (13.8 percent) only during the world depression of the early 1930s; even then, the average farm worker had two-and-one-half times more real income to spend than his grandfather had had in the 1880s.[50] Gleason admits that because his calculations of rural income do not include rents there is a differential between the highest and lowest strata. Nevertheless, since we know that in the twentieth century tenant farmers' rice surpluses after paying paddy rent increased sharply—by 59 percent between 1905-1909 and 1935-1939 although yields grew by only 24 percent—and that real dry field rents actually fell absolutely—by 21 percent in these thirty years—tenant farmers must have increased their disposable income to a greater degree, and landlords to a lesser degree, than the average for these years.[51]

Tenant farmers had growing amounts of income at their disposal as the modern period unfolded, not only because better techniques brought improved yields and bigger profits on their farms, but also because industrialization provided non-agricultural job opportunities for members of farm households. Modern farming techniques made the cultivator efficient enough to harvest higher yields with less work than in the feudal era; this not only allowed him to till a larger area of land more effectively, but also freed some of his family members to work elsewhere. Modern factories, often like silk-reeling filatures, ones which used as raw materials produce from local farms, absorbed this extra labor to the benefit of the profit side of the rural household's balance sheet. Arlon Tussing, in a remarkable 1966 article, shows how in

[50] Gleason, "Economic Growth and Consumption in Japan," p. 414.

[51] *Ibid.*, p. 415; *Chōki keizai tōkei*, Vol. 8, pp. 135-136; Vol. 9, pp. 166-168, 216-217, 220-221.

[52] Arlon Tussing, "The Labor Force in Meiji Economic Growth: A Quantitative Study of Yamanashi Prefecture," *Journal of Economic History*, 26 (1966), reprinted in Ohkawa, *Agricultural and Economic Growth*, pp. 207, 210-211.

Yamanashi Prefecture in the Meiji era farm households significantly increased their non-agricultural income. The percentage of cultivators who farmed as a side occupation grew from 13.1 percent of all farm households in 1879 to 39.4 percent in 1920; silk-reeling filature workers increased from 3,116 in 1873-1877 to 19,285 in 1908-1911 (in a prefecture with about 75,000 full- and part-time farm households at the turn of the century); real wages per filature worker expanded by 98 percent between 1883-1887 and 1908-1911.[52] And Nakamura Takafusa has pointed out that the numbers of Yamanashi farm workers with secondary occupations grew from 33.1 percent to 45.3 percent of the total between 1879 and 1920.[53] Moreover, as we shall see in detail in the following chapter, thousands of Yamanashians migrated elsewhere to work, especially after the completion of the Chūō railroad line in 1903 breached the mountains and brought the Kōfu Basin within six comfortable hours of the Tokyo-Yokohama industrial region; in 1908, the Kōshin'etsu region of Yamanashi, Nagano, and Niigata prefectures provided more Tokyo workers than any other area in Japan outside the capital and its immediate environs. Although Yamanashi was, because of its silk industry, already a relatively advanced region in the 1870s, it was not unique in the development of non-agricultural sources of income for farm households. Local secondary employment for farmers increased in the Meiji era in almost all regions outside the backward northeast; even there, some farmers had secondary occupations, and many members of farm households supplemented their families' livelihoods (and lessened their expenditures) by migrating to other regions to work.[54]

---

[53] Nakamura Takafusa, *Economic Growth in Prewar Japan*, p. 113.

[54] *Ibid.*, pp. 112, 115-117, 125, 128. Nakamura gives data for the percentage of the agricultural population with dual occupations between 1897 and 1915 for thirteen prefectures. In three Tōhoku prefectures, Aomori (1897), Iwate (1904), and Fukushima (1913), 19.8 percent of farm workers had dual occupations. In three central/east prefectures, Chiba (1901), Niigata (1909), and Yamanashi (1915), the percentage was 28.3. In four central/west prefec-

One should not assume, as many contemporary journalists did and later scholars have, that work in these factories and filatures was necessarily more satanic than work in the villages.[55] The very fact that female workers left their villages for textile mills, Nakamura Takafusa writes, indicates that life in the silk filatures and cotton mills was no worse than life in the village.[56] And, as Tussing shows, the buying power of Yamanashi filature workers' wages rose from 2.54 *koku* of rice in 1885-1887 to 4.46 *koku* in 1908-1911. "On this basis," he writes, "toward the end of the Meiji era the earnings of one girl in the silk filatures could have supported a whole family at pre-Meiji standards."[57] Tussing, like Gleason, Hayami, and Yamada, believes that "the incomes of the common people rose substantially" in the Meiji era, and did so partly because of non-agricultural income.[58] The decline of agricultural income as a percentage of national income, therefore, should not be interpreted as reflecting the comparative impoverishment of farmers; by the 1920s most rural households received some of their income from non-agricultural sources.

The final evidence of an improving standard of living for all farmers, and thus in rebuttal to the overemphasis on polarization into richer and poorer households, is the increased purchase by farmers of modern conveniences like bicycles and electric lights; the expanded use of communication facilities like trains, telegrams, and the postal system; the more extensive use of modern health facilities like doctors, den-

---

tures, Wakayama (1908), Kagawa (1909), Tokushima (1909), and Kōchi (1899), the percentage was 30.7. Finally, in three prefectures in Kyushu in the far southwest, Fukuoka (1901), Kumamoto (1905), and Saga (1909), the percentage was 25.1. Although the northeastern region had the lowest percentage of its farm workers with secondary employ, still almost 20 percent brought home non-agricultural income.

[55] Nakamura Masanori, *Rōdōsha to nōmin*, pp. 78-86; Mikiso Hane, *Peasants, Rebels, and Outcastes*, pp. 173-193.

[56] Nakamura Takafusa, *Economic Growth in Prewar Japan*, p. 114.

[57] Tussing, "Labor Force," p. 217.

[58] *Ibid.*, p. 220.

tists, pharmacists, and hospitals; the widespread attendance at new forms of entertainment like moving pictures; and the greater commitment to the education of children. We shall deal with this phenomenon in more detail in the following chapter when we treat agricultural development in Yamanashi Prefecture. Still, to demonstrate the growth in the use of these modern facilities, let me state here that by the end of the Taishō era in 1925 the average Yamanashi household sent over 3 packages, 7 telegrams, 400 letters, attended 7 moving pictures, and took 31 train trips per year; 80 percent of the prefecture's households had electricity (100 percent by the early 1930s, when power lines reached both rich and poor in mountain villages); over one-quarter had bicycles (over one-half by 1939); and there was one dentist and pharmacist for each 1,000 families.[59] Clearly Yamanashi agriculturalists, who made up almost three-quarters of the prefecture's population in 1925, benefited from these new opportunities because they had risen far enough above the margin of poverty to have discretionary income to spend. And the same seems to be true nationwide. When one compares real per capita spending in 1935-1939 with that in 1879-1883, one finds an increase of 466 percent for clothing, 382 percent for medical treatment, 4,397 percent for transportation, 569 percent for recreation and education, 385 percent for beer, and 1,266 percent for tobacco, etc.[60] Although some of this increase in cash expenditures can be attributed to people buying what they formerly produced for themselves, most of it cannot. The size of the expansion, by four to 44 times, and the nature of some of the categories, like medical care and transportation, lead this observer to believe that more and more Japanese lived better and better because of rising incomes in the prewar modern era; it is hard to believe, given our other evidence, that tenant and owner tenant farmers were left behind completely.

[59] *Yamanashi tōkeisho*, 1925.

[60] Shinohara Miyohei, *Chōki keizai tōkei*, Vol. 6, pp. 132-135, 211, 222-227, 244-245, 250-251.

Perhaps the most dramatic non-monetary indicator of improving rural standards of living was the increasing enrollment of Japanese farm children in school. Although the government established compulsory education in the 1870s, in 1879 only 41 percent of eligible children, 58 percent of boys and 23 percent of girls, attended; many poor farm families could not afford to lose their sons, who worked in the fields, or their daughters, who helped with the farm work, minded the younger children, spun thread and weaved textiles in proto-industrial "factories," or functioned as servants in wealthy households, by sending them to school. But as the Meiji period progressed, school attendance increased. In 1890, 49 percent, in 1895, 61 percent, and in 1903, 93.2 percent of eligible children, 96.6 percent of boys and 89.6 percent of girls, attended school. By 1912, the final year of the Meiji era, 98.2 percent of all eligible children, 98.8 percent of boys and 97.6 percent of girls, went to school. And, from 1903 on, the *Education Ministry Yearbook* gives a rural-urban breakdown in enrollment which shows that attendance was consistently higher for country than city boys. A survey conducted in April 1924 of 5,583 people in 1,124 tenant union households in four Okayama counties indicates how pervasive education had become among poor rural families in the twentieth century. Altogether 99.6 percent of the boys and 99.4 percent of the girls between the ages of eight and fifteen attended school, and over 98 percent of men and 93 percent of women between the ages of sixteen and forty had studied in school. Although 70 percent of the unschooled respondents between eight and forty came from the pure tenant farmer stratum of local rural society, they were so few in number (10-15 men and 40-50 women) that we can probably safely conclude that by 1924 even the poorest Okayama tenant farmer households had at least one member who had been to school.[61] The doubling of the real value of produc-

[61] Kyoto daigaku bungakubu, *Nihon kindaishi jiten* (Kyoto, 1958), p. 920; Mombudaijin kambō, *Mombushō nempō*, 1905, p. 64; 1912, p. 73; Ōta Toshie, "Kosakunō kaikyū no keizaiteki shakaiteki jōtai," *Sangyō kumiai* 261 (1927), pp. 83, 100-102.

tion per farm worker and the increase in non-agricultural income between 1879 and 1912 must have played a role in allowing young people to give up full-time work for school. It would appear from all of this evidence about the breakup of estates and increased land reclamation, profit-minded tenancy, caloric intake, disposable income, secondary employment, expenditure on modern appliances, facilities and entertainment, and interest in education that, the spread of tenancy notwithstanding, rural class bipolarization was not as great as the proponents of differentiation would have us believe. The doubling of real rural income during the Meiji period seems to have raised even the poorest tenant farmer well above, rather than driven him toward or below, the margin of subsistence.

IMPROVING RURAL STANDARDS OF LIVING, 1900–1919

All but diehard supporters of the idea that a market economy by definition polarizes rural society into rich landlords and capitalists, on the one hand, and impoverished tenant farmers and wage laborers, on the other, agree that differentiation and tenant poverty reached their peak sometime around the years of the Russo-Japanese War and that rural living standards improved gradually from then until 1920, the end of the World War I economic boom. Domestic demand for food and foreign demand for raw silk expanded with the spread of industrialization and the growth of incomes at home and abroad—both rice market transactions and raw silk exports grew by almost five times between the late 1890s and the end of World War I—and because rice and sericultural products created two-thirds of Japan's value of agricultural production in 1919, this growth led to a sharp improvement in agricultural income per farm worker.[62] In the years between

[62] Lillian Li, *China's Silk Trade: Traditional Industry in the Modern World, 1842-1937* (Cambridge, 1981), pp. 86-87; Mochida Keizō, *Beikoku ichiba no tenkai katei* (Tokyo, 1970), pp. 52-53, 88-89; Nishida Yoshiaki, "Nōmin undō," p. 144; Ogura, "Niigata-ken beikoku keizaishi no isshaku," p. 607.

1900-1904 and 1915-1919, real value of agricultural production per farm worker expanded by 73 percent, an annual growth rate of 3.7 percent, compared to 58 percent and 2.3 percent in the two decades before the turn of the century. Because of the rapid expansion of industry in but a score of years, factories provided more non-agricultural secondary employment as well.[63]

Not only did farm incomes increase between 1900 and 1920 more rapidly than at any other time in pre-land-reform Japanese history, but also the poorer segments of rural society benefited from these gains. The evidence for this is four-fold: rents as a percentage of yields fell, allowing tenants to market a larger share of their produce, the spread of tenancy stagnated, the trend toward a larger amount of land tilled per farm worker continued, and one toward larger family farms began.

The government conducted a series of four surveys of tenancy practices between mid-Meiji and World War II and they indicate steadily increasing surpluses after rent for tenants. Between the 1908-1912 and 1916-1920 surveys, single crop paddy rents as a percentage of yields fell by 4.7 percent, double crop paddy rents fell by 3.2 percent, and mulberry field rents fell by 22.8 percent. Tenant surpluses after rent increased by 19.7 percent, 11.1 percent, and 67 percent, respectively, on the three kinds of fields.[64]

The growth of tenancy also slowed, almost to a standstill. In 1912, the first year of the Taishō era, tenants tilled 45.4 percent of Japan's arable land; ten years later, the percentage had reached only 46.4 percent. Tenancy spread by only two-tenths of 1 percent per year in a decade compared to 1 percent per year for the forty years before 1912. And it is even more likely that reclamation, not poverty, caused tenancy in the Taishō than in the Meiji years. While tenancy spread to

[63] *Chōki keizai tōkei*, Vol. 8, p. 135; Vol. 9, p. 146; Ohkawa and Shinohara, *Patterns of Japanese Economic Development*, pp. 293-294.

[64] Nōrinshō nōmukyoku, *Hompō kosaku kankō* (Tokyo, 1926), 1908-1912 survey, pp. 17-18, 23; 1916-1920 survey, pp. 67, 70, 174.

200,000 more *chō* of land, 320,000 *chō* of new fields came under the plow; thus, even if landlord/entrepreneurs financed and contracted with tenants to till only three fifths of the reclaimed land, no tenancy was caused by bankruptcy or mortgage foreclosures.[65]

But, even more significantly, this national slowing of the growth of tenancy conceals regional variations which run counter to the expectations of the differentiation theorists. Tenancy actually contracted in this period in three relatively commercial regions: Tōzan, which includes Yamanashi, Tōkai around Nagoya, and Sanyō in the Inland Sea area near Okayama and Hiroshima. It expanded most rapidly in the two most remote regions of the country excluding Hokkaidō, Tōhoku in the far north and Kyūshū at the southern end of the nation.[66] Even if one believes that commercialization was the primary cause of tenancy and poverty in the Meiji period, which I do not, one seems compelled to conclude that the market benefited rather than hurt poor farmers in the early Taishō years.

The broadening demand for rice, cocoons, and various new products like milk, chicken, pork, beef, grapes, and apples not only brought increased income to tenant farmers, but also turned them more and more into profit-minded petty entrepreneurs. By 1915-1920, most farm households in commercial regions had members who had received elementary-school educations and could read at least simple publications on farming techniques and make written budgets and plans; used commercial, and increasingly, chemical fertilizers; and had access to rice seed, silkworm, and mulberry types developed in the modern laboratory. This combination of increased demand, improved techniques, and greater ability to exploit them led to larger profits and more capital, and subsequently to even greater ability to invest in better techniques and gather still bigger gains. Because of the profits,

---

[65] Nakamura Takafusa, *Economic Growth in Prewar Japan*, p. 56.
[66] *Ibid.*

literacy, and techniques, farmers also found themselves able to produce larger crop yields in a shorter period of time than in the past, which stimulated them both to enlarge their farms and to dispatch some of the family's labor to non-agricultural jobs.

Farmers' improved standards of living in these decades are thus reflected in trends toward a greater area of land tilled per farm worker and per cultivating household and away from large landlord-run or servant-farmed estates; this is the "trend toward petty farming" and "commercial production tenant farming" which Kurihara and Nishida posit. Between 1908 and 1939, the area of land tilled per farm worker grew by 36.4 percent, from 3.38 to 4.61 *tan* of arable.[67] In the same three decades, small, fragmented farms of 5 *tan* (one-half *chō*) or less declined from 38.1 percent to 34 percent, and large landlord or extended family estates of 3 *chō* or more from 3.2 percent to 1.7 percent, of all farms. Middle-sized, family operated farms of 5 *tan* to 3 *chō* increased from 58.8 percent to 64.3 percent of the total. (See Table 1-4.)

One should not conclude, as some writers do, however, that the 34 percent who in 1939 still cultivated less than 5 *tan* were destitute. Many of them ranked among the farmers who by choice because of increased labor productivity farmed only part-time while working, or sending family members to work, in non-agricultural jobs. Nishida has found in his research of Hanabusa Village in Yamanashi Prefecture that tenants with small holdings earned one-quarter of their income outside of agriculture, compared to only 7½ percent for middle farmers.[69] Needless to say, unlike the

[67] *Chōki keizai tōkei*, Vol. 9, pp. 216-217; Ohkawa and Shinohara, *Patterns of Japanese Economic Development*, pp. 293-295. Over the sixty-five prewar years for which we have data, 1874-1939, area cultivated per farm worker increased by 55.7 percent, from 2.96 to 4.61 *tan* per worker.

[68] I have corrected Ōuchi's totals for the 1912 and 1927 data, which do not tally exactly with the data in the other columns. Ōuchi, *Nōminsō no bunkai*, p. 245.

[69] Nagahara, *Nihon jinushisei*, pp. 228-229.

TABLE 1-4
Area of Cultivation by Household, 1908-1939
(excluding Hokkaidō)

Year	5 Tan or Less	5 Tan- 1 Chō	1-2 Chō	2-3 Chō	Over 3 Chō	Total
1908	2,003	1,754	1,031	306	167	5,261
1912	1,998	1,793	1,045	297	146	5,279[68]
1917	1,954	1,805	1,090	305	130	5,284
1922	1,891	1,810	1,140	299	122	5.262
1927	1,871	1,861	1,169	295	106	5,302[68]
1932	1,854	1,894	1,215	297	94	5,354
1939	1,773	1,761	1,299	290	87	5,210

Source: Ōuchi, *Nihon ni okeru nōminsō no bunkai*, pp. 168, 245, 258. In thousands of households.

well-educated landlords, who also garnered much of their income from non-agricultural sources as managers, teachers, government officials, investors, or entrepreneurs (two owned small 40-50 basin filatures in the village), the members of tenant households tended to toil in jobs with comparatively low pay, as silk reelers or farm laborers. But even Nishida, who views these jobs as "insecure," admits that they provided secondary income for poor farmers which would not have been available without Japan's capitalist development; in fact, average real wages nationwide for female filature workers and for male and female farm workers grew by over 50 percent between the Russo-Japanese War in 1905, and 1920.[70]

It also seems likely that poorer farm households in Hanabusa and similar villages dispatched more members than did larger-scale farmers to live and work outside the village. Resident household size in Hanabusa fell by 10 percent and in highly commercial Naka Koma County by 5 percent in the

[70] *Ibid.*, pp. 236-239; *Chōki keizai tōkei*, Vol. 8, pp. 135, 243-245.

fourteen years of the Taishō era. This evidence, together with survey data for 1924 and 1925 which indicate that tenant households averaged one to one-and-one-half fewer resident members than did owner tenant and owner households (5.92 to 6.91 to 7.37) shows, I think, that members of small-scale tenant households were more likely than members of owner tenant and owner households to seek employ outside the village.[71] Although Nishida's Hanabusa data do not include this non-residential income, it is very likely that his small-scale cultivators and their counterparts elsewhere supplemented their household's income with periodic remittances from the city while at the same time cutting expenditures by having fewer mouths to feed. Income from both farming and non-agricultural jobs seems to have increased for poor farm households in the first two decades of the twentieth century even more strongly than it had between 1870 and 1900.

WAS THERE A RURAL RECESSION IN THE 1920s?

It was at the end of these 15-20 years of rising tenant living standards and narrowing rift between the incomes of the lower and upper strata of rural society that tenant disputes first erupted in the Japanese countryside. The initial disputes appeared in 1917-1919, extraordinarily, almost anomalously, prosperous years for farmers, reached their peak in tenant participation[72] during both the recession years of 1921-1923 *and* the strong years of 1924-1926, declined through the succeeding good years of 1927-1929, receded even further during the depression years of 1930-1933, resurged again during the recovery years in the mid-1930s, before disappearing

[71] Nagahara, *Nihon jinushisei*, p. 221; *Yamanashi tōkeisho*, 1912 and 1926; Nōrinshō nōmukyoku, *Nōka keizai chōsa*, 1924, p. 14; 1925, p. 13.

[72] As I shall explain in more detail in Chapter Five, I believe that the number of participants or amount of land involved in disputes in any one year gives a better idea of the degree of anti-landlord activity in that year than do the number of disputes.

after 1940. I shall argue in Chapters Five and Six that the primary causes of these disputes were not short-term economic ones—as we can see from the schematic presentation above, participation flowed and ebbed without apparent correlation in both good years and bad—but longer-range stimuli like rising levels of tenant farmer income, education, literacy, cultivating techniques, entrepreneurial management, power, and self-confidence. Still, we must ask whether or not there are any special characteristics of Japanese rural society after World War I which might account for the original appearance and subsequent growth of the tenant movement in this particular era. The answer is "yes," there is one economic trend which should be mentioned, although I shall argue one must assert its importance as a cause of disputes with care; rural economic growth slowed between 1920 and 1935 from Meiji and early Taishō levels before taking off once again in the mid-1930s.

Many economic historians, among them Ohkawa Kazushi, Nakamura Takafusa, Hayami Yūjirō, and Yamada Saburō, have pointed out the decline in the rate of agricultural growth after 1919. As we can see from Table 1-5, productivity contracted by 8.1 percent in 1920-1924 from the 1915-1919 level. Scholars have forwarded various explanations for this contraction after steady growth. Among those advanced most frequently are the adverse effect of the Finance Ministry's deflationary fiscal and monetary policies between World War I and 1932, the end of the profitable reclamation of new fields, the diminishing returns in productive yields from increased use of chemical fertilizer, the end of the spread of traditional farming methods, the reduction of domestic rice prices because of large-scale importation of Korean and Taiwanese rice after the 1918 Rice Riots, the world depression from 1930 to 1934, and the temporary collapse of silk prices between 1929 and 1936 because of the depression and the development of rayon.[73]

[73] Hugh Patrick, "The Economic Muddle of the 1920s," James W. Mor-

TABLE 1-5

Agricultural Value Added and Real Productivity per Agricultural Worker

Year	Farm Value of Agricultural Production*	Current Inputs*	Value Added*	Workers (in 1,000s)	V.A. per Worker (yen)	Rural CPI	Index of Productivity
1879–80	507	146	361	15,588	23.2	34.9	100
1900–04	1,035	219	816	15,850	51.5	49.5	157
1905–09	1,315	268	1,047	15,950	65.6	57.7	171
1910–14	1,695	355	1,340	15,853	84.5	62.4	204
1915–19	2,988	597	2,391	14,597	163.8	89.8	275
1920–24	3,955	789	3,166	13,800	229.4	137.1	252
1925–29	3,844	798	3,046	13,631	223.5	123.4	273

* In millions of yen.

Calculated from *Chōki keizai tōkei*, Vol. 8, pp. 135–136; Vol. 9, pp. 146–147, 183–184; Ohkawa and Shinohara, *Patterns of Japanese Economic Development*, pp. 293–295.

It seems logical that one of the underlying causes of tenant disputes between 1920 and 1935 was the frustration felt by tenant and owner tenant farmers over this decline in their incomes. If a farmer who has become accustomed to steadily rising income faces its stagnation, he might well try disputation as a way of lowering his rent and continuing to improve his livelihood. Nevertheless, for two reasons, the agricultural decline of the 1920s and its effect on tenant disputes may well be overstated. First, 1918 and 1919 were, because of straitened postwar conditions in Europe, anomalously good years for Japanese farmers. If one excludes those two years from one's calculations, the index of productivity for 1915-1917 is 231, and the 1920s show continued, albeit slower, growth, not contraction. Second, the growth of farm household incomes in regions with advanced market economies where tenant disputes broke out first and most frequently did not falter as much as the data in Tables 1-1 and 1-5 lead us to believe; thus, we should not overemphasize the importance of this "stagnation" in the face of "rising expectations" as a cause of the tenant movement.

Although data for all Japan show a slowing of growth, statistics for highly commercialized areas like Naka Koma County in Yamanashi Prefecture demonstrate continued expansion, except during the recession years of the early 1920s and the depression years of the early 1930s. As we can see from Table 1-6, real value of production per farm household nationwide stagnated between 1919 and 1935 (the 1917-1921 period includes three excellent and two recession years); in Naka Koma, real value of agricultural production increased steadily until the world depression, and then took off again

ley, ed., *Dilemmas of Growth in Prewar Japan* (Princeton, 1971), pp. 213, 217, 255; Jung-Chao Liu and Daniel B. Suits, "An Econometric Model of a Rice Market," *Tunghai Journal*, 4-1 (Taiwan, July 1962), pp. 183-201; Hayami and Yamada, "Agricultural Productivity," p. 115; Ohkawa, "Phases of Agricultural Development and Economic Growth," p. 11; Nakamura Takafusa, *Economic Growth in Prewar Japan*, p. 29; Hayami Yūjirō, *A Century of Agricultural Growth in Japan* (Minneapolis and Tokyo, 1975), pp. 60-64.

TABLE 1-6

Indices of Real Value of Agricultural Production
per Farm Household for Japan and Naka Koma County,
1909-1939 (Japan 1909 = 100)

Year	Japan	Naka Koma
1909	100	97
1912-16	121	133
1917-21	139	155
1925-29	134	179
1930-34	114	141
1935-39	162	220

Calculated from *Chōki keizai tōkei*, Vol. 8, pp. 135-136; Vol. 9, pp. 146-147, 218-219; Ohkawa and Shinohara, *Patterns of Japanese Economic Development*, p. 388; *Yamanashi tōkeisho*.

in the late 1930s. Yet it was in prosperous areas like Naka Koma, not in the stagnant, depressed regions, that the most tenancy disputes occurred during the interwar years.

Farmers in regions like Naka Koma swam strongly in a sea of economic troubles because commercial experience and attitudes, capital, railroads, and proximity to markets allowed them to diversify when rice prices fell and rice productivity stagnated after World War I. The Japanese government, frightened by urban riots in the summer of 1918, imported Taiwanese and Korean rice to increase the supply and lower its price at home in order to lessen the possibility of future unrest. Jung-Chao Liu and Daniel B. Suits have calculated that each 1 percent increase in rice imports reduced the domestic price by 1.75 percent.[74] If one sets 1919, the apex of the World War I boom, as 100, Japanese rice prices when adjusted for inflation slumped to 71 in 1933, before rising to 103 in 1939.[75] No wonder that rice yields, which had climbed to 1.88 *koku* per *tan* in 1915-1919, did not ad-

[74] Liu and Suits, "Rice Market," p. 194.

[75] *Chōki keizai tōkei*, Vol. 8, pp. 135-136; Vol. 9, pp. 146-147, 216-217.

vance significantly until 1935-1939, when they jumped from 1.9 *koku* in 1930-1934 to 2.03 *koku* in 1935-1939.[76] It would seem that the stagnation of rice yields in the 1920-1934 period and their resurgence after 1935 were as much functions of farmers' conscious decisions to shift some of their resources to other crops or to non-agricultural work (and then back) as they were the result of nearing the productive limits of available and affordable cultivating techniques.

The stagnation of rice and the slow but steady transition to other crops, especially in regions like Naka Koma, is demonstrated by the data in Table 1-7. The real value of production of all staple grains fell between 1915-1919, and 1930-1934. Conversely, vegetables, livestock, poultry, and fruit production expanded; in 1915-1919, these four products represented 10.7 percent, but, in 1935-1939, 15.1 percent of total farm value. We see here the beginnings of the changes away from customary eating habits which we usually associate with the post-World War II era.[77]

TABLE 1-7

Index of Real Value of Agricultural Production for Primary Crop Categories, 1915-1919 to 1935-1939

Year	Rice	Seri-culture	Grain	Vegetables	Livestock & Poultry	Fruit
1915-19	100	100	100	100	100	100
1920-24	89	77	73	104	135	117
1925-29	89	105	81	104	173	135
1930-34	78	68	71	104	187	149
1935-39	114	84	119	120	234	187

Calculated from *Chōki keizai tōkei*, Vol. 8, pp. 135-136; Vol. 9, pp. 146-147; Ohkawa and Shinohara, *Patterns of Japanese Economic Development*, p. 388.

[76] *Ibid.*, Vol. 9, 166-168, 216-217.

[77] These products represented only 5.4 percent of total value of production in 1874-1878, but rose to 32.1 percent in 1959-1963.

Cocoons also provided farmers with a source of non-grain income in the 1920s and 1930s, especially in sericultural prefectures like Yamanashi. In the late 1920s, sericulture provided about 17-18 percent of total farm value nationwide although it slumped to 12-13 percent during the world depression, when weak American demand for silk stockings and rayon cut into raw silk exports (one must keep in mind, however, that rayon thread was not used to make stockings and did not affect stocking-raw silk exports). Sericulture made a partial recovery in the late 1930s because a renewed market for silk stockings in the United States stimulated exports once more. Farmers in areas like Naka Koma, which, as we have seen in Table 1-6, recovered strongly from the depression, received even greater benefits from silk's resurgence; sericulture provided 55 percent of income in the 1920s, but 60 percent in the late 1930s, which were even more prosperous. It was DuPont's introduction in 1939 of nylon, which was used in stockings, and the wartime end of Japanese-American trade in 1941, not the depression and rayon, that killed Japan's and Yamanashi's raw silk industry.[78] In commercial areas especially, crop diversification lessened the adverse effects of the stagnation of rice and *mugi* yields and profits; still, it was these areas with highly developed market economies, not the backward and depressed areas like Tōhoku, which had the most active and widespread tenant movements.

Farmers not only switched to other crops to avoid the ill effects of rice stagnation; they also shifted to other work. In the 1920s industrial output grew slowly but steadily and in the 1930s it expanded more rapidly than in any other decade of the prewar modern era.[79] Accordingly, as we can see from Table 1-8, non-agricultural jobs grew in number; during the twenty-five years between the outbreaks of the two world

[78] Jesse W. Markham, *Competition in the Rayon Industry* (Cambridge, 1952), p. 33. By 1959-1963, sericulture represented only 3 percent of total farm value of agricultural production nationwide.

[79] Patrick, "Muddle," pp. 214-215.

TABLE 1-8

Population and Workers in Agriculture and Non-Agricultural
Jobs, 1910-1939 (in 1,000s)

Year	Population	Agriculture	Non-Agriculture
1910-14	50,223	15,853	9,657
1915-19	53,669	14,597	11,846
1920-24	57,403	13,800	13,576
1925-29	61,639	13,631	14,773
1930-34	66,416	14,061	15,949
1935-39	71,014	13,461	17,981

Sources: Ohkawa and Shinohara, *Patterns of Japanese Economic Development*, pp. 293-295, 392-393.

wars, while population grew by 1.4 percent per year, the
number of non-agricultural workers increased by even more,
by 2.5 percent per year, whereas that of farm workers contracted. In 1900 only 3½ percent of Naka Koma County's
80,000 registered residents (*honseki*) lived and worked outside
the county, but by 1920 the percentage had risen to 10 percent of 100,000, by 1930 to 15 percent of 113,000, and in
1935, 25,000 people, or about 21 percent of those whose *honseki* was in Naka Koma, resided and worked outside the
county all year around; another 3,700 lived away from their
home villages, but within the county.[80] Clearly a great number of farmers in Naka Koma and elsewhere turned to commercial, manufacturing, and service jobs to supplement their
agricultural incomes in these two decades. In fact, one can
argue that a shortage of farm labor because of profitable non-
agricultural employment opportunities may have led to stagnation in rice production to as great an extent as the stagnation caused farmers to seek jobs elsewhere.

Ron Napier has presented a convincing analysis of the im-

[80] *Yamanashi tōkeisho.*

pact of this "transformation of the Japanese labor market" in the 1920s and 1930s. As more farm workers became industrial workers, not only did farm household incomes rise, but also, according to Napier, the position of labor improved steadily, until after World War I it reached the "turning point," the place where surplus labor disappeared so that the "marginal productivity of labor in the traditional sector exceeds the subsistence wage level."[81] Because at this point labor became scarce rather than plenteous, employers had to pay workers more money to attract them; thus wages for both industrial and farm workers increased (Table 1-9). Real manufacturing wages increased by 2.8 percent per year between 1915-1919 and 1935-1939. Real wages for landless farm workers, the lowest stratum of rural society, increased by 1.3 percent per year and declined only during the depression years—although even then wages averaged 10 percent higher than during the years of the World War I boom.

The combined effect of non-agricultural job opportunities, labor scarcity, and higher wages, needless to say, benefited tenant farmers. If it had not, the tenant would have joined

TABLE 1-9

Indices of Real Wages for Manufacturing and Male
Annual Agricultural Workers, 1915-1939

Year	Agricultural	Manufacturing
1915-19	100	100
1920-24	121	142
1925-29	130	153
1930-34	110	176
1935-39	130	174

Calculated from Napier, "Labor Market," p. 346, and Ohkawa and Shinohara, *Patterns of Japanese Economic Development*, pp. 390-391.

[81] Napier, "The Transformation of the Japanese Labor Market, 1894-1937," pp. 343-345.

"a queue to become a [farm] wage worker," to borrow Napier's apt phrase.[82] The tenants' relative security in income and dearth in numbers allowed them to refuse to till a landlord's land (i.e., to strike) in order to force him to make concessions on rents, land tenure, and contract terms. The new conditions and disputes also brought success in achieving these goals. In the 1920s and 1930s rents fell steadily, tenants were evicted only infrequently, and landlords agreed to contracts which gave tenants increased freedom of action. Tenants kept 59 percent more rice after paying paddy rents in 1935-1939 than 30 years earlier; real dry field rents fell by 21 percent, while real value of production for cocoons and *mugi*, the two primary non-paddy crops, increased by 73 percent and 65 percent in three decades (Table 1-10).[83] Landlords evicted tenants unconditionally in 5.3 percent, and with conditions in only 39 percent more of landlord attempts to use their own private property as they wanted.[84] Tenants won the right to sublet, sell the right of tenancy, plant what they wanted, and otherwise use the landlord's land more or less as if it were their own.[85] So much power had tenants gained before the land reform in 1946-1948 that when the Yamanashi Electric Railroad Company purchased its right-of-way in the western part of the Kōfu Basin in 1929-1931, it paid tenants over one-third of the price it offered the landowners.[86] Non-agricultural job opportunities and the end of a labor surplus in Japan after World War I gave tenant farmers

[82] *Ibid.*, p. 349.

[83] Farmers grew both rice and winter grains in many of their paddies, but paid rent only on the rice crop. Accordingly, the 59 percent increase in surplus after rent refers only to rice; any growth in area of double cropped paddy or in yields of *mugi* also added to the tenant's surplus. Thus, tenants benefited from reduced rent in the twentieth century to a greater extent than this evidence indicates.

[84] *Kosaku chōtei nempō*, 1925-1926; *Kosaku nempō*, 1927-1939; *Nōchi nempō*, 1940.

[85] Nōrinshō nōmukyoku, *Hompō kosaku kankō; Kosaku jijō chōsa* (Tokyo, 1938).

[86] Kyōchōkai, *Kosaku sōgichi ni okeru nōson jijō no henka* (Tokyo, 1934), p. 77.

TABLE 1-10
Rents, Yields and Value of Production, 1905-1939

| | Paddy (in koku) | | | Dry Fields | | |
| | | | | | | |
Year	Rent	Yield	Surplus	Real Rent	Real Sericulture Income	Real Mugi Income
1905-09	0.966	1.64	0.674	100	100	100
1910-14	0.984	1.72	0.736	108	111	130
1915-19	1.043	1.88	0.837	102	204	137
1920-24	1.041	1.89	0.849	79	158	101
1925-29	0.971	1.88	0.909	89	214	113
1930-34	0.954	1.90	0.946	81	138	98
1935-39	0.960	2.03	1.070	79	173	165

Source: *Chōki keizai tōkei*, Vol. 8, pp. 135-136; Vol. 9, pp. 146-147, 167-168, 220-221. The same data, excluding 1938-1939, is presented in a slightly different form in Napier, "Labor Market," p. 357.

the leverage to continue to improve their standards of living even during a period of slowed economic growth.

Not surprisingly, therefore, tenancy declined in the 1920s and 1930s. Nationwide, the percentage of tenant-farmed land decreased 1.1 percent from 46.4 percent of all arable land in 1922 to 45.9 percent in 1940, and in four commercial regions it ebbed considerably more: by over 10 percent in Kinki around Kyoto and Osaka, and by 7½-10 percent in Tōzan, Tōkai, and Sanyō, the three commercial areas where tenancy had ebbed even from 1912. Tenancy in backward Tōhoku increased by 7-8 percent over these eighteen years, but even there it waned from 1932 after the tenant movement spread to the northeast.[87] It would seem that a combination of commercial farming, higher tenant and farm worker incomes, a shortage of labor, and tenancy disputes made landlordism increasingly unprofitable, and this allowed tenants, with

[87] Nakamura Takafusa, *Economic Growth in Prewar Japan*, p. 56.

governmental help, to buy land cheaply to cultivate it as owner farmers. And conditions improved to the greatest degree for tenant farmers in the very commercial regions where, according to the theory of differentiation, the market should have pauperized the lower rural economic strata and turned petit bourgeois smallholders into tenants and rural proletarian wage workers.

Rural borrowing patterns also underline this trend toward the middle (i.e., away from differentiation). If most borrowing had been done by poor farmers to keep their marginal farms afloat, one would expect it to increase in bad times and decrease in good, and would expect tenant farmers to be more deeply in debt than owner farmers. But the opposite seems to be true in both cases. Farmers took out one-third fewer loans in the depression year of 1933 than they had in the relatively prosperous year of 1928, and, as Table 1-11 demonstrates, borrowing rose steadily from the time of the Russo-Japanese War as real farm value per farm worker increased, and fell sharply only as the depression set in at the end of the 1920s.[88]

Nationwide surveys of budgets in selected households conducted by the Agriculture Ministry in the 1920s and 1930s reveal that the average owner farmer borrowed 42 percent more than the average tenant farmer.[89] (See Table 1-12.) Owner tenants borrowed more than owner farmers, but the surveys also show that the former tilled larger farms; thus, they needed more capital. All in all, indebtedness appears to have been a sign of good farm management, not of imminent poverty. In fact, one could argue that the *low* rather than the *high* level of tenant farmer borrowing signified their relative indigency; because they had less land to use as security for loans, tenants could not borrow to improve tech-

---

[88] *Ibid.*, p. 230; Gōtō Shin'ichi, *Nihon no kin'yū tōkei* (Tokyo, 1970), pp. 136-137, 140-141.

[89] As early as 1937, Kawada Shirō pointed out that owner farmers borrowed far more than tenant farmers. *Nihon shakai seisaku* (Tokyo, 1937), pp. 349-350.

TABLE 1-11
Indices of Real Borrowing in which Farm Land
Was Used as Security and Real Farm Value of
Agricultural Production, 1900-1933

Year	Index of Real Farm Value per Farm Worker	Index of Real Borrowing in which Farm Land Was Used as Security
1900-04	100	100
1905	92	73
1910	107	140
1915	128	145
1920	156	166
1925	190	185
1926	173	236
1927	164	243
1928	167	282
1929	170	255
1930	131	228
1931	125	230
1932	147	188
1933	170	149

Calculated from *Kōsaku nempō*, 1934, pp. 9-11; *Chōki keizai tōkei*, Vol. 8, pp. 135-136; Vol. 9, pp. 146-147, 218-219; Ohkawa and Shinohara, *Patterns of Japanese Economic Development*, pp. 293-295.

TABLE 1-12
Indebtedness by Category of Farm Household,
1925, 1928-1940

Owner Farmer	664 *yen*
Owner Tenant Farmer	752
Tenant Farmer	467

Calculated from *Nōka keizai chōsa*, 1925, 1928-1935; *Nōka keizai chōsa hōkoku*, 1936-1940.

niques and expand production as rapidly as could their more well-to-do owner tenant and owner farmer compatriots.

Although tenant farmers took out fewer loans than did more well-to-do cultivators, tenants used a higher percentage of their resources to manage their farms, which partly compensated for their lower borrowing power.[90] The 1921-1940 surveys show that the tenant farmer's income after rent and taxes was 70 percent of that of an owner farmer; the owner tenant fell in between, 88 percent of the owner farmer's level. But if one looks at their expenditures per household for land, land improvement, tools, seeds, seedlings, feeds, and fertilizers, the primary farm expenses aside from rent, taxes, interest, and debt repayment, one finds a much narrower gap. (See Table 1-13.) The surveys reveal that tenant farmers invested 77 percent, and owner tenants 94 percent of owner farmers' outlays to manage their farms. The details of these surveys indicate that tenant cultivators saved on non-productive expenditures like those for entertainment, ceremonial occasions, housing, and clothing, but invested more heavily in food and farms.[91] In other words, although

---

[90] It is reported in Nōgyō hattatsushi chōsakai, *Nihon nōgyō hattatsushi*, Vol. 4 (Tokyo, 1954), p. 54, that farmers in the middle and late Meiji period sold their rice and ate mugi and millet mixed or imported rice, which they purchased. Ōuchi Tsutomu, *Nōgyōshi*, p. 90, interprets this to be a sign of the tenants' financial distress. Since there is no reason to believe that Japanese rice is superior nutritionally to *mugi*, millet, or imported rice, one can also view this trend as reflecting poor farmers' good farm management; they sold a crop which brought good profits and bought equally nutritious but cheaper ones to eat. Japanese rice seems to hold symbolic importance for some Japanese scholars. Nakamura Masanori, in his discussion of the suffering of female filature workers, considers it a deprivation that they were required to eat Taiwanese, Chinese, or Korean rather than Japanese rice. *Rōdōsha to nōmin*, p. 82. A non-Japanese scholar, Susan B. Hanley, argues that farmers had more nutritious diets when they ate coarse grains rather than polished rice. "A High Standard of Living in Nineteenth Century Japan: Fact or Fantasy?" *Journal of Economic History*, Vol. 43-1 (1983), p. 188.

[91] The following table, which indicates the percentage of owner farmer expenditures made in each category by owner tenant and tenant farmers, shows how poorer farmers saved on non-essentials to spend on farming. Compared to farm management outlays, non-farm management expendi-

TABLE 1-13

Index of Average Expenditures for Farm Management
Excluding Rent, Taxes, and Interest; and Repayment
of Capital on Loans by Category of Household,
1921-1940

Category	Income	Farm Expenditures
Owner Farmer	100	100
Owner Tenant Farmer	88	94
Tenant Farmer	70	77

Calculated from *Nōka keizai chōsa*, 1921-1935; *Nōka keizai chōsa hōkoku*, 1936-1940.

tenant farmers borrowed less than owner tenant and owner farmers, they used a higher percentage of their income and indebtedness to run their farms and a smaller percentage non-productively. If tenant farmers were falling increasingly into debt and if they were not becoming increasingly entrepreneurial in their approach to farm management, one would not expect them to run their farms in almost the same way with almost the same outlays as owner farmers; yet they did.

If tenant farmers faced increasing poverty, one would anticipate a large gap in income between owner and tenant farmers, but, surprisingly, one does not find it in the survey

tures were relatively lower for tenant farmers in every category except food, which was obviously not a luxury.

	Owner	Owner Tenant	Tenant
Income after Rent and Taxes	100	88	70
Farm Management	100	94	77
Food	100	96	86
Clothing	100	84	65
Entertainment	100	71	48
Ceremonial	100	81	52
Housing	100	74	59

data. According to the surveys, the income gap between small landlord-owner farmers, the rural upper middle class, and tenant farmers was not as great as one would expect in a highly stratified society. In the 1921-1930 surveys, an average tenant household's net income after deducting all agricultural expenses including rent and taxes was 63 percent of an owner farmer's; in the more broadly based 1931-1940 surveys, it was 72 percent. Owner tenants fell in between with 81 percent and 90 percent of owner farmer households' income in the two decades.[92] A society in which the lower class earns three-fifths to three-quarters, and the lower middle class eight- or nine-tenths of the income of the upper middle class after rent and taxes (especially since some of the upper middle class were landlords) does not seem highly stratified to me.[93] In addition, the surveys indicate that the differential between the three groups narrowed over the two decades. Table 1-14 presents data on net income after excluding all agricultural expenses (household expenses being part of the self-employed farmer's "salary") and shows that owner tenants' incomes rose from 81 percent to 91 percent, and tenant farmers' incomes from 62 percent to 76 percent of owner farmers' incomes between 1921-1925 and 1936-1939. To the extent that the Agriculture Ministry's surveys accurately reflected rural economic conditions, they demon-

[92] *Nōka keizai chōsa*, 1921-1935; *Nōka keizai chōsa hōkoku*, 1936-1940.

[93] Ōuchi points out that these surveys must be used with extreme care and I agree. The samples, especially in the early 1920s, are small (1921 includes only 100 households); farm size for cultivators in each category are larger than national averages; and the households surveyed, in that they kept the necessary records to be included, are atypical. Nevertheless, as he points out, we use these surveys because they provide our best information on household budgets by class of farmer in the interwar years. Moreover, as Ōuchi recognizes, the surveys for the 1930s have larger samples (280-290 households) and from 1931 on include part-time farm households, thus bringing farm size per surveyed household more into line with national averages for all farm households. *Nōminsō no bunkai*, pp. 165-166. It was in the late 1930s, with its more accurate surveys, that net tenant income vis-à-vis net owner farmer income reached its highest levels in the interwar decades.

TABLE 1-14
Net Income after Deducting All Agriculture Expenses Including
Rent and Taxes as a Percentage of Owner Farmer Income,
1921-1939

Years	Owner Farmer	Owner Tenant	Tenant Farmer
1921–25	100	80.6	62.0
1926–30	100	82.2	64.2
1931–35	100	88.3	73.5
1936–39	100	90.5	76.2

Calculated from *Nōka keizai chōsa*, 1921-1935; *Nōka keizai chōsa hōkoku*, 1936-1939.

strate that tenant and owner tenant farmers' livelihoods improved vis-à-vis the rural elite in the interwar years.

Finally, the surveys indicate that all three categories of farmer turned a profit throughout the 1920s and 1930s except during the worst depression years of 1930-1931 when owner, owner tenant, and tenant farmers' total expenditures exceeded total income by 2.7 percent, 3.2 percent, and 4.4 percent, respectively; tenants also took a loss of one-hundredth of one percent in 1929, but their profits in the succeeding depression years of 1932-1933 more than compensated for the 1929-1931 losses. Owner farmers made profits of 7-8 percent in 1921-1928, of 11 percent or more in 1932-1935, and of 22 percent in the second half of the 1930s; owner tenants also made profits of 7-8 percent in the 1920s, 9-10 percent in the late depression years, and of almost 20 percent in the last five years of the 1930s; even tenant farmers stayed in the black by 5-6 percent in 1921-1928 and again in 1932-1935, and by over 15 percent between 1935 and 1940.[94] Even if these surveys do not present a completely accurate morphology of economic conditions in the Japanese countryside, owner tenant and tenant farmers seems to have kept their

[94] *Nōka keizai chōsa*, 1921-1935; *Nōka keizai chōsa hōkoku*, 1936-1940.

heads well above water during the so-called stagnation years of the interwar agricultural economy.[95]

THE WORLD DEPRESSION AND JAPANESE FARMERS

There was, of course, one quinquennium with particularly bad economic conditions during these two decades, that of the world depression of 1930-1934, and we must look at its effects before ending our discussion of agricultural growth in modern Japan. After the American stock market collapsed in the fall of 1929, economic disaster spread around the world like influenza, and caused unemployment in cities and greatly reduced incomes in the countryside everywhere it touched. Japanese rice, *mugi* and cocoon prices fell by 37 percent, 20 percent, and 55 percent, respectively in 1930 and did

[95] Nakamura Masanori, in his critique of Nishida Yoshiaki's work, objects to the latter's claim that his owner tenant and upper tenant farmers earned a profit from their farms. Nakamura avers that Nishida finds a profit only because he does not calculate labor costs when he computes his farmers' balance sheets. If unpaid labor charges are added to farm management costs, Nakamura writes, Nishida's industrious farmers of the 1920s did not make a profit. Nakamura, *Jinushiseishi kenkyū*, p. 238. Nakamura might make the same objection to the data presented here from the 1921-1940 surveys, but if he did so his criticism would not be valid. Although the surveys do not show labor costs per se, they do include among expenditures those things which most people buy with their salaries or wages: food, clothing, entertainment, etc. The outlays listed under those budget items included in the surveys' balance sheets as household expenditures, as distinct from farm management disbursements, represent the wages the farmer paid to himself and his family members. Thus, the profits shown above have been calculated after unpaid labor costs (the self-employed farmers' equivalent of wages) are subtracted and meet Nakamura's definition of a profit. I might add here that farm management expenditures include the farmer's capital expenditures for farm equipment, etc., as well as his spending on current inputs; thus, that part of his profit which he reinvests in his farm business would be enumerated under the farm management expenditure rather than the profit and loss category of the surveys. In other words, the average surveyed farmer's capital accumulation was larger than the profits reported above.

not recover until the middle of the decade.[96] In the view of Nakamura Masanori, "the Japanese village, which had rice and cocoons as its two pillars, was thrown into the midst of unprecedented poverty."[97] Without question, Japan's living standards fell to a level lower than at any time since the beginning of the World War I boom. (See Table 1-15.)

Nakamura's hyperbole notwithstanding, one should remember that poverty is relative. Although rural Japanese suffered during the depression—real value of production per farm worker was 17 percent lower in 1930-1934 than it had been in 1925-1929—they still had more buying power than they had had in 1910-1914 and over twice as much as their grandparents had had in the boom years of 1879-1880 just before the Matsukata Deflation. Moreover, because of the reductions in rent which tenants received in the 1930s and because they still on average marketed only half of their produce, tenant incomes fell much less than 17 percent. Although a 5-10 percent reduction in income over five years was certainly not welcomed and tenant-farmed land increased by about 140,000 *chō* (2 percent of all arable land) between 1927 and 1932, conditions did not fall to the extremes that they had in eighteenth- and nineteenth-century crises, or to the extent that one would expect in a depression if one followed the differentiation of classes approach.[98] To begin with, the greatest suffering occurred in the least commercial region of the country, Tōhoku, where the impact of the depression coincided with a series of bad rice harvests. Second, suffering even there was light compared to the effects of famine in the mortality crises of the eighteenth and nineteenth centuries. Mikiso Hane, a writer whose inclination is to emphasize the damage to "the underside of Japan"

[96] *Chōki keizai tōkei*, Vol. 9, p. 161; the price of rice reached the 1929 level again in 1934, *mugi* in 1936, but cocoons not until 1939.

[97] Nakamura, *Jinushiseishi kenkyū*, p. 261.

[98] Between 1927 and 1932, 115,000 *chō* of new land came under the plow; thus, all the newly tenanted land cannot be attributed to foreclosures and bankruptcies caused by the depression.

TABLE 1-15

Agricultural Value Added and Real Productivity per Agricultural Worker

Year	Farm Value of Agricultural Production*	Current Inputs*	Value Added*	Workers (in 1,000s)	V.A. per Worker (yen)	Rural CPI	Index of Productivity
1879–80	507	146	361	15,588	23.2	34.9	100
1910–14	1,695	355	1,340	15,853	84.5	62.4	204
1920–24	3,955	789	3,166	13,800	229.4	137.1	252
1925–29	3,844	798	3,046	13,631	223.5	123.4	273
1930–34	2,556	546	2,010	14,061	142.9	95.0	227
1935–39	4,290	930	3,360	13,461	249.6	114.1	330

* In millions of yen.

Calculated from *Chōki keizai tōkei*, Vol. 8, pp. 135-136; Vol. 9, pp. 146-147, 183-184; Ohkawa and Shinohara, *Patterns of Japanese Economic Development*, pp. 293-295, 388.

caused by the modernization process, writes that during "the famine of 1934 . . . in Iwate prefecture about half of the 900,000 people were on the verge of starvation." Even if his assessment is not exaggerated, this contrasts starkly with "the hundreds of thousands of people" who, he writes, starved to death in "the 1730s, the 1780s, and the 1830s."[99] Oddly, given the adverse effects of the depression and crop failure in Iwate and the rest of Tōhoku in 1934-1935 that Hane reports, 63.8 percent and 65 percent of eligibles respectively passed the conscription physical examination, compared to 58 percent in Yamanashi, 54.7 percent in Tokyo, and 61.4 percent nationwide.[100]

Let me also reemphasize something here which should be clear from the data in Table 1-15; when farm value dropped by 33.5 percent during the depression, the value of current inputs fell too, by 31.6 percent. In other words, although farmers' incomes contracted in 1930-1934, so too did their expenses. Nakamura Masanori writes that farmers had smaller harvests during the depression because the cost of commercial fertilizers, which made up the majority of the fertilizer used, did not fall when crop prices did—the fertilizer companies had the power to set prices.[101] The fact of the matter is that fertilizer prices did fall, and fell sharply to about the same extent as the price of rice and to a much greater extent than the consumer price index. From 1925-1929 to 1930-1934, the cost of the four primary commercial fertilizers (83 percent of all commercial fertilizers in 1929) fell by 33.3 percent, while rice and cocoon prices and the consumer price index fell 33.3 percent, 53.6 percent, and 23 percent, respectively.[102] In spite of the adverse effects of the depression on rural household incomes, farmers, instead of economizing on fertilizer, took advantage of lower prices to use 18 percent more chemical fertilizer in 1930-1934 than

[99] Hane, *Peasants, Rebels, and Outcastes*, pp. 7, 114-115.

[100] *Rikugunshō tōkei nenkan*, 1934-1935.

[101] Nakamura, *Jinushiseishi kenkyū*, p. 264.

[102] *Hiryō yōran* (1936), pp. 20-21.

they had in 1925-1929. Accordingly, in the depression era the production of rice and cocoons did not shrink as Nakamura states it did, but rose by 2.7 percent and 5.1 percent, respectively; the production of profitable cash "crops" like livestock (swine 24.6 percent), poultry (hens 19.8 percent, hens' eggs 59.9 percent), and dairy products (cow's milk 40 percent) expanded even more.[103]

Finally, farmers during the depression continued to supplement their income with non-agricultural wages and this helped cushion the shock of adversity. As we can see from Table 1-16, the shift toward non-agricultural employ persisted during the depression. From 1925-1929 to 1930-1934, non-agricultural workers increased in percentage more rapidly than did the population as a whole; the number of ag-

TABLE 1-16
Population and Number of Workers, 1925-1934
(in 1,000s of workers)

Year	Population	Umemura LTES Agricultural Workers	Umemura Patterns Agricultural Workers	Non-Agricultural Workers
1925-29	61,639	13,942	13,631	14,773
1930-34	66,416	13,867	14,061	15,949
	+7.7%	−0.5%	+3.2%	+8%

Calculated from *Chōki keizai tōkei*, Vol. 9, p. 219; Ohkawa and Shinohara, *Patterns of Japanese Economic Development*, pp. 295, 392-393.

[103] *Chōki keizai tōkei*, Vol. 9, pp. 168, 181. Fertilizer, needless to say, is not used in the process of raising silkworms, swine, hens, hens' eggs, and cow's milk, but in the growing of mulberry and feed which the silkworms and animals eat. Since the sources give no data on mulberry or feed grain yields, I have substituted cocoon, animal, poultry, and dairy product yields, which could not have increased unless mulberry and feed production grew. These data raise doubts about the validity of Nakamura's contention that poor farmers in hard times practiced self-exploitation. *Jinushiseishi kenkyū*, pp. 264-265.

ricultural workers either deceased absolutely or expanded to a lesser degree than did population, depending on which of Umemura Mataji's two sets of data on farm workers one follows. But, either way, these statistics support Nakamura Takafusa's contention that once laborers emigrated to urban jobs they did not return to work in their villages again. In fact, Nakamura writes that even female textile operatives, who normally worked for only a few years, did not go home after completing their terms in the filatures or cotton mills, but rather married urban workers. Thus, to Nakamura, the slight rise in rural work force during the depression (if there was one), does not indicate that urban workers returned to their villages during times of economic hardship, but rather represents normal population growth and reduced emigration to the cities.[104] These statistics and this interpretation contrast with the view of Nakamura Masanori and Ann Waswo that large numbers of unemployed laborers went home during the depression, placing greater pressure on a limited amount of arable land and thus threatening the livelihoods of farm households.[105]

Not only did farm households persist in having family members work at non-agricultural jobs during the depression, but also they still earned reasonably good wages, considering the bad times. Real industrial and manufacturing wages increased by 12.8 percent and 14.3 percent, respectively, in spite of economic adversity worldwide; real wages for female filature workers fell only by either 3 percent or 6.9 percent (depending on source), in spite of the depression and rayon. Only real wages for service jobs, which included household servants, the kind of job many teenagers from tenant households might be likely to hold, fell sharply, by 20.6 percent, but even in this case the number of service jobs increased by over 13 percent during the depression.[106] Al-

[104] Nakamura Takafusa, *Economic Growth in Prewar Japan*, pp. 29, 128.

[105] Nakamura Masanori, *Jinushiseishi kenkyū*, p. 262; Waswo, *Japanese Landlords*, pp. 128-129.

[106] Ohkawa and Shinohara, *Patterns of Japanese Economic Development*, pp. 390-394; *Chōki keizai tōkei*, Vol. 11, p. 302.

though the quinquennium from 1930 to 1934 was a straitened time for rural Japanese, it does not seem to have been a period when the "village . . . was thrown into the midst of unprecedented poverty."

RURAL RECOVERY AFTER 1935

The five or six years which immediately followed the depression brought rural Japan unprecedented prewar prosperity. A combination of Finance Minister Takahashi Korekiyo's stimulative fiscal policies, military spending, a depreciating yen foreign-exchange rate, higher raw silk and cocoon prices, and changing domestic eating patterns led to a sharp growth in productivity. Productivity per farm worker (Table 1-15) grew by 45.4 percent from 1930-1934 to 1935-1939 and reached its highest level before the mid-1950s. Renewed prosperity must have relieved most of the suffering that farm villages had felt during the depression.

Data on increases in productivity alone do not reflect the benefits to tenant farmers of the economic revival of the mid-1930s. As we have seen in Table 1-10, tenants also garnered a larger share of the results of this comeback than did their economic superiors, the landlords. In the five immediate post-depression years, the tenant farmer's rice surplus after paddy rent increased by 13.1 percent; real dry field rents fell by 2.5 percent, while the real farm value of production for the two primary dry field crops, cocoons and *mugi*, increased by 25.4 percent and 68.4 percent. (The reader should also remember that farmers grew *mugi* as a second crop on many of their paddies, but paid none of it in rent; thus, the 13.1 percent expansion of rice surplus understates the benefits which accrued to paddy-tenant farmers in the late 1930s.) Although we have no cumulative data on landlords' rent income, materials about Sekimoto, one of Hanabusa Village's leading landlords, indicate that he received 2.8 percent less rent rice per *tan* of paddy, and, amazingly, 56.8 percent less

[107] Nagahara, *Nihon jinushisei*, p. 313.

rent income when adjusted for inflation per *tan* of dry land in 1940 than in 1930.[107] Data for paddy rent charged by Oku-yama Genzō in Kasugai Village in the Kōfu Basin indicate that yields increased by 9 percent but rent by only 4½ percent between the early and late 1930s.[108] If these examples are at all representative, then tenant farmers gained larger and larger slices of a growing economic pie in the Japanese countryside during the early years of World War II.

The advantages which accrued to tenants, at least compared to their urban brethren, continued through the end of World War II. While Japan's cities suffered grievously from American bombing in 1945, the countryside, the army's "electoral constituency," as Tokutomi Soho called it, paid a much smaller price. Agricultural production remained high in spite of conscription, the recall of reservists to active duty, the battlefield deaths of thousands of villagers, and the shortage of farm tools, chemical fertilizers, and pesticides. Rice production was only 15 percent lower in 1945 than it had been in 1933, the best prewar harvest; *mugi* production in 1939-1940 reached its highest level in history up until that time, and in 1941, 1942, and 1944 outputs bettered any other years except a few during World War I.[109]

A major reason for this stability in grain output during the war was the government's policies to stimulate production which benefited producers, and thus tenants, more than it did non-producing landlords. The government introduced a double-pricing system for rice, by which it paid a higher price to producer/sellers than it did to landlord/sellers. When a landlord in 1941 or 1942 marketed rent rice, he received 44 yen per *koku*, but when a producer, whether he was owner farmer or tenant farmer, sold it, he garnered 49 yen (Table 1-17). By the immediate postwar months in early 1946, a tenant-producer-seller received five-and-one-half times more money than did a landlord-rent collector-seller.[110]

---

[108] *Ibid.*, p. 216.
[109] *Chōki keizai tōkei*, Vol. 9, p. 168.
[110] Nishida, "Jisakunō sōsetsu iji seisaku no rekishiteki seikaku," Hayama

TABLE 1-17
Double-Pricing System for Rice during World War II

Year	Price Paid to Landlord	Price Paid to Producer
1941	44 yen	49 yen
1942	44	49
1943	47	62.50
1944	47	62.50
April 5, 1945	55	92.50
November 17, 1945	55	150.00
March 31, 1946	55	300.00
1946	75	550.00

Source: Nishida Yoshiaki, "Jisakunō sōsetsu iji seisaku no rekishiteki sei-kaku," in Hayama Teisaku et al., *Dentōteki keizai shakai no rekishiteki tenkai*, Vol. 1 (Tokyo, 1983), p. 270.

At the same time that the government encouraged owner and tenant farmer production through the double-pricing system, it also liberalized the terms of the 1926 program to encourage tenants to become owner farmers by allowing them to buy land cheaply with guaranteed loans. It mandated that land be sold at a controlled land price, the 1939 assessment of each plot. As the value of land appreciated during the wartime inflation, the tenants could buy land at lower and lower real prices. In 1943, a tenant who purchased a *tan* of middle-grade paddy bought it for about 20 percent less than the market value; by 1945, he purchased it even more cheaply. Not surprisingly, tenants bought as much land under the government's program during the inflation of 1944–1946 as they had in all eighteen years between 1926 and 1943.[111] Tenant farmers even before the land reform had rid-

Teisaku et al., *Dentōteki keizai shakai no rekishiteki tenkai*, Vol. 1 (Tokyo, 1983), p. 270.

[111] Between 1926 and 1946, tenant farmers bought 382,165 *chō* of land, about 13-14 percent of all tenanted land in the mid-1920s, under the terms of this program. *Ibid.*, pp. 263, 270-271.

den the wave of rising agricultural productivity, through the trough of 1930-1934, to their highest pre-1948 level of prosperity. The striking transformation of the countryside between 1868 and 1948 turned peasants into farmers. General MacArthur and his land reform only iced the cake.

TWO

The Commercialization of
Agriculture in Yamanashi

THE Kōfu Basin, the heart of modern Yamanashi Prefecture
and of medieval Kai Province, is a small agricultural plain in
the mountains 80 miles to the west of Tokyo. One reaches
the basin and Kōfu, its principal city, by a two-and-one-half-
hour train ride along narrow river valleys through precipi-
tous mountains. After one's train leaves the Kantō Plain and
Tokyo's crowded suburbs at Hachiōji, it begins a steady
climb to Lake Sagami and into Yamanashi at the old post
town of Uenohara. From here the railroad follows the Katsura River westward through a valley not much wider than
the railbed, with a highway, a few houses, and the stream.
At Ōtsuki, the primary city of the province's easternmost
Tsuru region, and the transfer station for vacationers headed
for Mt. Fuji, the river curves to the southwest toward the
renowned volcano; but the visitor to Kōfu and its environs
continues to travel through the mountains to the Sasago
Pass, ten miles to the west. In Tokugawa times, this 3,600-
foot-high corridor slowed considerably the traveler walking
from Edo to Kōfu, but today one of the marvels of turn-of-
the-century Japanese engineering, a 2.9-mile-long tunnel, allows the train to glide easily into the Kōfu Basin.[1]

The view that meets the eye as the train emerges from the
mountains at Katsunuma is stunning: early in summer, one
sees Yamanashi's central plain covered with sparkling rice
paddies, lush grape vines, and fruit-laden peach and persimmon (and before World War II, gnarled mulberry) trees, and

[1] Yamanashi-ken shihan gakkō, *Sōgō kyōdo kenkyū* (Kōfu, 1936), (hereafter
abbreviated as *SKK*), p. 455.

surrounded by rugged mountains. But the express does not plunge onto the plain directly and speed straight to Kōfu. Rather, it curves to the north and then coasts westward around the perimeter of the basin. Thus, the visitor's view of the valley is panoramic; he can look from the train, moving around the basin's eastern and northern slopes on the one side, to the southern and western foothills 8-10 miles away on the other.

One can see a striking vista from any elevated spot in Kōfu, located as it is on the north-central edge of the basin. Standing on the balcony outside the lunch room of the Yamanashi Prefectural Library, for example, one can see the Sasago Pass and the 6,750-foot Mt. Daibosatsu to the east, the Chichibu Mountains to the north, the jagged, snow-capped, 9,000-10,000-foot peaks of the Southern Alps to the west, and the white cone of Mt. Fuji to the south. And within the confines of these encircling mountains lies the basin, a small delta of farmland fed by the Fuefuki River from the northeast, the Ara River from the north, and the Kamanashi River from the northwest, all of which flow into the Fuji River near the town of Ichikawa Daimon at the bottom point. These geographical features, the small plain, the broad rivers, and the rugged mountains, provide the natural setting within which Yamanashi's agricultural history has unfolded.

The prefecture, one of the more intensely cultivated agricultural regions in Japan in the past century, contains diminutive and fragmented farms on the base of a tiny area of arable land.[2] Yamanashi ranks thirty-second in size among the nation's forty-seven subdivisions and covers only one eighty-sixth of Japan's surface. Within these narrow confines little arable land is found; in 1930, fewer than 200 square miles, the size of one self-respecting Texas ranch, about 11 percent of the prefecture's total area, supported 68,000 full-

[2] In 1930, Yamanashi had double the national average in the percentage of total income derived from agriculture, and more than half again as high a percentage of households devoted to agriculture as the rest of the country.

time and 13,500 part-time farming households. Each of Yamanashi's prewar agricultural families cultivated an average of only 1.5 acres (about 0.6 *chō* or hectare), a small farm even by Japan's minute standards; farms in the four surrounding prefectures, Nagano, Saitama, Kanagawa, and Shizuoka, were one-third larger. In addition to cultivating only a scant amount of land, the normal farm family did not have a unified holding, but had its fields scattered throughout the village. The Yamanashi farm consisted of 20 or more plots, each about 490 square yards in size, less than the area between two successive 10-yard stripes on a football field, and, incredibly, paddy fields averaged only 338 square yards, about the size of an American house plot.[3]

Not only were the farms small and disjointed, but also the productivity of the land, because of its quality, slope, and water supply, varied from region to region. Good harvests depended on innovative methods and hard work. Farmers in the central valley around Kōfu, where 58 percent of Yamanashi's population lived on 5-6 percent of its land, tilled flat, comparatively large, and well-watered fields and produced higher yields per worker and per unit of land than those in the surrounding highland plateaus and hills. Although cultivators in the basin had to overcome problems like sandy, gravelly, or otherwise infertile soil, and inadequate or excessive water, their peers in the mountains faced much greater difficulties. Most of them cultivated land at high elevations. Some fields were 3,000 feet or more above sea level and had short growing seasons, icy water in their paddies, killing frosts for their mulberry trees and silkworms, and required their tillers to construct and maintain hillside terraces in the places where the climate allowed them to grow rice. Since the soil in cold, mountainous regions like Mukawa in the northwest was better than in the basin, when farmers did successfully cultivate rice, they received an excellent price in the market. But paddies on these and other highlands were

---

[3] *SKK*, pp. 188, 525-526; *Yamanashi tōkeisho.*

uncommon, and tillers had to develop special methods for warming the mountain water at rice-transplanting time in the spring. To overcome these difficulties of scale, climate, elevation, fertility, and irrigation, agronomists and farmers in both the mountains and the basin, even before postwar mechanization, did research and recommended and made technological improvements to increase yields.[4] But it was not agricultural technology alone which allowed Yamanashi farmers on these small and precarious plots to improve both their yields and their levels of living in the seven decades between the Meiji Restoration and World War II; government encouragement, the growth of a commercial market for their products, improved transportation, increased capital, and the farmers' responsiveness to these opportunities also spurred agricultural growth.

The cumulative effect of these opportunities and efforts was striking. In 1884-1888, yields of rice and of the three *mugis* (barley, wheat, and rye), the staples of the farmer's diet, were 1.51 and 1.01 *koku* (1 *koku* = 5.1 bushels or 180 liters) per *tan* (0.245 acres or about one tenth of one hectare), well above the national average (1.31 for rice). Output of cocoons, together with rice one of the two primary cash crops, was 1.23 *koku* per producing household. Fifty years later, in 1935-1939, when expanded foreign demand had increased its dominance as the major commercial crop, cocoon production reached 7.65 *koku* per household, and rice and *mugi* 2.45 and 1.75 *koku* per *tan*, an increase of 522 percent for the primary marketed crop, and of 62 percent and 73 percent for the two types of grain. Not only did the region's agriculturalists increase yields, but also their real income. When adjusted for the inflation of commodity prices, cocoon income per household more than tripled, and rice income per *tan* almost doubled from the 1880s to the 1930s. In the six-and-one-half decades between 1872 and 1935-1939, the real

[4] *SKK*, pp. 125, 290-292; Tsuchihashi Riki and Ōmori Yoshinori, *Nihon no minzoku—Yamanashi* (Tokyo, 1974), pp. 52-53.

value of production per agricultural household in Yamanashi increased by 410 percent. Even in 1930-1934, the nadir of the world depression, the average farm family's real value of production was three times larger than in the opening years of the Meiji era. Transportation, technology, commercial opportunity, industriousness, entrepreneurship, and the resultant capital allowed Yamanashi farmers to overcome the problems of farm size, fertility, location, slope, and lack of water.[5]

Water, when available, caused serious environmental problems which were overcome only with great difficulty. The same rivers which irrigated Yamanashi's fields also inundated them periodically. Between 1890 and 1910, seven floods occurred, and the worst in 1907 destroyed 760 hectares of farmland, 12,000 houses, and caused 232 people to drown. Although similar calamities had occurred even in medieval times, they had a new cause in the Meiji period: the destruction of timber land. In Kai as elsewhere much woodland, traditionally exploited by local cultivators for firewood, charcoal, and green fertilizer, became publicly

---

[5] *SKK*, pp. 185-188; *Yamanashi tōkeisho*, 1884-1888, 1930-1939. The primary source for statistical data on Yamanashi agriculture, *Yamanashi tōkeisho*, is a government publication and thus presents official statistics. When using these data, we must keep in mind James Nakamura's contention that the official statistics for the Meiji period understate both yields and land under cultivation; he writes that the government's statistics gradually became more accurate, but that underestimation does not disappear altogether before 1920. In this book, I follow scholars like Hayami, Ohkawa, Shinohara, and Umemura, who accept as valid Nakamura's critique of the accuracy of the Meiji statistics, but think he overstates his case. Hayami, *A Century of Agricultural Growth in Japan*, p. 43; Francks, *Technology and Agricultural Development*, pp. 21-22; *Chōki keizai tōkei*, Vol. 9. Ohkawa and Shinohara, *Patterns of Japanese Economic Development*, p. 101, write that underestimation ended with the government's cadastral survey of 1885-1889, for example. Thus, my figures for yields and area of land under cultivation are probably somewhat low for 1872, slightly too low for 1884-1888, but accurate for 1935-1939. Since almost all the data which I draw from the *Yamanashi tōkeisho* postdates 1890, I think we can trust the accuracy of these official statistics.

owned when villagers could not prove title to it in the 1870s. This land, 850,000 acres in mountainous Yamanashi (about three-quarters of the prefecture), eventually fell into the hands of the imperial family, whose agents randomly harvested the timber. The deforestation, destroying Yamanashi's watershed and intensifying its flooding, led to the disasters at the turn of the century. We can see their impact from prefectural statistics on rice harvests: yields for the seven flood years fell 11 percent below those for the normal years between 1890 and 1910; those for 1907 and 1910, the two most disastrous flood years, fell 16 percent below the 20-year average. After the 1910 flood, the prefecture petitioned for the return of the land, received an imperial "gift" of 164,000 hectares, introduced more scientific forest management, built new dikes along the Fuefuki and Kamanashi rivers, and eliminated flooding as a major environmental problem.[6]

Rugged mountains, after tiny farms and broad rivers, the final segment of our tripartite geographical setting, also influenced the development of Kai agriculture before 1900; they tended to isolate the province from the nation's primary markets in Kyoto, Osaka, and Edo and from its main transportation arteries, such as the Tōkaidō Road. Although Yamanashi made brief forays onto the national scene, especially in the mid-sixteenth century when Takeda Shingen, whose immense bronze image guards the south entrance to Kōfu Station, won a series of battles against Uesugi Kenshin, Oda Nobunaga, and Tokugawa Ieyasu, the region was a backwater for most of its history. Only foreign demand for raw silk in the late nineteenth century, and the breaching of the mountains by the railroad and the modern highway in the early twentieth century, drew the prefecture tightly into the mainstream of the nation's economic and political life.

[6] *Yamanashi kensei gojūnenshi* (Kōfu, 1942), p. 507; Isogai Masayoshi and Iida Ban'ya, *Yamanashi-ken no rekishi* (Tokyo, 1973), pp. 243-245.

THE PREMODERN LEGACY TO YAMANASHI'S
MODERN AGRICULTURAL DEVELOPMENT

In spite of its relative isolation, Yamanashi had a long and significant involvement in the nation's history. Numerous archaeological excavations of Jōmon, Yayoi, and Tomb-period remains point to its prehistory, and Nara records show that today's four primary subdivisions—Tsuru in the eastern mountains, Yamanashi in the north-central region, Yatsushiro in the south, and Koma in the center and west, as well as the province of Kai itself—were established officially by the "Chinese"-style government at the time of the Taika Reform in the seventh century. The central authorities also organized villages below the four counties, nationalized, ordered, and taxed fields according to the continental model (traces of this *jōrisei* still remain in Yamanashi today) and over the next several hundred years, as river-control projects on the basin's flood plain allowed reclamation, established new agricultural communities.

The growth of private authority at the expense of public government, which in the ninth and tenth centuries led to the reorganization of villages into aristocratically controlled estates called *shōen*, had its impact in Kai as elsewhere. Important Kyoto families like the Fujiwara began to take over direct proprietorship of "national" land which previously had produced the income for their official salaries and consequently became increasingly independent of the central government in which they served. The Fujiwara, who dominated national politics for two centuries between 900 and 1100, created *shōen* in Kai as early as 900 and used members of the Genji family as their estate managers. In the twelfth century, one of these men, Nobuyoshi, took the surname of the "Kai Genji," Takeda, and began the process through which his family gradually replaced local Fujiwara hegemony and governed the province with varying degrees of control for most of 400 years. Nobuyoshi and his son aided

111

Minamoto-no-Yoritomo when he defeated the Taira and organized his national military government in Kamakura in 1185; supported Yoritomo's successors, the Hōjō, in suppressing the Emperor Go-Toba's "revolt" in 1221; and thus became the officially reorganized military government of Kai.

The Kai Genji played an active role in both local and national politics under the Hōjō and the Muromachi regimes, and, more important to our narrative of Kai's agricultural history, they did not neglect their economic base at home. The Takeda not only took over control of the Fujiwara manors on which they had previously served as managers, but they also created new *shōen*, especially in the river delta of the Kōfu Basin. The most important of these was Inazumi-shō, a manor which included two primary subdivisions, Inazumi and Kamada, of twelve and eight "villages" each; thus, medieval records indicate that at least parts of our twentieth-century village, Ōkamada, already existed in the thirteenth century.

The political and economic organization of these communities changed as the years of Takeda rule progressed. What had been "public" villages under the authority of the national and provincial bureaucracy in the Nara and early Heian periods gradually became "private" manors, increasingly independent of central authority. Control over these estates in the late Heian period was divided among absentee proprietory temples and families such as the Fujiwara, resident managers such as the Takeda, and sub-manor level elites, in Kai either cadet lines of the Takeda or other local warrior families. Under the Kamakura regime proprietorship of the estates moved increasingly from Kyoto to Kai. Although the organization of the *shōen* was still complex (a number of families shared proprietorial, managerial, and the new stewards' rights), the Takeda, their branches and their allies, gradually simplified matters by absorbing most of these prerogatives. In the succeeding Muromachi epoch, the Takeda remained preeminent in Kai, and the *shōen* became unified subfiefs on which one resident family combined proprietorial and managerial functions as the Takeda's vassals; one should bear in mind, however, that the Takeda, like many military governors in the Muromachi era, had serious problems controlling their vassals and maintaining their regional hegemony.

Finally, during the civil wars of the sixteenth century, Nobutora and Shingen, father and son, reconsolidated Takeda authority and reorganized their domain for economic and military efficiency; the Takeda built a castle in the central city of Kōfu, and began the processes of separating their vassals from the land, and thus from their economic base, and of converting these former subfiefs into villages (*mura*) under firmly centralized regional control. Although on the surface the uniform local governmental system of the late sixteenth century seemed to return to its earliest seventh-century form, in fact it was quite different; while Nara-period villages had been subordinated to a remote and loosely enforced central authority, Takeda-Tokugawa control of these "public" villages was firm and backed by highly visible military power. All in all, Kai's isolation could not prevent it from feeling the impact of changes taking place elsewhere in Japan.[7]

For a short time in the sixteenth century, Kai influenced the rest of Japan as well when between 1540 and 1573 Takeda Shingen strove to increase his regional and then national power. In the process, Shingen proved himself a ruthless politician, a brilliant general, and an expert at logistics. Born in 1521, he took charge of Kai's affairs in 1540 when, hearing of his father's plans to disinherit him in favor of his younger brother, Shingen arrested Nobutora and placed him under house arrest in an ally's castle. Shingen then consolidated Kai, brought Shinshū Province to the west under his control through a series of famous battles between 1553 and 1564 against the other "Zen" general, Uesugi Kenshin, seized Su-

[7] *Yamanashi-ken no rekishi*, p. 68; *SKK*, pp. 86-89, 201-203, 214.

ruga Province to the southeast, and moved against the remaining barriers between himself and national hegemony, the Oda and the Tokugawa to the south. Shingen defeated Tokugawa Ieyasu at Mikatagahara near Hamamatsu in December 1572, passed into the province of Mikawa, and captured Noda Castle in February 1573. The way to Kyoto and the shogun's title looked open when during the final stages of the seige at Noda, Shingen fell seriously ill; he died two months later, before he could return to Kōfu.

Shingen's son Katsuyori fell heir to his father's titles, territory, and army, but not to his ability. Awe of Shingen's ruthlessness, military ability, and daring—he lived up to his motto, borrowed from the Chinese military sage Sun Tzu, "swift like the wind, quiet like the forest, aggressive like the fire, immovable like the mountain"—kept his vassals in line. The impetuous Katsuyori did not command his subordinates' respect as his father had, and his alliance began to crumble quickly. Within a few years of Shingen's untimely death at the age of fifty-three, the epigone's allies were gone, his and his father's hopes for national hegemony dead, and finally the family destroyed.[8]

Shingen's thirty years of glory and Katsuyori's subsequent downfall had a significant impact on Yamanashi's farmers. Although bringing new land under the plow had been a preoccupation of the Takeda throughout its long reign in Kai, Shingen, to finance his expensive campaigns, carried out land reclamation much more extensively and systematically than any of his predecessors, especially along the riversides in the Kōfu Basin. Much of the land on the banks of the Kamanashi River in the western part of the basin flooded frequently and could not be cultivated, but Shingen's engineers created the "Shingen dikes" and increased taxable production dramatically. Even today dozens of place names in the area include the words *shinden*, "new field," and *arai*, "new residence," and attest to his efforts.

[8] *Yamanashi-ken no rekishi*, pp. 119-128, 143-146.

Shingen's taxation and monetary systems were as important to agricultural change as were his dikes. He introduced an arrangement called "large-small portions" (*daishōgiri*) under which landowners paid two-thirds of their taxes in produce (*daigiri*) and one-third in money based on the price of rice (*shōgiri*). This step allowed Shingen to mobilize for war more quickly than under the old system in which taxes were paid only in kind; it also compelled Kai farmers to sell part of their harvest, and thus sped the spread of commercial agriculture to Kai even more quickly than in other areas of Japan. In order to facilitate these commercial transactions and provide the cash for tax payments, Shingen gave four Kōfu merchant houses the authority to coin money. Although corruption and favoritism led the Tokugawa to change the number and even the families of the minters from time to time, they too issued "Kai money" (*Kōshūkin*) throughout the 1600-1868 period. This monetary system, disunified as it became after 1600, when as many as 136 different kinds of money were in circulation at one time, helped commercialize agriculture in Yamanashi.[9]

The Tokugawa shoguns took charge of Kai after they came to power in 1600 and for all but two decades of their 270-year rule governed the province through bureaucrats (*daikan*) sent out from Edo. Although Tokugawa-branch family heads served as daimyo occasionally in the seventeenth century, the central government's bureaucrats still exercised real power since none of these relatives of the shogun was willing to sacrifice the pleasures of the capital to visit, much less live in, their domain. Because of this absentee governance, Kōfu Castle fell into desuetude between its seizure by the Tokugawa in 1600 and the visit to Kōfu in 1704 of Ogyū Sorai, lieutenant of the temporary daimyo, Yana-

[9] Amemiya Yuzuru, "Yamanashi-ken Kubo Nakajima buraku ni okeru nōmin undō no kisoteki kaimei," unpublished undergraduate thesis at Chūō University in the mid-1950s, pp. 23-24. The author is the son of Amemiya Ishizō, a tenant farmer in Kubo Nakajima. *Yamanashi-ken no rekishi*, pp. 103-146; *SKK*, p. 90; *Gojūnenshi*, pp. 37, 43.

gisawa Yoshiyasu; the uninhabited building functioned only as an awe-inspiring symbol of governmental authority.

Control of Kai served the Tokugawa well. Its strategic location immediately to the west of Edo made the province defensively important, and its agricultural productivity gave the region economic value. Although Kai's ring of mountains prevented easy access, the Edo government did exploit the province's productive capacity, assessed at 236,000 *koku* of rice per annum in 1603, and 306,000 *koku* one hundred and fifty years later. Control of the wealth of the central basin from which most of Kai's produce came (Koma, which included most of the basin, produced 42 percent of the province's rice in 1603, and 46 percent in the 1750s) and of water transport between Edo and the Fuji River port of Kajikazawa allowed the Tokugawa to take advantage of the region, albeit with difficulty.[10]

The Takeda demise and the Tokugawa victory had a direct impact on Yamanashi's rural society and economy. The suicide of Katsuyori and the annihilation of his family in 1582 left Kai with a surplus of unemployed samurai. Although some found jobs as warriors elsewhere or became merchants, many became farmers and landlords. Moreover, since the Takeda's effort at separating the samurai from the land was unfinished in the 1580s, many farmer-warriors chose to remain on their land as rich peasants. The ancestors of the Sakurabayashi and the Takamuro, two of the leading landlord families in Ōkamada in the twentieth century, for example, were ex-warriors who stayed in their villages as local leaders in the early seventeenth century. The highly developed patron-client (*oyabun-kobun*) relationships found in modern rural Yamanashi are traced to this phenomenon.

Tokugawa officials intensified the growth of commercial agriculture by increasing the percentage of taxes to be paid

[10] *Gojūnenshi*, p. 42; *Yamanashi-ken no rekishi*, pp. 148-159. These assessments indicate a growth rate of one sixth of a percent per year; more commercial Koma had a growth rate of over one quarter of one percent per year.

in money. Their *daishōgiri* system called for the taxpayer to pay in money one-third of the two-thirds previously paid in kind under the Takeda. Thus, the landowner submitted five-ninths of his taxes in cash. The basis for determining his payment differed for the new and old monetary levies. The Tokugawa continued to assess the old Takeda tax at the fixed rate of one *ryō* for each 4.14 *koku* of rice; they based their new tax on an average of the rice prices in October of each year at the basin's four primary markets. In other words, the Tokugawa bureaucrats were cautious: they collected one part at a fixed rate, insuring adequate revenues in years when prices fell, and the other at the market price, guaranteeing increased revenues when prices rose. The taxpayers received the same insurance; only one part of their taxes went up in years when rice prices rose, and only one part stayed high in years when rice prices fell. Either way, after 1600 land-owners had to market over half of the rice they paid in taxes, about one-sixth of what they produced or collected in rent, and this speeded the development of commercial agriculture.[11]

When Japan began to enter the modern world in the 1850s, Kai's agricultural economy and society had six basic characteristics which, together with the impact of foreign trade and of the new central government's endeavors at modernization and industrialization, provided the basis for the province's economic growth after 1870, its rising levels of living at least after 1890, and ultimately its tenancy disputes in the 1920s. First, the average farm family cultivated a small, fragmented farm, even compared to those in other areas of Japan. Second, Kai had attained a high degree of internal commercialization because of its taxation system.

Third, in spite of its physical isolation, Kai was linked to the national market. Although rugged mountains ringed the

[11] Amemiya, pp. 24, 153; Hagiwara Tametsugu, *Suhadaka ni shita Kōshū zaibatsu* (Tokyo, 1932), pp. 10-11; Furushima Toshio, *Kazoku keitai to nōgyō no hattatsu* (Tokyo, 1947), p. 320; *Gojūnenshi*, p. 43; *Yamanashi-ken no rekishi*, pp. 198-206.

province and limited trade, there were five major and five minor routes in and out of Kai, and these allowed a triangular, Edo/Osaka—Kōfu Basin—Tsuru—Edo/Osaka trade (see Map). Most imports came by boat up the Fuji River from Iwabuchi in Suruga Province in the south to Kajikazawa, the northern terminus, ten miles downstream from Kōfu. This route, which Shingen developed to support his campaigns in the 1560s and 1570s, was only forty-four miles long, but back-breaking. The trip from Kajikazawa to Iwabuchi lasted only nine hours, but the returning boat, hauled by three men's brawn against the current, took four or five days, depending on the depth and swiftness of the river. Moreover, arrival at either terminal did not complete the journey. At Iwabuchi, stevedores packed the outgoing goods onto horses for the over-land haul to the ocean port of Kambara; from there, freight went by coastal boat to Shimizu and then by ship to Edo or Osaka. At the northern river port, handlers loaded the cargo onto shallow-bottomed boats for shipment to Kōfu, Nirasaki, or Isawa, Kai's primary cities, and then onto backs for redistribution. Although hauling goods to Kai took at the very least a week, compared to a day or two for goods going out, imports (salt, sugar, salted fish, soybeans, oil, and cotton textiles) far exceeded exports (tobacco and rice) along this route throughout the Edo and Meiji periods. As late as 1892, three years after the government completed the Tokyo-Osaka railroad, which had a station at Kambara, and only a decade before the railroad between Tokyo and Kōfu went through, the yen value of imports at Kajikazawa exceeded exports by four-and-one-half times.

The imbalance was made up by trade over the Kōshū Highway, which the Tokugawa government developed to link Edo with its regional administrative headquarters in Kai Province. The mountains and ravines along this road, which, like the modern railroad, ran from Edo and Hachiōji up the Katsura River to Ōtsuki and then across the Sasago Pass (the railroad, of course, runs through it) to Kōfu, limited the use

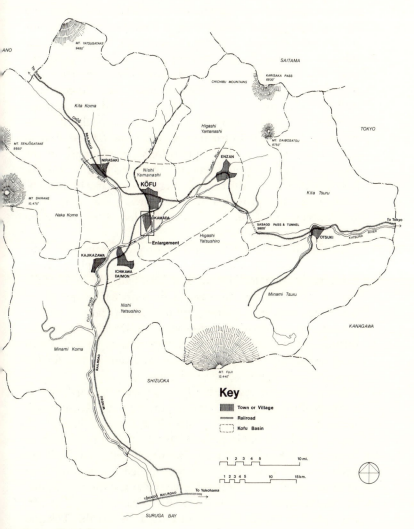

MT. YATSUGATAKE
9480'

ANO

SAITAMA

KARISAKA PASS
6930'

CHICHIBU MOUNTAINS

Kita Koma

Higashi
Yamanashi

TOKYO

MT. DAIBOSATSU
6750'

MT. SENJŌGATAKE
9950'

NIRASAKI

Nishi
Yamanashi

ENZAN

KŌFU

Kita Tsuru

MT. SHIRANE
10,475'

Naka Koma

ŌKAMADA

SASAGO PASS & TUNNEL
3900'

To Tokyo

Enlargement

Higashi
Yatsushiro

OTSUKI

KATSURA RIVER

KAJIKAZAWA

ICHIKAWA
DAIMON

Minami Tsuru

Nishi
Yatsushiro

KANAGAWA

Minami Koma

MT. FUJI
12,440'

SHIZUOKA

Key

Town or Village

Railroad

Kofu Basin

1 2 3 4 5   10 mi.

1 2 3 4 5   10   15 km.

TŌKAIDO RAILROAD   To Yokohama

SURUGA BAY

amanashi Prefecture

of its rugged western segment to officials, travelers, and light-weight goods. In fact, even in the 1890s, after the completion of Governor Fujimura's campaign to improve Yamanashi's roads, freight wagons still could not cross the pass. Goods had to be unloaded, carried over the pass, and reloaded on the other side. Thus, to make the road commercially useful, it was necessary to develop a trade in commodities which were not too heavy. The growth of the silk textile industry in the Tsuru region across the Sasago Pass in eastern Kai provided this opportunity; increasingly in the eighteenth and nineteenth centuries, cocoons harvested in the basin's easternmost districts of Higashi Yamanashi and Higashi Yatsushiro provided the raw material for the spinners and weavers of Tsuru. This traffic established the second leg of Kai's trade triangle.

The third major route, the Fuji Road, together with the eastern segment of the Kōshū Highway, completed Kai's commercial triangle. The Fuji Road ran from the heart of the Tsuru silk district at the base of the northern slope of the famed volcano, through the region's administrative center at Yamura, to the road's junction with the Kōshū Highway at Ōtsuki. These roads enabled Kai merchants to sell Tsuru cloth in the national market at Edo, and thus to pay for the imports which came up the Fuji River.

In the closing decade of the Tokugawa era, a fourth artery, the Kamakura Highway, replaced the Fuji and Kōshū roads as the major egress for Kai silk. The foreign demand for Tsuru textiles and for raw silk reeled in both the Gunnai (Tsuru) and Kuninaka (Kōfu Basin) regions, which developed after the port of Yokohama opened for commerce in 1859, required a direct route between Kai and the treaty port. The Kamakura Highway ran over the eastern slope of Mt. Fuji to the Tōkaidō Road (and after 1889, to the Tōkaidō Main Railroad Line) at Numazu and provided this link. The Fuji River—Fuji and Kōshū Highway—Kamakura Highway triangles functioned as Kai's major trade arteries from 1700 until the completion of the Chūō Railroad Line in 1903.

The final major road, the Shinshū Highway, ran along the Kamanashi River and linked Kōfu with the Suwa and Matsumoto regions to the west. This artery allowed for the haulage of goods from Kōfu and Nirasaki to towns in western Kai and southern Shinshū. Use of this road, however, was expensive. The Kamanashi River above Nirasaki was too shallow for boats, and everything went on the backs of horses or men, usually the latter. The price of salt was 27 percent higher in Nirasaki than in Kajikazawa, only fifteen miles away. One can imagine the cost of a *koku* of salt after it was carried all the way to Suwa or Matsumoto. Thus, the road led to few commercial opportunities for Kai merchants. Until the 1880s, when Yamanashi girls began to travel the Shinshū Highway to Suwa to work in the filatures there, only officials, occasional peddlers, and silk technicians took this route. Although the terrain was the least arduous of all Kai's highways, the road did not play an important part in Kai's Tokugawa period trade; it did, as we shall see in the following chapter, play a role in the development of Yamanashi's sericultural technology.

The other routes to Kai, the Minobu Road, which paralleled the Fuji River, the Ōme Highway over the 6,200-foot Daibosatsu Pass to the east, the Chichibu Road over the 6,800-foot Karisaka Pass to the northeast, and the Hosaka and Saku roads through the mountains to the north northwest, did not play an important part in Kai's economic history; if traveling the major roads was hiking, traversing these minor roads was mountain climbing. "Going to Kai is like going into exile," the saying went. Except for the triangular trade in the southeast, Yamanashi was cut off from the rest of Japan after the 1570s; but, luckily for Kai, that premodern textile and raw-silk trade helped to provide the basis for its modern prosperity.[12]

Fourth, the social structure of Kai's villages was highly

stratified. Nevertheless, because of its nature, the stratification not only did not inhibit, but actually enhanced, commercialization, the acceptance of new technology, and in the long run better living standards for tenant farmers, and the diminution of this very stratification. Patron-client (*oyabun-kobun*) relationships, through which a small number of rich and powerful landlords came to exercise considerable control over the lives and livelihoods of a larger number of tenant farmer families, blossomed in the region from the proto-capitalist late sixteenth century.[13] The patron guaranteed his clients' livelihood in time of flood, famine, or other emergency, and provided a number of less dramatic economic benefits at marriage, house-building, childbirth, sickness, death, and other times in the regular life cycle. In return, he received labor service and subservience; the *kobun* came hat in hand through the kitchen door and used honorific language when approaching his *oyabun*. The client traded freedom for security. Although the need for a secure livelihood provided its basic underpinning, the relationship was not strictly economic. Even critics of the system write that the paternalistic patrons gave their clients important emotional support as well. These affective ties, based on mutual feelings of benevolence and obligation, ameliorated the harshness of hamlet life in the Tokugawa and Meiji eras, and even

---

[13] Researchers studying the practice in ten villages in Yamanashi in the 1930s, found that 395 *oyabun* serviced 2,553 *kobun*. This indicated an average of five *oyabun* and thirty-two *kobun* per hamlet, the level at which most of their activities took place; it is not surprising, therefore, that Kubo Nakajima's actual figures of four resident *oyabun* and thirty-four *kobun*, representing all the hamlet's households but two, a Buddhist priest and a non-conformist who spent 1924-1945 under an ostracism sanction, matched the investigators' averages almost exactly. *SKK*, p. 615; Hattori Harunori, "Kubo Nakajima buraku ni okeru shakai kōzō to kaisō," unpublished manuscript, hereafter abbreviated as *KNJ*, pp. 134-135. *KNJ* is a study of social stratification in Kubo Nakajima written by Hattori Harunori of Yamanashi University and based on research conducted in 1954 by Professors Hattori, Fukutake Tadashi, Matsubara Haruo, and Morioka Kiyomi under the guidance of Ariga Kizaemon.

helped limit the goals of the disputing tenants of the 1920s and 1930s to economic and political rather than social issues.

Oyabun-kobun relationships in Yamanashi differed from those in many other areas of Japan, particularly those in the Tōhoku region in the northeast. Because a market economy appeared earlier in Kai, the patron-client system there pervaded the lives of its members and limited their economic and social freedom and opportunity to a lesser degree than it did in Tōhoku. In the northeast, patron-client linkages and the extended family (*dōzoku*) were intimately interwoven. Because the *oyabun-kobun* system there developed before the appearance of commercial agriculture and its concomitant landlord-tenant contractual ties, both of which generally tended to undermine extended families, the client households became branches (*bunke*) and their members served as agricultural workers and servants for real or fictive patron-relatives (*oyabun* and *honke*), who often controlled entire one-family villages. In Kai, on the other hand, the burgeoning of cultivation for the market in the sixteenth century started to destroy the extended family and to promote an economic system based on landlords and tenants before patron-client relationships began to appear. Thus, although Yamanashi landlords often served as the *oyabun* of their tenants, extended families were less common than in Tōhoku. For example, twenty-five of thirty-nine households in Kubo Nakajima hamlet shared the surname Ishihara. Hence, a hamlet-wide extended family may have existed there at some time in the past. But by the end of the Tokugawa period at least, it no longer did; the twenty-five Ishiharas represented seventeen different and unrelated families.

Because the patron-client system in Kai developed as farming for the market began to replace agricultural self-sufficiency, it did not inhibit the development of relatively businesslike landlord-tenant relations in the Tokugawa period or the modernization of agriculture in the nineteenth and early twentieth centuries. With the assistance of regional officials, landlord patrons helped their tenant clients improve yields and income in the Meiji period for the benefit of all three groups. And when in the twentieth century, because of this help, the tenants' livelihoods became more secure and they struck out on their own technologically and entrepreneurially, *oyabun-kobun* ties became less economic and more ceremonial. Although an improved standard of living, achieved with landlord help, gave Yamanashi tenant farmers more freedom than ever before, they continued to ask their landlords to serve as *oyabun* and marriage go-betweens even when the tenants challenged their landlords' economic supremacy in the hamlet during the disputes of the 1920s and 1930s. In the more tightly organized and self-contained Tōhoku villages, where extended family ties were more personal and farmers cultivated less for the market, the incentives to modernize were fewer because the commercial opportunities to improve one's livelihood were limited. The Tōhoku patron-client-extended-family system, unlike the Kai patron-client-stem-family arrangement, slowed the spread of new agricultural methods, commercial agriculture, and a tenant farmer, anti-landlord movement. (One must recognize that the reverse was also true; the *dōzoku* system not only inhibited commercialization and tenancy disputes, but also reflected their relative absence.)[14]

Landownership and tenancy data also reveal stratification in Yamanashi at the beginning of the modern era, but again it, like the patron-client system, did not block agricultural improvement. Our earliest data on prefectural and county tenancy come from the 1880s, and at that time Yamanashi Prefecture ranked fourth nationally in the proportion of tenanted land under cultivation, and the Kōfu Basin area had the highest degree of tenancy in the prefecture. In Naka Koma County in 1883, tenants worked 70 percent of all arable land, and in 1887 only 14 percent of the county's farm-

[14] *SKK*, pp. 614-616; *KNJ*, pp. 134-135; Nakamura Masanori, *Rōdōsha to nōmin*, p. 72. Francks argues that extended families like the Tōhoku ones could not benefit from new technology. *Technology and Agricultural Development*, p. 64.

THE COMMERCIALIZATION OF AGRICULTURE

ers owned all the land they cultivated. Table 2-1, which shows the government's estimates for tax purposes of rice produced per household on owned land (*kokudaka*) in Kubo Nakajima hamlet (one paid taxes only on owned land) in 1685 and 1870, demonstrates the Kōfu Basin's stratification. Eight *tan*, the area of land necessary to produce 8-9 *kōku*, was the average size farm in the hamlet. Twenty-eight and twenty-six households, respectively, had their rice production on owned land assessed at seven *koku* or less; since most of these households could not have lived on such a small quantity of rice, they must have rented extra land to cultivate. Thus, two-thirds or more of the Kubo Nakajima families in 1685 and 1870 were tenant farmers. At the same time, the family paying taxes on over 50 *koku* was clearly a landlord one, as were probably several of the 10- to 50- *koku* households. Stratification in neighboring Futsuka Ichiba was even more pronounced. Of the forty-four families residing there in 1870, 37 had *kokudaka* of 10 *koku* or less and 4 had *kokudaka* of 50 *koku* or more. The Meiji land settlement of the early 1870s recognized officially the Tokugawa era's social stratification.[15]

TABLE 2-1

Government Estimate for Tax Purposes of Rice Production per Household on Owned Land in Kubo Nakajima Hamlet in 1685 and 1870

	1685	*1870*
Total Number of Households	37	39
50 *koku* or more	0	1
10-50 *koku*	8	7
7-10 *koku*	1	5
5-7 *koku*	3	1
0-5 *koku*	25	25

Source: *KNJ*, pp. 11-15.

[15] *SKK*, p. 65; Amemiya, pp. 25-26; *KNJ*, pp. 11-15.

The same stratification and tenancy which impoverished many farmers in Tokugawa and early Meiji Yamanashi paradoxically set the stage for a better level of living for tenant farmers in the twentieth century. As Ronald Dore writes, Tokugawa stratification produced well-educated and prosperous landlords, who, when encouraged by the government in the late nineteenth century, poured time and money into agricultural improvement and education.[16] Yamanashi landlords were not atypical. Although self-interest—their desire for greater rent income from higher yields—undoubtedly provided part of the landlords' motivation, the tenants also benefited from these efforts. After the Yamanashi countryside began to recover in the late 1880s from the impact of the Matsukata Deflation, household income rose steadily while tenancy's expansion slowed and then contracted. And it was this higher standard of living which provided a base for and an impetus to tenancy disputes. The landlords' efforts at improvement, which would not here have been possible without the surplus income, time, and education produced by stratification, ultimately provoked the challenge to their predominance.

Fifth, Kai had a tradition of sericulture, of cocoon, raw silk, and silk textile production. As early as the sixteenth century, Takeda Shingen had encouraged the fabrication of textiles as exports to pay for military imports and to acquire specie. For over one hundred years after the Takeda's demise, their successors who were outsiders made no effort to promote Yamanashi industry; its prosperity meant nothing to them so long as Kai paid its taxes. But when Yanagisawa Yoshiyasu became daimyo in 1704, he and his adviser, Oygū Sorai, once again encouraged silk. Under their sponsorship, peasants in the Yamanashi and Yatsushiro districts in the eastern part of the basin became suppliers of cocoons for the Tsuru district's reelers and weavers. From this time, "Kai

---

[16] Ronald P. Dore, "Agricultural Improvement in Japan," pp. 69-91.

silk" became Yamanashi's primary export and provided the terrain on which local entrepreneurs, and especially the Kō-shū *zaibatsu*-to-be, Wakao Ippei, Nezu Kaichirō, and Ame-miya Keijirō, built financial empires, and in which Yama-nashi's commercial agriculture grew.[17]

Sixth, farmers from a number of villages in the highlands which encirlced the Kōfu Basin worked as itinerant peddlers in the winter off-season. Men from these areas, as Mizoguchi Tsunetoshi has shown for the Midai River alluvial delta in western Naka Koma County, although faced with less extensive tenancy than in the central areas, became peddlers because they made smaller profits on their farms and had fewer opportunities for local secondary employ.[18] The most daring entrepreneurs covered long distances. They traveled by foot on several-hundred-mile journeys as far as Shinshū, Kōzuke (Gumma Prefecture), and Edo to sell goods both from their own areas and from villages and towns along their routes. Some of these peddlers combined great physical endurance and strength with speculative daring. When opportunity knocked in the guise of foreign demand for raw silk and silk textiles after 1859, Wakao, Amemiya, and others answered and became some of the richest men in Yamanashi.

These six characteristics of Kai in the late Tokugawa era: small, fragmented farms, commercialization, both integration into the national market and isolation at the same time, a stratified rural society, a premodern silk industry, and the existence of peddler-entrepreneurs, supplied the roots for the growth of modern Yamanashi's economy and society. But they could not have done so without proper nourishment, and this necessary fertilizer was provided by two new stimuli: foreign demand for raw silk and silk textiles after 1859, and encouragement of modernization and economic development by the new government after 1868. It is to a discus-

---

[17] *SKK*, p. 297.

[18] Mizoguchi Tsunetoshi, "Midaigawa senjōchi hatasaku nōson ni okeru gyōshō katsudō, *Jimbun chiri*, 28 (1976), pp. 27-56.

sion of demand and encouragement, therefore, that we turn next.

The Coming of the West, the Meiji Reforms, and Yamanashi's Agricultural Development

In the 1850s, the military and diplomatic pressure of a handful of European and American powers forced Japan, after two hundred years of relative isolation, to open her doors to political and economic intercourse with the West. In the 1850s and 1860s, treaties established a number of ports where foreigners could trade with indigenous merchants, and Japan entered the world of international commerce. As one can imagine, foreign supply and foreign demand, reinforced by foreign coercion, deeply influenced Japan's productive world, made up as it was of handicraft industries. Some, like cotton, required to compete with the steam-driven looms of Lancashire, languished (temporarily); others, like raw silk and tea, able to fill a Western need, flourished. Raw silk, which remained Japan's major export for three-quarters of a century after 1859, especially prospered because of outbreaks of silkworm disease in France and Italy in the 1840s and 1850s; the Taiping Rebellion, which partly disrupted China's raw silk industry between 1850 and 1864; the opening of the Suez Canal, which reduced transportation costs to England and France; and the subsequent emergence of the United States as the primary market for Japanese raw silk. Between 1859 and 1868, Japanese raw silk output doubled; between 1868 and 1912, it increased by twelve times; and between 1913 and 1929, it grew by 3½ times more. Raw silk exports (and thus, demand) grew by 24½ times in the Meiji period, and by 3½ more times between 1912 and 1929. And the value of exports grew even more rapidly: by 130 times in the sixty years after the Meiji Restoration. The foreign, and particularly the American requirement for raw silk (85 percent of all exports) provided the demand for almost one-third of the value of Japan's total exports between 1860 and

1929; it is only a slight exaggeration to say that the American woman's habit of wearing silk stockings paid for Japan's prewar economic growth.[19]

This foreign demand had a remarkable effect on the economies of agricultural prefectures which like Yamanashi had and further developed raw silk industries and sericulture. By 1933, Yamanashi filatures employed 21,761 people, 68 percent of the prefecture's industrial work force; another 5,361 workers, 17 percent, fabricated silk textiles. By the same year, 59,751 families, 85 percent of Yamanashi's farm households, raised cocoons, compared to 34,884 and 63 percent in 1883. In the 1860s, cocoons ranked as Kai's third crop after rice and the three *mugis*; by World War I, sericulture held first place, and by 1925, it provided over half of Yamanashi's total value of agricultural production. And the largest increase in income from sericulture and raw silk fabrication came in central areas of the Kōfu Basin like Naka Koma County, where almost no one raised cocoons in 1859. As late as 1883, only 26 percent of Naka Koma's farm households bred cocoons; by 1933, 78 percent did so. In 1909, 35 percent of the value of production of the average Naka Koma farm household came from sericulture; by 1929, it provided 59 percent of the value. And, finally, in 1860 there was hardly a filature in all of Kōfu City or Naka Koma

[19] At the beginning of the Meiji era, Japan's raw silk export trade was significant, but still small compared to China's (490 tons for Japan compared to 3,430 tons for China in 1870). By 1909, Japan's exports had surpassed China's (9,450 tons to 9,100 tons for China). By the late 1920s, Japan's raw silk exports had tripled China's (35,000 tons to 12,000 tons per year in 1925-1929). Japan's raw silk exports grew by 7.4 percent per year between 1870 and 1929); China's expanded by 2.1 percent per year. Lillian Li, *China's Silk Trade*, pp. 72, 86-88; Shinohara Miyohei, "Economic Development and Foreign Trade in Prewar Japan," in C. D. Cowan, ed., *The Economic Development of China and Japan* (New York, 1964), pp. 226-227; Tōyō keizai shimpōsha, *Nihon bōeki seiran* (Tokyo, 1935), pp. 53-55; G. C. Allen, *A Short Economic History of Modern Japan*, pp. 28, 65-67, 118; William W. Lockwood, *The Economic Development of Japan* (Princeton, 1968), pp. 338, 357, 366, 374.

County. By 1934, Kōfu mills employed 29 percent of all Yamanashi filature workers; Naka Koma employed 24 percent more. In other words, foreign demand played an important part not only in the commercialization and development of Yamanashi agriculture, but also in bringing about a shift in the geographical center of the prefecture's sericultural economy and prosperity. In the 1920s, thanks to cocoons and raw silk, Naka Koma County had the highest per capita income of Yamanashi's counties; it also had the most tenancy disputes.[20]

Foreign military, economic, and diplomatic pressure not only obliged Japan to traffic with the West, but also helped to generate a change of government, which took place in 1868. The new Meiji regime, motivated by fear of this extrinsic force and at the same time using it as a model, set about remaking Japan; these modifications had a sharp, positive effect on Yamanashi's agricultural economy. We have introduced in Chapter One many of the government's reforms and their impact on rural Japan: the abolition of seigneurial rule and warrior privilege, the new system of landownership and taxation, systems of local government and education, the encouragement of modern industry, transportation and commerce, etc. Accordingly, I would like to single out here for special emphasis only those aspects of these reforms which most deeply and directly influenced Yamanashi's agriculture and agriculturalists.

One must begin a discussion of the impact of the new government's reforms on Yamanashi farmers with another look at the Meiji land settlement. In the early 1870s, the Meiji government abolished the Tokugawa regime's laws which banned cultivators from buying and selling land; issued deeds of title to those persons, usually peasants but occasionally merchants, whom local custom recognized as the sub-warrior class landholder; assessed the land's value; and

---

[20] *Yamanashi tōkeisho*; *SKK*, pp. 189-190, 318, 528; *Yamanashi-ken sanshi-gyō gaishi* (Kōfu, 1959), pp. 72, 82, 117, 185.

then introduced the 4 percent (after 1877, 3 percent) land tax. Since under seigneurial rule the feudal lord had held legal title to all his domain's land, the new settlement took ownership from the dispossessed samurai ruling class and gave it to those non-warrior households which through the chance of birth, successful management, usury, good luck, and reclamation had become "landholders" within the feudal system. Those farmers who, through the ability to rise out of serflike bondage, bad fortune, inefficient farm management, foreclosure, and the decision to expand production by renting land from one of the reclaimers, had no clear title to their land before 1868 became tenants after. Students of the Japanese countryside generally believe that this settlement increased the power of the landlords and made the tenants, "to a great extent ignored by the government, . . . more vulnerable to exploitation than ever before."[21] The critics also write that owner tenant and owner farmers, who under the new system had to sell crops to earn money for paying taxes, fell increasingly into debt in the Meiji period; this subsequently led to a dramatic increase in tenancy between the 1870s and World War I.[22]

This position has been overstated for Yamanashi just as it has been for Japan as a whole. When one judges the Meiji land settlement to have been more exploitative than the Tokugawa system, one must have in mind an accurate picture of what the feudal system was like, but many writers seem not to. Implicit in Tokugawa-Meiji comparisons, as Ōuchi Tsutomu points out, is the view that at some time during the Tokugawa period the Japanese countryside was peopled uniformly by owner farmers, many of whom became tenant farmers as they were drawn into a market economy.[23] The Meiji settlement, according to its critics, speeded up this process by turning owner farmers into owner tenant farmers and owner tenant farmers into tenants.

---

[21] Waswo, *Japanese Landlords*, p. 21.   [22] *Ibid.*, pp. 12-23.

[23] Ōuchi, *Nōminsō no bunkai*, pp. 1-2.

This view misrepresents Tokugawa reality. Although we do not have comprehensive pre-1868 data on landownership, it is probably safe to say that at no time in the 1600-1868 era did all Japanese or Yamanashi cultivators own the land they tilled.[24] Rural Japan was also widely inhabited by farmers who worked in varying degrees of servitude to local masters. This was true in Yamanashi for reasons discussed above. From the demise of the Takeda in 1582, Kai was governed by outsiders and had no samurai elite of its own. Many of the former warrior followers of the Kai Genji, like the Sakurabayashi and Takamuro in Ōkamada, gave up their swords to become peasants and stay in their villages as local economic and political overlords.[25] Thus, some of the subsequent growth of tenancy in their villages reflected, not the fall of owner farmers from, but the rise of agricultural servants to, tenancy. Accordingly, when Furushima Toshio writes that landlords controlled 27 percent of Japan's arable land in 1868, this does not necessarily indicate that owner farmers worked the other 73 percent; when Waswo tells us that the percentage of land controlled by landlords had risen to 36 percent of the total in 1883, this does not necessarily mean that tenancy rose by one-third at the expense of owner farming.[26] Some of the spread of tenancy in areas like Tōhoku and some parts of Yamanashi, which had traditions of extended family "serfdom," can be viewed as liberating rather than increasingly exploitative.

In Yamanashi as in Japan as a whole, the opening of new fields must also have accounted for a considerable part of the growth of tenancy. In Naka Koma, the highly commercial county in the heart of Yamanashi's Kōfu Basin, tenancy grew by 749.6 *chō* of land, 8.5 percent of the county's total, between 1883 and 1912. Over the same three decades, area

[24] Smith, *Agrarian Origins*, pp. 1-35; Ōuchi, *Nōgyōshi*, p. 27; Francks, *Technology and Agricultural Development*, p. 64.

[25] Amemiya, pp. 23-24; Hagiwara Tametsugu, *Suhadaka ni shita Kōshū zaibatsu*, pp. 10-11; *Yamanashi jinji kōshinroku* (Kōfu, 1940), p. 1,623.

[26] Waswo, *Japanese Landlords*, p. 16.

of arable land expanded by 781 *chō*.[27] Since it is widely accepted, even by followers of differentiation theory, that rich landlord and merchant entrepreneurs, not small-scale cultivators, financed most reclamation of arable land and contracted with local farmers to till it as tenants, a significant part of the growth of tenancy must have come about, not because of the tax system, commercialization, and bankruptcy, but because of the desire of poorer farmers to till these newly opened fields. The growth of tenancy in Yamanashi may be more a sign of the tenants' using their growing labor productivity to increase their income than of their sinking poverty.

In Yamanashi as elsewhere tenants also tilled rented land voluntarily, not because they were falling, but because they were rising—to further augment their production and income. Greater labor efficiency or additional farmhands allowed them to increase their area of cultivation, and these tenants did not have sufficient capital to buy more land, or if they did no land was available, or they wanted to expand their farms only temporarily, or they decided rationally that they took fewer risks in renting than in buying additional land. Two of twenty-two Ōkamada farmers who answered a questionnaire distributed in the summer of 1969 reported that they rented out and borrowed land at the same time in the 1930s. One was a small, twenty-*tan* landlord who leased twelve *tan* of land for his own cultivation from other landlords rather than evict his own tenants whom he might want back in a few years.[28] (Let me add here parenthetically that

[27] *Yamanashi tōkeisho*, 1883 and 1912.

[28] Twenty-two former members of the Ōkamada branch of the Imperial Military Reserve Association answered a questionnaire distributed in the village in the summer of 1969 to gather information about local reservist activities. The questionnaire included questions on prewar landholdings from which these data are culled. The respondents include two landlords, five owner farmers, three owner tenant farmers (owned 50-90 percent of the land tilled), nine tenant owner farmers (owned 10-50 percent of the land tilled), and three pure tenant farmers (owned less than 10 percent of land tilled).

the belief that, when a surplus of potential tenants exists, landlords freely evict old and contract with new tenants is erroneous. Customary and kinship connections aside, some tenants, because they are particularly hardworking, bring both themselves and their landlords good returns on their investments; a wise landlord avoids evicting such a tenant even if it means the landowner has to rent other land to till himself.)[29] Three of 39 households in Kubo Nakajima, a hamlet within Ōkamada, also fit into this category. As we can see from Table 2-2, one was a landlord cultivator, but the other two were tenant owner farmers. Although this phenomenon occurred mostly in the twentieth century and seems to have been somewhat limited in extent, it must have accounted for some of Yamanashi's tenancy in the Meiji period. In the absence of clear statistical evidence, I would posit conservatively that a large part of Yamanashi's growth of tenancy in the Meiji period took place, not because of bankruptcy and foreclosure under the impact of an expanding market caused by the land settlement and tax system, but

TABLE 2-2

Landlord-Owner-Tenant Farmers in Kubo Nakajima

Farmer	Land Rented Out	Owner Cultivated	Rented In
Ishihara Toshiharu (2)	16.2 *tan*	14.9 *tan*	2.1 *tan*
Ishihara Taizō (4)	4.4	7.8	9.0
Ishihara Toyokichi (13)	4.0	4.1	10.7

Source: *KNJ*, p. 162.

[29] The practice of tenant farmers' subleasing their rented land to other tenants for short periods was also practiced in Naka Koma County. Thus, farmers who had sons leave the village for military service or to work in the cities or who for some other reason suffered from a temporary labor shortage could maintain their tenancy tenure until they needed the land again. Subleasing was most prevalent in the areas like Ōkamada with the highest incidence of tenancy disputes. *Kosaku jijō chōsa*, pp. 139-141.

because of reclamation, entrepreneurial tenancy, and the breakdown of servitude.

Whether or not the land settlement and tax system created conditions which hastened the spread of tenancy, they certainly indicated the new government's recognition of a good part of the rural status quo, a continuation of the preexisting stratified peasant order sans samurai, and this has brought the Meiji regime much criticism. But while it is easy to look back to the 1870s from our egalitarian vantage point a century later and chastise the nineteenth-century government for not turning all farmland over to the cultivators, or, worse yet to many Japanese scholars, for not collectivizing all agricultural land, the Meiji settlement was, to borrow Kurihara's phrase to describe another rural phenomenon, "advanced for its day." One should be surprised enough to find a government made up almost entirely of samurai taking ownership away from its own class's members and turning it over to peasants.

Ronald Dore argues, in developing his "reactionary thesis," moreover, that the stratification which the land settlement recognized and the tax system may have exacerbated benefited Japanese agriculture. Because landlords in the Meiji period had the knowledge, status, contacts, motivation, and capital necessary to improve farming techniques, and tenants did not, agricultural production increased to the extent it did in modern Japan because of stratification. A more egalitarian society in the nineteenth century, Dore thinks, would have slowed development. Only in the 1920s did tenants have the necessary prerequisites—capital, education, motivation, etc. —to make land reform work.[30] It is not surprising, therefore, that it was in the 1920s that tenants in advanced regions sought to reform the system; the efforts of the well-to-do leaders of the Meiji era's stratified rural order in improving agricultural methods so benefited their less well-to-do fol-

---

[30] R. P. Dore, "Land Reform and Japan's Economic Development," pp. 382-386.

135

lowers that it put the latter in a position to challenge the former after World War I. Chances are, as Dore implies, that a more equitable rural society in 1875, because it would not have stimulated growth, would have led to a poorer and ironically perhaps even less equitable society in 1925.[31] A maximal conclusion about the impact of the land settlement on rural Yamanashi and Japan might be that the Meiji government did owner and tenant farmers a favor by not carrying out a complete land reform (and certainly by not collectivizing agriculture) in the 1870s. A more conservative, safer, but still heterodox, conclusion would be that the new system made poorer farmers much less vulnerable to exploitation than is generally believed.

The Meiji government's new tax system, which required landowners to pay 4 percent of the assessed value of their agricultural land (3 percent after 1877), seems not to have raised Yamanashi taxes significantly before 1877 and seems to have lowered them sharply after. Kozo Yamamura calculates that the Yamanashi tax rate after the reform came to 28.97 percent (the highest in Japan) of the value of production per piece of arable land and that this was 2.1 percent higher than the average Kai tax before the reform.[32] Accordingly, the 25 percent tax reduction in 1877 meant that farmers in 1878 paid 21.7 percent of their value of production in taxes and that this was 23 percent lower than the feudal tax. Although we do not have tax data for the middle Meiji years, our twentieth-century evidence, presented in Table 2-3, which indicates that farmers in 1907 and 1911 paid less than 10 percent of the value of production in taxes, would seem to demonstrate that the burden in Yamanashi, as in Japan as a whole, fell steadily throughout the Meiji era.[33]

In Yamanashi, as in other regions of Japan, there was spo-

---

[31] Ibid., pp. 382-384.

[32] Yamamura, "Meiji Land Tax Reform," Tables 14.2 and 14.3.

[33] A Kubo Nakajima Tenant Union document from 1929 indicates the taxes that landowners paid on one tan of rice paddy. Unfortunately, we do not have comparable evidence for mulberry orchards or mugi fields. Taxes on one tan of medium quality paddy in 1929:

TABLE 2-3
Percentage of the Value of Agricultural Production
Paid in Taxes by Yamanashi Farmers,
1907–1935

Year	Percentage
1907	9.3
1911	9.3
1917	7.3
1919	5.7
1921	12.5
1919–23	9.9
1925	8.4
1924–28	9.9
1930	14.3
1935	9.2

Calculated from *Yamanashi tōkeisho*; *SKK*, p. 497; Ame-miya, p. 157.

radic resistance to the new Meiji tax system, but the unrest came before the government carried out its reassessment of land values and well before it began to collect its new taxes. In the summer of 1872, Yamanashi peasants petitioned the

---

1. National Land Tax: 4.5 percent of the paddy's estimated value of 42.7 yen — 1.92 yen
2. Prefectural Tax: 139.8 percent of the National Land Tax — 2.68
3. Village Tax: 66 percent of the National Land Tax — 1.27
4. Village House Tax (*kosūwari*): 6.7 percent of 10 yen, estimated income from one *tan* of paddy (see actual rice income per *tan* for 1925–1929 in Table 2-16) — 0.67
5. National Income Tax: 9.5 percent of 14 yen, estimated income from one *tan* of paddy (see 4 above, and actual income per *tan* for 1925–1929 in Table 2-16) — 1.33
6. Additional Prefectural Tax: 40.5 percent of National Income Tax — 0.54
7. Agricultural Association dues: 15 sen per *tan* of land owned, and 10 sen per 1 yen of land tax — 0.34

Total tax per *tan*: — 8.75 yen

government for the continuation of the existing *daishōgiri* system. Governor Doi refused, and in August the so-called Daishōgiri Uprising took place. Peasants in 97 villages from the eastern section of the Kōfu Basin arose, marched on Kōfu, looted and burned the home of Wakao Ippei, the rich raw silk merchant who donated money to the new regime, and again petitioned the government to continue the old method of taxation. Officials again refused, brought in troops from nearby prefectures to suppress the uprising, and harshly punished the participants. The three principal leaders were executed, four received three years' imprisonment and 4,000 others were fined.[34] (Cf. much lighter punishments in the tenant disputes of the 1920s.) Since the Daishōgiri affair occurred before the government instituted the Meiji tax system in Yamanashi, the participants could not have risen to resist the actuality of new, higher taxes; moreover, since Kai taxpayers already paid five-ninths of their taxes in money, fear of forced involvement in the market could not have impelled them to rise. Rather, it would seem that the fear of harsher taxes, which turned out to be unfounded, motivated this peasant uprising. Yamanashi peasants must have breathed a collective sigh of relief in 1878 when taxes began to fall from Tokugawa and early Meiji levels.

The new government also began to create a public school system and legislated compulsory education in the 1870s, and these too influenced rural Yamanashi. Ronald Dore estimates that about 40-50 percent of Japanese boys and 15 percent of girls received some kind of schooling at the end of the Tokugawa era, although his evidence does not allow him to state with precision who had become how literate.[35] But, assuming that everyone who went to school was literate and that all samurai and most merchants matriculated, then only 30-40 percent of Japan's peasants could have achieved any

---

[34] *Gojūnenshi*, p. 43.

[35] Ronald P. Dore, "The Legacy of Tokugawa Education," in Marius B. Jansen, ed., *Changing Japanese Attitudes Toward Modernization* (Princeton, 1965), p. 100.

degree of literacy when the Meiji regime came to power, and these people probably tended to come from the rural well-to-do who had the time and money to study. In 1870, a majority of owner tenant and tenant farmers must have been illiterate.

One of the new government's first reforms was to establish schools. Officials, with landlord support, founded schools in Yamanashi as early as the summer of 1873, and the prefectural government reported in 1878 that over 33,000 young people attended 275 schools. Even if we make adjustments for the possibility of exaggeration in the data—the 1881 and 1887 figures were slightly lower, about 31,500 students, than those for 1871—the statistics reveal that half of the prefecture's school-age children attended school in the late 1870s and 1880s. Since Yamanashi had few ex-samurai and merchants in the early Meiji era, one can safely assume that most of the students were peasants becoming farmers. From 1887 on, the school population increased steadily, until by the end of the Russo-Japanese War in 1905, the enrollment of male youths in elementary schools exceeded 98 percent.[36]

The Ōkamada experience reinforces the prefectural one. The village's first school was established in 1873 in Futsuka Ichiba hamlet, with its most prominent landlord, Mikami Hachiemon, in charge, and in 1875 another was set up in nearby Tōkōji temple in Ōsato. By 1925, the village had one central school, in Ōsato, with eight grades, 434 students, close to 100 percent enrollment, and a 95 percent rate of attendance.[37] Moreover, it appears that in the 1920s and 1930s almost all male children, rich and poor alike, studied for eight years, although law made but six years compulsory. Only one of our twenty-two questionnaire respondents in

[36] Yamanashi records show that in 1906, 98.8 percent of eligible boys and 95.5 percent of eligible girls matriculated in elementary schools; overall, 97.2 percent of eligible children enrolled in school. *Yamanashi tōkeisho*, 1906; *SKK*, pp. 899, 904.

[37] *Naka Koma gunshi* (Kōfu, 1928), Section 8, pp. 7, 25-33, 53.

Ōkamada, all of whom were educated between 1905 and 1930, and of whom fifteen were owner tenant or tenant farmers, ended his education after six years, and he was one of the five owner farmers in the sample. By the early 1900s, almost every farm household must have included one literate person; by the 1920s, almost every male under the age of thirty must have had the ability to read and write.[38]

The impact of literacy on the countryside was great. To begin with, the men who joined the tenant-farmer movement after World War I were able to write petitions and reports, to pass information within the local organization, from hamlet union to hamlet union, and back and forth to regional and national headquarters more easily because they could read and write. Literacy also allowed the movement's outside sympathizers, the movement's non-farmer "leaders," like national tenant union officers, labor leaders, and radical intellectuals, to influence the village. Although I think that some scholars overemphasize this influence and that villagers tended to resist those exogenous forces which did not use the hamlet's cohesiveness to enlist support, literacy made the outsiders' potential more powerful than ever before.[39]

Literacy had an even greater impact on technology, farm management, and economic attitudes than it did on tenancy disputes. Landlords took the lead in the spread of agricultural and sericultural technology in the early and middle Meiji period, often teaching by example, but, after the turn of the

---

[38] The questionnaire of reservists described in footnote 28 also included a question on the respondent's level of education. Of the twenty-two men who answered, twenty had attended higher elementary school (eight years of study), one had left school after elementary school (six years of study), and one (another owner farmer) had matriculated in a technical school after completing his compulsory education. The 1924 survey of tenant union households in four Okayama counties indicates that in the early 1920s 71 percent, in the 1910-1920 decade 66 percent, and in the first decade of the twentieth century 53 percent of eligible young tenant farmer males attended school for the extra two years. Ōta Toshie, "Kosakunō kaikyū no keizaiteki shakaiteki jōtai," p. 102.

[39] Nakamura, *Jinushiseishi kenkyū*, pp. 244-246.

century, tenant farmers relied less and less on landlords to learn new techniques. Tenants' increased ability to read and write, and the publication of technical periodicals written in simple language like *Yamanashi Silkworm and Mulberry News*, which catered to that ability, allowed farmers to learn new methods without the landlords' guidance.[40] Literacy also allowed farmers to keep financial records, order goods by using catalogues, deal directly with buyers, banks, and government officials, read contracts and insurance policies, serve as village and hamlet officers, and perform independently many functions for which they had had to depend on their landlords in the past. In other words, literacy freed tenants from much of their customary economic and political dependence on their landlords.

The skills that owner tenant and tenant farmers learned in school also helped these less well-to-do men develop positive attitudes of independence and control over their own lives. The literate tenant farmers of the twentieth century were less likely to resist change and more likely to switch from subsistence to more profitable commercial crops, were more self-confident than their fathers and grandfathers had been. By the 1900s, Japanese farmers were no longer peasants concerned only with subsistence; they had become farmers who managed their own farms and lives. The Meiji government's educational system and its concomitant literacy played an important part in this transformation.[41]

The renowned economic reforms of the Meiji government aimed at building a "rich country and a strong army," which Western scholars have discussed extensively, also had a dramatic effect on Yamanashi's agricultural economy.[42] Too

[40] *Yamanashi Silkworm and Mulberry News (Yamanashi sansō jihō)* was a periodical published privately from 1905 to the end of World War II in Yamanashi to disseminate sericultural techniques.

[41] Ronald P. Dore, *Education in Tokugawa Japan* (London, 1965), p. 292.

[42] See, for example, Thomas C. Smith, *Political Change and Industrial Development in Japan: Government Enterprise, 1868-1880* (Stanford, 1955) and G. C. Allen, *A Short Economic History of Modern Japan.*

much cannot be said of the positive effect on the prefecture's farmers of raw silk filatures powered by inanimate energy, agricultural and sericultural research stations, a new banking system which brought the cost of capital down from over 20 percent to under 10 percent per annum, and of modern transportation facilities which moved people and goods cheaply and quickly. We shall return to these reforms later. But here I would like to emphasize a government policy which may have been more influential than any of these concrete modifications: the Meiji regime created a milieu in which entrepreneurship, experimentation, the exchange of ideas, and self-improvement were encouraged. Hundreds of landlords, petty businessmen, and technicians nationwide, stimulated by this atmosphere, set out to help themselves, Japan, and their home regions and villages simultaneously. Late-nineteenth-century Yamanashi had its share of men who, encouraged by the prefectural government, gambled great amounts of time, effort, and money for returns which could not have seemed certain at the time. Wakao Ippei, who was an itinerant peddler when the port of Yokohama opened in 1859, is a primary example of a man who, encouraged by successive governors of Yamanashi, took risks, prospered, and affected his home region. Admittedly, Wakao is an extreme case; he ranked among the richest men in Japan when he died in 1913. Nevertheless, he is worth singling out as a prototypical rural entrepreneur, at least partly because sources to elucidate his career are available.

Wakao was born in 1820 as the son of the village headman of Zaikezuka, an upland village in the Midai River region in western Naka Koma County, an area famous for its traveling salesmen. His childhood was not one of privilege in spite of his father's position. Ippei was sickly and he had neither father nor mother for much of his youth. His father was away from home constantly because of continual litigation with the next village over a longstanding water dispute, and Wakao's mother died when he was two years old. Thus, in spite of his family's status, Wakao did not enter school until he

142

was twelve, when his father remarried; two years later, Wakao's stepmother died also, and he was forced to drop out of school to replace her at home. He cooked and cleaned, and studied, Abe Lincoln style, at night. Only when he turned seventeen did Wakao finally get a chance to strike out on his own; because he considered himself too weak physically to farm, he decided to follow his childhood ambition and become a warrior. Thus, in 1837, Wakao left for Edo to study sword-fighting and find a position as an apprentice samurai. But he had less success as a soldier than as a student; the closest Wakao got to his apprenticeship was a menial post in a Honjō lumberyard. This frustration and his knowledge that a boyhood friend who had become a "samurai" wore two swords, but in fact worked as a servant for a high-ranking warrior family, induced Wakao to renounce his martial ambition and turn instead to the life of a traveling merchant.

One would like to say that Wakao's decision in 1841 led directly to his riches. Alas for him, it did not. His career as a merchant, like his earlier attempts as a student and warrior, went through many vicissitudes before he finally achieved great wealth in the new atmosphere of the Meiji period. As a matter of fact, the triumphs and defeats in Wakao's entrepreneurial ventures, usually the result of his good or bad knowledge of the market, timing, luck, daring, ruthlessness, and, after 1868, government encouragement, were not unlike those of other merchants from Kai (and elsewhere) and are probably worth recounting in some detail.

When Wakao began his career as a peddler at the age of twenty-one, he lacked one important prerequisite for the merchant's life: capital. Nevertheless, he was a pragmatist who believed in making do with what he had. Since the family's only visible marketable assets hung on twenty peach trees, Wakao picked the fruit and set off on the Shinshū Highway past Lake Suwa to the neighboring province. After an exhausting one-hundred-mile walk, he arrived in the castle town of Matsumoto; when he unpacked his peaches to display them to a prospective customer, Wakao found that they had spoiled. He went home chastened, his return trip financed by a gift from the wholesaler to whom he had attempted to sell his rotten fruit.

Ippei decided to turn next to trading in his region's tobacco, and for a few years his efforts met with extraordinary success. He borrowed three *bu* (four *bu* = one *ryō*, which in 1870 = one *yen*) from his father to purchase his first crop and sold tobacco all over Kai—as far as Mukawa, halfway to Shinshū in the west, and Tsuru, near Mt. Fuji in the east. He returned home with silk textiles and other regional products which he marketed around Kōfu. Through these efforts, he turned his father's three *bu* into 150 *ryō* in just five years. Perhaps overly enboldened by his success, Ippei abandoned tobacco for the seemingly greater profits to be made in the cotton textile trade, and by 1854, eight years later, he was back where he started in 1841, flat broke. But his thirteen years of back-breaking effort apparently had not been in vain; Wakao's reputation as a merchant enabled him to borrow fifty *ryō* to set himself up carrying tobacco and other goods between Kōfu and Musashi, Edo's province. By 1857, he had built this loan into 800 *ryō*. Too sickly to be a farmer, he was still strong enough to bear tobacco with a shoulder-carrying pole across the treacherous Sasago Pass and down the Kōshū Highway to the capital and its environs.

The opening of the treaty port at Yokohama in 1859 proved a boon to Wakao and dozens of other enterprising young Japanese merchants; Morimura Ichizaemon, the maker of Noritake china; Ōkura Kihachirō, of hotel fame; Amemiya Keijirō, Yamanashi's renowned steel, railroad, flour, and electricity speculator; and Wakao stand out as the best known in a large group of energetic entrepreneurs.[43]

Ippei's reaction to this new opportunity shows how he could quickly revise his misconceptions and adapt to new

[43] Yasuzō Horie, "Entrepreneurship in Meiji Japan," in Lockwood, *The State and Economic Enterprise in Japan*, p. 192.

market forces. When Ippei heard of the arrival of the foreign merchants in Yokohama, he and his brother Ikuzō raced there with a load of dried radishes to sell to the Chinese. This was a decision based on not knowing who the foreigners were or what they wanted to buy. Although the Wakaos' first trip ended in failure, Ippei and Ikuzō took away knowledge of the European and American demand for raw silk and silk textiles, both produced in their home province, and quickly exploited their opportunity. At first they dealt with the foreigners through their Yamanashi compatriot Shinohara Tadaemon, who maintained an establishment in Yokohama and functioned as a middleman in selling the Wakaos' goods to the foreigners. But soon Ippei and Ikuzō struck out on their own. Within a year they had amassed so large a profit selling Kai's raw silk in Yokohama and British cotton textiles in Kōfu that they could expand and organize their business; Ippei ran the Kōfu end, Ikuzō served as his agent in the treaty port, and a small army of employees carried their goods back and forth.

This system allowed the Wakao family to exploit changes in the market at both ends of their business. One example of this flexibility took place on Christmas night of 1860, when Ikuzō overheard a foreign merchant telling Shinohara of his willingness to pay a high price for Kai crystal. Ikuzō raced to Hachiōji, where his brother had gone on other business, and told him the gist of his eavesdropping. Ippei and Ikuzō literally ran back to Kai, bought cheaply as much crystal as they could carry on their backs, sped to Yokohama, and in the middle of the night went straight to the foreign merchant's house before Shinohara arrived. The brothers then made several more round-trips, amassed additional profits, and stopped only when they had sated the crystal market. While the Wakaos traveled back and forth to Kai, their bearers continued to supply the foreigners with raw silk and silk textiles, for which there was a more secure and less volatile demand. By 1868, Ippei had amassed enough wealth to contribute 1,350 *ryō* to the loyalist, anti-Tokugawa army when it entered Kai.[44]

When the Meiji period opened, the Wakao brothers were already well-to-do businessmen, but Ippei accumulated the bulk of his fortune because of the new atmosphere and opportunities. In 1875, the two brothers divided their business; Ikuzō took the Yokohama part and Ippei the Kōfu end. From that time on, Ippei invested in various kinds of enterprises: banking, Western-style industry in both Tokyo and Yamanashi, raw silk filatures, sericultural technology, and agricultural land. His investments, whether modern like railroads and electricity, or "hybrid" modern-traditional like sericulture and agriculture, and his extensive participation in politics all had a direct effect on Yamanashi's economy.[45]

Wakao's involvement in modern enterprise began when he bought a Western-style silk reeling machine in Maebashi in the early 1870s and then hired a number of women to operate it and the other similar machines he had built. Wakao's involvement in hybrid enterprises started in 1878 when he set up a research and training center under the leadership of his older brother Rinzaemon to advise farmers in sericultural matters. He then established the Tenth National Bank in Kōfu and a few years later became a managing director of the Yokohama Specie Bank. From his banks, which he used to finance Yamanashi's raw silk industry and its exports, he turned to railroads, which helped to transport cocoons and raw silk. Wakao invested heavily in railways after the mid-1880s, urged their construction when he became a member of the House of Peers in 1890, and had a major role in directing the Tokyo Horse Railway Company (later the Tokyo Tramcar Company), which built the capital's first trolley car lines. Moreover, it was only a small step from Tokyo tram-

---

[44] Saitō Toshiya, ed., *Kyōdoshi ni kagayaku hitobito*, Vol. 2 (Kōfu, 1969), pp. 105-126; Naitō Bunji, *Wakao Ippei den* (Yokohama, 1972), passim.

[45] See Kazushi Ohkawa and Henry Rosovsky, "A Century of Japanese Economic Growth," in Lockwood, *The State and Economic Enterprise in Japan*, pp. 66-67, for a definition of the term "hybrid."

cars to the Tokyo Light Company which Wakao founded and which drew on the abundant power of Yamanashi's rivers. The first hydroelectric plant was built in the region in 1900, and by 1933 Wakao's company was the largest electric producer in Yamanashi. The prefecture ranked sixth nationally in the generation of electric power in that year, although only 10 percent of it was consumed at home; Wakao's Tokyo Light Company and the Tokyo-Yokohama Electric Company sold the rest in the capital's metropolitan area. Thus, electricity, which in Japan was generated primarily by waterpower until the late 1950s, became an important export and created employment at home and helped to pay for Yamanashi's extensive imports, especially of fertilizer, in the twentieth century.[46]

This self-made and multi-faceted entrepreneur by the mid-Meiji period became Yamanashi's largest landowner; Wakao owned property in six counties and twenty-six towns and villages, although his family's holdings in the Tokugawa era had been confined to small ones in Zaikezuka Village. According to a 1924 survey by the Agriculture and Commerce Ministry, the Wakao household owned 423 *chō* of land, two-and-one-half times more than its nearest Yamanashi competitor and enough to rank it as the forty-seventh largest land-owning family in Japan outside Hokkaido.[47]

Wakao obtained the foundation for his farmland holdings because of a daring speculative act in 1877, in which he during a period of inflation gambled his entire estate that the government would be compelled to introduce deflationary measures, and won—after a wait of half a decade. The Meiji government's fiscal policies created inflation during the closing years of its first decade in power because it succumbed to the temptation of deficit financing and of expanding the nation's money supply when confronted with the cost of liq-

---

[46] Saito, *Kyōdoshi ni kagayaku hitobito*, Vol. 2, pp. 105-126; *SKK*, pp. 237-238, 387-389.

[47] *Gojū chōbu ijō no daijinushi* in *Nihon nōgyō hattatsushi*, Vol. 7 (Tokyo, 1956), p. 745.

uidating the old regime, industrializing, modernizing, and suppressing rebellions. These policies not only debased Japan's currency, but also reduced the buying power of the government's tax resources. Although the cost of commodities rose considerably between 1877 and 1881, the government's tax revenues, 2.5 percent of the value of land assessed before 1877, stayed the same. Moreover, while the government suffered, farmers flourished; they paid a lower percentage of the value of their production in taxes than before the inflation. But the cultivators' abnormally good times were short-lived. In 1881, the fiscally conservative Matsukata Masayoshi became Finance Minister, introduced a program of retrenchment and monetary stabilization, and laid the foundation for Japan's subsequent economic growth. In 1877, when inflation was just getting up a full head of steam, Wakao, gambling that the government would be forced to stop rising prices and make paper money convertible into silver at par, mortgaged his home and fields to borrow 110,000 yen in silver and exchanged the specie for almost double its amount in inflated paper money. When Matsukata's deflationary policies took hold after 1881 and paper money once again became convertible with specie, Wakao had nearly doubled his original investment (and saved his property). But this was only the first half of his speculative coup. The drop in the prices of agricultural commodities caused by the deflation forced many farmers who had overexpanded in their inflationary good times to borrow money by using their land as security to keep their farm businesses afloat. In Yamanashi, the newly enriched Wakao was able to supply many of these loans, and when some of these farmer-borrowers subsequently defaulted, Wakao foreclosed. The lands gained in this way, together with those garnered through his investments in opening new fields, made Wakao Yamanashi's major landowner.

Wakao's investment in land, needless to say, had a significant impact on the development of Yamanashi's agricultural economy. To begin with, it reinforced his commitment, already formed when he began to sell raw silk in Yokohama in the *bakumatsu* period, to improving the quality of the region's sericulture. After all, good raw silk offered Ippei double profits: increased farm rents as well as better prices in Yokohama. The national and prefectural governments and local landlords, of whom Wakao was only one, albeit a very rich one, poured time, energy, and money into raising the quality of the region's raw silk, mulberry trees, silkworm eggs, and cocoons. Wakao's contribution to the semi-modern sericultural industry was recognized by the government; late in both their lives the Meiji emperor decorated Wakao for his efforts.

Second, Wakao's landownership, as well as his commitments to modern factories and transportation, led him to play a role in introducing sericulture into areas of the prefecture where in the 1870s and 1880s the primary cash crop was rice. In the early Meiji period, most cocoons came from either the mountainous Tsuru region or the upland villages on the eastern periphery of the basin. With the establishment after 1880 of large-scale filatures using inanimate energy in Kōfu City, where Wakao lived (he served as the city's first mayor in 1889), and in nearby villages in Naka Koma, Nishi Yamanashi, and Higashi Yamanashi counties, and with the development of modern transportation which centered on the city and these counties, sericulture moved to the lowland villages nearer to the prefectural capital. It is not surprising, therefore, that most of Ippei's tenants operated farms in centrally located villages, and that these communities increasingly turned to sericulture and sent family members to work in the mills. Finally, the Wakaos unwittingly had an impact on Yamanashi agriculture when their bank failed in 1928. In an attempt to avoid bankruptcy, the family liquidated most of its assets. This included selling their farmland to their tenants at low prices; several Kubo Nakajima tenants became tenant-owner farmers in the opening years of the Shōwa era because of the collapse of the Wakao empire. Fortunately, Ippei did not live to see his family's fortune, much like that

149

of an earlier famous Kai clan, the Takeda, rise and fall within two generations. He had died in 1913 at the age of 93.[48]

Wakao was only one of many Yamanashi landlord-entrepreneur-experimenters who flourished in the congenial atmosphere of the Meiji period. Countless others tried their hand at improving the prefecture's raw silk industry and their own profits: Amemiya Keijirō (1840-1911), "one of a kind Amemiya" as a later prime minister, Ōkuma Shigenobu, called him, speculated in raw silk and silkworm eggs between 1859 and 1876 and served as director of twelve Tokyo companies before he died. Hatta Tatsuya (1854-1916), a landlord, mayor of Ukai Village near Kōfu and prefectural assemblyman, devoted his life and wealth to the study and spread of sericultural technology. Kazama Ishichi (1821-1907), who worked for a pawnbroker in Kōfu before 1859, traded in silk in Yokohama between 1859 and 1868 and established a modern filature in Kōfu with French-style reeling machinery in 1876. Kazama Kanehachi (1855-1907), Ishichi's son, managed his father's filature, investigated American cotton mills on a trip there in 1887, and wrote a book entitled "The Principles of Making Raw Silk," in which he explained his adaption of American cotton-spinning techniques for use in Japanese silk filatures. Natori Masaki (1814-1900), who invented a silk-reeling machine in the early Meiji period, managed the prefecture's model filature which was established by Governor Fujimura in 1874. Nezu Kaichirō, who served as village assemblyman and mayor of Shōtokuji Village to the east of Kōfu, became Yamanashi's second leading landowner, an entrepreneur of railroads and electricity, a member of the House of Peers, and a famous art collector and museum founder. Ichinose Masuyoshi (1865-1921), who served as mayor of Ueno Village and as prefectural assemblyman, founded a raw silk filature, developed one of Japan's best mulberry strains, and involved himself throughout his

[48] *Kyōdoshi ni kagayaku hitobito*, Vol. 2, pp. 122-126; *Wakao den*, pp. 205-242; Saitō Yoshihiro, *Kōshū zaibatsu monogatari*, Vol. 2 (Kōfu, 1976), pp. 11-15, 20-24, 55-64, 147-156.

adult life in Yamanashi's agricultural and sericultural development. And there were many other such entrepreneurs of agriculture too numerous to mention.[49]

The literate landlord-businessman-experimenter, whose interests in agricultural and industrial improvement before 1868 had been somewhat frustrated by feudal restrictions, burst into practical action after the Meiji government swept away the rules which inhibited contact with foreigners and Japanese from other regions and urged economic development. Stimulation came not only from the national government, with its banks, schools, and model factories, but also from regional headquarters, where officials appointed by the Tokyo regime encouraged improvement in agriculture and small-scale industrial production. Successive governors of Yamanashi in the Meiji era, members of the same clique of lower samurai who ruled in Tokyo, played an active role in creating a new atmosphere for change in Kōfu. Fujimura Shirō, governor of Yamanashi for thirteen years, was one such example.

Fujimura, who was born into a warrior family in Kumamoto in Kyushu in 1845, received his appointment as governor in 1874 at the age of twenty-nine as a reward for his service to the loyalist cause. As one of the "men of sincerity" of the *bakumatsu* period, Fujimura (while still a teenager) had abandoned his feudal obligation to his lord in Kumamoto to join the Chōshū domain in its successful effort to topple the Tokugawa regime. When Governor Doi resigned in 1873 to accept responsibility for the Daishōgiri peasant uprising, Fujimura received the Kōfu appointment. He immediately set out to improve Yamanashi's economy through three programs: development of the raw silk industry, of roads, and of schools. One of Fujimura's first acts was the establishment of a model filature in Kōfu with Natori Masaki in charge. Beginning in the late 1870s, Fujimura dispatched students to

[49] Yamanashi nichinichi shimbunsha, *Yamanashi hyakka jiten* (Kōfu, 1972), passim; *Sanshigyō gaishi*, passim; *Kyōdoshi ni kagayaku hitobito*, Vol. 3 (Kōfu, 1970), pp. 1-24.

other parts of Japan to study sericulture and silk reeling. One of the students, Muramatsu Bokusuke, returned from Fukushima in 1883 with a technique which was to revolutionize Yamanashi cocoon raising: the heated cultivating room. In 1883, Fujimura helped to establish the Yamanashi Sericultural Society, a semi-official organization which performed sericultural research, conducted teaching seminars, and published a newsletter to disseminate new techniques. In 1885, he founded a sericultural school and the Sericultural and Silk Reeling Association with the landlord, local politician, and sericultural experimenter, Hatta Tatsuya, as president. This society played a role in the spread of technological information and in raising the quality of silkworm eggs. Throughout his governorship, Fujimura strove to develop the Kōshū and Ōme highways as roads for the export of Yamanashi raw silk, and to build elementary schools; the Kōshū Highway was widened to twenty-five feet in the basin and thirteen feet at the Sasago Pass, and the students of Ōsato School, who first met in a local Buddhist temple, moved into a new building within a year of the school's founding in 1875, for example.[50] Although Fujimura's effectiveness waned after 1881 when his arbitrary methods of governing aroused stiff opposition from the People's Rights Movement and its representatives in the prefectural assembly, he did create an atmosphere conducive to experimentation and to technological improvement in Yamanashi's key industry, sericulture. Entrepreneurs like Wakao and Amemiya built a market for Kai's raw silk; officials like Fujimura encouraged its improvement; and, as we shall see in the next chapter, landlord-businessmen-experimenters like Hatta, Ichinose, and Wakao himself invested much of their time, energy, and money in sericultural development in the sympathetic milieu of the Meiji period.

[50] *Yamanashi hyakka jiten,* pp. 685; *Sanshigyō gaishi,* pp. 34, 74-76; *Yamanashi kan,* pp. 125-126; *Naka Koma gunshi,* Sec. 8, pp. 7, 25-33, 53; *Yamanashi-ken no rekishi,* pp. 220-222.

Silk and Yamanashi's Economic Growth

Yamanashi entrepreneurs used the region's advantages: proximity to Yokohama's foreign demand; small, family-operated farms which could switch to labor-intensive sericulture profitably because of this demand; some farmers who had experience in sericulture and others who were receptive to new techniques; market networks because of the developed commercial agriculture by premodern standards; a large number of tenant farmers who welcomed a cash crop which lessened their rent burden; abundant water, and later hydroelectric, power; and raw materials and labor to create modern raw silk filatures and successful sericultural farms. In 1868, when the modern era opened, all of Yamanashi's raw silk was hand-reeled in small one- and two-basin, "proto-industrial" workshops, usually farmers' houses. But Wakao, Kazama Ishichi, and Amemiya Kihei established the first modern filatures in Kōfu in the 1870s; Fujimura and Natori followed with their "official" mill; and by 1879, the prefecture had over 80 filatures with ten or more basins powered by inanimate energy, in this case water. Less than twenty years later. Yamanashi contained 201 modern factories which employed an average of 53 workers each. In 1894, technicians introduced steam-powered reeling machinery, and by the turn of the century it had replaced water as the primary type of motive power in the larger filatures. But steam's days were also numbered. At about the same time, Wakao established his hydroelectric plant at Ashikawa, and gradually the modern filatures converted to electricity.[51] In 1896, the raw silk industry provided slightly over 10,000 jobs in Yamanashi. By 1911, 16,636 men and women

---

[51] Electricity makes its first appearance as a motive force for textile- and fiber-making machines in 1899. In 1918, it passed the steam engine as the primary method of powering these machines, and in 1920 it provided 53 percent, in 1930 81 percent, and in 1940 92 percent of the horsepower used to run spinning and weaving machinery. *Chōki keizai tōkei*, Vol. 12, p. 223.

worked in the prefecture's filatures. Raw silk provided half of all non-agricultural jobs in Kai.[52]

Although the growth of Yamanashi's raw silk industry was substantial before the turn of the century, it took off even more dramatically after 1900 because of another policy of the modernizing Meiji regime, the laying of railroads. In 1903, Nezu Kaichirō built the Chūō Line, which tied central Yamanashi to the rest of Japan, and the government nationalized the railroad two years later. Not only did the new line transport passengers from Kōfu to Tokyo in six hours, and after electrification in 1931, three-and-one-half hours, but, even more importantly, it moved large quantities of industrial and farm goods cheaply and quickly (Table 2-4). Other modern transportation facilities followed and reinforced the effect of the Chūō Line: in 1928, the Minobu Line in the south linked Kōfu with the Tōkaidō Line at Fuji; in 1929, the Ōtsuki-Fuji Yoshida Electric Railroad in the east tied the Tsuru Region to the Chūō Line; and after the late 1920s, trucks began to complement and even replace railroads as a means of handling freight.[53]

The railroads, trucks, and continued modernization of sericultural and silk-reeling techniques led to a sustained increase in production and in large-scale filatures after 1903, as Table 2-5 indicates. By 1934, Yamanashi housed 252 ma-

TABLE 2-4

Freight Handled at Chūō Line Stations in Yamanashi in Tons

	1906	1910	1922	1927	1937
Out	72,660	109,305	353,881	429,057	323,600
In	153,910	189,704	369,402	440,308	337,807

Source: *Yamanashi tōkeisho.*

[52] *Sanshigyō gaishi*, pp. 59, 105; *SKK*, p. 190.

[53] *SKK*, pp. 452-460, 468. Note in Table 2-4 the decline in freight handled on the Chūō Line from 1927 to 1937. Most of the difference was taken up by the new Minobu Line or truck transport.

TABLE 2-5
Filatures and the Value of Production, 1902 and 1934

Year	Machine Filatures	Value of Production in Machine Filatures (in 1,000s of yen)	Hand-Reeling Filatures	Value of Production in Hand-Reeling Filatures (in 1,000s of yen)
1902	111	4,166	10,497	1,260
1934	252	18,627	3,062	717

Source: *SKK*, 318-319.

chine-operated filatures with an average of 65 workers each; 214 of the mills had more than ten basins, and 54 over 100 basins. The products of these modern, electrically powered facilities, with their higher and more uniform quality of raw silk, dominated production and exports. In 1922, machine filatures turned out 85 percent of Yamanashi's raw silk (96 percent in 1934). In 1923, they produced 99.9 percent of its exports, most of which went for American silk stockings, which required raw silk of uniform quality. Even in the depression year of 1933, raw silk provided over 5,000 more jobs than a quarter of a century earlier; 21,761 people worked in filatures, more than 80 percent in machine filatures.[54]

[54] *SKK*, pp. 318, 528; *Sanshigyō gaishi*, pp. 138-140. In the nineteenth and early twentieth century, Yamanashi was one of the leading prefectures in the use of silk-reeling machines powered by inanimate energy. In 1879, it ranked behind only Nagano and Gifu, much larger and more populous prefectures, in the number and size of modern filatures utilizing water power to drive their spinning machines. In 1896, 80 percent of all the prefecture's exportable raw silk came from machine filatures, compared to 53 percent nationally. By 1936, when output both nationally and in Yamanashi had increased dramatically (12 times nationwide, 14 times in Yamanashi), machine filatures produced 97 percent of exportable raw silk in both places. Raw silk made from duplion cocoons, those cocoons spun by two silk-

Because it fed this ravenous raw silk machine, Yamanashi agriculture was also transformed. The number of sericultural households grew by 24,500, from 64 percent to 85 percent of all farm families, between 1883-1887 and 1933-1937, and the amount of land planted in mulberry per sericultural household expanded from 2.9 to 3.7 *tan* over the same period. Household income from cocoons was seven times greater in 1933-1937 than in 1893-1897 and double when adjusted for higher consumer prices, a real growth rate of 2.0 percent per year.[55] Even at the nadir of the world depression in the early 1930s, real cocoon income per household was 70 percent higher than in the 1890s.

Thanks to this shift toward sericulture and to constantly improving technology, cocoon output increased by 43 times between 1872 and 1938-1942, eight times before the Chūō Line went through, and another five-and-one-third times afterward. Land planted in mulberry expanded three-and-one-half times between 1883-1887 and 1938-1942. The earliest data for mulberry yields date from 1906, but from that year until 1939 they expanded by over 500 percent.[56]

The growth of mulberry acreage and cocoon output for the raw silk industry came at the expense of other crops, as Table 2-6 shows. By the 1920s, half, and by the 1930s, two-thirds, of Yamanashi's dry field acreage and some of its paddy was devoted to mulberry at the expense of millet, soy-

---

worms, which were not regular enough in quality to be used to make raw silk for silk stockings (although many of Japan's most beautiful silk textiles were and still are made from duplions, they were not exported and thus brought a smaller return on the market than regular cocoons), must be reeled by hand, but are excluded from these calculations. They made up a very small percentage of production (about ½ percent in Yamanashi in 1934). *Chōki keizai tōkei*, Vol. 11, pp. 294-295; *Nōshōmushō tōkeihyō*, 1896; *Nōrinshō tōkeihyō*, 1936; *SKK*, p. 319; Ishii Kanji, *Nihon sangyōshi bunseki* (Tokyo, 1972), p. 129.

[55] Real cocoon income per household in Yamanashi Prefecture grew at an annual rate of 2.9 percent per year between 1893-1897 and 1923-1927 (before the depression set in in 1930).

[56] *Yamanashi tōkeisho; Sanshigyō gaishi*, pp. 72, 117, 185.

TABLE 2-6
Production of Dry-Field Crops, 1885-1934

Year	Millet*	Soybeans*	Soba*	Cotton	Tobacco (in 100s of kan)	Indigo	Mulberry Area in chō	Cocoons (in 100s of koku)
1885	544	221	113	3,841	734	1,200	5,513	364
1895	651	322	180	2,368	1,376	224	12,692	784
1905	495	332	165	896	1,108	6	13,600	817
1915	275	220	112	234	257	0	14,913	1,875
1925	121	238	89	13	0	0	16,826	3,268
1934	76	147	50	1	0	0	21,517	4,099

* In 100s of koku.
Source: *Yamanashi tōkeisho; SKK*, 237-240.

beans, buckwheat (*soba*), cotton, tobacco, indigo, and eventually even rice. (Cotton, tobacco, indigo, and soybeans lost out not only to mulberry, but also to cheaper and better imports.) As Table 2-7 indicates, before World War I cocoon production surpassed, and then in 1930s doubled, rice as the prefecture's primary crop. The process that foreign demand and Wakao and his peers began in the 1860s bore dramatic fruit in the twentieth century.

TABLE 2-7

Percentage of Total Value of Production of the Four Major Categories of Crop in Yamanashi, 1905–1939

Year	Rice	Cocoons	Mugi	Other
1905	31	28	18	22
1910	26	34	18	22
1915	30	35	13	22
1920	31	37	14	18
1925	27	53	8	12
1930	27	48	8	16
1935	27	49	8	16
1939	24	59	7	10

Calculated from *Yamanashi tōkeisho*.

But if Yamanashi's industrial and agricultural concentration on sericulture gradually expanded after the Meiji Restoration, that of the central area of the prefecture, the Kōfu Basin, exploded. In 1870, except for the easternmost districts bordering on Tsuru, the premodern silk-textile-producing region, raw silk, cocoons, and mulberry were almost nonexistent in the basin; by the 1920s, Kōfu and its environs were dominant. The central city and closeby towns and villages housed Wakao, Kazama, and Amemiya Kihei's first modern filatures in the 1870s, most of the steam-operated filatures at the turn of the century, and virtually all of the large, electrically propelled filatures in the 1920s and 1930s.

In 1925, Yamanashi contained 104 modern raw silk facilities with 50 or more basins; 27 in Kōfu, 20 in Naka Koma, and 19 in Higashi Yamanashi, the basin's primary counties (Yamanashi in 1925 was made up of one city and nine counties). The two remote Tsuru counties had none. And the concentration of filatures with 100 or more basins was even greater: of 41, 14 were in Kōfu, 10 in Naka Koma, and 8 in Higashi Yamanashi. Moreover, Kōfu housed the two largest filatures, with 520 and 350 basins; Naka Koma had the next two with 274 and 250 basins; and Higashi Yamanashi had the sixth, seventh, and eighth largest with 231, 210, and 200 basins each. In 1934, 76 percent of the value of machine-made raw silk produced, 73 percent of the machine basins, and 72 percent (2,202 of 3,062) of Yamanashi's proto-industrial hand centered in Kōfu, Naka Koma, and Higashi Yamanashi, and machine filatures produced 96 percent of the prefecture's raw silk. As Table 2-8 shows, the number and scale of operations in these three central jurisdictions was much larger than in Kita and Minami Tsuru.[57] Although the two Tsurus had only seven small "modern" filatures, each with an average of 13 basins and workers, these two counties contained 72 percent (2,202 of 3,062) of Yamanashi's protoindustrial hand filatures, each with an average of 1.1 basins and workers.[58] And, finally, work-force data reflect not only the growth of

[57] If we could disaggregate out data for raw silk production within counties, we would find that the Kōfu Basin's dominance was even greater than it appears here. Although Kōfu, Naka Koma, and Higashi Yamanashi occupy most of the Kōfu Basin, parts of Nishi Yamanashi, Minami and Kita Koma, and Higashi and Nishi Yatsushiro counties also touch the basin. One found large filatures in such basin towns as Kajikazawa in Minami Koma, Ichikawa Daimon in Nishi Yatsushiro, Nirasaki in Kita Koma, and Isawa in Higashi Yatsushiro. Minami Koma County, for example, had only 12 filatures in 1934, but they operated on as large a scale as Naka Koma's 42: 106 workers, 86 basins, and 122,000-yen production per facility. Kajikazawa and its environs housed all four of Minami Koma's largest filatures, each with over 200 basins and workers.

[58] *SKK*, pp. 318-319; *Yamanashi-ken no rekishi*, p. 173; *Sanshigyō gaishi*, pp. 106, 138-139; Ishii, *Nihon sangyōshi bunseki*, pp. 137-138. Takano Gikyō, *Yamanashi sanshi yōkan* (Kōfu, 1934), p. 368.

TABLE 2-8

Raw Silk Production by Machine in Modern Filatures in
Kōfu, Naka Koma, Higashi Yamanashi, and Kita and
Minami Tsuru Counties, 1934

	Kōfu	Naka Koma	Higashi Yamanashi	Kita and Minami Tsuru
Filatures Using Inanimate Energy	80	42	41	7
Workers per Filature	67	102	59	13
Basins per Filature	60	93	52	13
Yen Value per Filature (in 1000s of yen)	83	124	57	15

Calculated from SKK, 318-319.

the Kōfu Basin's modern filatures, but also the decline of Tsuru's premodern, household silk-reeling establishments. Between 1920, the year of Japan's first national census, and 1930, the year of its third, the industrial work force in Naka Koma grew by 27 percent; over the same decade, it shrank by 39 percent in Minami Tsuru and 24 percent in Kita Tsuru.[59]

Not only did Kōfu and its surrounding communities become the center of Yamanashi's raw silk industry, but also they came to dominate the prefecture's cocoon and mulberry production as well (see Table 2-9). Naka Koma County farmers produced no cocoons to speak of at the time of the Meiji Restoration and only 5 percent of the Yamanashi total yields in 1883-1887, but by 1913-1917 Naka Koma turned out 17 percent and from the early 1920s until the late 1930s, 25 percent or more. The production of and income from cocoons per household of Naka Koma sericulturalists expanded, compared to the rest of the prefecture, as well. Their

[59] Kokusei chōsa hōkoku, Yamanashi volume, 1920 and 1930.

TABLE 2-9

Production, and Productivity and Income from Cocoons per Household in Naka Koma County and the Rest of Yamanashi, 1883–1887 to 1935–1939

Year	Yamanashi Excluding Naka Koma County				Naka Koma County			
	Sericultural Households (in 100s)	Cocoon Production (in 100s of koku)	Cocoon Production per Household (in koku)	Income per Household (in yen)	Sericultural Households (in 100s)	Cocoon Production (in 100s of koku)	Cocoon Production per Household (in koku)	Income per Household (in yen)
1883–1887	311	420	1.35	—	37	20	0.54	—
1893–1897	415	759	1.83	51.8	54	54	1.00	27.6
1903–1907	411	1,028	2.50	108.8	67	118	1.76	80.7
1913–1917	445	1,707	3.84	166.5	78	350	4.51	231.1
1923–1927	485	2,382	4.91	380.4	94	774	8.20	656.5
1933–1937	486	3,151	6.48	276.5	107	1,075	10.09	457.9
1935–1939	478	3,331	6.97	401.9	103	1,116	10.81	651.1

Calculated from *Yamanashi tōkeisho*.

averages were only 55 percent of those for the rest of Ya-manashi in 1893-1897, but reached equality just before World War I, and were 55-70 percent higher after the early 1920s. Real sericulture income per household expanded by 4.8 per-cent per year between 1893-1897 and 1935-1939, double the 2.1 percent rate of growth for the rest of Yamanashi.[60]

The greater growth of sericultural production and income per household in the Kōfu area did not happen only because the region's farmers committed more and more of their land to mulberry, and more and more of their time to raising cocoons. In fact, in the 1920s and 1930s, the average Naka Koma sericulturalist's mulberry acreage was about the same as the prefectural average, and Ōkamada farmers, who had higher outputs and made greater sericultural profits per *tan* of mulberry than most other Naka Koma cultivators, had fewer mulberry fields.[61] The dramatic increase in output and income also came about because the dissemination of im-proved sericultural technology, which was widespread everywhere in Yamanashi, was more pervasive in the basin than in the surrounding hills and plateaus. Farmers in Naka Koma and Higashi Yamanashi, the primary basin counties, because they lived closer to their market and transportation and had more capital from greater profits, tended to grow higher-quality mulberry, raise better varieties of silkworm,

[60] Real cocoon income per household in Naka Koma County grew at an annual rate of 6.4 percent per year between 1893-1897 and 1923-1927; this remarkable growth rate compares with one of 2.3 percent for the rest of Yamanashi Prefecture. See also Takano, *Yamanashi sanshi yōkan*, pp. 365-366, 372-382.

[61] In 1933-1937, Yamanashi, Naka Koma, and Ōkamada sericulturalists tilled an average of 3.7, 3.8, and 2.9 *tan* of mulberry per sericultural house-hold. The average acreage rose from 1883-1887 figures of 2.9 *tan* for the whole prefecture and 0.3 *tan* for Naka Koma. We do not have Ōkamada data before 1927, but we have no reason to believe that Ōkamada farmers in the 1880s cultivated more mulberry than other Naka Koma farmers. Be-tween 1900 and 1930, total mulberry acreage in the more technically ad-vanced Naka Koma County quadrupled; in the prefecture as a whole it increased by 40 percent; in Minami Tsuru County it shrank by 36 percent.

spread more fertilizer, and to a greater extent use labor-saving techniques like close harvesting (*negari*) and branch feeding (*jōsōiku*). (See the following chapter for a discussion of changing sericultural techniques.)

Accordingly, farmers in the basin counties not only produced more cocoons per household, but also had much higher cocoon outputs per *tan* of mulberry land and per egg card than did their peers in the remote areas. In 1920, 1925, and 1930, for example, Naka Koma sericulturalists produced two-and-one-third, and in 1935, three times as many cocoons per *tan* of mulberry land as did their counterparts in Minami Tsuru County.[62] In the spring cocoon season of 1921, Naka Koma and Higashi Yamanashi sericulturalists produced 1.34 and 1.15 *koku* of cocoons per egg card, respectively, compared to 0.94 *koku* in the rest of the prefecture and 0.87 and 0.75 *koku* each in Minami and Kita Tsuru counties.[63] Thus, the establishment of raw silk filatures in Kōfu and its environs, and the laying of roads and railroads which most benefited this area, led not only to an increased investment of land, capital, and time in mulberry and cocoons, but also to a greater concern for more modern sericultural techniques. The ease with which farmers in the central part of the basin could get their cocoons to the expanding market led to the development of techniques by which they could produce more and more of a better and better product; those farther from the market had less incentive to follow suit.

The impact of the remarkable growth of sericulture in Naka Koma is seen clearly by comparing data for the farm value of agricultural production for all crops in Naka Koma County with that for the rest of Yamanashi (Table 2-10), and

[62] Minami Tsuru cocoon yields per mulberry *tan* were 0.61, 1.06, 1.12, and 0.85 *koku* in 1920, 1925, 1930, and 1935 respectively. In the same years, Naka Koma yields were 1.41, 2.48, 2.57, and 2.65 *koku* per mulberry *tan*. *Yamanashi tōkeisho*.

[63] *Yamanashi tōkeisho; Yamanashi sansō jihō*, 197 (September 1921), pp. 23-24.

TABLE 2-10

Value of Agricultural Production per Household,
Naka Koma County and the Rest of Yamanashi Compared,
1909-1939, in Yen at Current Prices

Year	Naka Koma	Rest of Yamanashi	Difference
1909	231	289	− 20%
1912	363	378	− 4%
1915	291★	224★	+ 30%
1919	1,180	873	+ 35%
1921	722	551	+ 31%
1925	1,117	760	+ 47%
1929	939	645	+ 46%
1931	449	309	+ 45%
1934	518	337	+ 54%
1937	926	607	+ 53%
1939	1,936	1,180	+ 64%

★ There was a sharp, unexplained increase in the number of farm households reported in 1915, and this accounts for the drop in income.

Calculated from *Yamanashi tōkeisho*.

by introducing an index of the growth of the real value of agricultural production for the county in the twentieth century (Table 2-11). Because of the development of the raw silk industry and sericulture there, the value of agricultural production per household in Naka Koma County, the most highly commercial county in Yamanashi, more than quadrupled between 1909 and 1935-1939; the value of production adjusted for the growth in consumer prices expanded by 85 percent between 1909 and 1925-1929, and by 127 percent between 1909 and 1935-1939, in spite of the impact of world depression in the early 1930s. It seems, contrary to many interpretations of the spread of commercial agriculture, that the market brought a higher average level of living to this highly commercialized district than it did to those nearby

TABLE 2-11

Index of Real Value of Agricultural Production in Naka Koma,
County, 1909-1939

Year	Value in Current Yen per Household	Agricultural Consumer Price Index	Index of Real Value
1909	231	56.98	100
1912-16	349	62.74	137
1917-21	800	123.2	160
1925-29	924	123.4	185
1930-34	558	95.0	145
1935-39	1,048	114.1	227

Calculated from *Chōki keizai tōkei*, Vol. 8, 135-136 and *Yamanashi tōkeisho*.

districts where production for the market was less advanced.[64]

Income per household increased even more sharply than the value of agricultural production per household that Tables 2-10 and 2-11 indicate because advances in output per man/day allowed household size to shrink.[65] Improved rice, mulberry, and silkworm types, chemical fertilizers and insecticides, better irrigation systems, electric pumps and pedal threshers, and new methods of utilizing them, reduced the number of hours spent tilling the soil and feeding silkworms, and freed family members to find employment elsewhere so as to supplement their household's income. Members of rural families in regions of the Kōfu Basin like Naka Koma,

[64] For a discussion of the adverse effect of commercialization on rural communities, see James C. Scott, *The Moral Economy of the Peasant*. For a critique of Scott's position, see Samuel L. Popkin, *The Rational Peasant* (Berkeley, 1979).

[65] Average household size in Naka Koma fell from 6.49 members in 1906 to 6.06 members in 1935.

165

where the surplus farm laborers were close enough to the raw silk filatures to commute to work by train, bus, bicycle, and foot, were especially likely to find non-agricultural jobs.

Penelope Francks has assembled data for changes in labor requirements in rice cultivation in the Saga Plain area of southern Japan. She has found that the output per man/day doubled between 1857 and 1922, and tripled between 1857 and 1938.[66] Although it is dangerous to use material for rice cultivation from a distant region to describe changes in Yamanashi agriculture, to such a large extent sericulture, Professor Francks' data are suggestive. If, because of modern technology, especially the adoption of an electric irrigation pump in the 1920s, rice yields per man/day tripled in Saga, it seems safe to assume that given new sericultural techniques, output per man/day in Naka Koma improved as well. Thus, outputs increased, and at the same time farm labor was freed for other tasks.[67] There was an increase of 96 percent in cocoon production per *tan* of mulberry orchard in Naka Koma between 1912 and 1939; since the number of agricultural workers in the county fell by 39 percent over the same period, production per worker increased by 221 percent. Annual rice yields increased by 61 percent between 1912 and 1939; when recalculated for the diminishing agricultural work force, the output per worker grew by 164 percent in 27 years.[68] The growth in the real value of

[66] Francks, *Technology and Agricultural Development*, p. 289.

[67] Penelope Francks, "The Development of New Techniques in Agriculture: The Case of the Mechanization of Irrigation in the Saga Plain Area of Japan," *World Development*, 7 (1979), pp. 531-539.

[68] The number of farm workers in both Yamanashi and Naka Koma increased during the Meiji period, but much more rapidly in the latter jurisdiction, with its more highly commercialized agriculture. From around 1910, however, the size of the agricultural work force contracted steadily in both places, and this trend continued even during the world depression, when, according to some writers, large numbers of unemployed urban workers returned home. Waswo, *Japanese Landlords*, p. 128; Nakamura, *Jinushiseishi kenkyū*, p. 262. The Yamanashi and Naka Koma agricultural work forces contracted by 12 percent and 3.8 percent respectively from 1925-1929 to 1930-1934.

agricultural production per agricultural household (Table 2-11), when adjusted for the falling number of workers per household, grew by 169 percent between 1909 and 1925-1929, and 253 percent between 1909 and 1935-1939, not the 85 percent and 127 percent shown in the table.[69] (And our Naka Koma data reveal nothing about reduced work days for which we have no Yamanashi data like Professor Francks' for Saga.)

Where did all of these workers who were no longer needed on the farm with its limited acreage go? The answer is—to the factory. The increase in real farm value in Naka Koma between 1909 and 1939 reveals only part of the county's prosperity. The money saved because absent mouths did not have to be fed, and the money gained because family members sent home part of their wages or lived at home and commuted to work, also bolstered Naka Koma's agricultural economy.

One aspect of the Kōfu Basin's raw silk industry, which distinguished it from neighboring Nagano's, was that many of its female workers did not live in dormitories, but traveled daily back and forth to the filatures. The development of the region's modern transportation system, the centrally located silk-reeling industry in Kōfu and its environs, the proximity of Naka Koma to the filatures, and the central basin's high labor productivity all allowed local girls, and to a lesser degree men, to commute to work. As we have seen, Yamanashi industry provided 11,000 jobs in 1896, and 31,000 in 1931, in a prefecture with 110,000 households. Even during the world depression, there was one worker in every three or four families. In 1930, Naka Koma had 7,946 industrial workers and 16,518 households, one worker in two households. From 1920, approximately one million passengers boarded Chūō Line trains in Kōfu Station each year. Two million traveled by Chūō Line trains to and from other

[69] The number of farm workers in Naka Koma declined from 77,235 in 1910 to 63,480 in 1912 to 38,738 in 1939. The number of workers per farm household fell from 5.27 in 1910, to 5.16 in 1912, to 3.68 in 1925-1929, and to 3.44 in 1935-1939.

towns in the basin like Enzan, Nirasaki, and Kusakabe, all of which had filatures, and many more by Minobu Line trains to towns and villages like Kajikazawa and Kokubo, Ōkamada's neighbor, which housed a large Kanebō filature after 1921 and a railroad station after 1928. And, finally, by the 1930s, over 500 cars and busses and 45,000-60,000 bicycles were registered in Yamanashi. When one adds tens of thousands of feet, one can visualize a small army of rural commuters to the urban and semi-urban mills.[70]

It has become standard in recent years for scholars to decry the treatment of the young women who worked in raw silk filatures, and it is impossible to deny that sometimes they were badly paid and housed. But wages and working conditions, like poverty, are relative, and, as Table 2-12 indicates, however poorly the girls were paid, in the Taishō and early Shōwa eras their wages normally ran well ahead of those for female agricultural workers. Their wages also added significantly to their households' incomes. During World War I, 15,000 to 20,000, and during the 1920s and 1930s, 18,000 to 23,000, young women worked annually at reeling silk in Yamanashi, and a high percentage of them came from Naka Koma County with its large filatures and proximity to Kōfu. Certainly the county's 16,500 households and 12,000 farm families benefited from this extra income.[71]

Naka Koma County's increased labor productivity did more than free people to commute to factories and filatures in the Kōfu Basin; it also allowed men and women to travel to the surrounding regions for semi-permanent and seasonal employ. In 1935, 24,847 people or about 21 percent of those whose permanent place of residence was in Naka Koma lived

[70] *SKK*, pp. 180-181, 460, 468, 495-496, 565-566; *Yamanashi tōkeisho; Kokusei chōsa hōkoku*, 1930.

[71] *SKK*, p. 322. See Nakamura, *Rōdōsha to nōmin*, pp. 78-105, for a description of the harsh life of female filature workers. See Tussing, "The Labor Force in Meiji Economic Growth," pp. 70-96, for a discussion of the part female filature workers' wages played in supplementing Yamanashi farm households' incomes.

TABLE 2-12

Annual Wages of Female Filature Workers Compared to Wages
for Female Agricultural Workers in Yamanashi, and to the Value
of Agricultural Production per Agricultural Household in
Yamanashi and Naka Koma County, 1890–1935 (in yen)

Year	Female Agricultural Worker's Wages[72]	Female Filature Worker's Wages[73]	Yamanashi Value of Agricultural Production	Naka Koma Value of Agricultural Production
1890–92	(16)	31	—	—
1893–95	(15)	37	—	—
1913–15	25	42 (50)	292	318
1916–18	42	65 (87)	494	733
1919–21	133	156 (234)	673	834
1922–24	137	242 (267)	685	—
1925–27	140	280 (310)	689	910
1928–30	(154)	176	569	729
1931–33	(101)	93	411	584
1933–35	(103)	100	467	670

Calculated from *SKK*, pp. 189, 193, 323; *Sanshigyōshi*, p. 142; *Yamanashi tōkeisho*.

[72] I do not have Yamanashi data for the wages of female agricultural workers' wages before 1915 and after 1926. Thus, I have used the national averages presented by Umemura Mataji in Volume 9 of *Chōki keizai tōkei*, p. 220, for the pre-1915 and post-1926 entries. These figures are presented in column one in parentheses to set them off from the Yamanashi data. Also, the agricultural worker's wage for 1913–1915 represents that for 1915 alone; the 1925–1927 wage represents 1925 and 1926 only.

[73] Yamanashi filature wages are calculated on the basis of 200 working days of 10–12 hours each per year. One source states that the girls worked 250 days per year; if so, all filature wages must be increased by 25 percent. *SKK* gives two separate sets of figures for the daily wages of spinners. In column two I have multiplied both sets of figures by 200 and presented the lower figure without parentheses and the higher figure in parentheses. If both the higher figure and the 250-day working schedule are correct. Yamanashi female filature workers earned from 38.75 yen per annum in 1890–1892 to 387.5 yen per annum in 1925–1927.

outside the county year around; another 3,725 or 3 percent lived outside their home village but within the county. Both the numbers and the percentages had increased steadily since the turn of the century, when only 2,000 and 3 percent lived and worked elsewhere. Most of these people were male workers, who worked in factories in the Tokyo-Yokohama area, and their families. Also, some 15,000 to 25,000 seasonal workers left Yamanashi each year, and many were from Naka Koma and other regions of the Kōfu Basin. In addition to the 18,000 female filature workers in Yamanashi in 1921, for example, about 19,000 more young women traveled each spring to work for part of the year in silk-reeling mills else-where, especially in the Suwa region of southern Nagano; Naka Koma provided 4,000 of them.

A survey of farm families in the Kōfu Basin for the 1931-1935 period, the worst years of the depression, when indus-trial jobs were the hardest to find and filature wages, as Table 2-12 attests, low, reveals that the average farm family earned over one-quarter of its income from non-agricultural sources. If one takes the figures for the value of agricultural production per household for the 1930s presented for Naka Koma County in Table 2-10 and adds this income, one can see how increased agricultural labor productivity allowed farm households' levels of living to improve through the ad-dition of non-agricultural income.[74]

The Growth of Rural Prosperity in
Twentieth-Century Yamanashi

Many students of rural Japan (and of rural societies in gen-eral) interpret the commercialization of agriculture through government encouragement, entrepreneurship, new tech-niques, and improved transportation as a force which "pau-perized" already poor families. According to these scholars,

---

[74] *Yamanashi tōkeisho; SKK*, pp. 180-181, 243, 322, 496; *Sanshigyō gaishi*, pp. 565-566.

market agriculture inevitably widens the gap between the well-to-do and the "immiserizated," even when, as in the case of the impact of sericulture and commercialization in Naka Koma, per capita income grows. The rich get richer and the poor get poorer, and the more commercial the agriculture the worse the poverty.[75] One might forward this view for Naka Koma in the wake of the Matsukata Deflation in the 1880s, when foreclosures occurred and tenancy increased, although with the reservations of reclamation, the decline of servitude, and entrepreneurial tenancy in mind, but it does not seem applicable at all to the region after the turn of the century, when foreclosures were rare and tenancy declined. A variety of evidence leads one to conclude that the growth of an industry based on agriculture and of its related commercial farming, in Naka Koma of raw silk production and sericulture, and of job opportunities in Suwa, Tokyo, and elsewhere, allowed tenant and owner tenant as well as owner farmer households to improve their livelihoods. After 1900, "poor" farmers became in Nishida Yoshiaki's words "commercial production tenant farmers," and began to manage their farms rather than simply react to landlord initiatives and uncontrollable market forces.

The keys to the "pauperization" approach are harsh rents and their accompanying indebtedness and tenancy. Poorer cultivators, usually tenant owner or owner tenant farmers, forced to pay excessive rents normally and buffeted by falling rice and cocoon prices in deflation years like 1884 or 1930 periodically, borrowed money and when they could not repay the principal, forfeited their security and went into bankruptcy. This kind of analysis does not fit Yamanashi and Naka Koma for a variety of reasons.

[75] See Nakamura Masanori, *Jinushiseishi kenkyū*, passim, and especially Appendix I, "A History of the Debate Over the Landlord System" and Appendix II, "Studies of the Landlord System and I"; Yasukichi Yasuba, "Anatomy of the Debate on Japanese Capitalism," *The Journal of Japanese Studies*, 2 (1975), pp. 63-82. More generally, see Scott, *The Moral Economy of the Peasant*, and Popkin, *The Rational Peasant*.

To begin with, foreclosure rarely led to immediate bankruptcy because the average farmer tilled twenty to thirty discrete fields and used only one per loan as security. A foreclosed mortgage might drive him more deeply into tenancy, but, unlike a present-day, midwestern American farmer, it did not ruin him completely. Kubo Nakajima hamlet's experience is a case in point. The hamlet at the end of the Meiji period in 1912 had 42.4 *chō* of arable land divided into approximately 1,160 plots of land, about 1.1 *chō* and 30 plots per farm household. Between 1877 and 1902, owner, owner-tenant, and tenant farmer households borrowed money from their landlords with land as security 200 times or about 5½ times per borrowing household. The borrowers subsequently defaulted in 96 cases. This figure does not prove, however, that Kubo Nakajima's 36 non-landlords fell into bankruptcy on an average of 2.7 times per household between 1888 and 1912. Rather, it indicates that 7.5 percent of the hamlet's arable land, 96 of its 1,160 plots and 3.2 *chō* of its 42.4 *chō* switched hands as a result of these foreclosures and became tenant rather than owner farmed.[76]

Second, a considerable amount of the increase in tenancy must have come about for the reasons discussed above: reclamation, the end of servitude, and entrepreneurial tenancy. In the case of Kubo Nakajima, for example, landlords took title to between 4.1 and 6.1 *chō* of arable land from cultivators between 1884 and 1912.[77] In the same three decades, a conservative estimate is that 10-11 *chō* of new land came under the plow and that the total area of tenancy increased by 11 *chō*. Thus, 45-65 percent of the new tenancy came about

[76] *Yamanashi tōkeisho*, 1913; *KNJ*, pp. 38, 211.

[77] I write between 4.1 and 6.1 because of the nature of my data. We know that landlords gained 6.1 *chō* of Kubo Nakajima land between 1884 and 1912; we know that they gained 4.1 *chō* of it from cultivators. Since we do not know the provenance of the other 2 *chō*, we can only state that landlords may have gained it from cultivators. At the same time, it might be part of the 10-11 *chō* of newly reclaimed land or may have been bought from other landlords.

because of reclamation, not foreclosures or forced sales. If we transpose the Kubo Nakajima percentages to the Naka Koma County tenancy data presented earlier in the chapter, reclamation is responsible for between 340 and 480 *chō* of the 749.6 *chō* expansion in tenant-farmed land.[78]

Third, fewer and fewer Yamanashi farmers supported themselves from agriculture alone as Japan's modernization and industrialization process progressed. More and more farmers took outside jobs, or farmed as secondary work, or sent family members to other employment both locally and in distant regions. Farmers turned to non-agricultural jobs, not because they sought ways to escape poverty, but because their increased labor productivity, the physical limitations on the profitable reclamation of arable land, and the availability of new jobs because of the nation's and the region's economic growth made this a profitable route to follow.[79] Why stay on the farm and be underemployed when Suwa's, Kōfu's and Naka Koma's filatures and Tokyo's and Yokohama's heavy industries beckoned? The trend toward postwar *san-chan* agriculture (farming by grandmother, mother, and daughter while father and son work elsewhere) was under-way in the 1930s, when farm families in the Kōfu Basin earned one-quarter of their income from non-agricultural sources. (Admittedly in the prewar era, the daughter, one of the three *chans*, brought in some of the outside income by working in a silk filature.)

[78] See footnote 27 above, and footnotes 47, 59, and 62 in Chapter Four.

[79] Area of arable land in Naka Koma County increased from 8,040.6 *chō* in 1883, the earliest year for which we have data, to 9,273.3 *chō* in 1925, the peak year. It stayed at about that level (9,234.7 *chō* in 1937) before declining in the early war years. One assumes, therefore, that by 1925 all the land in the county which could be cultivated profitably had been reclaimed. Since labor productivity, as we have seen, improved steadily even after 1925, the economic incentives to leave the farm were great. It is not surprising that the agricultural work force contracted by 9 percent, and the full-time agricultural work force by 13.3 percent between 1925 and 1937; or, stated the other way around, the area cultivated per farm worker increased by 9.2 percent in 12 years.

Fourth, rents in Yamanashi were not "harsh" enough to prevent tenants from keeping increasingly larger surpluses as yields rose (Tables 2-13, 2-14, and 2-15). Three of the Agriculture Ministry's four surveys of tenancy practices contain precise data on rents for various types of field by prefecture for 1908-1912, 1916-1920, and 1933-1935.[80] If one uses as a base the earliest, 1885 survey, which indicates that Yamanashi paddy rents (for both single- and-double-crop paddy) averaged between 47 percent and 65 percent of rice harvests in 1885, the tables show both that rents as a percentage of yields fell and that surpluses after rent rose steadily.[81] According to Table 2-13, which presents data for single-crop paddy, the tenant's surplus for marketing and consumption rose by 38.1 percent between 1908-1912 and 1916-1920, and by 76.6 percent between 1908-1912 and 1933-1935.

TABLE 2-13

Yamanashi Paddy Fields Rents Compared to Rice Yields and Surpluses in *Koku* of Unhulled Rice per *Tan* in Single-Crop Paddy, 1908-1912, 1916-1920, 1933-1935

Year	A Rent	B Yields	A as a Percentage of B	Surplus
1908-12	1.761 *koku*	3.186 *koku*	55.3%	1.425 *koku*
1916-20	2.095	4.063	51.6	1.968
1933-35	1.740	4.256	40.9	2.516

Calculated from *Hompō kosaku kankō*, 1912, p. 16; 1921, p. 65; *Kosaku jijō chōsa*, 1938, p. 22.

[80] Most of the materials from the 1885 study were lost when the Agriculture and Commerce Ministry's archives were destroyed during the Kantō Earthquake of 1923. Waswo, *Japanese Landlords*, pp. 9-10.

[81] Other data support the view that rents as a percentage of yields fell in this period. According to *Yamanashi-ken ni okeru kosaku jijō*, found in Volume Eleven of *Nōsei shiryō*, unpublished data on modern agriculture housed in the library of Tokyo University's Social Science Research Institute, paddy rents fell from 54 percent to 43 percent of rice yields between 1922 and 1935.

TABLE 2-14
Yamanashi Paddy Fields Rents Compared to Yields of Rice and a
Second Grain Crop in *Koku* of Unhulled Rice and Hulled Grain
per *Tan* and Surplus in *Yen* and Index of Real Surplus
in Double-Crop Paddy, 1908-1912, 1916-1920, 1933-1935

Year	Rent koku	Rice Yield koku	Grain Yield koku	Surplus at Current Prices-yen	Index of Real Surplus
1908-12	2.638	3.981	1.44	21	100
1916-20	2.510	4.350	1.55	47	124
1933-35	1.930	4.476	1.75	49	144

Calculated from *Hompō kosaku kankō*, 1912, p. 18; 1921, p. 68; *Kosaku jijō chōsa*, 1938, p. 25; *Yamanashi tōkeisho; Chōki keizai tōkei*, Vol. 8, pp. 135-136.

Table 2-14 presents data for double-crop paddy, which is defined in the survey as fields where one crop of rice and one crop of some other grain (usually winter wheat, rye, or barley) were both tilled in one year. Tenants here as those on single-crop paddy paid all of their rent in kind, in the primary crop, rice (rents ran to 66 percent, 58 percent, and 43

TABLE 2-15
Yamanashi Mulberry Orchard Rent per *Tan* Compared to
Cocoon Income per Mulberry *Tan* in *Yen*, 1908-1912,
1916-1920, 1933-1935

Year	A Rent	B Value of Cocoons	A as a Percentage of B	Surplus B - A	Index of Real Surplus
1908-12	9.7 yen	38.2 yen	25.4%	28.5 yen	100
1916-20	22.0	109.4	20.1	87.4	169
1933-35	11.6	75.8	15.3	64.2	139

Calculated from *Hompō kosaku kankō*, 1912, p. 21; 1921, p. 172; *Kosaku jijō chōsa*, 1938, p. 72; *Yamanashi tōkeisho; Chōki keizai tōkei*, Vol. 8, pp. 135-136.

percent of rice yields in *koku* respectively in the three time periods), but kept the complete harvest of the secondary grain.[82] Here again we see significant growth in the tenant's surplus. When one adds to this another five or six yen for the value of the vegetables that most cultivators grew as additional crops on both types of paddies, and on which no rent was levied, one can see that these surveys indicate an improving level of living, not increasing poverty, in the twentieth-century Yamanashi countryside.

But the evidence which runs most strongly counter to the pauperization view, with its emphasis on harsh rents, is that for mulberry orchards, as the evidence in Table 2-15 corroborates. Because tenant sericulturalists marketed all their cocoons, paid all their rent in cash, and because of rapidly rising cocoon yields and prices, the opportunities for profit were great. Mulberry orchard rents were only one-quarter of cocoon income per *tan* of mulberry in 1908-1912, fell to one-fifth in 1916-1920, and then to less than one-sixth in 1933-1935. Mulberry orchard rents thus took a considerably lower percentage of yields and left a larger surplus than did rents for either type of rice paddy throughout the 1908-1935 period. In 1916-1920, the cocoons produced from a *tan* of mulberry earned farmers 86 percent more profit after rent than did the surplus grain from a *tan* of double-crop paddy. Even during the world depression, when rayon began to cut into silk exports and sericultural prices declined, the surplus cocoon income after rent from a *tan* of mulberry was still 31 percent higher than that from a *tan* of double-crop paddy. (And one must remember that sericulture began its comeback in the following year, 1936.) Moreover, tenant farmers had the added advantage that they earned most of their sericultural income in the late spring and summer months (compared to the last month of autumn for rice), but did not pay their cash rents until the very end of December, and that

[82] In 1924, farmers planted winter wheat, rye, or barley, that is *mugi*, in 51.4 percent of Yamanashi's and 51.8 percent of Naka Koma's paddy fields. *Yamanashi tōkeisho*, 1924.

they faced no penalties for late payment of cash rents. Thus, sometimes tenant farmers could invest their cocoon earnings in postal savings and make a few extra yen.[83]

Fifth, the diversification of agriculture—that is, the shift toward the production of crops other than rice and *mugi*— took place in Yamanashi as it did elsewhere in Japan in the twentieth century. We have already seen how sericulture expanded until cocoons supplanted grain as the primary product of Yamanashi and especially Kōfu Basin farms in the 1920s and 1930s. But other crops followed as grain yields stagnated in the 1920s and as sericulture itself suffered temporarily from falling prices in the early and mid-1930s. Between 1912 and 1939, the cultivation of grapes, already the prefecture's leading fruit crop at the end of the Meiji period, expanded sharply. The number of vines increased by four times, the weight of production by five times, and the real value of production by six times, so that in 1939 grapes ranked as Yamanashi's fourth leading crop behind, albeit well behind, only cocoons, rice, and *mugi*. Over the same period, cherries became one of the prefecture's leading cash crops, and persimmon cultivation more than doubled.[84] Beginning in 1925, a new type of farming, vegetable cultivation in greenhouses, made its first appearance in the Kōfu Basin. In one village, Nishino in the Midai River area on the plateau of western Naka Koma, for example, farmers between 1925 and 1935 constructed 186 such facilities covering over 3 *chō* of land.[85]

Although fruit and vegetable production represented only a small percentage of the basin's agricultural income before World War II, these and other similar signs of diversification indicate, I think, the increasing attentiveness of Yamanashi

[83] See Katō Yuzuru, "Sources of Loanable Funds of Agricultural Credit Institutions in Asia," *Developing Economies*, 19 (1972), pp. 133-136, for a discussion of successful efforts beginning in the 1890s to encourage "petty" Japanese farmers to save.

[84] *Yamanashi tōkeisho; SKK*, pp. 240-246.

[85] *SKK*, p. 242.

farmers to market changes, and show that the post-World War II trend toward wider multi-crop farming began as early as the post-World War I epoch. When raw silk and cocoons increased in profitability in the 1920s, farmers turned to sericulture; mulberry land under cultivation grew by 7,100 *chō* between 1915 and 1930, its peak year, cocoon output per *tan* of mulberry increased 75 percent, land planted in *mugi* contracted by 11,000 *chō*, and the expansion of rice and *mugi* yields slowed. When the world depression and rayon threatened sericulture, fruit and vegetable truck farming began to expand and rice and *mugi* made comebacks. Rice yields in Yamanashi, which had stagnated in the 1920s after expanding at a rate of 1.2 percent per year from the 1880s until the end of World War I, rebounded to a growth rate of 1 percent per year in the 1930s; the area of *mugi* fields under the plow expanded by 3,160 *chō* between its low point in 1930 and 1939, while the mulberry orchard area declined by 2,400 *chō*.[86]

These changes in the nature of Yamanashi agriculture showed themselves even more sharply in the highly developed, commercial farm areas of the Kōfu Basin. If Yamanashi cultivators in general responded to market changes, basin farmers did so even more quickly and clearly. In Naka Koma, for example, grape vines under cultivation, output, and real value of production expanded by 4.8, 6.7, and 7.5 times, respectively between 1912 and 1939 (compared to 4, 5, and 6 times for all Yamanashi). Cherry output rose from 7 *kan* to 50,000 *kan*, and the aforementioned Nishino greenhouses were in Naka Koma. Production of other fruit and vegetable crops, like persimmons, cucumbers, watermelons, tomatoes, onions, and apples, also expanded in this quarter-century.[87]

Naka Koma's mulberry land under cultivation more than doubled, from 1,830 to 4,326 *chō* between 1915 and 1930, at

---

[86] *Yamanashi tōkeisho.*

[87] *Yamanashi tōkeisho,* 1912, 1939; *SKK,* pp. 240-242.

an annual growth rate of 5.9 percent, more than triple the 1.7 percent in the rest of Yamanashi. As elsewhere, most of these new mulberry orchards were remade dry fields; *mugi* land contracted by 44 percent, 2,000 *chō*. But, more startlingly, Naka Koma farmers did something non-basin farmers dared not to do; they turned 15 percent of their rice paddy, 785 *chō*, into mulberry orchards.[88] Moreover, the county's farmers used this additional land for mulberry although their rice and *mugi* yields did not stagnate; in 1928-1932, Naka Koma farmers harvested 12.6 percent more rice and 18.2 percent more *mugi* per *tan* of land than they had in 1913-1917. What motivated them to plant mulberry trees in *mugi* and rice fields were market forces; in the years between 1913-1917 and 1925-1929, the last predepression quinquennium, cocoon income per sericultural household expanded by 124 percent while rice income per *tan* grew by 91 percent and *mugi* income per tan by 83 percent.[89]

What we see here are cultivators making continual, often long-range decisions about which crops to plant—mulberry and fruit trees, for example, took two years or more before they began to earn their keep—and how best to allocate their resources. Needless, to say, if farm households tilled 25-30 fields and had increasingly more productive workers, they could adjust to changes in the market gradually, a few fields at a time, or send family members out to work one at a time. The farmers' ability to adjust to changes in the market's or their household's situation at any given time allowed all but the poorest and most remote farmers to remain well above the margin of poverty. In other words, what we see in the Kōfu Basin are Nishida's "commercial production farmers."

[88] Area of paddy under cultivation decreased for other basin counties like Nishi Yatsushiro (20.5 percent), Higashi Yamanashi (19.1 percent), Higachi Yatsushiro (10.5 percent), and Minami Koma (10.5 percent), but actually increased in non-basin ones like the two Tsurus (17.8 percent) and Kita Koma (5.1 percent). Only the southeastern corner of Kita Koma County was in Kōfu Basin.

[89] *Yamanashi tōkeisho.*

(And keep in mind that Hanabusa, the home of one set of Nishida's petit bourgeois producer farmers, was in the Kōfu Basin.)

Sixth, although the world depression brought hardship to Yamanashi and the Kōfu Basin, it did not bring permanent poverty and thus cannot be used as evidence of increased differentiation and "immiserization." As we saw in Table 2-11, the real value of agricultural production per household in Naka Koma fell by 21.6 percent during the depression, certainly a significant drop, but rebounded by 56.5 percent in the quinquennium afterward to a level 22.7 percent higher than in the late 1920s. Table 2-16 reflects the reasons for this comeback after the depression. The real value per *tan* of cocoons, rice, and *mugi* in both Naka Koma and the rest of Yamanashi increased by 50-70 percent in the late 1930s; if we had similar evidence for grape, cherry, and hothouse vegetables, we would undoubtedly find the same revival of income.

Seventh, our available evidence shows that Yamanashians spent increasing amounts of money on what would certainly be termed luxuries in a subsistence economy. Between 1906 and 1939, utilization of a wide variety of modern facilities (Table 2-17) like the mail, telegraph, and school systems, electric lights, bicycles, railroads, and moving picture

TABLE 2-16

Value of Production per *Tan* of Three Primary Crops, Naka Koma County and Rest of Yamanashi Prefecture, 1925-1939 (in *yen*)

Year	Naka Koma			Rest of Yamanashi			Rural CPI
	Cocoons	Rice	Mugi	Cocoons	Rice	Mugi	
1925-29	187.2	68.1	19.9	119.2	64.3	20.3	123.4
1930-34	88.2	44.6	14.7	55.4	42.3	13.4	95.0
1935-39	172.1	82.0	26.2	113.7	76.1	25.8	114.1

Calculated from *Yamanashi tōkeisho*, 1925-1939.

TABLE 2-17

Utilization of Modern Facilities in Yamanashi, 1906–1939 (in 1,000s)

Year	Packages Delivered	Letters Delivered	Telegrams Sent	Households with Elec Lights	Number of Light Fixtures	Moving Picture Attendance	Railroad Passengers	Bicycles	Elementary School Students	Prefectural Population
1906	119	11,981	238	—	—	—	814	0.07	76	548
1909	171	16,081	290	3.7	13.6	—	1,051	0.3	85	589
1915	182	17,556	323	25.6	55	—	1,281	9.2	91	613
1920	300	33,902	654	80.2	163	—	2,536	27.5	104	633
1925	377	48,791	821	94.4	235	798*	3,470	30.9	108	661
1930	376	39,812	621	111.6	288	1,178	3,612	45.8	111	683
1935	421	34,926	571	124.4	361	1,372	3,360	57.5	119	697
1939	624	40,014	951	126.5	398	1,452	3,945	65.9	121	705

* 1926
Source: Yamanashi tōkeisho.

theaters indicates the growth of discretionary income. One might argue that city dwellers and non-farmers were the ones who spent money in this way, but since Kōfu, Yamanashi's only city, housed less than 10 percent of the prefecture's households and two-thirds of Yamanashi's population farmed, it is unlikely that cultivators never rode trains and bicycles, mailed letters, or went to school or the cinema. Moreover, by the mid-1930s every household in Yamanashi, no matter how remote, had electric lights; although city dwellers and landlords may have had more fixtures (we do not know that they did), they certainly did not monopolize the new technology.[90]

Finally and probably most conclusively, tenancy in commercial Yamanashi and even more commercial Naka Koma declined in the twentieth century. In 1883, 48 percent of Yamanashi's land was cultivated by tenants; by 1912, the year in which the Emperor Meiji died, it had risen to 56 percent, but by 1939 it had fallen back to the 1883 level. From 1905 to 1939, the percentage of owner tenant households increased by 54 percent and of tenant households declined by 28 percent; from 1917 to 1936, the number of owner farmer households increased by 41 percent. The decline of tenancy in Naka Koma County was even more striking. From its high point in 1903, when tenants tilled 77 percent and 6,466.2 *chō* of the county's arable, the percentage of tenant-farmed land fell to 60.7 percent and the area of land to 5,285.5 *chō* in 1939, 9 percent and 329.5 *chō lower than the 1883 level*. (And farmers tilled 760 *chō* more land in 1939 than in 1883.) From 1906 to 1939, the percentage of owner tenant households increased by 87 percent and of tenant households decreased by 37 percent. Moreover, contrary to the expectations of those who believe that polarization occurs to the greatest degree in

[90] Use of transportation and communications' facilities declined during the depression in the early 1930s, but, oddly, motion picture attendance and electrification continued apace. This might indicate that the contraction in use of the postal and railroad systems can be attributed to competition—telephones, busses, bicycles, and automobiles—as well as to the depression.

the most highly capitalistic regions in the hardest economic times, tenancy contracted in highly commercial Naka Koma even during the world depression. In 1925-1929, tenants tilled 6,397 *chō*, 69.4 percent of Naka Koma's land; in 1930-1934, they tilled 6,115 *chō*, 66.2 percent. In 1939, tenants tilled 1,062 *chō* less land than they had in 1930.[91] If some students of the countryside interpret expanding tenancy as evidence of "pauperization" and growing differentiation, then to be fair they must view tenancy's diminution as a sign of "enrichmentization" and a reversal of the trend toward polarization. Thus, in the Kōfu Basin and Yamanashi, as, I think, in most of the rest of Japan, owner tenant and tenant farmers had more secure livelihoods in the late 1930s than ever before in modern Japan.

[91] *Yamanashi tōkeisho*; Shihōshō chōsabu, *Setai chōsa shiryō* (Tokyo, 1939), Vol. 9, pp. 26-27.

THREE

Sericultural Technology in Yamanashi, 1870–1940

MUCH of Yamanashi's and Naka Koma's prosperity occurred because the technology of sericulture became increasingly sophisticated between 1870 and 1940. This was a period when landlords, raw silk entrepreneurs, prefectural officials, and in the twentieth century even tenant farmers encouraged, conducted, and used new research; disseminated information; and generally encouraged improvement in every aspect of the sericultural process. Enterprising young men studied and experimented with ways to raise silkworms and harvest mulberry, with mulberry and silkworm egg selection, hybridization, storage, and disease prevention, with silk-reeling technology, meteorology, financing and marketing, and accordingly were able to produce more and better raw silk for the expanding western market. Foreign demand as measured by raw silk exports abroad increased by 4½ times in the first twenty years of the Meiji era and continued to grow steadily until 1929. Accordingly, cocoon production expanded by 16 times and 95 times, and cocoon productivity per unit of land by 4 and 6 times in Yamanashi and Naka Koma between the mid-1880s and 1939. The cultivation of new mulberry orchards and technological improvement allowed sericulturists to increase production and productivity and thus to garner larger profits; between 1891, the first year with adequate data available, and 1939, real cocoon income per sericultural household expanded by 543 percent in Yamanashi and 1,671 percent in Naka Koma.[1]

---

[1] *Yamanashi tōkeisho*, 1885, 1891, 1929, 1939; *Sanshigyō gaishi*, pp. 53, 60.

The increase in yields of mulberry, cocoons, and raw silk and in financial returns came about because farmers made small but significant improvements in existing techniques. Man's primary labor-saving contribution to modern technology, the harnessing of inanimate energy, water, steam, electricity, and petroleum, was used only in the industrial part of the fabrication of raw silk; the prior sericultural process continued to depend largely on animate energy. Within this limit, however, farmers brought about enormous increases in cocoon and mulberry yields. Moreover, the improvements made by Yamanashi sericulturalists were for the most part not based on either new (at least before World War I) or indigenous methods. In the 1870s, farmers in other regions, like Fukushima's Shindatsu and Nagano's Suwa and Shimo Ina (and also in other countries like China), had more advanced methods, and it was largely on their ideas that Yamanashi farmers drew—eclectically, one idea from here, another from there. By the turn of the century, when Yamanashi had drawn abreast or ahead of Nagano, Gumma, and Fukushima, and well ahead of the technologically recumbent Chinese, local sericulturalists turned to the national government's research institutes and their own practical experience.[2] In 1936, Yamanashi, one of Japan's smallest and least populous prefectures, was fifth in Japan in total production of cocoons, but first in production per farm household by 10 percent and 40 percent, over its two closest rivals, Gumma and Nagano prefectures.[3]

Yamanashi (and other Japanese) sericulturalists raised the quality and quantity of raw silk by learning to better control what was a natural cycle, the metamorphosis of egg to worm to moth to egg again; thus, a brief description of the sericultural process will give the reader a better understanding of the kind of advances made. The process begins when the silkworm, at first a small, black, hairy, antlike creature

[2] See Vlastos, *Peasant Protests and Uprisings*, and Lillian Li, *China's Silk Trade*, especially Chapter One, "The Technology of Silk."
[3] *Yamanashi tōkeisho*, 1936.

(called in Yamanashi a *kego* or hairy insect), breaks out of its egg. After hatching, the worm goes through five stages of four, four, five, six, and eight days, respectively, during each of which it eats mulberry leaves, and between each of which it rests and sheds its skin. At the end of its four-week life, it has eaten an immense amount of mulberry leaves, grown to ten thousand times its original weight, and changed color from opaque black to translucent light brown. After the fifth stage, the silkworm does not shed and rest once again; rather, it spends two or three days spinning its cocoon. Then a chrysalis and finally a moth develop inside; if heat is not applied to kill the pupa at this stage, the moth breaks out, lays more eggs, and the process begins anew. The complete life cycle from egg to egg takes about forty-eight days, the sericultural part of the cycle from egg to cocoon about thirty.[4] The sericulturalists' efforts, especially in the ten days before cocoon spinning, when the worms must be fed five or six times a day (and night), are exhausting; one who has heard the sound of thousands of silkworms munching mulberry knows how voracious their appetites are.[5]

Manipulating this cycle is not easy because, unlike many other types of farming which are precarious enough, sericulture requires the coordination of two separate natural processes, that of the silk worm and that of the mulberry. Farmers who produce cocoons have to time maturation of their eggs and mulberry crop to insure that the leaves are ready to be eaten when the worms are ready to eat. Thus, many of the Meiji-Taishō innovations were developed to allow seri-

---

[4] Li, *China's Silk Trade*, pp. 19-20, and Vlastos, *Peasant Protests and Uprisings*, p. 95, each describe the cycle slightly differently. Not only did different kinds of silkworms have diverse life cycles, but also variations in temperature could cause inconsistencies in the length of the cycle. Vlastos reports that in late Tokugawa Shindatsu the cycle "ranged from a maximum of fifty-one to as few as thirty-seven days."
thirty-seven days."

[5] The author had this experience in June 1977 when with Lillian M. Li of Swarthmore College and Kazuko Yoshida Furuta of Tokyo University he visited cocoon farms in Gumma Prefecture's Niiharu and Kawaba villages.

culturalists to control the two processes: experimenters discovered ways, for example, of slowing and even regulating egg hatching, and of propagating mulberry varieties which were resistant to cold and thus matured in time for the spring cocoon season, so that the cycles operated more or less synchronously. Although researchers never solved this problem entirely, they came close in the 1920s with the development of artificially hatched eggs. The difficulties faced before that time are illustrated by the plight of Yamanashi sericulturalists in 1884-1888, when during a five-year period the mulberry price index fluctuated from 100 to 177. This wavering transpired when a series of natural occurrences upset the balance between the supply of mulberry leaves and silkworm eggs. In 1885, a bumper egg crop was hatched after a cold spring which slowed the mulberry's growth and increased the price of leaves by 20 percent; in 1886, fewer eggs were hatched, but a warm spring led to a large mulberry harvest so that prices fell by 23 percent; in 1887, spring frost damage and the consequences of overharvesting leaves the fall before for a large 1886 autumn cocoon crop to compensate for the bad spring production of that year cut down the spring yield so that prices rose by 11 percent; and in 1888, the silkworm eggs hatched before much of the mulberry budded, and the consequent shortage of leaves increased mulberry prices by 56 percent.[6] As this example indicates, in the Meiji period improvement in the technology of sericulture was essential if farmers were to reap the profits to be made from the growing foreign demand for raw silk.

IMPROVEMENTS IN MULBERRY TYPE AND USE

The two most important natural ingredients in the making of silk, obviously, are silkworms, which weave the cocoons, and mulberry leaves, which the worms eat, and it is to improvements in their cultivation and quality which we must

[6] *Sanshigyō gaishi*, p. 73.

turn first. In the 1860s, five mulberry varieties—*aoki, haku-sōsei, takahashi, yotsume,* and *nezumigaeshi*—were important in Yamanashi, and, of these, *takahashi* was particularly so; it represented 80 percent of the trees grown in the Kōfu Basin. *Takahashi* and the others did not yield particularly large harvests, but there was no need for them to do so; before the opening of Yokohama to foreign trade in 1859, the small domestic demand for silk limited cocoon production to one spring crop per year. Moreover, the method of raising silkworms, fed with carefully plucked and deveined leaves on the second floor of one's farmhouse, was so labor-intensive that, given the available number of farm workers, productivity could not be raised without developing new techniques.

But opportunity is the mother of innovation—at least in a receptive milieu—and the new foreign demand led both to new methods and to new mulberry types.[7] The first breakthrough came in 1872, when Yamanashi farmers, learning from their Suwa neighbors who had begun forty years earlier, started to cultivate two cocoon crops each year, in spring (*harugo*) and summer (*anago*) or early fall (*ochiba*), and by the 1920s in all three, plus occasionally in late fall (*shimo no shita*) as well. (By the 1920s, the summer and fall harvests combined produced one-half of total cocoon yields.)[8] Thus, sericulturalists expanded mulberry acreage to meet this new demand—by 33 times in Naka Koma and 3 times in the rest of Yamanashi between the 1880s and 1930s. At first, the new fields tended to be on unused or marginally productive land in swampy or badly irrigated areas in the basin, and in villages with late final and early first frosts in the mountains.

---

[7] Li demonstrates that at the beginning of the period of Japan's sericultural modernization Japan was more backward than China. By the 1920s, Japan's sericultural technology had moved onto a new plane while China's had hardly changed at all. The difference is that the Japanese government created a milieu which encouraged innovation, but the Chinese authorities did not. *China's Silk Trade*, pp. 35-36.

[8] *Nihon sanshigyō taikei* (Tokyo, 1961), Vol. 5, p. 186; *Yamanashi tōkeisho,* 1920, 1925.

In the twentieth century, however, increased demand for raw silk impelled the transformation of regular dry fields and even rice paddies into mulberry orchards.[9] The use of marginal fields necessitated the development of mulberry types which resisted frost and excessive dampness or dryness, the transformation of existing fields compelled the discovery of ways to propagate mulberry seedlings quickly and in great number, and both required new variants which produced higher yields of better leaves.

A number of Yamanashi sericulturalists, who in most cases in the Meiji period were well-to-do landlords with time and money to invest, joined like-minded people throughout sericultural Japan—Gumma, Nagano, Saitama, Fukushima, etc.—to gather and exchange samples of mulberry seedlings from various regions. From these they selected the best strains for their use and propagation; by the early 1900s, the region's farmers had available 500 types of mulberry, of which eight were singled out for special improvement and cultivation. Of these eight, five—*ichinose* (32 percent), green bud *takahashi* (12.4 percent), improved *rosō* (8.6 percent), improved *nezumigaeshi* (5.3 percent) and *kozaemon* (3.9 percent)—captured over 60 percent of the market; the traditional varieties which had dominated the fields in 1870 represented less than 10 percent of the mulberry used in 1931. (*Takahashi*'s share had fallen to 5.3 percent in 1932).[10]

(1) *Kozaemon.* This was the only one of the five new mulberry types to be brought into Kai before the Meiji Restoration, but it did not become important until the 1870s. Ichikawa Kozaemon, an itinerant merchant from the southern part of the Kōfu Basin, first had imported this variety in 1850 from southern Shinshū, where it was called "Shinshū

---

[9] Chinese farmers tended to grow mulberry only on hills, canal and rice-paddy embankments, along walls, and in other areas where rice could not be grown. Li, *China's Silk Trade*, pp. 11-12. In Yamanashi, on the other hand, mulberry became the primary dry-field crop, and became so profitable that farmers turned paddies into mulberry orchards. *Yamanashi tōkeisho.*

[10] *Gojūnenshi*, p. 553; *Sanshigyō gaishi*, p. 192.

early bloom," and marketed it in the mountainous Tsuru region near Mt. Fuji. Because *kozaemon* resists cold and matures quickly, it spread rapidly in Tsuru, where the region's late spring often prevented the slowly maturing regular types of mulberry from being ready for the June cocoon season. In the early Meiji period, sericulturalists in the foothills around the Kōfu Basin also adopted this variety, renamed *kozaemon* after its importer, and its use increased; only in the twentieth century, when even better cold-resistant mulberry varieties were developed did *kozaemon*'s market share shrink to 3.9 percent.[11]

(2) Improved *rosō*. In the 1800s, Ono Motobē (1857-1919), a landlord from Hikawa Village to the east of Kōfu who, following in the footsteps of his father, devoted his life and fortune to sericulture, gathered 140-150 mulberry types from all over Japan in order to select the ones with the best yields and growing characteristics. After testing, Ono selected *rosō*, a Chinese mulberry, as the variety most suitable for the newly cultivated summer and fall silkworms, and in 1884 purchased 20,000 seedlings from the government's Mita Nursery in Tokyo. Ono found four different leaf types among these seedlings and experimented with them to find out which gave the best yields. He concluded that those with round leaf tips were the most productive and singled them out for propagation. In 1885, therefore, he christened his *rosō* variety "improved *rosō*."[12]

Ono, empirical student of sericulture that he was, did not rest here. He then began a testing program to compare improved *rosō*'s yields and profitability with those of the customary *takahashi*. Ono planted both types in his fields and kept careful records of their costs of production, yields, and profits which he later published in one of his pamphlets on

[11] *Sanshigyō gaishi*, p. 121.

[12] *Ibid.*, p. 47. Hagiwara Yoshihira, ed., *Kai shiryō shūsei*, Vol. 11 (Kōfu, 1934), p. 455; *Rosō* is the Japanese pronunciation of *lu-shang*, one of the two primary mulberry types cultivated in Kiangnan in China. Li, *China's Silk Trade*, pp. 12, 273.

sericultural methods.[13] Ono, whose itemized cultivating expenses included labor, fertilizer, and rent, found that improved *rosō* showed a profit from the second year onward, and brought in an average income of 14.7 yen per *tan* per year over the four years required for a mulberry tree to reach maturity; *takahashi*, on the other hand, made no money until the third year, and lost an average of 4.8 yen per *tan* per year over the four-year maturing period.[14] Ono's findings on the advantages of improved *rosō* were even more compelling for the mature trees, as Table 3-1 shows. Although Ono invested almost half again as much in labor and fertilizer to raise improved *rosō*, his yields and income outgained *takahashi* by an even larger margin. The annual net profit from

TABLE 3-1

Ono Motobē's Findings on the Comparative
Profitability per *Tan* of Mature Improved *Rosō*
and *Takahashi* Mulberry per Year in the 1880s

Costs	Improved Rosō	Takahashi
Rent	25 *yen*	25 *yen*
Labor	26.5	22.5
Fertilizer	22	11
Total Costs	73.5	58.5
Gross Profits	173.5	88
Net Profit	100	29.5

Source: Ono, *Jikken Onoshiki rosō saibaihō*, pp. 68, 72.

[13] *The Ono Method of Cultivating Rosō Mulberry* (Jikken Onoshiki rosō saibaihō) is an 82-page pamphlet complete with detailed instructions on how to propagate, grow, and utilize *rosō*. It is written in an easily understandable style.

[14] Ono, *Ono Method*, pp. 65-74. Since Ono's balance sheets include both labor and rent costs, the profits per *tan* are those for a tenant, not an owner farmer household, and meet Nakamura Masanori's definition of a profit. See footnote 95, Chapter One. Since Ono himself was a landlord, he must have included the rent costs in order to demonstrate to tenant and owner tenant farmers the benefits of *rosō*.

one *tan* of the new mulberry was more than three times larger than for the customary variety.

In spite of the clarity of the evidence, Ono's hard-nosed empiricism did not carry the day without a fight. A rumor spread that Ono's *rosō* was a "poison mulberry" that killed silkworms, and it took years of hard effort on his part to overcome the superstitious fears of some of his critics.[15] By that time, other mulberry types had become even more productive than improved *rosō*, and, although it was important, improved *rosō* never matched *ichinose* in its widespread cultivation.

(3) Green bud *takahashi*. One day in the late 1880s, Okuyama Shichirōemon, a landlord of Kanōiwa Village in the eastern region of the basin, while on a walk along the banks of the Nikkawa River accidentally discovered green bud *takahashi*, a variety of the customary Yamanashi mulberry, growing as a weed. Since the leaves appeared to be larger and fleshier than those of most *takahashi*, Okuyama carried the plant home, cultivated, propagated, and tested it, and found it superior as a spring mulberry type to its progenitor. Compared with *takahashi*, green bud *takahashi* matured faster, had higher yields, had later burgeoning buds, which made it comparatively free from frost damage, was otherwise cold-resistant, and grew well even in infertile soil. In 1890, the prefectural sericultural research officials selected

---

[15] Superstitions abounded among Yamanashi's sericulturalists, as the following examples indicate: since silkworms do not like the smell of fish, one does not cook fish during the silkworm's growing seasons; since silkworms fear snakes, one calls them long insects in the presence of silkworms; since the bitter smell of pepper poisons silkworms, one does not boil pepper leaves near the silkworms; since tobacco and paulownia trees are poisonous, one does not grow mulberry near them; since the silkworm deity likes wisteria flowers, one uses them to decorate the silkworm room; since silkworms like to return to the remains of their egg cards during thunderstorms, one does not throw away the cards from which the eggs originally came until the cocoons are formed. Tsuchihashi and Ōmori, *Nihon no minzoku—Yamanashi*, p. 69. For similar superstitions in China, see Li, *China's Silk Trade*, pp. 22-23.

green bud *takahashi* as a mulberry variety to be developed and promoted, and by 1932 it was the second most important mulberry type in Yamanashi.[16]

(4) Improved *nezumigaeshi*. Less is known about the provenance and introduction of improved *nezumigaeshi* than of the other important mulberry types. Although its parent plant, *nezumigaeshi* proper, came from Yamanashi's neighboring Shinshū Province, the improved form apparently originated in Kumamoto Prefecture in the south. How it got there is unclear, but it is known that in 1900 a farmer from Kumamoto who wanted to spread improved *nezumigaeshi's* use distributed samples to fellow sericulturalists, and some of it somehow reached Yamanashi. It proved to have a low resistance to cold, but to produce many large, fleshy leaves. Because of its high yield, local farmers adopted it as a summer-fall season mulberry—cold-resistant strains had no advantage after the spring season—prefectural officials fostered its use, and by 1932 it was the fourth most extensively cultivated variety in Yamanashi.[17]

(5) *Ichinose*. In May 1916, the Nishi Yatsushiro County Agricultural Society sponsored one of the many *concours* held all over Japan in the Meiji and Taishō eras to encourage agricultural improvement, and in the mulberry competition, Ichinose Masuyoshi (1865-1921), a landlord from the village of Ueno on the southern edge of the Kōfu Basin, stunned the judges with the quality and productivity of his mulberry. He presented a hitherto unknown variant of *nezumigaeshi* mulberry, which bristled luxuriantly with large, meaty leaves and evidence of stunningly large yields. Ichinose's records indicated that in 1915 he produced 860 *kan* of high-grade mulberry on 1.6 *tan* of orchard; his fields generated triple the average yields of Yamanashi orchards, double those of the relatively fecund Naka Koma County fields, and almost double the *highest* yields in China at this time.[18] In fact,

---

[16] *Gojūnenshi*, p. 553; *Sanshigyō gaishi*, pp. 48, 121.

[17] *Sanshigyō gaishi*, p. 121.

[18] While mulberry yields per unit of land expanded rapidly in Japan during

his results so impressed the judges that both the prefectural governor and Prince Kan'in, the honorary president of the Greater Japan Sericultural and Raw Silk Association, decorated him.

Ichinose first discovered his prize-winning mulberry in 1901, the year after he bought 1,000 *nezumigaeshi* seedlings from a Nagano nurseryman and found that two of the seedlings were particularly productive, and made cuttings to plant more. As he increased the number of his seedlings, he distributed them to other Ueno farmers (probably his tenants) so that by the time of the 1916 competition the number of sericulturalists who cultivated this variety, named *ichinose* in his honor by prefectural technicians in the year of his triumph, was fairly large.

Ichinose mulberry combined the features of all the other mulberry types discussed above, and its use spread quickly both within Yamanashi and without. It resisted cold and disease, grew well in a dry climate, and had yields of high quality and weight. Unlike *kozaemon* and green bud *takahashi*, spring mulberries, and improved *rosō* and improved *nezumigaeshi*, summer and fall mulberries, *ichinose* could be used in all seasons; this feature made it particularly important in the 1920s, when Yamanashi sericulturalists began to cultivate three or four cocoon crops per year. In 1932, one-third of all Yamanashi, and over half of the Kōfu Basin's mulberry acreage, was planted in *ichinose*, and because of its high yields it generated an even greater percentage of mulberry produced by weight. *Ichinose* also provided 23 percent of the mulberry used nationwide in the 1930s, and even today is the most important mulberry variety in Gumma, Japan's one remaining important sericultural region.[19]

---

the Meiji, Taishō, and early Shōwa eras, they seem to have contracted in China. Li, *China's Silk Trade*, p. 16. Thus, the average Naka Koma yields in 1925 were as great as the highest yields in China. By 1935, average Naka Koma yields were 45 percent higher, and by 1939 70 percent higher than the largest Chinese yields.

[19] *Gojūnenshi*, p. 553; *Sanshigyō gaishi*, pp. 96-99, 121, 192.

The improvement of mulberry did not depend on the development of more productive and manageable varieties alone; sericulturalists also devised new methods for propagating, cultivating, and harvesting mulberry, all of which extended productivity considerably. One of the keys to the development of new mulberry strains was propagation. If new plants could not be produced quickly and inexpensively, the rapid expansion of production was impossible—this was particularly so because new methods of harvesting leaves allowed farmers to plant as many as 1,000 trees per *tan* by the 1900s. A number of sericulturalists worked on this problem. One, a farmer named Kawanishi from Mitsue Village in Naka Koma County, developed a way of taking cuttings without damaging the parent tree. A shoot was pruned just above the root and carefully prepared by trimming and shaping with scissors so that only three buds remained and the base was opened up for rooting "like a horse's hoof"; the prepared cutting was then inserted into the seedling bed, a well-ventilated rice paddy, in the spring before the rainy season set in in June. The propagator readied the bed as well: he turned the soil over in the winter, allowed it to dry out, treated it two or three times with manure, and then just before planting built up ridges two or three inches high for the seedlings. After the farmer inserted the cuttings, he partly covered them with straw to protect the shoots from the direct sunlight and used irrigation to regulate the water supply. This method impressed other sericulturalists and prefectural officials, who disseminated its details through newly developed educational channels, formal and informal, official and unofficial. Kawanishi's method remained the orthodox one until the beginning of the twentieth century, and clearly it and its successors were necessary. The number of *chō* of mulberry under cultivation in Yamanashi increased from 5,500 in 1883 to 14,500 in 1900 to 24,700 at the peak of Yamanashi's sericultural activity in 1930. If one posits a conservative average of 300 trees per *tan* (3,000 per *chō*) before 1900 and 750 trees per *tan* thereafter, and excludes any replacement planting or expansion in number of trees in existing fields, twenty-seven million new mulberry trees were planted between 1883 and 1900, and another seventy-five million between 1900 and 1930. Clearly methods of propagation like Kawanishi's had an impact on modern Yamanashi sericulture.[20]

Equally important to the growth of sericulture was the development of new methods of harvesting mulberry leaves. Increased demand for raw silk led to the cultivation of more and better mulberry trees, and sericulturalists needed a technique for pruning which facilitated this expansion. They found it in "close harvesting" (*negari* or "root pruning"). The traditional "standing" (*tachitōshi*) method, by which farmers harvested individual leaves one by one, and the transitional method of "high harvesting," by which farmers cut leaves and small branches at heights of 8-9 feet or more above the ground, were suited to the old method of feeding silkworms leaf by leaf. But as sericulturalists turned to "branch feeding" (*jōsōiku*), a method by which they fed whole branches of mulberry to silkworms, the new harvesting technique in which complete limbs were pruned close to the trunk and only one foot from the ground (or, at most, under *nakagari* or the "middle harvesting" method, 2 to 5 feet from the ground) came into vogue. The observer who has seen a mulberry field after close harvesting knows what it entails. The orchard resembles a devastated area; nothing can be seen but dozens of short gnarled leafless stumps.

Close (and middle) harvesting had two advantages for the betterment of cocoon yields and household prosperity; it saved labor in pruning and silkworm feeding, the two most arduous tasks in the sericultural process, which could be shifted to increased production or even nonagricultural employment, and it allowed farmers to increase production by

[20] *Sanshigyō gaishi*, pp. 45-46; *Yamanashi tōkeisho*. Chinese sericulturalists planted their trees more sparsely than did the Japanese. Li reports that in Wusih, farmers planted about 300 trees per *mou* (450 trees per *tan*). Li, *China's Silk Trade*, footnote 26, p. 213.

planting many more trees per *tan*. Since mature trees trimmed in this way resemble *bonsai* more than spreading trees, sericultural researchers recommended no fewer than 600, and as many as 1,000 trees per *tan*. In 1883, the average Yamanashi *tan* of mulberry contained 193 plants; five years later in 1888, 290; and by the 1920s, many *tan*-sized fields in the Kōfu Basin had 1,000 trees or more. As anyone who has observed wine-making in Bordeaux or the Napa Valley, or has even gardened in his own backyard, knows, this drastic pruning did not lead to an equally marked drop in leaf yields per tree; unlike the scraggly "normal" trees, the pruned ones grew much more luxuriantly and compactly. In fact, their small size itself saved the farmer's labor; he needed to use no ladders or to engage in no dangerous tree climbing to harvest his mulberry.[21]

By 1932, 77 percent of Yamanashi's orchards were "close harvested" and most of the less productive middle (19 percent), high (3 percent) and standing (0.16 percent) harvesting took place in the mountainous Tsuru district, where cocoon yields and sericultural income were the lowest.[22] This region, close to Edo and the Tōkaidō Road, had been Yamanashi's primary silk-producing area in the Tokugawa period, but became its most backward one in modern times. Conversely, Kōfu Basin counties like Naka Koma, relative newcomers to sericulture, used close harvesting almost exclusively and had much higher mulberry and cocoon productivity. As Table 3-2 shows, in 1930 mulberry and cocoon productivity in Naka Koma, which contained a few mountain as well as basin villages, were 14 percent and 33 percent above, and in Ōkamada Village in the exact geo-

---

[21] Vlastos reports no branch feeding or close harvesting for Shindatsu in the 1860s. *Peasant Protests and Uprisings*, pp. 97-99. Although Li indicates that some mulberry trees in China were as small as two or three feet high, her picture on p. 14 of farmers picking mulberry leaves, from a late-seventeenth-century book, shows the harvesters climbing precariously up tall trees to pick the leaves.

[22] *Sanshigyō gaishi*, pp. 122, 192.

TABLE 3-2

Index of Cocoon and Mulberry Production per *Tan* of
Mulberry Orchard, 1930 (Yamanashi Average = 100)

Jurisdiction	Cocoon Production	Mulberry Production
Yamanashi Prefecture	100	100
Naka Koma County	133	114
Ōkamada Village	157	139
Minami Tsuru County	60	55

Calculated from *Yamanashi tōkeisho*, 1930.

graphical center of the Kōfu Basin, 39 percent and 57 percent
above the prefectural averages. Minami Tsuru County, conversely, was 40 percent and 45 percent below. In fact, Ōkamada sericulturalists, although they cultivated only three-
quarters of the average size mulberry orchard, earned more
from cocoons than their counterparts elsewhere in Yamanashi. The more commercial and modern sericulturalists in
the Kōfu Basin developed and used close harvesting and
other new techniques to a greater extent than Tsuru farmers,
and accordingly produced higher yields and income.[23]

Mulberry yields increased in the Meiji period not only because more productive trees were planted more closely together, but also because more and better fertilizer was applied. Before 1900, the sericulturalist in January carried out
"cold fertilizing," which consisted of applying to the orchard
night soil, soybean cake, rice bran, and, if extra money was
available, the more expensive dried sardines. He added wine
dregs, oil cake, or more rice bran in April to encourage bud-
ding, and silkworm droppings, soybean cake, or wine dregs
in June after the harvest. Before the introduction of chemical
fertilizers around 1900, dried sardines were the most effica-

[23] See Chapter Four, pp. 250-251.

198

cious fertilizer, but, as Table 3-3 indicates, also the most expensive.[24]

In the twentieth century, as foreign demand, capital, railroads, and new sericultural technology allowed even more expansion of the raw silk industry and cocoon production, commercial fertilizer use, and especially chemical fertilizer (also the product of modern technology) use, developed. Between 1909 and 1937, the weight of commercial fertilizer applied in Yamanashi swelled by 843 percent. In the same three decades, the inorganic fertilizers utilized multiplied by 17¼ times. Cocoon production leaped forward too; during World War I it passed 10 *kan* per *tan* for the first time, halfway to the 21 *kan* level it reached in 1935-1939; in Naka Koma it passed 10 *kan* a decade earlier and reached 29 *kan* in the late 1930s. This rapid growth in cocoon harvests was made possible at least partly because the use of fertilizer allowed mulberry yields to grow proportionately, from 88 *kan* per *tan* in 1906-1910, to 154 in 1915-1919, to 304 in 1935-1939 for the prefecture, and from 130 *kan* per *tan* to 220 to 421 for Naka Koma County in the same years. Moreover, the real unit cost of fertilizer fell also, from an index figure of 100 in 1906-

TABLE 3-3

The Weight or Volume of Fertilizer Purchasable for One *Yen* in the mid-1880s

Type	*Volume or Weight*
Wine Dregs	59.3 kilograms
Oil Cake	21.1 kilograms
Dried Sardines	5.3 kilograms
Soybean Cake	25.5 liters
Rice Bran	84.8 liters

Source: *Sanshigyō gaishi*, p. 51.

[24] *Sanshigyō gaishi*, p. 51.

1910 to 71 in 1921-1925 to 64 in 1931-1935. It would seem that fertilizing paid dividends.[25]

Although the greater application of increasingly cheaper commercial fertilizer allowed Yamanashi sericulturalists to enlarge productivity per unit of land and per worker, one should not think of it as a totally unmixed blessing. Fertilizer brought the rapid growth of mulberry yields between 1909 and 1939, but they still increased more slowly than did commercial fertilizer use. After World War I, even cheaper real fertilizer costs could not keep the sericulturalists' capital outlay for commercial fertilizer from growing more rapidly than did his income from cocoons. Between 1909 and 1939, income from cocoons grew by 900 percent, but the cost of fertilizer grew by 1,300 percent.[26]

The causes of this slowing in the relative rate of growth of cocoon income vis-à-vis fertilizer expenditures are twofold: the decision of farmers to shift household resources from one part of the agricultural and sericultural process to others or to non-agricultural employment, and the extremely intensive nature of the cultivation of mulberry. To begin with, the 843 percent increase in the weight of commercial fertilizer between 1909 and 1939 does not mean that farmers used 843 percent more fertilizer at the end of the period; it indicates, rather, both an increase in fertilizer applied *and* a decision to replace non-commercial with commercial fertilizer. The use of the latter cost the household more money, but saved it time; farmers in the twentieth century, because their profits gave them more capital, spent less time collecting animal and human feces, green manure, and other locally available non-commercial fertilizers. The labor thus saved could be utilized for more profitable agriculture tasks and in jobs off the farm. In other words, the expanded use of commercial fertilizer in the twentieth century lowered labor costs and this is another indicator of increasingly rational farm household management and of greater amounts of capital available.

[25] *Yamanashi tōkeisho*, 1909-1939.   [26] *Ibid.*

The other reason for this relative slowing of the growth of mulberry yields has to do with the intensity of mulberry cultivation. By 1910, as we have seen, close harvesting and branch feeding allowed farmers to plant 1,000 trees on a single *tan* of land (remember that a *tan*, 993 square meters, is about the size of the area between the two forty-yard lines of an American football field), but this dangerously depleted the fertility of the soil so that the continued rapid growth of harvests was threatened. The solution to this predicament lay in more chemical fertilizer. Although chemical fertilizer improved mulberry yields in the short run, it caused certain kinds of leaf-shrivelling blights and over the long run depleted the fertility of the soil. Thus, sericulturalists applied some chemical fertilizer to maintain productivity and more to continue its expansion. With government support, they made efforts to break out of this vicious ecological cycle of diminishing soil fertility and greater applications of commercial fertilizer—most sericulturalists grew *vicia sativa*, a leguminous manure plant, in their mulberry orchards to cut down their dependence on chemicals. But it seems safe to say that the gradual agricultural diversification toward vegetable gardening in greenhouses and fruit cultivation which began in Yamanashi as the world depression and rayon began to cut into the silk market in the 1930s, and which grew rapidly after the introduction of nylon and the outbreak of World War II, probably would have taken place to some extent without the blights of depression, synthetic fibers, and war.[27] Yet, for the 1870-1940 period, fertilizer along with improved mulberry varieties and new methods for their propagation, cultivation, and harvesting led to increasing mulberry and cocoon yields and income, to greater labor

---

[27] *Sanshigyō gaishi*, pp. 51, 123; *SKK*, p. 300. Skeptical that farmers could actually plant 1,000 mulberry trees between the two forty-yard lines of an American football field, i.e., on one *tan* of land, I visited Ōtsuki and Ōkamada in Yamanashi and Kami Moku in Gumma in the spring of 1984 to check. After repeated pacings and countings, I found *tan*-sized fields with as many as 1,200 miniature mulberry trees.

productivity, and thus to the opportunity to shift workers to other forms of agriculture or to non-agricultural work.

IMPROVEMENTS IN SILKWORM VARIETIES, STORAGE, AND CULTIVATION

Similar attention was paid to developing better varieties of silkworms and new ways of handling them, but this experimentation proved more complicated and required greater scientific knowledge than did improving mulberry. Thus, although landlord sericulturalists played an important role, government technicians contributed more, and, as with rice, the most consequential breakthroughs came after 1910, when scientists had developed laboratories and skills equal to the intricacies of crossbreeding silkworms. Yet, researchers made significant improvements in the quality of Yamanashi silkworm eggs in the earlier Meiji period through four kinds of efforts: new varieties were intromitted from elsewhere in Japan, quality testing was introduced, the tempo of egg hatching was better controlled, and traditional silkworm types were improved.

Too much emphasis cannot be placed on the importance of intranational communication among like-minded, well-to-do, "experienced" farmers and regional officials in the development of Japanese agriculture and sericulture in the late nineteenth century. In the Tokugawa era, government policies had not always encouraged the free exchange of ideas from province to province, but with the onset of the Meiji era in 1868 the nation's new leaders turned to building national wealth and power, demolished regional barriers, and, to speed economic growth, promoted the exchange of technical knowledge. Members of the rural elite, freed from feudal restrictions and inspired by a desire to serve their country and region (and to make money), traveled throughout the country in greater numbers than ever before to teach and learn about unfamiliar types of mulberry trees, techniques of raising silkworms, and silkworm varieties. Yamanashi received a number of new egg types in this way.

Before the Meiji Restoration, Yamanashi had produced few of its own egg cards, and imported the rest from the contiguous Suwa and Matsumoto regions in the south of the neighboring Shinshū Province, a region which in the Tokugawa era had a more advanced sericultural industry than Kai. (Several important Meiji period innovations in Yamanashi were already standard practice in Shinshū in the closing years of the Tokugawa era.) But experienced Yamanashi farmers in the 1870s and 1880s began to look beyond Kai and Shinshū for silkworm eggs, and, as they did, they did not import eggs as in the past, but rather brought them back for experimentation and mass reproduction at home. Although Yamanashi sericulturalists developed only a few silkworm strains themselves, by 1887 they were successful in breaking their dependence on Shinshū and in producing at home half of the eggs used in the prefecture. Moreover, it was the more advanced areas like Naka Koma which used the new eggs, while the more backward regions like Tsuru continued to depend on Shinshū.[28]

A number of new silkworms were introduced to Yamanashi in the Meiji era, some successfully and others not. Egg sellers from Tokyo introduced the first new type, an Italian strain, in 1872, and it was successfully reproduced in Yamanashi. This was followed by eggs from Hokkaidō in 1874 which were divided for testing between four sericulturalists, including Ono Motobē and Okuyama Shichirōemon, who also played important roles in the development of better mulberry varieties. They found the Hokkaidō eggs superior to the reigning Shinshū type, and in 1885 local producers began to process them for widespread use. The Hokkaidō eggs were followed in 1875 by a Chinese variety which the Japanese consul in Shanghai obtained, reproduced, and shipped to Yamanashi Prefecture's Board to Encourage Industry. Unfortunately these silkworms failed to spin cocoons in their new environment and were rejected. The Fukushima Prefectural office's sericultural bureau sent a variety called

[28] *Sanshigyō gaishi*, p. 67.

Ōshū to its Yamanashi counterpart in 1881, and the government distributed the eggs for testing among thirty of its efficient farmers; they found the new eggs, like the Hokkaidō variety, superior to the Shinshū eggs, and Yamanashi egg merchants also began to produce Ōshū in the mid-1880s. A well-to-do farmer from the southern part of the Kōfu Basin imported and experimented with Iwate eggs, but abandoned them when he found them good, but inferior to the Fukushima variety.[29] This is far from a complete catalogue of the silkworm varieties introduced, tested, and accepted or rejected by Yamanashi sericulturalists in the first half of the Meiji era, but even this abbreviated list illustrates two important points to be made about the improvement of silkworm eggs in the Meiji period. First, a wide variety of people played roles in the process. Sericulturalists, egg producers and sellers, government bureaucrats, and even Japanese diplomats in far off places like Shanghai and Italy participated in the drive to enhance their own profits and to aid in Japan's economic development. Second, sericulturalists who searched for better silkworm eggs turned more to identifying better existing varieties than to the development of new types. Although some new types were developed in the Meiji era, it was only in the twentieth century that researchers fashioned better kinds of silkworms through systematic and controlled crossbreeding in the laboratory.[30]

Prefectural officials with the active support of sericulturalists played an important role in the improvement of silkworms by introducing in the mid-Meiji period a system for the inspection of the eggs. Traditionally the farmer had bought his silkworm eggs from either itinerant peddlers or the producers themselves, and he had little protection from dishonest dealers who sold defective eggs—caveat emptor. The buyer did not lose everything from silkworms which did not spin cocoons because of his method of settlement: he paid half on receipt of the eggs and half after the harvest, or

[29] *Ibid.*, pp. 67-68.   [30] *Ibid.*

he made payment based on the size of the cocoon yield, but this system of remittance did not compensate him for the loss of a season's income. And, more importantly from the point of view of the government's officials, diseased eggs provided a weak foundation for increasing productivity prefecture-wide. Accordingly, in 1886, the Yamanashi government promulgated the Silkworm Egg Inspection Regulations, which required the licensing of silkworm egg producers and sellers, and the inspection of their products. Under these rules, in 1887 officials established inspection stations in each sericultural district, staffed them with graduates of the Agriculture and Commerce Ministry's Sericultural Testing Station in Tokyo, and began to test eggs. These inspections significantly reduced the number of diseased eggs and defective cocoons and assisted in the expansion of the region's cocoon production.[31]

The most ingenious technique for increasing sericultural production in the late nineteenth century was the introduction of a method of controlling the onset of the silkworms' life cycle through the cold storage in mountain caves of the eggs to be used in the summer and autumn cocoon seasons. Farmers began to produce both summer and fall cocoon crops in the 1870s, but the scale of these operations was limited because of the farmers' difficulty in finding silkworm eggs ready to start their life cycle at the appropriate time—the eggs' natural time of hatching, after all, was in the spring. As early as 1872, Matsumoto egg dealers, who had first developed this technique in the 1830s, suggested the use of caves to store eggs in order to slow down their maturation. In the late 1870s, Mimori Chūzaemon, a well-to-do farmer from a village in the foothills to the east of Kōfu,

---

[31] *Ibid.*, pp. 69. *Gojūnenshi*, p. 557. The importance of the prevention of silkworm disease can be seen from a comparison with China. Li reports that in the 1920s between 75 percent and 95 percent of Chinese silkworm eggs were diseased. As we have seen, Japanese raw silk exports went from being less than 20 percent of China's in the early 1870s to tripling them in the 1920s. Li, *China's Silk Trade*, pp. 23, 86-87.

discovered a cave along the slopes of a nearby mountain ravine which was fifty to sixty days behind the basin in the melting of spring snow and used the cave to store autumn silkworm eggs through the spring and early summer. He got good results in his succeeding fall harvest, and in 1879 received official permission to begin commercial storage. By 1881, Mimori had 400 customers. Hatta Tatsuya (1854-1916), another of Yamanashi's eminent landlord sericulturalists, seeing even greater opportunities in the larger caves in the hills near Mt. Fuji, also decided to go into the business. Gradually that area took the lead in cold storage. Hatta's company at its peak had customers from as far away as Shimane, Hiroshima, Mie, and Yamagata prefectures; the caves in the east and near Mt. Fuji soon stored almost all the eggs used in Yamanashi's summer and fall cocoon seasons, and continued to do so until after World War I. Only the development around 1915-1920 of artificial means of refrigeration and of hybrid egg types for which hatching could be controlled preempted the utility of cold storage in caves.[32]

The final improvement which led to higher quality and more productive silkworms in Yamanashi before the end of the nineteenth century was the propagation by Mimori and Okuyama of a late-developing silkworm type for use in the fall cocoon season. Sericulturalists found from experience that they generated better cocoons in the late autumn, when the days were drier and cooler, than in the warmer and more humid summer or early fall. To produce late in the year, however, farmers needed silkworm eggs, and faced a dilemma: on the one hand, cold storage past early summer often damaged the eggs, and, on the other, if sericulturalists brought their eggs out of storage at the normal time in June or early July, they matured too fast to be used in late autumn. Mimori and Okuyama found a way out of this predicament by successfully breeding a new hybrid silkworm which started the egg-worm-cocoon cycle later than normal.

---

[32] *Sanshigyō gaishi*, pp. 70-71; *Gojūnenshi*, p. 552.

It did not begin its life cycle when it was brought out of cold storage in early July; rather, it remained dormant until September. The two experienced farmers called their new variety "Kai Province *shimonoshita* Late Fall Silkworm Variety" (*shimonoshita* is the Kai term for late-fall cocoon production), and sold it all over Japan. In fact, Mimori and Okuyama met with such success that new inns went up near Kusakabe Station (present-day Yamanashi City) to accommodate the merchants who came to buy the eggs.[33]

In spite of these important Meiji period contributions to silkworm productivity, the revolution in egg technology both nationwide and in Yamanashi occurred in the Taishō era, and came about because of advanced scientific knowledge and facilities available after 1910. In 1911, the Agriculture and Commerce Ministry established the National Institute of Silkworm Egg Production in Tokyo to experiment with new silkworm egg types; in 1917, Yamanashi Prefecture followed suit and established a similar facility in Kōun near Kōfu to test the aptness to Yamanashi conditions of the new egg varieties developed in Tokyo. These genetic researchers both introduced pure Chinese and Italian egg cards, and successfully created fertile and disease-resistant Japanese-foreign hybrids, which led to better cocoons and which fitted the needs of each region in each of the three or four cocoon seasons more productively. One found the Yamanashi government encouraging the use of the following kinds of Japanese-Chinese-European hybrids, all of which could be controlled by artificial incubation:

Spring Cocoons

1. Japan-China One Generation Hybrid, a silkworm egg which produces white cocoons and is a hybrid of Nationally Produced Japan #1 and Nationally Produced China #4.

2. China-Europe One Generation Hybrid, a silkworm egg

---

[33] *Sanshigyō gaishi*, p. 71.

which produces white cocoons and is a hybrid of Nationally Produced China #4 and Nationally Produced Europe #3.

3. China-Europe One Generation Hybrid, a silkworm egg which produces yellow cocoons and is a hybrid of Nationally Produced China #7 and the outcome of crossing Nationally Produced Europe #7 and #10.

Summer and Fall Cocoons

1. Two Metamorphoses, One Metamorphosis, One Generation Hybrid, a silkworm egg which produces white cocoons and is a hybrid of the outcome of Nationally Produced Japan #10 and Nationally Produced China #9, crossbred with the product of Nationally Produced Japan #107 and Nationally Produced China #9.

2. Two Metamorphoses, Two Metamorphoses, One Generation Hybrid, a silkworm egg which produces white cocoons and is a hybrid of the product of Nationally Produced Japan #107 and Nationally Produced China #101, crossbred with Nationally Produced Japan #106 or #107 over two metamorphoses.

3. *Sangenkō* Hybrid, a silkworm egg which produces white cocoons and is the complex hybrid of the outcome of crossing the product of Nationally Produced Japan #106 crossbred with the outcome of crossbreeding Nationally Produced China #9 and #101, and the product of crossing Nationally Produced Japan #107 with the outcome of crossbreeding Nationally Produced China #9 and #101. (NPJ 106 X the outcome of NPC 9 X 101 crossbred with NPJ 107 X the outcome of NPC 9 X 101.)

As the names and contents of these hybrids indicate—and this is only a sampling of the silkworm egg types under study and employ—Japanese technicians conducted research into various types of foreign and domestic silkworm strains and crossbred them to create new hybrids which were suitable to each region's climatic, topographical, and market needs.[34]

---

[34] *Ibid.*, pp. 129-136; *Gojūnenshi*, pp. 558-559. See Kiyokawa Yukihiko,

The research which was done in Tokyo and Kōun and at public and private centers all over Yamanashi and the other sericultural prefectures, often at the county and village level with local funding, was not limited to the laboratory. Only the most intricate and technical investigations were done there. After the Tokyo technicians bred new hybrids, and the Kōun technicians studied them for local appropriateness, they had to be proven for their efficacy on the farm. Prefectural researchers assigned different egg cards to various local sericulturalists to be tested at their own expense and risk with their own mulberry (which was also under experimentation). In 1917, Tsukamoto Jirō and six others received spring egg cards, and Furuya Hisamasa (1861-1933), a landlord from the eastern Kōfu Basin, and three others, fall egg cards to cultivate and verify. New varieties of silkworm eggs did not win the prefectural government's seal of approval unless they had received high grades in the Kōun laboratory and passed this empirical test on the farm.

The impact of these fecund and artificially incubated egg varieties—by 1923, they represented 97 percent of all silkworm eggs nationwide—and the introduction of refrigeration to the process in 1919 were important. To begin with, man-induced hatching eliminated the predicament of coordinating the mulberry and silkworm cycles which cave storage and new varieties of cocoon and mulberry had only mitigated. Accordingly, cocoon productivity, already high in 1913-1917, continued to rise steadily, particularly in the more advanced districts like Naka Koma County and Ōkamada Village. In 1927, cocoon production per *tan* of mulberry land for the prefecture, county and village was 16, 24, and 39 *kan*, respectively, an increase of 38 percent and 27 percent each in ten years for the two larger jurisdictions. (We have no 1917 data for Ōkamada.)[35]

"The Diffusion of New Technologies in the Japanese Sericulture Industry: the Case of the Hybrid Silkworm," *Hitotsubashi Journal of Economics*, 25 (1984), pp. 31-59, for a history of the development of hybrid silkworms in Japan.

[35] *Yamanashi tōkeisho*, 1917, 1927; Kiyokawa, "Diffusion," p. 57.

These innovations changed the nature of Yamanashi sericulture as well as the quality of its product. The founding of Satō Saburōemon's Yamanashi Silkworm Egg Refrigeration Company in 1919 for the safe storage of eggs marked the beginning of the rapid demise of the cave storage companies. The spread of the use of artificially hatched eggs came at the expense of the older varieties; Yamanashi's contribution to the world of silkworm eggs, Mimori and Okuyama's *shimonoshita* late fall, for example, could not compete with the new, more scientifically developed and managed varieties, and its use and the prosperity of the inns at Kusakabe gradually faded.[36]

Sericulturalists not only improved mulberry and silkworms, but also altered the conditions under which they raised the silkworms, and this too facilitated the achievement of higher outputs per *tan* of land, per worker and per unit of time. In the 1880s, cocoon farmers began to heat their silkworm-raising rooms, and this allowed sericulturalists to protect the silkworms from frost and dampness, to increase their appetites, thus shortening the process, economizing on mulberry, and saving labor, and to know in advance the exact length of the cycle, thus enhancing planning.[37] Customarily Yamanashi farmers had cultivated cocoons only in the spring, on the second floor of their houses—in eastern Yamanashi many houses even now have distinctive, towerlike second floors in the center of their structures for this reason—and had done so without attempting to control the temperature of the silkworms' environment. This had hindered the growth of productivity since silkworms produce better cocoons when raised in fairly constant and moderately warm temperatures; 20 to 28 degrees centigrade (68° to 83°F.) is normal, higher in the first stages, lower in the later.[38] The uncontrolled environment had also made them

---

[36] *Sanshigyō gaishi*, pp. 71, 136.

[37] Shōji Kichinosuke, *Kinsei yōsangyō hattatsushi* (Tokyo, 1964), p. 92.

[38] Sericulturalists in Niiharu and Kawaba villages in Gumma Prefecture in 1977 used cooperatively owned and operated incubators to keep the tem-

susceptible to destruction by sudden spring frosts, which even in the basin districts of Yamanashi fall as late as mid-May.

In 1883, in the halcyon days of government-efficient farmer cooperation, Governor Fujimura sent three young farmers to study "temperature-controlled" cultivation (*ondōiku*) in Fukushima Prefecture, a cold northern region where sericulturalists had heated their silkworm rooms since the late eighteenth century.[39] On their return, Hatta Tatsuya invited Muramatsu Bokusuke, one of the three, to Ukai Village near Kōfu to teach him the new method. To adopt the temperature-controlled process, Hatta renovated his room for raising silkworms by installing a brazier for heat, an exhaust system to avoid suffocating the silkworms with charcoal fumes, and building an enclosure appropriate to the new equipment. Hatta, pleased with the results of using this method in 1884, placed an advertisement in a local newspaper expounding its virtues and received responses from 2,000 sericulturalists interested in his new technique. Hatta, thus encouraged by both the popular response and the support of Governor Fujimura (whose paternalistic view of government was receiving heat elsewhere from the prefecture's people's rights' movement), kept a record of his experiences and published it as a pamphlet entitled *Sericultural Diary* (*Yōsan nikki*), which he distributed at his own expense to more than 1,000 interested readers.[40]

A survey of Yamanashi sericultural practices conducted in 1888 shows that the idea of a controlled environment for raising silkworms caught on quickly. Although only 10 percent of Yamanashi sericulturalists used the pure temperature-controlled method at that time (the capital investment to renovate or build anew a room for silkworm cultivation must have discouraged all but wealthy farmers in the mid-Meiji

---

perature of the silkworms within this range in the early stages of their growth.

[39] Vlastos, *Peasant Protests and Uprisings*, p. 95.

[40] *Gojūnenshi*, p. 552; *Sanshigyō gaishi*, pp. 38-39.

period), fully 80 percent used some kind of heat-controlled environment. By World War I, with the development of rural prosperity, greater literacy, a deeper understanding of the new technology, and more simplified and cheaper ways of creating a controlled environment for silkworms, almost all Yamanashi farmers had adopted the temperature-controlled method of producing cocoons. Not surprisingly, the new method caught on most quickly among sericulturalists in the Kōfu Basin, whereas the 20 percent who clung to the traditional "cool" method (*seiryōiku*) lived mostly in the more backward Tsuru region.[41]

Sericulturalists also changed the methods by which they fed mulberry to silkworms by introducing branch feeding (*jōsōiku*), a method by which they fed the maturing silkworms whole branches of mulberry rather than carefully pruned leaves in the traditional manner. This way of feeding the worms, also called "tower feeding" (*yaguragai*) because the branches when piled in the feeding trays with two running one direction and two above them the other, gradually formed a tower, saved farmers hours of labor. Not only was feeding faster, but so too was the concomitant close harvesting. In the late 1880s, branch feeding became the usual mode of raising silkworms in the fifth and final eight-day stage of their lives; by the turn of the century, it was used also in the fourth six-day stage, and by 1929, 95 percent of Yamanashi's sericulturalists used this method of feeding for fully half the month-long life of the worms.[42]

In spite of the obvious labor-saving benefits of branch feeding, prefectural officials, silk reelers, and even a few of the powerful "efficient" farmers like Hatta Tatsuya opposed its introduction vigorously (and in vain). The opponents, by attacking the new method as "careless raising" and "slothful raising," even added a moral dimension to their claim that it led to reduced quality and quantity in yields. For a time, the efforts and hard evidence of the supporters of branch feeding

[41] *Sanshigyō gaishi*, pp. 38, 125; *Gojūnenshi*; p. 552.
[42] *Sanshigyō gaishi*, pp. 88-89.

212

could not persuade its enemies. In 1897, Furuya Hisamasa, a landlord and influential sericultural innovator, published a pamphlet about the most up-to-date sericultural techniques in which he argued that branch feeding did not affect the quality of cocoons. In 1911, Nakashima Kikuhira, a sericultural technician in Kita Tsuru County of the Gunnai region, studied a sample of households using both the customary and the new methods, and found that the latter produced 5-10 percent higher yields per egg card than its traditional counterpart. And Takabe Wakatarō, editor of *Silkworm and Mulberry News*, a newsletter which between its founding in 1905 and its demise during World War II played a central role in the diffusion of technical information, worked diligently to spread the word. In 1910, his journal even put out a special issue on branch feeding.

In the closing years of the Meiji era, the debate came to a head in a most unJapanese way at a conference of egg manufacturers sponsored by prefectural officials. Furuya, who had a financial and psychic investment in branch feeding, argued to these specialists in silkworm eggs that his method led to higher quality eggs because it reduced the danger of microbe infection. Kanō Takashi, a prefectural sericultural technician, disagreed, and the two began a heated public argument. Takabe came to Furuya's support. Hatta came to Kanō's, and demanded that Takabe, who was a recent convert to branch feeding, recant. He declined and tried to explain his position; Hatta refused to listen to Takabe, impelling the latter to retort that "the truth will be the final victor." Whether or not truth won out, branch feeding triumphed. In a period of rapidly increasing demand for silk and of other opportunities for workers, techniques which saved labor as dramatically as branch feeding and close harvesting did could not be resisted; by the 1920s, as we have seen, everyone used them, and still do today in Gumma Prefecture.[43]

Another area of innovation in sericultural technology was in quality control. This took two forms, one in silkworm

---

[43] *Ibid.*, pp. 90-91, 124-125.

eggs, which was successful, the other in cocoons, which was considerably less so. The prefectural government, with the support of the efficient sericulturalists, established egg-inspection stations in 1887 in an attempt to eradicate the brokers' selling of diseased silkworm eggs. Sericulturalists welcomed this system because it guaranteed the quality of one of the two major inputs of their cocoon crop. In fact, farmers so benefited from disease-free eggs that cocoon cultivators successfully coerced officials to reinstate three of the five inspection stations eliminated by the government to save money in 1918. Officials, pressed by "sericultural representatives" in the prefectural assembly, like Tsukahara Suijirō of Mitsue Village, took the face-saving step of replacing the abolished centers with "temporary" ones—which remained temporarily in operation until the end of World War II.

The effort at establishing a system for the inspection of cocoons was less successful than that for silkworm eggs, however, largely because it represented an attempt to control one of the farmer's salable products rather than one of his inputs, and accordingly he was less interested in its quality control. Chōda Akira, a rich landlord and powerful politician from Futagawa, Ōkamada's neighboring village, as part of his continuing battle to make cocoon marketing transactions more efficient, encouraged the prefectural government to establish a cocoon inspection system in the late Taishō era. Methods to improve the selling of cocoons were welcomed even by the poorer farmers, but attempts to enforce standards of quality received a less enthusiastic response. Sericulturalists feared that they might receive a reduced price or nothing at all for cocoons that did not reach the minimum standards. Thus, when Yamanashi officials established Japan's first inspection system for cocoons in 1926, they made it voluntary and won only a limited response—in 1927, 3 percent, and in 1931, 6 percent of Yamanashi cocoons were sold through the inspection system.[44]

[44] *Ibid.*, pp. 69, 149-150, 239-240.

Marketing and Financing of Sericulture

Yamanashi efficient farmers, in their efforts to raise yields and profits, strove not only to improve mulberry, silkworm eggs, and cocoon cultivation and quality, but also to better the methods by which they marketed their finished product, cocoons, and financed their operations. Smooth and equitable transactions, and adequate and affordable capital, were as important to producers as new technology. Traditionally, individual farmers had sold their output to itinerant merchants who, as the representatives of the silk-reeling companies, made the rounds of the various sericultural districts. At the turn of the century, it was not an uncommon sight at the end of the spring cocoon season in mid-June to see clusters of men bargaining around the hearth of Yamanashi farmhouses. The brokers had several distinct advantages over the farmers in these dealings. First, because they moved from village to village to conduct their business, the merchants possessed better information about harvests and prices elsewhere than did the sellers. Second, because they represented relatively large companies and were few in number, and because they could collude to fix the limits of their purchasing prices, the brokers avoided competition and played off the sericulturalists one against another. Accordingly, they were able to keep prices low. Third, until early in the twentieth century, farmers sold most of their cocoons "live," that is, with the pupa still living and the cocoon undried. Since most reeling companies but few cultivators owned expensive drying equipment, the buyers were in a much better position than the producers to bide time for more favorable prices.[45] Clearly what the "many" sericulturalists needed was a collective method of dealing with the "few" reeling companies and brokers. As in the case of technology, well-to-do efficient farmer landlords supplied the needed organizations.

In 1908, Tanabe Tamotsu, a prosperous sericulturalist

---

[45] *Ibid.*, p. 74.

from Ōfuji Village in the northeastern district of the Kōfu Basin, founded the Marujū Consignment Company in the nearby town of Enzan to market cocoons produced in his home county, Higashi Yamanashi. The producers consigned their cocoons to Tanabe; he then sold them collectively, and thereby established a stronger bargaining position than did individual farmers. But his company not only created the opportunity for large-scale marketing; it also lent money to producers at relatively low interest rates and provided its clients access to the most advanced drying equipment of the time, the Imamura-type Drying Machine. This apparatus allowed them the same opportunity as the buyers to wait for favorable price fluctuations. Clearly Tanabe's idea was well received; as Table 3-4 demonstrates, his company's business grew by almost thirty-eight times, and the share it marketed of the total prefectural cocoon production increased from 1.1 percent to 9.9 percent between 1908 and 1940.

Various well-to-do sericulturalists quickly established similar companies in other parts of the prefecture after Tanabe formed Marujū, and all vied to have the best drying facilities

TABLE 3-4

Volume of Cocoons in *Kan* Sold by the Marujū Consignment Company and Its Share of the Total Yamanashi Market, 1908-1940

Year	Volume of Cocoons Sold	Market Share
1908	15,000 *kan*	1.1%
1912	35,000	2.0
1916	55,000	2.4
1921	81,615	3.3
1926	189,734	6.2
1934	396,769	9.7
1940	566,447	9.9

Calculated from *Sanshigyō gaishi*, pp. 147, 234.

and to promote improved sericulture: Marusan and Central Cocoon in Kōfu City, Maruichi in Enzan, Isawa Cocoon in Isawa, Yamako in Nirasaki, Yatsushiro Farm Produce Warehouse in Kajikazawa, Saruhashi Cocoon in Saruhashi, and Naka Koma Cocoon and Raw Silk and Yamanashi Trading Companies in Naka Koma County. By the 1930s, most employed sericultural technicians to work with village agricultural associations, gave low-interest fertilizer loans, published pamphlets and organized lectures and seminars on mulberry and cocoon production, and provided baskets and bags free and truck transportation at cost to haul cocoons to market. In 1931, consignment companies sold 37 percent of the prefecture's cocoons, and the share sold directly to brokers at the producer's home had fallen to only 26 percent.[46]

Another method for the collective marketing of cocoons came through the Producers' Association (*sangyō kumiai*) movement begun at the turn of the century. A number of Home Ministry bureaucrats, under the influence of their knowledge of German cooperative unions, to help small farmers and manufacturers, engineered the parliament's passage of the Producers' Association Law of 1900, which provided for establishment of buying, selling, utilization, and credit cooperatives all over Japan. The movement spread quickly—in 1932, 3,500,000 farm households, drawn more or less evenly from all strata of rural society, belonged. Later, during the agricultural depression of the early 1930s, the government increased its control over the local branches until in 1943 it made membership compulsory. It is the activities of the wartime years which gave the unions a bad name; one student of the movement, Iinuma Jirō, calls the Producers' Association's branches the "building blocks of fascism."[47]

[46] *Ibid.*, pp. 147-149, 231, 234.

[47] Masumi Junnosuke, *Nihon seitōshiron*, Vol. 5 (Tokyo, 1979), pp. 348-352; Fujiwara Akira, Imai Seiichi, and Ōe Shinobu, eds., *Kindai Nihonshi no kiso chishiki* (Tokyo, 1974), pp. 158-159, 386-387; The "building blocks of fascism" phrase was used by Professor Iinuma during a presentation in the

Whatever the politics of the nationally controlled organization during the Pacific War, the association did help sericulturalists market their cocoons in the prewar twentieth century and served as the basis for a flourishing postwar cooperative movement. Although the Yamanashi sources do not inform us how much of the remaining marketing of cocoons was done by these associations, we do know that in 1935, 51,378 households, almost 86 percent of the prefecture's sericulturalists, belonged to 1,630 hamlet-level cooperatives. In addition to marketing cocoons, they helped members purchase fertilizer, and provided cocoon drying, freight hauling, medical facilities, and low-cost electricity. They also made cheap credit available.[48]

Financial institutions also became more modern in the late Meiji and early Taishō eras and benefited sericulturalists, especially those seeking capital to expand production. As the data in Table 3-5 show, the volume of Yamanashi farm loans increased by sixty times between 1885 and 1915 (and over thirty times in real terms), a tremendous increase in short-

TABLE 3-5

Yamanashi Farm Loans, 1885-1915, by Category of Lender, in *Yen*

Year	Pawnbrokers	Loan Companies	Banks
1885	299,000 *yen*	—	—
1890	479,000	—	423,000 *yen*
1895	519,000	—	1,407,000
1900	681,000	848,000 *yen*	4,405,000
1905	636,000	1,364,000	6,674,000
1910	495,000	2,286,000	10,666,000
1915	—	3,600,000	14,660,000

Source: *SKK*, p. 192.

autumn of 1974 to Professor Inoue Kiyoshi's seminar on the early Shōwa era held at Kyoto University's Institute of Humanistic Studies.

[48] *SKK*, pp. 541-543.

and long-term capital investment in agriculture, and we can safely assume that a large percentage of these new resources went into sericulture since it was Yamanashi's primary cash crop. The share of loans contributed by the traditional lenders, pawnbroker landlords, fell precipitously from over 50 percent in 1890 to under 4 percent twenty years later, and these were replaced by the more modern banks and loan companies. Although banks did not give money away easily or cheaply, their interest rates, unlike those of the pawnbrokers, were not usurious. Between 1912 and 1934, the bank lending rate fluctuated around 10 percent, and in 1935, it had fallen to 8.4 percent. Over the same decades, the Agricultural and Industrial Bank and the Hypothec Bank offered even lower interest rates, of about 8.7 percent and 7.5 percent. Interest rates for loans from individual lenders remained higher, at about 11½ percent, but even they indicated that pawnbrokers' and landlords' interest rates fell, at least after the turn of the century. All in all, in 1912, 35 percent of all farm loans nationwide had interest rates under 10 percent, and 80 percent under 15 percent; by 1935, the percentages were 63 percent under 10 percent, and 93 percent under 15 percent, a far cry from the standard late Tokugawa and early Meiji rate of 20 percent, the mid-Meiji rate of 15 percent or more, and Ralph Nickleby's rate of five-and-twenty percent per annum. Moreover, the banks regularized their procedures for making and terminating loans and for foreclosing on the security of the defaulters; the borrowers knew where they stood vis-à-vis the lenders. Modern banks gave sericulturalists and farmers in general better and more secure terms for obtaining capital than did traditional pawnbrokers and landlords.[49]

---

[49] *SKK*, p. 192; Ōuchi, *Nōgyō mondai* (Tokyo, 1961), pp. 286-287; Sakisaka Itsurō, *Nihon shihonshugi no shomondai* (Tokyo, 1947), p. 261; Asakura and Tobata, *Nōgyō kin'yūron*, p. 56; Smith, *The Agrarian Origins of Modern Japan*, p. 158. Paul Mayet writes that the Izu debtors' party in the 1880s considered 13 percent a "benefit." *Agricultural Insurance* (London, 1893), pp. 68, 127.

Credit cooperatives under the umbrella of the producers' association movement also helped provide low-cost capital to sericulturalists in Yamanashi. In 1935, the Yamanashi *sangyō kumiai* advanced 7½ million yen in loans, about 10 percent of Yamanashi farmers' indebtedness. (Since farm households depended on cocoons for most of their cash income, one assumes that a large share of this borrowing went into sericulture.) One may wonder why a cooperative movement which provided low-interest capital did not capture a larger share of the prefecture's credit. The answer seems to lie in the nature of the organization. As a cooperative, the credit union depended on its members' savings to provide most of the capital for lending. In 1935, savings reached only 4.7 million yen; thus, the productive associations did not have the resources to claim more than 10 percent of the lending market. The *kumiai* did seem to do better in highly commercial areas like Naka Koma, however. The average Naka Koma household borrowed 139 yen from the credit association compared to only 105 yen per household in the rest of Yamanashi.[50] In credit as in technology, centrally placed villages had an advantage.

Although the credit unions of the producers' association movement did not replace banks as the major lending organ for Yamanashi sericulturalists before World War II, they did supply some of the capital needed to finance the expansion of sericulture and laid one of the foundation stones for the expansion of agricultural credit and thus productivity after 1945. Moreover, the lending activities of the producers' associations cast a shadow on one standard belief of scholars who study Japanese rural society: that modern landlords exploited their tenants. Nationwide in 1926, the deposit-to-loan ratio of landlords in credit associations was 169 to 100, that of owner farmers 96 to 100, of owner tenant farmers 81 to 100, and of tenant farmers 73 to 100. By depositing

---

[50] *SKK*, pp. 540-542; *sangyō kumiai* provided 17 percent of agricultural credit nationwide in 1935. Asakura and Tobata, *Nōgyō kin'yūron*, p. 56.

money in cooperative agricultural credit unions, landlords provided capital for low-security, low-interest loans for less prosperous farmers.[51]

DISSEMINATION OF SERICULTURAL TECHNOLOGY

Not only did a number of efficient farmer-landlords and their allies in the prefectural government develop these various ways of augmenting sericultural productivity and selling and financing their product, but they also devised ways of disseminating the new technology. The educational effort was twofold: they taught the methods to both the relatively affluent, to the other landlords and owner farmers, and, more importantly, to the relatively poor tenants, most of whom in the early Meiji period were illiterate. In the nineteenth century, efficient farmers used oral persuasion based on their traditional ascendancy over the tenants to induce them to adopt new techniques; but as the poorer farmers became increasingly literate and concomitantly increasingly entrepreneurial throughout the modern period, the more formal organs of education influenced the tenants as well.[52] The sericultural societies and schools, itinerant teachers, study trips, pamphlets, newsletters, mulberry and cocoon competitions, and seminars which spread technical knowledge to landlords and owner farmers in the Meiji period also educated tenant farmers in the late Meiji, Taishō, and Shōwa eras.

One of the earliest methods for acquiring and spreading sericultural knowledge in the 1870s and 1880s was the study trip. Many young Yamanashi farmers and technicians traveled to other parts of Japan to learn new techniques and then returned to teach them in Kai. For example, Ono Motobē, age 21-23, at his father's expense spent many months in 1878-1880 traveling and learning about sericulture in Shin-

[51] Yuzuru Katō, "Sources of Loanable Funds of Agricultural Credit Institutions in Asia," *Developing Economics*, X-2 (1972), pp. 131-132.
[52] *SKK*, p. 899.

221

shū; in 1883, Governor Fujimura, committed to stimulating the prefecture's economy and thus its agricultural productivity, sent three young men, Muramatsu Bokusuke, Yadosawa Kiyomi, and Takano Takashi, to Fukushima to study the temperature-controlled method of raising silkworms. On their return, Muramatsu was invited by Hatta Tatsuya to his home village of Ukai, where, as we have seen, Hatta studied the new method and built himself a room for silkworm cultivation in which he could control the temperature and ventilation. Other young men similarly studied in Fukushima, Gumma, Nagano, and at the central government's new sericultural research center in Tokyo, and then returned to Yamanashi to impart to other farmers what they had learned.[53]

A coterie of itinerant "sericultural instructors" (*yōsan kyōshi*), who traveled from region to region to instruct farmers about silkworm cultivation, emerged alongside the young farmer-student-technicians in the late nineteenth century. These men, some of whom were landlords who taught part-time out of civic duty, and others of whom earned their livelihood as full-time teachers, introduced idea after idea into the faddish world of sericulture. Successive vogues, each appealing to part of the agricultural community, succeeded one another in the late Meiji and Taishō eras; the heated, but well-ventilated environment of the Hatta-Muramatsu temperature-controlled silkworm room gave way among a few farmers to one which was heated but unventilated; this then surrendered, again among a few, to an enthusiasm for outdoor cultivation made possible in the 1920s by the new types of silkworm eggs which could be artificially incubated, and of mulberry which resisted frost. Although most of these instructors' ideas improved the existing practices, or at least broadened their variety, some did not. In spite of the inefficacy of some of the notions taught by these *yōsan kōshi*, one should not think of those with the less fruitful ideas as charlatans or opportunists. Rather, one should view the sericul-

---

[53] *Sanshigyō gaishi*, pp. 38-39; Hagiwara, *Kai shiryō shūsei*, Vol. 11, p. 455.

tural world as a vital one of constant experimentation and discovery; some ideas which promised utility on paper and were disseminated before their value was confirmed did not work well in the silkworm room; but others, most of them, did. One also should keep in mind that some teachers were more able than others. It was to ensure uniformly high standards of performance among sericultural teachers that the prefecture established rules to regulate and license them in 1923; in 1925, the Yamanashi Sericultural Teachers' Research Association enrolled 375 licensed *yōsan kyōshi*.[54]

In the Meiji period, Yamanashi efficient farmers and governmental officials also established a variety of sericultural societies, schools, research centers, and seminars to increase and disseminate knowledge of improved sericultural technology. In 1883, Governor Fujimura established the Yamanashi Sericultural Society to stimulate the production of cocoons; in 1885, he founded a school in Kōfu to teach practical sericultural subjects like silkworm and mulberry disease prevention, meteorology, soil analysis, the construction of improved silkworm-raising rooms, and the storage of eggs and cocoons. This school was the first in a long line of public, semi-public, and private sericultural teaching facilities. For example, the Yamanashi Sericultural Training Center, established in Isawa in 1895 by the private contributions of farmers from Higashi Yamanashi and Higashi Yatsushiro, and similar institutions founded in 1903 in Kita Koma, Naka Koma, Minami Koma, Nishi Yatsushiro, and Minami Tsuru counties gave short courses of between four months and two years' duration in sericultural techniques and rudimentary science. Although they enrolled few students at first—15 to 20 per year—these centers helped create a cadre of trained sericulturalists among the sub-landlord class of Yamanashi farmers.

During World War I, the quality of these local schools was improved to spread more and better technology more fully

----

[54] *Sanshigyō gaishi*, pp. 126-129.

to more of the newly literate owner tenant and tenant farmers. The schools upgraded their entrance requirements in 1915 to eight years of elementary school; the compulsory education law required only six; but by the 1920s most rural young men in Yamanashi and Japan, whatever their socioeconomic background, were receiving eight years of schooling. When school officials raised the prerequisites for enrollment, they also improved the curricula of the schools; by the 1920s, students studied basic science, zoology, botany, economics, silkworm dissection, the use of microscopes, and practical sericulture.[55]

Public organizations and, more frequently, private citizens, published pamphlets, articles, and newsletters to disseminate sericultural techniques in the 1870-1925 period. For example, at least six influential pamphlets, written by landlord-model farmers in five cases and by a sericultural "journalist" in the other, appeared in the Meiji and Taishō periods. The first of these, Hatta's *Sericultural Diary*, first advertised the use of temperature control and heat in the silkworm cultivating room in the 1870s. The second and third, Ono Motobē's *The Ono Method of Cultivating Rosō Mulberry*, and *A Method for Raising Fall Silkworms, the Eggs of which were Stored in Caves*, in the 1880s, explained how best to use caves to store eggs and to exploit the *rosō* mulberry which Ono perfected for the fall cocoon season. The fourth, Naganuma Benjirō's *A New Book on the Principles of Practical Mulberry Cultivation*, called for planting at least 600 mulberry trees per *tan* when trimming was done by close harvesting, again in the 1880s. The fifth, Furuya Hisamasa's *The New Twentieth-Century Method of Silkworm Feeding*, published first in 1897 and reissued in 1913, taught branch feeding of silkworms and close harvesting of mulberry, two ideas which Furuya vigorously supported. The last, *The Essentials of Yamanashi Sericulture and Silk Thread*, written by Takano Gikyō, the editor of Yamanashi's important private newsletter, *Yamanashi Silk-*

[55] *Ibid.*, pp. 74-75, 111-112, 152-153.

worm and Mulberry News, described what one might call the state of the craft in mulberry and cocoon production in the late 1920s. Each of the six reached a goodly audience, and the last, Takano's pamphlet, published in the Taishō period, reached the newly literate owner tenant and tenant farmers as well as owner farmers and landlords.[56]

Newsletters, or should we say, *the newsletter* had even more influence than pamphlets in spreading technical sericultural information to farmers of non-landlord background in the twentieth century. Although Governor Fujimura's sericultural society began publishing an official newsletter in 1883, it was the non-official monthly newspaper, *Yamanashi Silkworm and Mulberry News*, which first appeared at the end of the Russo-Japanese War, that had the greatest effect on the spread of sericultural information. To begin with, the first editor, Takabe Wakatarō, who proselytized for both modern sericulture and Methodist temperance, proved himself to Yamanashi's non-landlord farmers because of his spirited defense of the labor-saving branch feeding when it came under attack in 1910. Takabe even put out a special issue of the journal to explain and defend the technique. Moreover, the newsletter's popularity among pragmatic farmers was enhanced in 1927 by the appointment as editor of Takano Gikyō, who had just published his pamphlet which described the newest sericultural technology in language that was easily readable for the marginally literate. But, most important, the magazine, in which the editors made extensive use of the phonetic syllabary alongside Chinese characters, contained a wide variety of practical information. A typical edition was about 25 pages in length and included six or

---

[56] *Sanshigyō gaishi*, pp. 38, 48, 89-90, 113; *Gojūnenshi*, p. 552. Although these six are the only sericultural handbooks to which I have found reference, there may well have been others. I have seen only three, Ono Motobē's two pamphlets, one of which is described above in footnote 13, and Takano's *Yamanashi sanshi yōkan*. All three are written in a straightforward, simple style and include phonetic readings (*furigana*) for most Chinese characters.

seven articles on sericultural techniques or problems and their solutions, advertisements for equipment, silkworm eggs and marketing and storage facilities, news reports of interest to sericulturalists, and poetry (*haiku*) written by the readers.[57]

Finally, the honor of winning prizes at national and even international competitions encouraged late-nineteenth-century landlord-cultivators to invest their time and money in sericulture and in the improvement of sericultural technology. The Meiji era was one in which a combination of government encouragement, patriotism, the freeing of the peasantry from feudal restrictions, and the idea of self-improvement stimulated literate landlord-cultivator-entrepreneurs to strive to expand agricultural productivity through the use of new technology; it is not surprising, therefore, that they took great pride in the more tangible and highly publicized rewards of their success. Between 1877 and World War I, a series of agricultural *concours* were held throughout Japan: for example, in 1879 at Shizuoka and Ueno, in 1882 at Kōfu and Kiryū, in 1887 in Mie Prefecture and at Hachiōji, in 1895 at Ueno again. Yamanashi competitors won their first gold medal when Natori Masaki, manager of the prefecture's model filature, earned one for raw silk in a four-prefecture competition before the home crowd in Kōfu in 1882, but the prefecture's crowning triumph came at the Paris World's Fair in 1889, when the Japanese government decided to test the level of Japanese sericulture internationally. Thirty-seven Japanese entered the competition, and fifteen Yamanashi entrants won prizes. The three most successful Japanese entrants came from Kai: Amemiya Kihei, a filature owner, won a silver medal for raw silk, Hatta Tatsuya won a silver medal for cocoons, and Ono Motobē won Japan's only gold medal, also for cocoons. Amemiya's, Hat-

[57] *Sanshigyō gaishi*, p. 113; *Yamanashi jinji kōshinroku* (Kōfu, 1928), pp. 582-583. The Local History Room of the Yamanashi Prefectural Library holds 149 issues of the journal, the first published in January 1908 and the last in March 1944.

ta's, and Ono's success brought honor to Yamanashi and celebrity to themselves. Ono traveled the Yamanashi banquet circuit in 1889-1890, and Hatta and Ono, before their deaths in the World War I era, became sericultural elder statesmen, recognized as such by being chosen judges for subsequent competitions and by receiving decorations from the imperial family.[58] And yet, in spite of this acclaim and their concrete financial success, Ono's and Hatta's prosperity was not preordained. When they undertook their efforts at technical improvement in the 1870s, the risks were great and the returns which they ultimately received not at all assured. Thus, it is important to close this chapter by tracing the landlords' (and tenants') motives for their involvement in sericultural improvement.

MOTIVATIONS FOR SERICULTURAL IMPROVEMENT

Scholars of rural Japan have suggested various motivations for the modern farmer's involvement in the advancement of new technology. Dore mentions a penchant for novelty, submissiveness, patriotism, and economic interest, and Waswo emphasizes the latter two, plus tradition and reformist zeal: all six reasons seem to have played a role.[59] Many premodern landlords had taken an active interest in agricultural improvement, as Thomas Smith points out, and their heirs and heirs' peers in the Meiji period, and their tenants in the Taishō era, continued and broadened this bent for a variety of reasons.[60] The desire to make Japan and Yamanashi rich and powerful (Kai "nationalism" emerged in the modern period as renewed pride in the region's sixteenth-century general, Takeda Shingen, reveals) in the face of foreign threats and competition, enthusiasm for self-improvement and for unusual techniques, the poorer farmers'

[58] *Sanshigyō gaishi*, pp. 77-78; Hagiwara, *Kai shiryō shūsei*, Vol. 11, p. 458.
[59] Waswo, *Japanese Landlords*, pp. 41-42; Dore, "Agricultural Improvement," pp. 84-91.
[60] Smith, *Agrarian Origins*, pp. 87-107.

227

willingness to accept the landlord's lead in the nineteenth century, and to join in the fervor for improvement themselves in the twentieth, and the desire of all farmers to raise their standards of living—all led in Yamanashi to rural prosperity in the twentieth century.

The zeal of Yamanashi and Naka Koma farmers for increasing their income through risk taking and mastering new techniques belies both James Scott's dictum that peasants prefer security to the dangers of entrepreneurship and profit maximization, and Ronald Dore's argument that the modern Japanese farmer did not take great risks in switching from the cultivation of rice, a subsistence *and* cash crop, to cocoons and other strictly marketed crops.[61] Sericulture, as we have seen, brought greater monetary returns than any other crop; on the other hand, it could not be eaten when prices and thus earnings dropped. In spite of this risk, Yamanashi and Naka Koma farmers turned to sericulture fearlessly in the 1885-1930 period. Prefectural mulberry acreage increased by 3.4 percent per year over the forty-five years; Naka Koma mulberry acreage increased by much more, 8.3 percent per year, over the same period. Moreover, Naka Koma sericulturalists did what Dore states Japanese farmers never do: turned paddy fields into mulberry orchards during the silk boom of the 1920s. Between 1919 and 1930, the county's paddy-field area decreased by 19.7 percent, 1,071 hectares, while mulberry orchards increased by 73 percent, 1,826 hectares.[62] In other words, the Yamanashi and Naka Koma evidence indicates, not surprisingly, that Dore and Waswo are correct in singling out economic interest as the primary motivation for agricultural improvement.

The basic point of this book, as must be clear to the reader by now, is that the modern Japanese farmer, whether rich or poor, was not merely a pawn to be buffeted by an unjust

---

[61] James C. Scott, *The Moral Economy of the Peasant*, pp. 5, 13-55; Dore, "Agricultural Improvement," p. 90.

[62] *Yamanashi tōkeisho*, 1885, 1919, 1930.

market system—as inequitable and onerous as that system at times might have been. Rather, the farmer was a positive actor, an "economic animal," a small entrepreneur, if you will, who increasingly made every effort to maximize profits by using new techniques to produce more and better cash crops. The market did not like a gigantic octopus ensnare the farmer in its tentacles and squeeze out his life's blood; rather, commercial agriculture and the other parts of Japan's modernization process allowed the cultivator to take greater and greater control of his own destiny. The rural market economy did not destroy the farmer; it freed him.

Nowhere are both the Japanese agriculturalist's accommodation to market forces and the risks involved more clearly demonstrated than in the Yamanashi farmer's adoption of sericulture and its new technology. In spite of the uncertainties of the new methods and the dangers of over-specialization, dozens of Yamanashi landlords gambled great amounts of time and money in new types of mulberry and silkworms in the late nineteenth century. Ono Motobē, for example, as we have seen, in 1880 set up a mulberry orchard and bought 140-150 different types of mulberry from all over Japan to test there. By 1884, Ono had selected *rosō* mulberry as the most productive of these, purchased 20,000 seedlings, and planted them in all of his and many of his tenants' non-paddy fields. But in the late 1880s, when the new mulberry finally began to produce a sufficient quantity of edible leaves to earn Ono a return on his immense investment, a rumor spread that *rosō* was a poison mulberry which inevitably led to cocoon crop failure. In spite of Ono's efforts to dissuade his neighbors from this view, dozens abandoned the new mulberry for more traditional ones and blamed him for their failures; even worse for him, some buyers stopped purchasing his cocoons. According to Ono, "I was attacked from every side. 'He is worthless,' 'He is crazy,' they said. Friends and relatives warned me that I would bankrupt myself if I didn't stop (cultivating *rosō*), but since my beliefs were based on my own experiments, I was convinced that I was correct."[63] Only when Ono's cocoons, spun by silkworms which fed on *rosō* mulberry, won their gold medal in Paris in 1889 was his investment saved.[64]

When Mimori Chūzaemon and Hatta Tatsuya invested in building stone vaults in caves to store fall-season silkworm eggs in the 1880s, they too faced great risks, but like Ono gambled on even greater long-range profits. In 1880, when the two men opened their storage businesses, they had no idea whether fall cocoon production would pay, whether the cold temperatures of the caves might not destroy the eggs, or whether they would attract many customers. Their worst fears were unfounded; at the peak of their business, before artificially incubated egg cards and refrigeration revolutionized the industry after World War I, most of Yamanashi's sericultural households stored their summer and fall egg cards with one or another of the cave consignment companies. Mimori, Hatta, Ono, and many others made substantial long-term profits from risky, short-term investments in new sericultural methods.

Tenant farmers also took part in this experimentation, although before World War I not always freely. Time and again, "efficient farmers" tested new techniques and their tenants, from necessity because of their traditional submissiveness to landlord authority, undertook the projects too. Ono's tenants had no choice but to plant many of his 20,000 *rosō* seedlings in the 1880s, and Ichinose Masuyoshi's tenants followed suit with his *ichinose* mulberry trees two decades later. And yet, what was done by these poorer farmers out of obedience to authority in the late Meiji period turned out to be profitable. The nineteenth- and early-twentieth-century innovations which landlords "forced" on their tenants—multi-seasonal cultivation, the new *rosō* and *ichinose* mulberry types, cave storage, branch feeding, close harvesting, and new silkworm egg types—helped to increase real sericultural income per household 3½ times in Yamanashi and 10 times in Naka Koma between 1891 and 1929; little landlord pres-

---

[63] *Sanshigyō gaishi*, p. 48.   [64] *Ibid.*, pp. 47-48.

sure must have been necessary after tenants recognized the rewards to be gained by changing some of their fields from grain cultivation to sericulture and to its improved technology.[65]

After World War I, tenants adopted the new technology freely without the need to follow the landlord's lead, much less his coercion. The newly and increasingly literate tenants without any landlord guidance whatsoever espoused the techniques which became the keys to the sericultural boom of the 1920s: artificially incubated silkworm eggs, more extensive use of more potent fertilizer, better mulberry types like *ichinose*, and increased adoption of collective methods of marketing cocoons, obtaining credit, and absorbing new techniques. In fact, in some communities in the late Taishō period tenants not only rejected landlord leadership in availing themselves of new methods, but also did not even share them with the landlords. In Kubo Nakajima, for example, the tenant union formed in 1921 became the hamlet cooperative, the agricultural association complete with its own agronomist, and thus the pipeline for assimilating new technology. Since the union/cooperative/association excluded landlords and owner farmers from its ranks, its tenant farmer members refused to share with the old elite any new agricultural techniques (or in fact any information) distributed by the regional and village governments and technical organizations through the hamlet agricultural association.[66] To summarize this lengthy discussion of farmers' motivations: both landlords and tenants turned to improved sericultural technology because it allowed them to increase their income and capital dramatically and steadily over a half century between 1880 and 1930. Landlords led the way in the Meiji period; tenants joined them and even took the lead after World War I.

[65] *Yamanashi tōkeisho*, 1891, 1927. The starting year 1891 is chosen for this comparison because it is the first year for which value of cocoon production is reported in the statistical yearbook.

[66] *KNJ*, pp. 118-124.

FOUR

Landlord-Tenant Relations in
Ōkamada Village

THE most productive farm communities in Yamanashi are found in a forty-square-mile triangle of fruitful agricultural land which lies within the larger triangles of the whole Kōfu Basin and the entire prefecture. Formed by the Fuefuki, Ara, and Kamanashi rivers and bounded in the north by the Chūō Railroad, this delta holds the Naka Koma villages which gained the most from the growth of a raw silk industry and a rural market economy, and from the ensuing improvement in rice, *mugi*, mulberry, and cocoon yields and quality. The "six villages of eastern Naka Koma"—Tatomi, Shōwa, San-chō, Inatsumi, Futagawa and Ōkamada—which filled the ten square miles in the toe of this small delta and which contained many rice paddies and mulberry orchards particularly benefited in modern times because of their proximity to markets and employment opportunities in the filatures in and near Kōfu.[1] Farmers here earned much higher agricultural incomes than their compatriots in the surrounding plateaus and hills.[2] Farmers in Ōkamada apparently had higher levels of living as well. Although indicators are few, we know that

[1] Hattori uses the phrase "the six villages of eastern Naka Koma" to describe that region where Yamanashi's tenant disputes first broke out. *KNJ*, p. 73. The six villages were in fact ten in the 1920s. In the early 1930s, Kokubo, Saijō, and Jōei merged to form Shōwa, and Hanawa, Shinobu, and Koikawa merged to form Tatomi.

[2] To cite an example, the value of production per agricultural worker in 1926-1929 was 21 percent higher, in 1930-1934 was 38 percent higher, and in 1935-1939 was 58 percent higher in Ōkamada than in Zaikezuka, Wakao Ippei's ancestral village, five miles to the west near the edge of the basin in the higher lands near the Midai River.

88 percent of Ōkamada's households owned their own homes, compared to only 68 percent in upland Zaikezuka in the middle triangle.[3]

Prewar farmers in the six villages tilled comparatively large farms: about 11 *tan* per household compared to 6 *tan* in Zaikezuka and its six neighbors which made up the "seven villages of the Midai," and compared to 8 *tan* for Naka Koma County as a whole. They also lived close to major transportation arteries and large machine filatures. After 1928, the Minobu Railroad Line had stations in Shōwa (Kokubo and Jōei) and Sanchō (Koikawa and Higashi Hanawa), and one of the two Kōfu-Ichikawa Daimon highways ran through Ōkamada, Inatsumi, and Sanchō, and the other through Shōwa and Tatomi. Shōwa housed the Kanebō Company's big, modern Kokubo filature (680 basins after the mid-1930s). Thus, in the 1920s and 1930s, farmers in centrally located villages like Ōkamada were able to earn higher agricultural profits than did tillers in less central Naka Koma villages like Zaikezuka, who in turn were more central, were served after 1932 by the Yamanashi Electric Railroad, and had more profitable farms than their counterparts in remote Minami Tsuru County villages. Thus also, in 1930, 44 percent of Kokubo's workers found employ in factories, compared to 17 percent in Zaikezuka.[4] The Midai area may have had fewer and smaller modern filatures than eastern Naka Koma, but it had many more and larger ones than Minami and Kita Tsuru.[5] Larger farms, relative proximity to markets and secondary jobs, and better transportation al-

---

[3] *Kokusei chōsa hōkoku*, 1950, Yamanashi volume.

[4] Not unexpectedly, Yamanashi's modern filatures tended to be close to railroads. Although Kokubo's Kanebō filature was established before the Minobu Railroad Line went through in 1928, it was made into a large-scale filature only in the 1930s.

[5] As late as the 1930s, almost one-third of the farmers of the Midai villages still worked part of the year, as Wakao Ippei had 100 years earlier, as itinerant merchants in order to supplement their incomes. Mizoguchi Tsunetoshi, "Midaigawa senjōchi hatasaku nōson ni okeru gyōshō katsudō," *Jimbun chiri*, 28 (1976), p. 46.

lowed farmers in eastern Naka Koma to achieve higher levels of living than those in Zaikezuka. Still, tenancy and tenancy disputes were far more prevalent in the east than in the seven villages in the Midai to the west.[6] Since, as we have seen in Chapter Two, the growth of an agricultural market economy in the Kōfu Basin region did not cause penury and intensify stratification, at least after the Russo-Japanese War, but led instead to rising incomes for most cultivators, tenants and owner farmers alike, I plan in this chapter to study economic and social life in Ōkamada, one of the "six," to analyze why tenancy and tenancy disputes were more common in relatively richer than in poorer Yamanashi villages.

ŌKAMADA VILLAGE AND ITS AGRICULTURAL DEVELOPMENT

Ōkamada, a village of 240-250 farm households and 250-260 hectares of arable land, located four miles to the south of Kōfu, looks like hundreds of other Japanese farm communities.[7] Like most, Ōkamada is not one village but a cluster of smaller villages arbitrarily joined by government fiat in 1874 and 1889. In each of these premodern hamlets, one found before World War II a cluster of unpainted, thatched (today tin, tile, or plastic) roofed houses, surrounded by its farmland. These fields, which in the flat terrain of Ōkamada, located as it is in the exact center of the basin, were mostly rice paddies (70 percent), looked particularly beautiful at rice-transplanting time in June. The pale green seedlings, reflected in the water of the tiny paddies, contrasted sharply

---

[6] 53 percent of all Midai region farmland was tilled by tenants in the 1920s; tenants farmed 75 percent of arable land in the eastern Naka Koma villages. Many writers have pointed out the high degree of tenant farmer contentiousness in eastern Naka Koma. See, for example, Nagahara et al., *Nihon jinushisei*, pp. 15-16; Amemiya, footnotes 7 and 9, p. 151.

[7] The number of households and area of arable land fluctuated slightly after World War I. In 1948, 245 farm households worked 259.6 *chō* of arable land.

with the brown trunks and dark green leaves of the gnarled, dwarfed mulberry trees nearby. But what is alluring to the outside observer is a matter of life and livelihood to the resident.

Ōkamada's nine hamlets, each before World War II the center of its inhabitants' cooperative economic life, covered the spectrum of Japanese village types.[8] At the one extreme the observer found Futsuka Ichiba, the village's largest hamlet, which lay along the Ara River and astride the Kōfu-Ichikawa Daimon Road in the northeastern corner of Ōkamada. Here one discovered a vertically organized, hierarchically "cooperative" hamlet dominated by one family. The households of the sake brewer and hamlet headman, Mikami Hachiemon, and of two of its five branches owned most of the riverine hamlet's land and ran Futsuka Ichiba like a fief. In 1870, these three households owned land assessed for tax purposes at producing 672 koku of rice per year, compared to 78 koku for the other three branches and 55 koku for the hamlet's remaining 38 households. Since Futsuka Ichiba had a total assessment of 370 koku, the Mikami held land producing at least 85 percent (315 koku or the complete 370 koku minus the non-Mikami 55 koku) of its total. Moreover, Hachiemon alone held a 1870 kokudaka of 485 koku, two-thirds of the Mikami total.[9] Although we do not know how much of each household's landholding was located in Futsuka Ichiba and how much in neighboring hamlets, it is

[8] Fukutake Tadashi, expanding on the work of Ariga Kizaemon, has presented the idea of two kinds of village structures, the vertically organized, feudal dōzoku type, and the horizontally organized democratic kumi type. Each arose from different economic conditions. Although the details of Fukutake's views are not universally accepted by scholars of the Japanese countryside, I have used the dōzoku-kumi idea here to convey the differences of hamlet organization within the one village of Ōkamada. Fukutake first presented his typology in Nihon nōson no shakaiteki seikaku (Tokyo, 1949). For a brief description in English, see Japanese Rural Society (London, 1967), pp. 138-145. For a brief analysis in English of Fukutake's view, see Chie Nakane, Kinship and Economic Organization in Rural Japan, pp. 177-179.

[9] KNJ, p. 157.

probably safe to conclude that Hachiemon, the head of the main Mikami line, was Futsuka Ichiba's largest landowner in 1870. Hachiemon's primogenitive descendants in the twentieth century migrated to Tokyo and lost much of their economic, religious, political, and patron-client leadership at home, but their power stayed in the family. A branch founded in 1850 by Hachiemon's younger brother Noboru dominated Futsuka Ichiba until the land reform of 1948.

A few thousand feet to the west of Futsuka Ichiba lies Kubo Nakajima, a much more egalitarian hamlet of 39 households. Kubo Nakajima before the Meiji Restoration contained only "titled" or "full-scale" farmers (*honbyakushō*), those cultivators who at some earlier time had held full membership in and had helped govern their villages. Most farmers in Futsuka Ichiba had been "petty" or literally "water-drinking" farmers (*mizunomi hyakushō*), whose small landholdings and relative newness to the village (most of course had been in the village for generations) had excluded them from full participation in hamlet life.[10] Although most of Kubo Nakajima's titled farmers at the Meiji Restoration were tenants to some degree, their landholdings were still considerably larger than those of their Futsuka Ichiba petty farmer neighbors. In 1870, Kubo Nakajima's non-landlord families had an average assessment of 4.4 *koku*, more than triple the 1.45 *koku* average in Futsuka Ichiba. Moreover, the "three Ishiharas," Kubo Nakajima's reigning resident landlords, had much smaller assessments, of only 57, 32, and 26 *koku* each, compared to the 485, 97, and 90 *koku* of the three leading Mikami households, and records from the Keichō era (1596-1611) show that Kubo Nakajima had no large landlords even then.[11]

Kubo Nakajima's political power, like its landed wealth,

---

[10] For definitions of the terms *mizunomi hyakushō* and *honbyakushō*, see Nakane, *op. cit.*, pp. 62-71; Keith Brown, transl., *Shinjō: The Chronicle of a Japanese Village* (Pittsburgh, 1979), p. 90; Ōtsuka shigakkai, *Shimpan kyōdoshi jiten* (Tokyo, 1969), pp. 530, 543.

[11] *KNJ*, pp. 12-15, 156-157.

was also less concentrated than Futsuka Ichiba's.[12] In the latter hamlet, Hachiemon's line and its primary branches provided successive headmen (nanushi), representatives of the farmers (hyakushōdai) and senior farmers (naga hyakushō).[13] In Kubo Nakajima, on the other hand, the positions rotated. Records for 1868, 1870, and 1872 show that three separate households held the position of headman: two of the three landlord Ishiharas (2 and 3), and the Kurosawa, a household which had the fifth largest kokudaka in 1870, but fell on hard times during the subsequent Meiji period and lost its land. The Komiyama, with the tenth largest assessment, served as representative of the farmers throughout the 1868-1874 period, and four households shared the senior farmer posts: one of the two Ishihara headmen (3) after he left that post, the Kurosawa headman before his promotion, the third of the "three Ishiharas" (1), who served for two successive terms between 1870 and 1874, and a fourth Ishihara, who paid taxes on a small assessment of only 2.4 koku.[14] These fragmentary records of tax assessments and office holding indicate that many more households shared wealth and power in Kubo Nakajima than in neighboring Futsuka Ichiba.

Ōkamada's other seven hamlets, situated more or less on a north-south axis along or near the Kōfu-Ichikawa Daimon Road, fell between these two extremes in the distribution of wealth and power. Emmanji, a small cluster of 13 households, Miyanohara, a large hamlet of 39 households, and Takamuro, of moderate size with 21 households, came under the hereditary domination of single families, the Gemma,

---

[12] KNJ, p. 23; Morioka Kiyomi, unpublished introduction to Ariga Kizaemon, Hattori Harunori et al., Wagakuni ni okeru shakaiteki seisō oyobi shakaiteki idō to shakai kōzō to no kanren ni tsuite, pp. 1, 8.

[13] The translations of these three terms come from Ronald P. Dore, Shinohata: A Portrait of a Japanese Village (New York, 1978), pp. 25-26.

[14] KNJ, p. 23; Morioka, Wagakuni, pp. 1, 8; Naka Koma gunshi (Kōfu, 1928), Vol. 1, pp. 88, 228, 238. For clarity because so many families shared the surname Ishihara, I identify each Kubo Nakajima household discussed in the text by number as well as by name. For a complete list of numbered households, see Appendix.

Sakurabayashi, and Takamuro, respectively, and like Futsuka Ichiba fell on the stratified end of the scale. The household of Kobayashi Jūhei (b. 1897), a small-scale landlord who invested considerable time and money in sericultural research, wielded a good deal of influence in Horinouchi, which with its 27 households fell on the scale between the stratified 4 hamlets and the others. Sekiguchi and Nakajō, with 14 households each, and Furu Ichiba, with 10 households, lacked predominating landlords and were relatively egalitarian, but less so than Kubo Nakajima[15] (see Map).

Table 4-1 shows the landholdings in the 1920s of Ōkamada's largest landowners and, for purposes of comparison, of the six Kubo Nakajima families that rented out land. None of Ōkamada's five leading landlord households had holdings even one-tenth as large as that of Wakao Ippei, but all could support themselves through rent collection, and by area of land owned fell at least into the upper 5-6 percent of Japanese landlords in the 1908-1940 period.[16] Conversely, none of Kubo Nakajima's households which rented out land met even Ronald Dore's minimum definition of landlord, a person who rented out 5 *chō* or more of land. Ishihara Yasuzō (1), a sericultural researcher who leased out 4.7 *chō* and cultivated 1.95 *chō* himself, came closest, but even he and certainly the others, including the remaining two households of the "three Ishiharas," were not landlords. Toshiharu (2) and Ichitarō (3) might best be called owner cultivators who rented out some land, rather than landlords.[17]

---

[15] Amemiya, p. 73, footnote 75, p. 161.

[16] The Wakao family owned 423.4 *chō* of land in Yamanashi in 1924; the second leading landlord family, the Nezu, owned 160.0 *chō*; Nagahara, *Nihon jinushisei*, p. 513. Ann Waswo, in *Japanese Landlords*, p. 9, presents a table taken from Ōuchi Tsutomu, *Nōgyō mondai* (Tokyo, 1961), p. 207, in which she indicates that 5.7 percent of all landlords in 1940 owned 5 *chō* of land or more. Since all of Ōkamada's big five owned over 10 *chō*, they probably fell into the upper 2-3 percent of landlords.

[17] Dore, *Land Reform in Japan*, p. 29; Shimizu Tsugutama, the priest of Fukusenji, neither fit Dore's definition of a landlord nor cultivated himself. Since Dore argues that a non-cultivating landlord needed to rent out 6½ *chō* of land to earn the same income from rent that a schoolteacher earned in

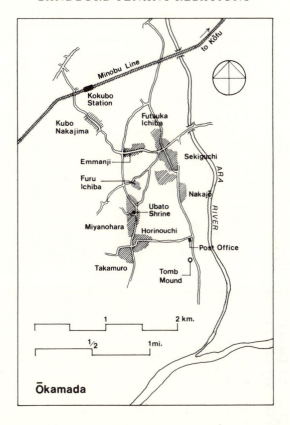

Ōkamada

Although Ōkamada has an ancient and medieval past, few documents remain to verify its history before 1850. A prehistoric tomb rises above the southern end of the village, and records reveal that at least Futsuka Ichiba, Miyanohara, Furu Ichiba, Horinouchi, and Takamuro fell into Kamada-shō, the early medieval manor over which the Kai Genji had held proprietory rights. The Ubato Shrine in Miyanohara, reputedly founded in the eleventh century by an immediate ances-

---

salary, Shimizu with his 2.2 *chō* lived far from the lap of luxury. Perhaps this was fitting for a Zen priest.

TABLE 4-1

Ōkamada's Largest Landlords and Kubo Nakajima's Households Renting Out Land, by *Tan* of Land Owned, Owned and Cultivated, Rented Out, and Rented In, in the 1920s (10 *tan* = 1 *chō*)

Landlord	Hamlet	Land Owned	Land Cultivated	Rented Out	Rented In
Mikami Keichō (Hachiemon)	Futsuka Ichiba	309.6 *tan*	1.7 *tan*	307.9 *tan*	0 *tan*
Mikami Saburō (Noboru)	Futsuka Ichiba	297.3	1.9	295.4	0
Takamuro Gorō	Takamuro	175.0	0.8	174.2	0
Sakurabayashi Hokaku	Miyanohara	150.0	0.93	149.07	0
Gemma Yoshinori	Emmanji	107.0	2.7	104.3	0
Ishihara Yasuzō (1)	Kubo Nakajima	66.5	19.5	47.0	0
Ishihara Toshiharu (2)	" "	31.1	17.0	16.2	2.1

Ishihara Ichitarō (3)	" "	24.9	21.9	3.0	0
Shimizu Tsugutama (Fukusenji)	" "	21.8	0.0	21.8	0
Ishihara Taizō (4)	" "	12.2	16.8	4.4	9.0
Ishihara Toyokichi (12)	" "	8.1	14.8	4.0	10.7

Source: *KNJ*, pp. 26–27, 118, 162; Amemiya, footnote 75, p. 161.

tor of the Takeda, and the illustrious lineage of two of the Ōkamada's twentieth-century landlord families, one of which officiated at the shrine, attest at least to their antiquity and the continuity of leadership in the village. Both the priestly Sakurabayashi in Miyanohara (the word *miya* means shrine) and the Takamuro in Takamuro, a hamlet which bears their name, descended from the Ogasawara, a twelfth-century branch of the Kai Genji, established by one of the early leaders of the Takeda line. The Sakurabayashi served not only as priests of Ubato Shrine but also as doctors (Chinese-style until the nineteenth century, when they trained in Western medicine), warrior retainers of the Takeda family before its demise in 1582, then followers of Tokugawa Ieyasu at the seige of Osaka Castle in 1614, village headmen of Miyanohara from the 1580s until the Meiji Restoration, and hamlet chiefs, village assemblymen, landlords, and ritual patrons thereafter. On two occasions in the interwar period, the sixth and last prewar Sakurabayashi Hokaku, who, unlike his predecessors, gave up medicine to become a professor of German literature at Kōfu's higher school, served as mayor of all Ōkamada; his son still lives in Miyanohara and practices medicine at a clinic immediately across the street from the Ubato Shrine.[18]

The Takamuro also trace their lineage to the Ogasawara in the twelfth century, but not in Takamuro hamlet. They arrived in Ōkamada only in 1531, when Nobutora, Shingen's father, rewarded Takamuro Masahide with land there. The successive descendants of Masahide, who himself died in combat in 1561 during the fourth of Shingen's five battles with Uesugi Kenshin at Kawanakajima, served as Takeda and then Tokugawa retainers, village headmen, landlords, patrons of many clients, after the Meiji Restoration hamlet representatives to the village council, and, like the Sakurabayashi, doctors (they too switched medical styles in the

---

[18] Beginning in 1724, each head of the Sakurabayashi household took the name Hokaku when he succeeded his father. Amazingly, there were only five Hokaku between 1724 and 1936.

Meiji period). Gorō, the last pre-land-reform Takamuro patriarch, wedded the younger sister of the last Hokaku; thus, the two of Ōkamada's five most powerful landlord families with illustrious lineages were intermarried. (Given the difficulty they must have faced in finding mates with suitable ancestry, and given the longstanding family connection—the first Hokaku studied medicine with Takamuro Masami in the 1740s—this marriage was clearly not the first Takamuro-Sakurabayashi merger.)[19]

Ōkamada becomes more visible in the Momoyama and early Tokugawa eras. To begin with, the other powerful Ōkamada families, the Mikami and the Gemma, first enter the written record here. The Mikami make their initial appearances in our documents in the last decade of the sixteenth century, when they already owned large tracts of land, and in 1686-1687, when they provided political leadership in Futsuka Ichiba.[20] In 1850, Mikami Hachiemon set up his younger brother Noboru as a branch household, and by the twentieth century the cadet family, headed by Noboru's adopted son Masaru, and then his adopted son Saburō, surpassed the main line in local wealth, power, and prestige. Noboru and Masaru in the mid- and late-nineteenth century acquired landholdings almost as extensive as the main household's (see Table 4-1). Saburō, after he married Masaru's daughter Riseyo, not only extended the Mikami estate (in 1929, he paid 774 yen in direct taxes and ranked first among Ōkamada's and ninety-eighth among Yamanashi's taxpayers), but also built himself a regional reputation as a doctor and medical researcher.[21] The "parasitical landlord"

[19] Amemiya, pp. 36-39; *Yamanashi jinji kōshinroku* (Kōfu, 1940), p. 1,623; *Naka Koma gunshi*, Vol. 1, p. 24; *Naka Koma gunchi* (Kōfu, 1926) p. 449; *Yamanashi hyakka jiten*, p. 464; *Yamanashi-ken no rekishi*, p. 65; Yamanashi-ken ishikai, *Yamanashi-ken ishikaishi* (Kōfu, 1969), p. 41; *Yamanashi-kenshi iji eisei shiryō*, unpublished materials, Vol. 11 (Naka Koma), no page numbers.

[20] Morioka, *Wagakuni*, pp. 1-2; *Naka Koma gunshi*, Vol. 1, p. 228.

[21] *Yamanashi jinji kōshinroku*, p. 1,702. *Kizokuin tagaku nōzeisha giin gosen jimmeibo*, A List of Persons Eligible to Vote for Large Taxpayer Members of the House of Peers, edited by Araki Moriaki and republished in 1970,

(*kisei jinushi*) studied parasitology (*kiseigaku*) and helped to isolate the cause and develop a treatment for "Japanese Blood Parasite Disease" (*Nihon jūketsu kyūchūbyō*), *Schistosomiasis japonica*, a disease which had long ravaged the Kōfu Basin; between 1915 and 1924 alone, it claimed 570 lives in the region.[22] Saburō's research and volunteer work as the Kokubo and Ōkamada school doctor brought him frequent awards from the governor and election as the head of the county and then the prefectural medical associations. Two of his sons became physicians in Tokyo.

The Gemma appear in the historical record for the first time in the seventeenth century, but not distinctly until the 1850s, when Gemma Genzaemon, like Mikami Hachiemon a landlord and sake brewer, served as Emmanji's headman. His son Naojirō and grandson Yoshinori continued to dominate Emmanji and to extend the family's landholdings into other hamlets in the twentieth century. Like Horinouchi's Kobayashi Jūhei and Kubo Nakajima's Ishihara Yasuzō (1), Naojirō, Yoshinori, and their cousin Hideyoshi, who stepped in as temporary family chief in 1930 when Yoshinori died, leaving an infant heir, played an active role in the development and introduction of new agricultural and sericultural techniques in Ōkamada. In 1916, Yoshinori founded and led the Ōkamada Sericultural Cooperative, and with his own money and time he built a cocoon storehouse so that members could stockpile their cocoons until the marketable supply fell and demand and prices rose. Beginning in 1917,

---

gives lists of taxpayers for seventeen upper-house elections between 1890 and 1941. Only Mikami Saburō among Ōkamada's landlords appears on the lists, and he only in 1929. In that year, he paid taxes in Ōkamada (over 85 percent), Kokubo and Kōfu, indicating that he probably had small landholdings outside of his home village, but not far away, in Kubo Nakajima's neighboring Kokubo. The Kōfu income probably came from his medical practice. Volume 19 (Yamanashi Prefecture), p. 110.

[22] Yamanashi-ken kōseibu, *Yamanashi-ken ni okeru chihōbyō no jittai* (Kōfu, 1974), pp. 3-5; *Yamanashi hyakka jiten*, p. 498; *Naka Koma gunshi*, Vol. 2, pp. 44-45. The disease was carried by a small water snail (*miyairi*) and attacked the portal system.

Hideyoshi headed Ōkamada's credit, purchasing, and utilization cooperatives, and in 1922 he became a director of the Naka Koma Agricultural Association and was elected to the first of four terms on the village council. In 1934, he became a prefectural assemblyman and secured funds to pave the Kōfu-Ōkamada section of the Kōfu-Ichikawa Daimon road. Certainly Hokaku (the fifth), Gorō, and Saburō profited from their medical practices; surely Yoshinori, Yasuzō, and Jūhei benefited from their sericultural activities; and self-interest must have prompted some of Hideyoshi's activities. Nevertheless, all seven men invested large amounts of their time and money in performing duties for their fellow villagers. Only Ōkamada's richest permodern landlord lineage, that of Mikami Hachiemon, headed after World War I by Keichō, a graduate of Waseda University who earned his doctorate at the University of Michigan and became the president of a Tokyo trading company, did not serve its village (or live in it) in the twentieth century.[23]

This landlord commitment to agricultural improvement, together with Ōkamada's proximity to markets and its favorable terrain, water supply, and farm size, provided the foundation for a striking growth in the value of agricultural production per household in the village in the twentieth century. Although the Ōkamada data for yields and value of production before 1925 are not as complete as those for Yamanashi and Naka Koma, the evidence we do have, when used together with the fuller prefectural and county materials, reveals a village which had one of the highest standards of living in the prefecture.

Table 4-2 shows rice yields and value of production per *tan* in Ōkamada, Naka Koma, and Yamanashi from 1906 until 1939. The data demonstrate that yields per *tan* grew at about the same rate (about 1.2-1.3 percent per year) in each of the three jurisdictions, except for a five-year period when

---

[23] *Yamanashi jinji kōshinroku*, 1918, pp. 727-728; 1940, pp. 1,207-1,208; *Yamanashi meikan* (Kōfu, 1926).

TABLE 4-2

Yields and the Value of Production per *Tan* for Rice in
Ōkamada Village, Naka Koma County, and
Yamanashi Prefecture, 1906-1939

	Ōkamada		Naka Koma		Yamanashi	
Years	Yields (koku)	Value (yen)	Yields (koku)	Value (yen)	Yields (koku)	Value (yen)
1906-09	1.89	—	1.78	26.6	1.64	31.0
1912-14	1.86	—	1.94	34.9	1.96	34.3
1915-18	1.80	37.7	2.18	49.6	2.08	46.7
1919-21	1.42	51.3	2.09	80.3	2.05	78.8
1922-24	No data		No data		2.20	71.6
1925-29	2.20	60.2	2.25	68.1	2.20	65.2
1930-34	2.28	41.0	2.38	44.6	2.34	42.8
1935-39	2.72	84.0	2.60	82.0	2.45	77.4

Calculated from *Yamanashi tōkeisho.*

Ōkamada's yields inexplicably fell precipitously (as low as 1.31 *koku* per *tan* in 1919) and the last four years surveyed, when Ōkamada and Naka Koma outstripped the rest of the prefecture.[24] This evidence for parallel growth does not disprove my hypothesis about Ōkamada's superior performance, however, because its farm households each cultivated a much larger area of paddy than households in either the rest of Naka Koma or of Yamanashi. Thus, as Table 4-3 informs us, equal or even inferior performance per *tan* led to a greater value of production per household. At the bottom of Ōkamada's productive slump in 1919-1921, when yields per *tan* fell to only two-thirds of average Naka Koma yields, Ōkamada still maintained an average value of production per household which was 14 percent higher, and per farm worker which was 23 percent higher, than the county aver-

[24] I can find no evidence to explain why Ōkamada yields were so low in the post-World War I years. The records give no indications of floods, droughts, or insect infestations.

ages.[25] In the 1920s, when Ōkamada's yields returned to equivalence with Naka Koma's, the village's farm households earned 70 percent more and then in the 1930s 100 percent more from rice than did the average county household. To make an even sharper contrast, in 1930-1934 and 1935-1939, rice yields and value of production per *tan* were similar in Ōkamada and Zaikezuka; because of the difference in the area of paddy that households in the two villages cultivated, the average Ōkamada farm had a value of production from rice which was 17-21 times greater than that of its Zaikezuka counterpart.[26]

One might expect that farmers in upland villages like Zaikezuka, with their relative wealth of dry fields (5.3 *tan* per household in Zaikezuka compared to 2.9 *tan* in Ōkamada in 1933-1937) and their dearth of paddy, would compensate for their lower value of production in rice by earning a greater income from dry-field crops like *mugi* and mulberry, the prefecture's major dry-field crops, and cocoons. They did make up some, but not all, of the difference. To begin with, Ōkamada's farmers, who had many more rice paddies to double crop (almost all dry fields were given over to mulberry in both places), earned 4-12 times more income from non-rice grain than did Zaikezuka farmers. And, on a larger scale, although Zaikezuka farm households planted almost twice as much land each in mulberry as did their Ōkamada neighbors in 1926-1939, they earned only one-quarter more income from cocoons. Ōkamada farmers had higher cocoon yields per *tan* of mulberry (70 percent in 1926-1929, 23 percent in 1930-1934, and 51 percent in 1935-1939) and produced better

[25] Ōkamada's value of production per farm household was probably 5-10 percent higher than indicated here. The Yamanashi statistical yearbooks give no data on the number of farm households in the village, and I have calculated Ōkamada's value of production per household on the basis of *all* village households; the statistics for Naka Koma give number of farm households so that the difference between Ōkamada and Naka Koma is greater than 14 percent.

[26] *Yamanashi tōkeisho*, 1930-1939.

TABLE 4-3

Tan of Paddy Field and Rice Value of Production per Household
in Ōkamada, Naka Koma, and Yamanashi, 1906-1939

Year	Ōkamada[27]		Naka Koma		Yamanashi	
	Tan per Household	Value per Household	Tan per Household	Value per Household	Tan per Household	Value per Household
1906–09	8.97	—	4.28	113 yen	3.45	107 yen
1912–14	8.34	—	4.13	144	3.32	114
1915–18	8.15	307 yen	4.58	227	2.93	137
1919–21	8.16	419	4.60	369	2.94	231
1922–24	No data		No data		2.87	205
1925–29	8.15	491	4.22	288	2.79	182
1930–34	8.02	329	3.75	167	2.60	111
1935–39	7.79	654	3.60	295	2.60	201

Calculated from *Yamanashi tōkeisho*.

[27] *Tan* of land and value of production per household for Ōkamada were even greater than these data demonstrate. See footnote 25, above.

quality cocoons (as judged by the higher price Ōkamada sericulturalists received for their cocoons: 11 percent in 1930-
1934 and 5 percent in 1935-1939). The Ōkamada farmer's
superior techniques for growing mulberry and raising silkworms brought him greater yields and income per unit of
land from sericulture, and this and his winter grain production almost compensated for his much smaller area of dry
fields.[28]

AN INTERPRETATION OF YAMANASHI'S AGRICULTURAL DEVELOPMENT

What I am presenting here is what one might call a concentric circle or, given the geographic picture drawn above,
concentric triangle view of Yamanashi agriculture. The innermost triangle, made up of the core villages in the heart of
the Kōfu Basin, villages like Ōkamada and its five neighbors,
had the closest proximity to the best markets, the most advanced sericultural techniques, and the highest value of production; those communities in the next triangle, on the outer
fringes of the basin and along the river valleys of Kita and

---

[28] Some readers may wonder why, if Ōkamada farmers had farms 80
percent larger and earned as high or higher value of production per *tan* for
all three major crops than their Zaikezuka compatriots, Ōkamada farm income was only 21-58 percent greater per farm worker than Zaikezuka's (see
footnote 2). The answer is that Zaikezuka farmers, by committing more of
their land and work time to sericulture, Yamanashi's most profitable cash
crop, partly compensated for their lower productivity and smaller farms.
Zaikezuka's less prosperous farmers thus took greater risks, although cultivators in neither village chose "safety first." See James C. Scott, *The Moral
Economy of the Peasant*, for a discussion of this principle, under which the
tiller "prefers to minimize the probability of having a disaster rather than
maximizing his average return" by cultivating subsistence rather than cash
crops. Scott, pp. 17-18. Scott's "safety first" principle is not universally
accepted. James A. Roumasset argues, for example, that there is no evidence
to support the assumptions either that the most profitable techniques of rice
production are more risky than the traditional ones or that fear of risk in-
hibits acceptance of techniques which maximize expected profits. *Rice and
Risk: Decision Making among Low-Income Farmers* (Oxford, 1976), p. 3.

Minami Koma counties, villages like Zaikezuka and its six neighbors in Midai, had the next best position, techniques, and value of production; villages in areas like Minami Tsuru, which by the 1920s had become an agricultural backwater, had inferior techniques, lower yields, and a smaller value of production. When one compares sericultural data for Yamanashi Prefecture, the complete triangle, for Naka Koma, which contained villages in the two inner triangles, and for Ōkamada in the center, the differences in productivity became readily apparent.

Table 4-4 contains data on cocoon yields and cocoon income per *tan* of mulberry planted in Ōkamada, Naka Koma, and Yamanashi. It indicates that consistently from 1926 to 1939, the years for which we have sericultural information for Ōkamada, yields and income per *tan* in the innermost triangle ran ahead of those in the middle and interior triangles combined, and far ahead of those for all three triangles together. In fact, as Table 4-5 reveals, Ōkamada farm house-

TABLE 4-4

Cocoon Yields (in *Kan*) and Income (in *Yen*) per *Tan* of Mulberry Planted, Ōkamada, Naka Koma, and Yamanashi, 1923-1939

	Ōkamada		Naka Koma		Yamanashi	
Year	Yields (kan)	Income (yen)	Yields (kan)	Income (yen)	Yields (kan)	Income (yen)
1923-27	No data		24.3	193	18.2	142
1926-29	34.0	227	25.1	170	18.4	119
1930-34	28.6	96	25.4	88	18.9	62
1935-39	36.6	227[29]	28.6	172	21.3	125

Calculated from *Yamanashi tōkeisho*.

[29] When calculated in real terms, the fluctuations in income from cocoons are not as great as they seem here. Ōkamada's real cocoon income dropped by 47 percent, not 58 percent, between 1926-1929 and 1930-1934, and recovered by 96 percent, not 136 percent, in 1935-1939.

TABLE 4-5

Average Income from Cocoons, and *Tan* of Land Planted in
Mulberry, per Sericultural Household in Ōkamada, Naka Koma,
and Yamanashi, 1923-1939

Year	Ōkamada		Naka Koma		Yamanashi	
	Income (yen)	Area (tan)	Income (yen)	Area (tan)	Income (yen)	Area (tan)
1923-27	No data		657	3.4	425	3.0
1926-29	512	2.3	599	3.5	390	3.3
1930-34	278	2.9	332	3.8	225	3.7
1935-39	633	2.8	651	3.8	446	3.6

Calculated from *Yamanashi tōkeisho.*

holds, in spite of planting fewer fields in mulberry, made ·
much more income from cocoons than Yamanashi sericultural households. In other words, households in peripheral
villages located outside Yamanashi's highly commercialized
core region did not make up through sericulture what they
lost in rice. Although farmers in villages like Ōkamada in
the inner triangle did not plant as much land in mulberry as
those in the two outer triangles, they received more income
per *tan* than their "outer" compeers. Sericulture reinforced
rather than undermined the economic advantage that the
core farmers held.

Table 4-6 introduces calculations of the value of production of rice, cocoons, and *mugi,* the three major crops, combined per household in Ōkamada and Naka Koma for the
years from 1926 to 1939, and discloses some startling results.
Ōkamada's value of production per household (keep in mind
that these data overstate the number of Ōkamada farm
households and thus understate its value of production per
household) for the three primary crops increased from 18
percent more in 1926-1929 and 1930-1934, to 44 percent
more in 1935-1939, than the value of production for all of
Naka Koma County. When one views these data in the light

TABLE 4-6

Value of Production in *Yen* and an Index of Real Value
of Production per Household for Rice, Cocoons, and
Mugi in Ōkamada and Naka Koma, 1926-1939

Year	Ōkamada		Naka Koma*	
	Value	Index	Value	Index
1926-29	948 yen	118	803 yen	100
1930-34	601	94	511	80
1935-39	1,330	173	924	120

* 100 = Naka Koma, 1926-1929
Calculated from *Yamanashi tōkeisho*.

of those presented in Table 2-10 which show that Naka Koma's value of production per household surpassed the prefectural average at the beginning of World War I and reached a level 64 percent higher in 1939, Ōkamada's growth is even more striking. The evidence indicates that while agricultural income grew only slowly if at all in the outer triangle of our region, it grew steadily in the middle triangle, and rapidly in the inner triangle. The highly commercialized and dispute-prone core region of Yamanashi, with its proximity to markets and transportation and its superior sericultural technology, seems in the 1920s to have achieved the highest value of production per household of any region in Yamanashi.

One might be tempted here to question whether Ōkamada's greater value of production reflects its farmers' higher levels of technology and labor productivity, or simply the ability of its households to mobilize more agricultural workers to operate larger farms. After all, as Table 4-7 shows, the average Ōkamada farm household tilled 30-40 percent more land than the average Naka Koma one. If Ōkamada's farms required and supported 30-40 percent more workers each, then its labor productivity would be no higher than the county's, and my concentric-triangle argument would be weakened. Our only sources for agricultural workers in both

TABLE 4-7
Average Farm Size in Ōkamada and Naka Koma, 1915-1939

Year	A Ōkamada	B Naka Koma	A/B
1915-18	10.47 *tan*	7.98 *tan*	131
1919-21	10.53	8.06	131
1925-29	10.70	7.64	140
1930-34	10.86	7.89	138
1935-39	10.75	7.86	137

Calculated from *Yamanashi tōkeisho*.

Ōkamada and Naka Koma, the national censuses of 1920 and 1930, do not indicate the number of agricultural households.[30] Nevertheless, by dividing the value of rice, *mugi*, and cocoon production for the two jurisdictions in 1930, as presented in the prefectural statistical annual, by the number of agricultural workers, as presented in the census, we can determine the value of production per worker for the three basic crops.[31] In 1930, each Ōkamada worker produced 188 yen worth of the three crops, compared to 161 yen for the average county worker, an advantage of 17 percent. (Each Ōkamada worker also produced a value of production 30 percent higher than his Zaikezuka counterpart.)[32] If we compare the 1930 data for farm workers with 1926-1929 and 1930-1934 value-of-production statistics, as shown in Table 4-8, we find that the average Ōkamada farmer outproduced

[30] The Yamanashi prefectural statistical yearbooks give data on agricultural households and workers for counties, but not for towns and villages.

[31] The prefectural statistical yearbooks give only sporadic data for the value of crops other than rice, *mugi*, mulberry, and cocoons at the village level. Since in the years for which we have data, these crops produced about 10 percent of the total value of agricultural production, our calculations give a fairly good idea of labor productivity.

[32] Although the national government conducted prewar censuses in 1920, 1925, 1930, and 1935, only the decennial censuses provide information about the work force.

TABLE 4-8

Average Value of Production in *Yen* of Rice, *Mugi*, and Cocoons,
and Agricultural Workers Compared for Naka Koma and
Ōkamada, 1926-1929 and 1930-1934

Year and Place	Annual Value of Production	Agricultural Workers	Annual Value per Worker
1926-1929			
Naka Koma	9,237,809 *yen*	33,317	277 *yen*
Ōkamada	227,548	687	331
1930-1934			
Naka Koma	5,897,385	33,317	177
Ōkamada	144,198	687	210

Calculated from *Yamanashi tōkeisho*, 1926-1934, and *Kokusei chōsa hōkoku*, 1930.

the average Naka Koma farmer by 19 percent in both 1926-1929 and 1930-1934. Thus, Ōkamada's larger labor force accounted for only part of its advantage; both output per unit of land and per agricultural worker were greater in Ōkamada than in Naka Koma as a whole.

The value of production of Ōkamada farmers expanded not only because they worked more land and adopted better farming techniques, but also because they took advantage of the profits to be gained from sericulture by turning their dry fields and then some of their rice paddies into mulberry orchards. Because sericulture brought greater profits and cost lower rents than any other kind of agriculture, a shift to increased mulberry cultivation made sense. Ōkamada mulberry acreage grew from practically nothing at the turn of the century to 2.8-2.9 *tan* per household, representing 95 percent or more of each household's dry fields, in the 1930s. Over the same period, the acreage of paddy per household fell from 8.97 *tan* to 7.79 *tan*; 13 percent of Ōkamada's rice paddies apparently became mulberry orchards.

Given the apparent advantages of cocoons, one might

question why Ōkamada farmers did not transform even more of their paddies into mulberry orchards in the 1920s and 1930s.[33] A number of possible explanations can be adduced, but which ones are more important is difficult to assay. First, Ōkamada farmers had more productive mulberry orchards than did Naka Koma and Yamanashi sericulturalists; between 1925 and 1939, the average yield of a *tan* of Ōkamada mulberry orchard was 418 *kan*, compared to 375 *kan* in Naka Koma and 286 *kan* in Yamanashi as a whole. In Ōkamada 2.8 *tan* of orchard produced as much edible mulberry as did 3.8 *tan* in other parts of the prefecture; thus, Ōkamada sericulturalists, by stretching their mulberry further than did their counterparts in the outer triangles, did not need to plant as much of it.

Second, before the mid-1920s, when tenants through collective action successfully began to win the right to grow semi-permanent crops like mulberry in paddies, they often needed landlord permission to remake fields from paddy to dry. Needless to say, landlords hesitated to approve modifications which lowered their income. Third, farmers may also have hesitated to shift to mulberry because they could not harvest full crops for three or four years. Thus, some poorer farmers may have feared the short-term losses of income more than they anticipated the long-term profits. Because of these fears and because they tilled 25-30 separate parcels of land per household, Ōkamada farmers most likely moved to mulberry slowly, one piece of land every few years; this would explain the very gradual transformation of rice paddy into mulberry orchard.

Fourth, without accepting the moral economists' argument that peasants prefer tradition and security to innova-

[33] Since Ōkamada farmers produced 19 percent more cocoons, but only 11 percent more mulberry leaves, per *tan* of mulberry than average Naka Koma farmers, it is possible that the Ōkamada sericulturalist bought whatever extra mulberry he needed from farmers in neighboring villages rather than increase his own mulberry acreage. Unfortunately, we have no evidence to prove or disprove this possibility.

tion, profit, and "danger," one can argue, I think, that what we may see here are farmers weighing the potential financial benefits in sericulture not only against its costs but also against its risks, and deciding on a steady but slow transition to mulberry. Cocoons bring great profits, but, because they depend on foreign demand and cannot be eaten when prices fall, they are chancy. Farmers will gamble, but rationally they will bet only a small part of their stake at one time.[34]

Fifth, the cultivation of *mugi* as a second crop on rice paddies grew steadily in Ōkamada in the 1920s and 1930s; in 1925-1929, farmers grew winter wheat on 30 percent of the village's paddy; by 1935-1939, because of better drainage, they double-cropped 48 percent of its paddy. As the cultivation of rice paddy land became more profitable, the advantage to be gained from switching to mulberry production decreased, lessening the impulse to gamble and thus slowing the transition.

Sixth, Ōkamada encountered a shortage of labor in the interwar decades. Although the number of people per household, and therefore probably the number of agricultural workers per household, was greater in Ōkamada than in Zaikezuka (5.84 to 5.31 in 1930), the difference in farm size was even larger (10.7 to 5.8 *tan*); an Ōkamada farm household had only 10 percent more members, but over 80 percent more land. Thus, Ōkamada farmers spread their labor more thinly over a larger area. Although they had more capital and employed more progressive farming techniques compared to their fathers, grandfathers, and upland neighbors, Ōkamada cultivators used very little inanimate energy, and this limited the amount of land that even the most advanced and hard-

---

[34] Scott, in arguing the "safety first" principle, writes that "typically, the peasant cultivator seeks to avoid the failure that will ruin him rather than attempting a big, but risky, killing" (p. 4). Scott implies, therefore, that the peasant's choice is risk *or* security. Our tenant farmers, however, chose an intermediate position. By converting some of their fields to the profitable and risky sericulture, while keeping others in the less profitable and more secure rice, they chose risk *and* security.

working farmer could till successfully.[35] Cocoon production especially aggravated this labor problem because it demanded very intensive labor inputs during the three thirty-day silkworm-raising periods each year. Farmers in Zaikezuka, however, could afford to cultivate more mulberry and feed more silkworms because their small farms, hilly fields, and inadequate irrigation made it difficult for them to cultivate rice, and forced them to grow the less profitable *mugi* before the development of the basin's raw silk industry in the late Meiji period. Ironically, in spite of their advantage in workers per *tan* of arable land, Zaikezuka tillers, even after they converted their *mugi* fields to mulberry orchards, could not match their Ōkamada brethren in productivity. Or, stated the other way around, each individual farm worker in Ōkamada cultivated an area of land more than half again as large as each Zaikezuka farmer, but still tilled it more productively.[36] Unless Ōkamada farmers could introduce dramatically new labor-saving technology—gasoline-powered tractors or electric silkworm incubators, for example—they neared the limits of their productivity in the 1930s. The shift to mulberry and cocoons, marked as it was in Ōkamada, was slowed by the dearth of available labor.[37]

[35] Few Ōkamada farmers owned power tools of any sort before World War II. As late as 1958, only the following number of Kubo Nakajima households (of 40) owned power tools: thresher 29, gas motor 24, hand huller 20, cutter 9, electric motor 7, three-wheeled truck 5, cultivator (hand-operated tractor) 1.

[36] I do not mean to imply here that Ōkamada's farmers worked harder than Zaikezuka's or Tsuru County's. The key to Ōkamada's success must have been capital. Because the village's farmers had larger yields and earned more income from their crops, they had more money to buy fertilizer, seeds, tools, and weed killers than did their counterparts in Zaikezuka and Tsuru. Greater expenditures on these inputs led in turn to even greater yields and income, and thus to even larger future inputs. Greater access to outside markets and transportation, discussed above in Chapter Two, is what must have given rise in the late nineteenth and early twentieth centuries to Ōkamada's advantage in the first place.

[37] The development of this kind of equipment, of course, is exactly what happened from the late 1950s on. The invention of low-cost, inanimately

Finally, Ōkamada farmers probably made the transition to sericulture slowly not only because cocoons demanded intensive labor, but also because they exacted that intensive labor seasonally. The sericultural household needed a large work force for three separate thirty-day periods during the farming year, but required far less labor for the other five or six months of the agricultural cycle. Thus, Ōkamada farm households, with their extensive rice paddies, employed their work force effectively by fitting the labor-intensive cocoon-raising periods into the relative lulls in the rice-growing cycle; one cocoon crop just before rice transplanting, one after weeding of the rice paddies, and one just before the rice harvest. By adjusting the rate of their transition to sericulture to the speed at which its technology evolved, Ōkamada farmers mitigated the problem of supporting excess, seasonally unproductive, labor. Zaikezuka farmers, conversely, favored by a relative proximity to good markets (much closer and better than Minami Tsuru, but farther and less good than Ōkamada), but handicapped by their small farms, limited rice paddy, and underemployed labor, probably turned to more extensive mulberry cultivation and sericulture in order to solve a problem of *excess* labor.[38] Since Zaikezuka

---

powered equipment, the spread of owner farming after the land reform, government agricultural subsidies, and more highly capitalized cooperatives allowed farmers to own singly or jointly power tillers, rice-transplanting machines, and a host of other labor-saving devices. The sericultural cooperative of Niiharu, one of the Gumma Prefecture villages visited in 1977, for example, owned incubators and automatic machinery for feeding silkworms in the first 10-15 days of their month-long cycle, which cost over one hundred thousand U.S. dollars in the mid-1970s. Since Niiharu had four silkworm seasons, cooperative members used the equipment only eight weeks per year. Neither the technology nor the capital was available to develop or buy this kind of labor-saving machinery in the 1920s and 1930s.

[38] The Yamanashi Electric Railroad, which ran from Kōfu to Aoyagi in Minami Koma County by way of the Midai plateau villages, opened for service in December 1932. This brought Zaikezuka and its neighboring villages into closer contact with Kōfu, the prefectural center for administration, markets, and capital. Nevertheless, Zaikezuka already in the 1920s had been drawn into Kōfu's network by roads, busses, and trucks.

farmers tilled mostly dry fields, the non-mulberry produce of which used the least labor and earned the least return of any major crop, the transition to sericulture allowed them to increase income by using their underemployed labor force fully for *at least* three months of the farming year. Ōkamada's farm households were larger than Zaikezuka's, but they still faced a labor shortage, especially during the labor-intensive cocoon-raising periods, and this impeded the speed with which they made their paddy fields into mulberry orchards.

In the absence of tools powered by gasoline or electricity, one source of additional energy still existed for Ōkamada in the 1920s and 1930s: the labor of local permanent residents who left the village either semi-permanently or daily to work in non-agricultural jobs. In other words, given the village's relatively profitable farms and shortage of agricultural labor, one would expect far fewer members of Ōkamada than Naka Koma or Zaikezuka families to work in Tokyo and Yokohama factories, or Kōfu, Kokubo, and Suwa filatures. The evidence here indicates a split decision: Ōkamadans filled more semi-permanent, but fewer daily, industrial jobs than Naka Koma people. All in all, a greater share of Ōkamada's adults tilled the soil, and a lesser percentage worked in non-agricultural jobs than in Naka Koma as a whole; still, industrial and commercial employ supplemented the income of Ōkamada's households. In fact, given Ōkamada's paucity of cultivators, it comes as something of a surprise that large numbers of villagers lived and toiled away from home.

Table 4-9 shows the size of the permanently registered (*honseki*) and actual populations of the county and the village; the number of people whose *honseki* was in Naka Koma and Ōkamada, but who lived elsewhere, expanded steadily between 1900 and 1937, but apparently grew more rapidly in Ōkamada. I write "apparently" because for two reasons we must be wary of drawing facile conclusions from this evidence. First, the statistics on actual population include not only people whose place of permanent registration was in Naka Koma and Ōkamada, but also those whose place of

TABLE 4-9

Permanent Registrants and Actual Population Living in
Naka Koma and Ōkamada Compared, 1900-1937

Year	Naka Koma			Ōkamada		
	A Permanent	B Actual	B/A	C Permanent	D Actual	D/C
1900-04	80,967	77,821	96%	1,412	1,338	95%
1913-16	94,281	87,076	92	1,694	1,488	88
1917-21	100,426	89,771	89	1,765	1,400	79
1925-29	109,172	94,449	87	1,921	1,404	73
1930-34	116,133	97,468	84	2,078	1,505	72
1935-37	119,969	96,483	80	2,212	1,533	69

Calculated from *Yamanashi tōkeisho.*

permanent registration was elsewhere and who migrated *into*
Naka Koma and Ōkamada to live and work. The table,
therefore, does not present a completely reliable comparison
of non-agricultural employment elsewhere since many of the
county's villages housed large filatures which attracted outsiders, but Ōkamada housed and attracted none of either.
Second, we compare here kumquats and oranges; that is, we
contrast Ōkamada, one village, with a county of forty-one
villages. There must have been many Naka Koma people
who lived away from their *honseki* communities, but still
within the county; although they did not live at home, they
would have been adumbrated in both the permanent and the
actual population columns, thus skewing our comparison.
Nevertheless, Ōkamada families still appear to have had a
higher percentage of non-resident members than did Naka
Koma ones. Other data, for 1925-1926, show that 20 percent
of the permanently registered men and women in the county
lived outside their home villages.[39] Since Ōkamada's actual
population was 27 percent smaller than its permanently reg-

[39] *Yamanashi tōkeisho,* 1925, p. 96; 1926, p. 98.

istered population in 1925-1926, presumably Ōkamada households had about one-third more members living elsewhere, working at non-agricultural jobs and receiving non-farm income.

In contrast, Ōkamada, in spite of its proximity to transportation and filatures, lagged behind both Naka Koma and Zaikezuka in providing non-agricultural workers who lived at home and commuted to their jobs, as Table 4-10 indicates. But, as Table 4-10 also shows, the centrally located "six villages of eastern Naka Koma" in toto provided about the same percentage of resident non-agricultural workers as all of Zaikezuka's upland "seven villages of Midai" combined.

TABLE 4-10

Resident Workers and the Number and Percentage of Resident Workers in Non-Agricultural Jobs in Naka Koma and Selected Regions and Villages within Naka Koma, 1930

Village or Region	A Non-Agricultural Workers	B Resident Workers	A/B
Naka Koma	14,116	47,433	30%[40]
6 Eastern Villages	2,283	9,122	25
Ōkamada	99	786	13
Kokubo	1,219	2,014	61
7 Midai Villages	1,487	5,914	25
Zaikezuka	337	946	36
Hyakuda	230	1,528	15

Calculated from *Kokusei chōsa hōkoku*, 1930.

[40] Naka Koma as a whole provided a higher percentage of resident factory workers in its work force than did the six eastern or seven Midai villages because many filatures were located in or near Ryūō, the village which housed the Chūō Line station immediately to the west of Kōfu. Since this station had opened in 1903, almost three decades before the Minobu and Yamanashi Electric lines were completed, Kōfu's western suburbs developed filatures more quickly than its southern ones.

What we find in this data, in fact, are striking contrasts from village to village within the two regions. In eastern Naka Koma, only 13 percent of Ōkamada's, but 61 percent of neighboring Kokubo's, work force held non-agricultural jobs; in the Midai villages, fully 36 percent of Zaikezuka's, but only 15 percent of neighboring Hyakuda's, work force held non-agricultural jobs. The reason for these differences is simple enough to explain. Kokubo and Zaikezuka housed filatures in 1930, and Ōkamada and Hyakuda did not. What these data show are what other evidence confirms. Naka Koma benefited from two clusters of filatures, a larger one in villages like Kokubo with its Kanebō facility in the outskirts of Kōfu, and a smaller one on a north-south line from Nirasaki in Kita Koma County in the north, through the Midai region in Naka Koma to Kajikazawa in Minami Koma County in the south (see Map). People who traveled to filatures daily tended to work in mills in their home villages rather than commute even moderate distances.[41]

People in both the eastern Naka Koma and the Midai regions gained considerable and increasing income from jobs in local silk-reeling mills. Between 1920 and 1930, the number of industrial jobs in the eastern Naka Koma villages grew by 23 percent, in the Midai by 9 percent, and, not surprisingly, in the remote Minami Tsuru they decreased by 39 percent.[42] Farm households in villages like Ōkamada and Hyakuda may not have provided many workers for the bur-

[41] Although the census does not indicate how many Kokubo filature workers came from local farm families of long standing, apparently many were newcomers. But the Kanebō mill in Kokubo still differed from the "infamous" dormitory-style filatures elsewhere in that it seemed to attract whole families, not individual workers, to the village. Between 1920 and 1930, Kokubo's industrial workers increased by 100, from 695 to 795, its resident households also by 100, from 609 to 709, and its average household size by 0.26 people per household, from 5.19 to 5.45. In 1930, the average household size in predominately industrial Kokubo was larger than in predominately agricultural Ōkamada (5.45 to 5.40 people per household). *Kokusei chōsa hōkoku*, Yamanashi volume.

[42] *Kokusei chōsa hōkoku*, Yamanashi volume.

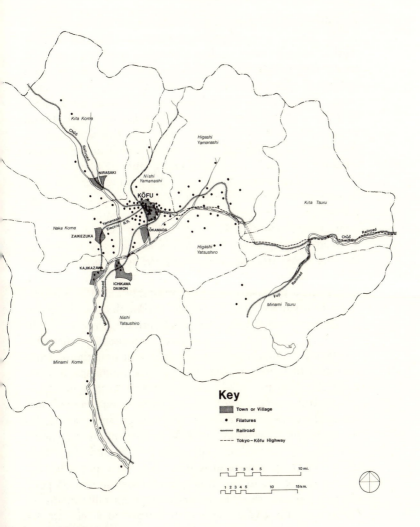

Key

    ▨ Town or Village

    • Filatures

    ⌇⌇⌇ Railroad

    - - - - Tokyo–Kōfu Highway

Kita Koma

Higashi
Yamanashi

NIRASAKI

Nishi
Yamanashi

KŌFU

Kita Tsuru

Naka Koma

ZAIKEZUKA

ŌKAMADA

Higashi
Yatsushiro

Chūō Railroad

KAJIKAZAWA

ICHIKAWA
DAIMON

Minami Tsuru

Nishi
Yatsushiro

Minami Koma

atures and Railroads in
manashi Prefecture

geoning filatures, but they benefited agriculturally because of the demand for cocoons that these raw-silk-spinning facilities created. And, finally, although Ōkamada sent relatively few people daily to work in factories (it did send some), 27 percent of its registered population lived elsewhere. One surmises that Ōkamada's demands for agricultural labor checked the tendency of its residents to commute to industrial jobs. One conjectures from Kokubo's experience that this would not have been the case if there had been a filature physically within Ōkamada. But one also concludes that the village's farm labor needs did not prevent over one-quarter of its permanent population from living and working elsewhere.

In the post-World War I period, not even a dearth of workers could prevent farmers in Ōkamada and the rest of the innermost triangle from tilling the soil more profitably than did farmers in Zaikezuka and the intermediate triangle, who in turn produced far more profitably than those in Minami Tsuru and the outer triangle. Although the tightness of the labor market did slow Ōkamada's transition from rice to sericulture, and thus to even greater agricultural profits, this shortage did not prevent Ōkamada's farm households from enlarging their total income through a combination of agricultural production and non-agricultural employment. In other words, what we see here are farmers, within the limits imposed by custom, landlords, technology, and available labor and capital, weighing alternative economic possibilities, and making rational choices about profit and risk. Rice brings much greater returns than *mugi*. Rice price fluctuations endanger household living levels less than cocoon price changes because rice can be eaten if prices fall too much. Cocoons bring greater returns than rice and *mugi*, but demand more labor seasonally. Cocoons lessen tenant dependency on landlords. Non-agricultural employ usually brings greater returns than rice, *mugi*, or even cocoons. Rice production meets a domestic demand which is less volatile than the demand for raw silk, which is foreign. When the Ōkamada farmer, with his somewhat larger farm, available capital, superior techniques, and relative closeness to markets and by-employment weighed all of these and other possibilities, he decided on a changing but balanced portfolio: rice, cocoons, by-employ, some vegetables, and *mugi*. He was a "rational farmer," not a "moral economist," but rationality required that the Ōkamada farmer balance profit and security.

His Zaikezuka counterpart undoubtedly made equally rational decisions, but he had more limited choices. A scarcity of land precluded larger farms, and topography and water supply allowed only token rice cultivation. The resultant lower value of production per household and per worker retarded capital formation and thus the introduction of new sericultural techniques and more extensive use of chemical fertilizer in mulberry orchards, which in turn perpetuated the lower value of production. On the other hand, proximity to filatures allowed the Zaikezuka farmer to earn non-agricultural income and to turn the majority of his fields into mulberry orchards. Since filature jobs and sericulture did not make up the difference completely, many Zaikezuka farmers also traveled as itinerant peddlers, but, even so, their levels of living and those of the middle triangle in general could not match those in Ōkamada and its neighboring villages. Nevertheless, Zaikezuka had a much higher standard of living than did villages in Minami Tsuru, which had few jobs in modern filatures, little modern sericulture, and practically no rice. Ōkamada and its neighbors had more tenancy disputes than Zaikezuka and the Midai; the upland Naka Koma villages, in turn, had far more tenancy and tenancy disputes than did the Tsuru region.

Social Stratification in Kubo Nakajima Hamlet

I have emphasized so far economic change in rural Japan as a cause of tenancy disputes. Now I would like to introduce a social ingredient in the chemistry of the Yamanashi farmers' movement, an element I have already hinted at earlier in the chapter: social stratification as a deterrent rather than as a cause of tenancy disputes. In my argument so far, I have challenged the standard interpretation by emphasizing agriculture for the market and *higher* levels of living as the primary causes of disputes. I would like here to introduce another point which challenges orthodoxy, namely, that the tenant farmers' movement was stronger and more successful in egalitarian than in hierarchical communities. In Ōkamada, for example, Kubo Nakajima had a tightly organized tenant union which successfully battled its landlords from 1921 until 1948, while Futsuka Ichiba had a loose, weak union with less endurance. From feudal times, Kubo Nakajima was a relatively egalitarian hamlet without big resident landlords; the villagers used their cooperative labor organization (*uma aite*), which had no powerful landlord leaders, as the basis for successful union organization. Futsuka Ichiba, on the other hand, was highly stratified, with one family, the Mikami, in command; its economic, social, and political power impeded the rise of the tenant farmer movement.[43] Still, the predominance of Futsuka Ichiba's landlord in modern times did not prevent the hamlet's farmers from improving their standard of living by producing for the market, nor from benefiting from their own moderate and others' more vigorous anti-landlord activities. On the one hand, for example, the Futsuka Ichiba ancestor of Fukada Hiroshi owned practically no land in 1870 (his *kokudaka* was 0.2 *koku*), but by the 1930s Hiroshi had become an owner tenant farmer who

[43] Waswo, drawing on Ushiyama Keiji, *Nōminsō bunkai no kōzō, senzenki: Niigata-ken Kambara nōson no bunseki* (Tokyo, 1975), pp. 100-101, argues persuasively that tenant unions were more frequent in "headless" communities, that is, those where "few if any landlords were in residence." Kubo Nakajima, with its semi-absentee landlords, fits into this category. She says nothing, however, about the effects of degree of equality of landholding among the farm households which actually resided in the communities. "In Search of Equity," p. 377.

owned 9.5 *tan* of land and rented in another 5 *tan* to create a farm of 14.5 *tan*. When he died in 1977, Fukada and his son owned 2,500 pigs. On the other hand, a 1927 survey of tenant disputes shows that both nationally and in eastern Naka Koma non-participants living in villages next to disputing villages received rent reductions of about one-half to two-thirds the size of those won by disputants themselves, and a 1930 Agriculture Ministry report indicates that through mediation "sixty-six" Futsuka Ichiba tenants (some were counted more than once since they dealt with more than one landlord) received rent reductions of 25 percent from four landlords.[44] On the basis of such evidence, I shall argue that more contentious tenant organizations tended to arise in hamlets with improving levels of living and relatively egalitarian social structures, but that disputes also conferred benefits on highly stratified hamlets with weaker or no unions. To set the stage for making this argument, I would like now to focus my attention on economic, political, and social change in the relatively egalitarian Kubo Nakajima.

Thirty-eight farm households cultivated 45 *chō* of arable land in twentieth-century Kubo Nakajima. Because the central basin's network of rivers provided ample water and the modern water control system allowed increasingly good drainage and flood protection, Kubo Nakajima, like its surrounding hamlets in the central basin, planted most of its land in rice. In the 1930s, paddy took up 32 of the hamlet's 45 *chō*, over 70 percent, and villagers cultivated mulberry in almost all of the rest.[45]

As with the whole of Ōkamada Village, Kubo Nakajima's

---

[44] Interviews at his farm with Fukada Hiroshi, July 3, 1969 and June 17, 1977; *KNJ*, p. 157; questionnaire completed by Fukada, July 1969; Teikoku nōkai chōsabu, *Kosaku sōgichi oyobi sono rinsetsuchi ni okeru kosakuryō narabi tochi baibai kakaku no hendō ni kansuru chōsa* (Tokyo, 1927), a mimeographed report of a survey of rent reductions in 528 disputing and neighboring villages in 41 prefectures, p. 11; *Kosaku sōgi oyobi chōtei jirei*, 1929, pp. 557–559. Oddly, one finds this 1930 mediation case in the 1929 issue of the annual; the actual date of publication appears nowhere in the volume.

[45] *KNJ*, pp. 2, 8-9, 13.

combination of paddies planted in rice and *mugi* and increasing cocoon yields seem to have led to a remarkable growth in the hamlet's value of production. Our sparse evidence for yields shows that, as in Ōkamada and Naka Koma, Kubo Nakajima farmers improved their productivity sharply in the late nineteenth and early twentieth centuries. (See Table 4-11.) Between 1887 and 1933, rice yields increased by 81 percent, *mugi* yields by 49 percent and cocoon yields by 136 percent.[46] Assuming that the price fluctuations for agricultural commodities in Kubo Nakajima paralleled those in the village and county, we can conclude that the hamlet's farmers benefited greatly from their augmented yields.

Nineteenth- and twentieth-century Kubo Nakajima farm households profited not only from harvesting larger yields per *tan*, but also from extending their arable land and from intensifying its use. An improved flood-control system near the hamlet, which as its name denotes was located on low-lying land between two streams, allowed the reclamation of unused wasteland. Although the number of households in the hamlet was the same in the 1930s as in the 1870s, the area

TABLE 4-11

Rice and *Mugi* Yields per *Tan* Planted and Cocoon Yields per *Tan* of Mulberry Planted in Kubo Nakajima, 1887-1933

Year	Rice	Mugi	Cocoons
1887	1.48 *koku*	1.1 *koku*	7.8 *kan*
1902	1.62	1.0	6.0
1912	2.08	1.67	14.1
1933	2.68	1.64	18.4[46]

Source: Amemiya, footnote 49, pp. 155-156.

[46] Given the cocoon output for Ōkamada as a whole, 28.6 *kan* in 1930-1934 (see Table 4-4), Amemiya's 18.4 *kan* figure for 1933 must be wrong and Kubo Nakajima's cocoon output must have been considerably higher.

of land under cultivation grew by at least 40 percent.[47] In the late Tokugawa era, the hamlet's large number of undrainable fields precluded double cropping or harvesting exceptional rice crops. But the Meiji and Taishō period efforts at improving irrigation and drainage helped bring increases in rice harvests, as the yields reported in Table 4-11 attest, and permitted more extensive double cropping. At the time of the Ariga study in 1952-1954, Kubo Nakajima's farmers grew winter wheat on more than half of their paddies.[48]

The physical layout of Kubo Nakajima was (and still is) not dissimilar from most Japanese hamlets (see Map). In the center one found the residential village complete with a narrow main street, in this case the east-west Kokubo-Futsuka Ichiba road, lined with similar walled-off or hedged-off house-barn complexes, a few side alleys with more houses and barns, a stream and a network of irrigation ca-

[47] We have no hard data on area of land under cultivation in Kubo Nakajima for 1870; thus, I have estimated the area of land for the early Meiji period by the following procedure: the 1870 *kokudaka*, or assessed value of rice production, was 312.3 *koku*. The average national rice yield per *tan* in 1874 was 1.18 *koku* per *tan*. (*Chōki keizai tōkei*, Vol. 9, pp. 166, 216.) If we assume this production figure held for the hamlet, it contained about 26.5 *chō* of rice land in 1870. Since in 1906-1909, before farmers began to turn paddies into mulberry fields (see Table 4-3), 35 of Kubo Nakajima's 42½ *chō* were paddies, I calculate that 8.5 *chō* of paddy were reclaimed, an increase of 32 percent. If we assume a similar increase for dry land under cultivation, farmers reclaimed 10.3 *chō* of land between 1870 and the end of the Meiji period, and 12.8 *chō* between the 1870s and 1930s. One might argue, following James Nakamura, that the 1870 *kokudaka* understates production and thus paddy land; on the other hand, farmers in advanced areas like Kubo Nakajima undoubtedly produced more than 1.18 *koku* per *tan*, the national average in 1874. (See footnote 62 below for an estimate as high as 1.50 *koku* per *tan*.) Thus, if anything, Kubo Nakajima contained fewer than 32.2 *chō* of land in 1870, as low as Hattori's estimate of 21-22 *chō*. (See footnote 59 below.) There was a 38 percent increase in taxable land in Okamada as a whole between 1874 and 1892. Shimazaki Hironori, *Yamanashiken shigunsonshi* (Kōfu, 1977 reprint), pp. 152-153. Thus, it does not seem unreasonable to posit a 32 percent increase in arable land in Kubo Nakajima between 1870 and 1906-1909.

[48] Morioka, *Wagakuni*, p. 8.

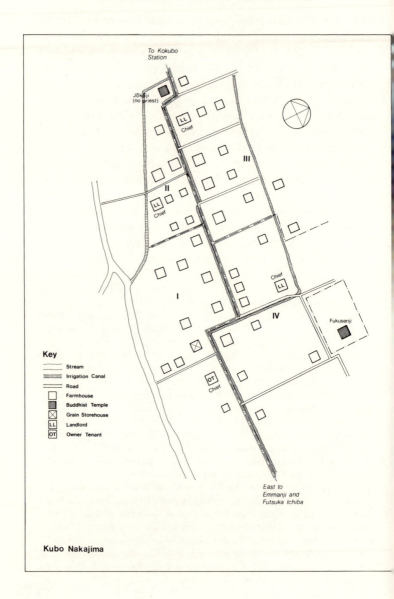

Key

‒‒‒‒‒	Stream
▦▦▦▦	Irrigation Canal
═══	Road
☐	Farmhouse
▦	Buddhist Temple
⊠	Grain Storehouse
LL	Landlord
OT	Owner Tenant

To Kokubo
Station

Jōkōji
(no priest)

LL
Chief

III

II

LL
Chief

I

Chief
LL

IV

Fukusenji

OT
Chief

East to
Emmanji and
Futsuka Ichiba

Kubo Nakajima

nals, a grain storehouse, and two Buddhist temples. (Unlike most hamlets, Kubo Nakajima had no discrete Shinto shrine.)[49] The hamlet was further divided into four subgroups (*kumi*). These clusters of ten, eight, twelve, and eleven households each provided the locus of most of the hamlet's cooperative labor.[50] Although the whole hamlet, excluding the three landlords, the one owner farmer, and the Shimizu at Fukusenji, functioned as one tightly knit, mutual self-help group, most of the actual labor exchange at the time of rice transplanting, harvesting, funerals, and weddings was done within the *kumi*. To carry out broader sub-hamlet-level functions, participation in the various agricultural associations, or upkeep of the roadside fertility statues (*dōsojin*), for example, the *kumi* merged to form two sub-hamlet organizations. Strangely, they combined differently for each job: in agriculture, I joined with II and III with IV into front (*omote*) and back (*ura*); in religion, I combined with IV and II with III into east and west. The four sub-groups also served as Kubo Nakajima's "neighborhood associations" during World War II.[51]

Again, as in hundreds of other Japanese hamlets, the place where the villagers actually earned their livelihoods, their plethora of small fields, ringed the central residential locale.[52] The average Kubo Nakajima farm household tilled 29-30 fields, which were scattered in various sections of the hamlet's acreage. Although we cannot recreate the layout of

---

[49] Fukusenji and its shrine to the kitchen god (*kōjindo*) provided the focus for the communal religious life of Kubo Nakajima farmers. Before the 1920s, one of the three small-scale landlords served as Fukusenji's "head of believers." After the tenant union took charge of hamlet political life, an owner tenant, union leader replaced one of the three Ishiharas as the hamlet's religious leader. Morioka, *Wagakuni*, p. 14.

[50] The Ariga group drew the map in the mid-1950s after two new postwar branches had brought the total number of Kubo Nakajima households from 39 to 41.

[51] *KNJ*, pp. 118-119.

[52] See Richard K. Beardsley et al., *Village Japan* (Chicago, 1959), pp. 147-148, for diagrams of the layout of a Japanese farm hamlet and its fields.

Kubo Nakajima's agricultural land in the 1930s, we can use a diagram taken from a 1934 Agriculture Ministry study of 13 farm households in Izumi Village near the Tone River in northern Saitama Prefecture, where, as in Kubo Nakajima, farmers specialized in rice and cocoons, to suggest the distribution of fields in our own hamlet (see Map). The farm household in this example tilled 24 fields, 15 rice paddies, 6 mulberry orchards, and 3 regular dry fields, an arrangement not unlike that in Kubo Nakajima. This Izumi farmer's 24 fields were scattered in 7 places among the hamlet's land, and he must have lost considerable work time in walking back and forth, especially to his more distant fields, which were over a quarter of a mile from his home and barn. We can see that farmers in prewar Izumi and, I think, in Kubo Nakajima and elsewhere as well, moved slowly in rearranging their fields in a more orderly fashion. The need for security from flood and drought seemed as important as efficiency. Our Izumi farmer, for example, tilled ten rice paddies in four locales (indicating some centralization) with good access to water, the prospect of good harvests in normal years, but the danger of flooding during typhoons or other excessively rainy weather. His five drier paddies, all in one cluster at the southern end of the hamlet, provided security against floods, but slightly lower harvests most of the time and the danger of even lower crop yields in drought years. Although local governments and regional entrepreneurs had built or improved flood control, drainage, and irrigation facilities in the late nineteenth and early twentieth centuries, the fear of flood and drought still slowed the farmer's reorganization of his arable land.[53] The cultivator in Kubo Nakajima, as in Izumi, practiced this balancing of efficiency with security; the rational farmer tried to increase his income, but without overly endangering his household's security.

Eight landlord families, four who lived in Kubo Nakajima and four who did not, dominated the hamlet economically,

---

[53] *Nōka rōdō chōsa hōkoku*, p. 8.

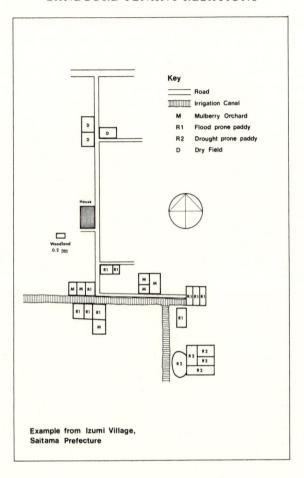

Example from Izumi Village,
Saitama Prefecture

politically, socially, and religiously before the land reform of
1948. The four resident landlords in the late Taishō period
all operated, as we have seen, on a small scale. Only Ishihara
Yasuzō (1), who rented out 4.7 *chō*, could be called a landlord. Ishihara Toshiharu (2), who leased out 1.62 *chō*, and
Ishihara Ichitarō (3), who rented out 0.3 *chō*, are more accurately described as owner farmers, and Shimizu Tsugu-

273

tama, the priest of Fukusenji who moved to the village from Kōfu's Kosenji Temple at the age of twenty-four in 1896, was a special case. His landholdings of 2.18 *chō* belonged to Fukusenji, the hamlet's primary religious institution, and their income provided his salary as Kubo Nakajima's priest. (In fact, after the postwar reformers confiscated Fukusenji's land, the villagers supported Shimizu by assessing each household.) All in all, three Ishiharas, each of whom cultivated a large farm himself, and Shimizu, who did not farm at all, owned 14.43 *chō* of the hamlet's land, about one-third of the total. If we deduct the 5.63 *chō* that the three Ishiharas owned and tilled, we find that the four resident landlords rented out 8.80 *chō* of land, about one-quarter of the total tenanted land in the hamlet.[54]

Most of the other three-quarters belonged to three "semi-absentee" and one absentee landlord. Mikami Saburō, the parasitologist of Futsuka Ichiba, owned 11.45 *chō*; Gemma Yoshinori, the sericulturalist of Emmanji who died in 1930 leaving an infant heir, owned 8.8 *chō*; Sakurabayashi Hokaku the fifth, the priest/doctor of Miyanohara who died in 1936, and his son the sixth, the priest/Ōkamada mayor/German professor, held 2.6 *chō*; Saburō's cousin Hatsu, whose adopted husband Akira managed a bank in Yokohama, owned 0.9 *chō*. The rest of Kubo Nakajima's tenanted land belonged to the two owner tenants mentioned above, Ishihara Taizō (4) and Ishihara Toyokichi (12) (8.4 *tan* in toto) and to the descendants of Wakao Ippei (a few *tan*). The Wakao land fell into the hands of his tenants when the Wakao's financial empire collapsed in 1928.[55]

The largest and most powerful landlords in Kubo Nakajima, therefore, were the three "semi-absentees," Mikami Saburō, Gemma Yoshinori (and, after 1930, his cousin Hideyoshi, who stepped in as temporary household head), and Sakurabayashi Hokaku, father and son, each of whom

[54] *KNJ*, pp. 20, 48, 162; Amemiya, footnote 68, p. 159.
[55] *KNJ*, pp. 19-20, 88, 162; Amemiya, footnote 68, p. 159.

274

ranked among Ōkamada's five largest landowners. These households owned 23 *chō*, just over half of the hamlet's land, and cultivated none of it. And yet, although they were fairly large-scale landlords and neither lived in nor tilled in Kubo Nakajima, the three resided in the same village, performed most of the functions of resident landlords, and thus cannot be classified as "parasitical landlords," the bête noire of scholars of the prewar countryside. Unlike the archetypal non-cultivating absentee landlord who did not live in the same village as his tenants, did not maintain paternalistic patron-client ties there, often resided in the city and invested in non-agricultural businesses or the stock market, had little interest in agricultural development, and charged his tenants exorbitant rents which he coolly calculated as investments, and gave nothing in return, all three lived in Ōkamada and contributed greatly to its well-being.[56] Admittedly, none of these households tilled more land than a small garden plot of a few *tan*, but one of them at least, the Gemma, involved itself in the village's agricultural life. As we have seen, Gemma Yoshinori founded Ōkamada's sericultural cooperative in 1916 and invested much of his time and money in a cocoon storage facility for the village. His cousin, Hideyoshi directed the village's farm and credit cooperatives after World War I, served on its public works committee, and became head of the county-wide agricultural society in 1922.

All three households made important non-agricultural contributions to Kubo Nakajima's life. On the psychic level, Mikami Saburō, Gemma Yoshinori, and Gemma Hideyoshi all enlisted clients in Kubo Nakajima although it was not their home hamlet. On the social service level, Mikami Sa-

---

[56] See Waswo, *Japanese Landlords*, pp. 81-93, and Nakamura Masanori, *Jinushiseishi kenkyū*, pp. 119-181, for discussions of the rise of absentee landlordism in Japan. Waswo, who unlike Nakamura does not excoriate landlords, writes that absentee landlords charged lower rents and made greater concessions to disputing tenants than did the resident landlords. Her description of the absentees' lack of interest in agriculture and agricultural improvement is similar to Nakamura's.

burō and Sakurabayashi Hokaku (the fifth) both worked as school doctors at the village's elementary school and devoted themselves to the study of the lethal Japanese blood parasite disease, which particularly attacked farmers who spent long hours wading in their rice paddies.[57] Mikami, who conducted his research and much of his practice at a hospital in Kōfu, also ran a clinic in Futsuka Ichiba for local patients; Sakurabayashi, like his grandson today, conducted his practice in Miyanohara. The sixth Sakurabayashi Hokaku, the Kyoto University graduate and scholar of German literature who succeeded his father as family head and chief priest of Ubato Shrine, Ōkamada's primary Shinto establishment, in 1936, also served as village fire chief and mayor. Gemma Hideyoshi was elected to the prefectural assembly in 1934. And representatives of all three households sat for generations on the village assembly and continued to do so in the 1920s and 1930s. The observer might argue that these men served their village and its constituent hamlets in a condescending, paternalistic way, from a sense of noblesse oblige, and he might well be right. After all, they had little in common with their fellow villagers. All but Gemma were university graduates, most wrote poetry, painted in a traditional style, or recited medieval dramatic texts. Several had traveled abroad. Nevertheless, in spite of their education and cosmopolitanism compared to the local farmers, Kubo Nakajima's absentee landlords continued to live in the village, albeit in neighboring hamlets, and to perform social, agricultural, medical, and political duties which benefited Kubo Nakajima's residents. Whatever their motives for service, the hamlet's "semi-absentee" landlords played a direct and important role in Kubo Nakajima's life and cannot be viewed as impersonal, exploiting absentees.[58]

---

[57] *Yamanashi hyakka jiten*, p. 458.

[58] In 1941, absentee landlords owned only 29.9 percent of all tenanted land in Japan outside Hokkaidō, and only 21.8 percent of all tenanted land in the highly tenanted Tōzan district, which includes Yamanashi. Waswo, *Japanese Landlords*, p. 87; *Nōchi kaikaku temmatsu gaiyō*, pp. 781-783. In 1927, 6 per-

How the Mikami, Gemma, and Sakurabayashi came to own so much of Kubo Nakajima's land is unclear, but interpretatively significant. Hattori and Amemiya, following a story told them by Ishihara Yoshinaga (16), a villager who headed the tenant union in the 1920s, write that outsiders owned little of the hamlet's land before 1870. According to Yoshinaga, at the time of the Meiji Restoration the Buddhist temple Fukusenji owned 13 *chō* of land.[59] In the mid-1870s, at the height of the anti-Buddhist movement, he continued, the head priest sold most of the temple's land to the three outside landlords. Mikami Noboru, the founder of Saburō's branch of the Mikami family, reputedly gained 6 *chō* of land in this way. The Mikami, Gemma, and Sakurabayashi then made loans to their new tenants and in the hard times after the Matsukata Deflation foreclosed and confiscated even more land. Thus, these households, which dominated their home hamlets paternalistically, became absentee landlords next door.[60] This explanation fits nicely with the *rōnōha* explanation of tenancy and the origins of the landlord system, which views them as the products of the development and nature of modern Japanese capitalism.

But there is good reason to doubt the memory of a tenant union activist who was born in 1879, after the event. Village records, which both Hattori and Amemiya introduce elsewhere in their manuscripts, indicate that Fukusenji owned 2.18 *chō* of land in 1685, had a *kokudaka* of 32.69 *koku* in

cent in Ōkamada and less than 1 percent in Kubo Nakajima of all tenanted land were owned by residents of other villages, towns, and cities. *Yamanashi tōkeisho*, 1927; *KNJ*, p. 88. Moreover, since many of the absentee landlords lived in neighboring villages or nearby towns and cities, the degree of absentee landlordism, that is, of "parasitical landlordism," has been overstated in the literature on the Japanese landlord system.

[59] According to Hattori, Fukusenji's 13 *chō* of paddy and dry land made up 60 percent of Kubo Nakajima's land in the late Tokugawa period; thus, the hamlet contained only 21-22 *chō* of land then, which if correct would indicate a doubling of the land under cultivation by the 1930s. See footnote 47, above.

[60] *KNJ*, pp. 17-20; Amemiya, p. 66.

1870, and owned 2.18 *chō* of land in the 1920s.[61] If we follow our production estimate of 1.18 *koku* per *tan* in the early Meiji period, Fukusenji owned about 2.8 *chō* in 1870.[62] Since Hattori uses Fukusenji's large-scale but relatively benign landlordship in the late Tokugawa period to explain Kubo Nakajima's egalitarianism (it had no harsh landlord before the 1870s), the 1870 *kokudaka* seems to contradict both Yoshinaga's story and Hattori's conclusion.[63] In addition, the Mikami, Gemma, and Sakurabayashi, as we have seen, had large landholdings outside their home hamlets in 1870. Mikami Hachiemon, for example, paid taxes on a *kokudaka* of 485 *koku*, and his two primary branch households on 97 and 90 *koku* respectively, but all three lived in a hamlet with a total *kokudaka* of 370 *koku*. If we again calculate that 11.8 *koku* equals one *chō* of land and if we assume that these three Mikami households owned all of Futsuka Ichiba's land, which is unlikely, they held at least 25 *chō* of land in other hamlets. It is highly possible that the Mikami, Gemma, and Sakurabayashi, who lived close by Kubo Nakajima, already owned a considerable amount of that hamlet's land before 1870. The Fukusenji story, and with it the idea that conditions worsened quickly in Kubo Nakajima when land passed from a lenient, resident religious landholder to exploitive, absentee, "parasitical" landlords, does not ring true.

It is clear, however, that even if our semi-absentee landlords already owned substantial amounts of land in Kubo Nakajima before 1870, as much as 20 percent of the hamlet's land passed into their hands in the Meiji and early Taishō periods. We have no data for their land accumulation before

[61] *KNJ*, pp. 11, 14, 20, 165; Amemiya, footnote 68, p. 159.

[62] If we posit that Fukusenji owned 2.18 *chō* in 1870 as in 1685 and the 1920s, which would not be illogical, the rice yield on their land in 1870 was 1.50 *koku* per *tan*. If this held for the whole hamlet, Kubo Nakajima contained 25.3 *chō* in 1870 and reclamation was more extensive (68 percent by 1912, 78 percent by the 1930s) than my conservative estimate in the text on page 269, but less extensive than that proposed in footnote 59.

[63] *KNJ*, pp. 17-18.

1884, but we have good data from that year on, and circumstantial evidence to indicate some transfers of land from cultivator to landlord between 1870 and 1884. We know that four households, including two owner farmers with the hamlet's fifth and sixth largest *kokudaka* in 1870, lost a total of 4 *chō* of land between that year and 1884. Some or all of this may have fallen into Mikami, Gemma, and Sakurabayashi hands.[64]

The evidence becomes more complete after 1884. Mikami Noboru (Saburō's line), Mikami Hatsu, and Gemma Naojirō (Yoshinori's father) accumulated 5.1 *chō* of land from unknown sources between 1884 and 1916. We also know that the same landlords and the Sakurabayashi gained 3.1 *chō* of land from Kubo Nakajima's *cultivators* between 1888 and 1916. Although we do not know how much of the 2 *chō* difference passed from cultivators to landlords between 1884 and 1888 (there are later records of transfers between landlords which make this a possibility here), this evidence indicates that at least 3.1 and at most 9.1 *chō* passed from cultivator to semi-absentee landlord hands between 1870 and 1916. The data allow two possible and not mutually exclusive interpretations of landlord accumulation in Kubo Nakajima. One is that the three semi-absentee and one absentee who owned 23 *chō* of land in the 1920s already in the late Tokugawa period held a great deal of the hamlet's land, as much as 13-14 *chō*. The other, undocumented, but highly likely, is that the landlords provided the capital for the land reclamation which took place in Meiji (and, for that matter, Tokugawa) Kubo Nakajima, and then collected rents on the new fields. If this were true, it would have benefited both landlords and tenants. The semi-absentee investors regained their original investment and more through rents; Kubo Nakajima's 38 farm families tilled at least 40 percent more land each in the Shōwa period than they had in 1870 and thus used their available labor more fully, increased profits, and,

[64] *KNJ*, pp. 27-28.

because of labor's relative scarcity, increased their power within the hamlet.

The provenance of the 3.1 *chō* of land which passed from cultivators to semi-absentee landlords, and the 2.1 *chō* of land which passed from cultivators to resident landlords between 1888 and 1916, is clearer and reflects the effects on Kubo Nakajima of the Matsukata Deflation of the 1880s and of the Ara River floods of the early 1900s. One has only to compare the data in Table 4-12 and 4-13 to grasp this. Cultivators borrowed from landlords with land as security 200 times between 1877 and 1902, largely in the aftermath of the Matsukata Deflation, and defaulted between 1888 and 1907 95 times. Landlords gained 3.79 *chō* of land from cultivators between 1888 and 1907. Floods severely damaged rice crops in 1907 and 1910, and landlords culled 1.4 *chō* more land from cultivators between 1908 and 1916.

I would like here to make a few remarks about these data, comments which have already been made in broader contexts earlier in the book. First, although the deflation of the 1880s clearly had a deleterious effect on Kubo Nakajima, we

TABLE 4-12

Land Transfers from Cultivators to Landlords in
Kubo Nakajima, 1888-1940

Years	To Resident Landlords	To Non-Resident Landlords
1888–92	0.3403 *chō*	0.6216 *chō*
1893–97	0.4328	1.3912
1898–02	0.2319	0.4103
1903–07		0.3615
1908–12	0.3129	
1913–16	0.7922	0.3016
1917–40		
Total	2.1101 *chō*	3.0862 *chō*

Source: *KNJ*, p. 36; Amemiya, p. 78.

TABLE 4-13

Landlord Loans to Kubo Nakajima Cultivators,
and Foreclosures, 1877-1940

Year	Loans	Foreclosures
1877-87	82	0
1888-92	80	12
1893-97	37	36
1898-02	1	22
1903-07	0	25
1908-12	0	1
1913-40	0	0
Total	200	96

Source: *KNJ*, p. 38.

cannot blame the effects of the recessionary policies of Finance Minister Matsukata on the growth of capitalism alone. The spending of the Meiji government, faced with overwhelming threats to its survival in the first decade of its existence, led to an inflation which would have been no less excessive in a communal, feudal, or socialist society. It is retirement bonds for warriors, the suppression of samurai rebellion, and the fear of foreign invasion, as well as industrialization policies (which of course were established because of threats of invasion and rebellion), which must be blamed for the foreclosures of 1888-1907.

Second, the direct effects of the Matsukata Deflation were not felt immediately; many farmers did not lose their land in the first few years of the recession. Rather, those whose farms fell into the red in 1881-1885 borrowed from their landlords, in some cases met further bad fortune, and subsequently defaulted and lost land. In many cases the land transfers took place as late as a decade or two after the deflation. In Kubo Nakajima, for example, as Table 4-13 indicates, defaulting farmers felt the most adverse effects of the 1881-1884 depression in the 1893-1897 period, when the economy had recovered, not in the deflation years themselves.[65]

Third, although I have written of increasing prosperity and improving standards of living for modern Japanese commercial farmers, I do not intend to portray them as absolutely well-off. The term "increasingly prosperous" is meant to indicate farmers who have attained higher standards of living than had their more communal and self-sufficient ancestors; farmers could be *more prosperous*, but *still poor*. The data for 1908-1916 underline this point. "Increasingly prosperous" as Kubo Nakajima farmers had become, some of them were not secure enough to save their fields or, more accurately, some of their fields, from the effects of two floods in four years; thus, 1.4 *chō* of cultivator-owned land, an average of 0.4 *tan* per tenant cultivator, fell into landlord hands.

Fourth, Table 4-13 corroborates the rural borrowing patterns discussed in Chapter Three. That Kubo Nakajima cultivators did not borrow from landlords after 1902 does not mean that farmers stopped taking out loans; after all, as farmers' living standards improved and their farm management became more economic, they borrowed to expand their operations, not just to stay afloat. Farmers after 1900 found that banks and farm cooperatives charged lower interest rates and gave better terms than did landlords; the data, or one might better say, the absence of data, in Table 4-13 support the view that lending practices became more modern and rational in the twentieth century.[66]

[65] Roger Bowen argues, on the basis of impressionistic evidence, that the Matsukata Deflation caused extensive immediate damage. According to him, over three million people went bankrupt because of the deflation. *Rebellion and Democracy in Meiji Japan*, pp. 104-105. Not only are his bankruptcy figures unlikely in a country that only had six or seven million households in the mid-1880s, but also his assertion about the immediate effects of the recession runs counter to the Kubo Nakajima evidence.

[66] See Chapter Three, pp. 218-219, for a discussion of the replacement of the rural wealthy by banks as the primary rural lending agency.

Professor Nakamura's interpretation of the development of the modern landlord system under capitalism reiterates the earlier orthodox writers' belief in the concept of the "differentiation of the rural classes" (*nōminsō bunkai*). According to this idea, the growth of an agricultural market economy, i.e., of rural capitalism, led to an increased concentration of land in the hands of non-cultivating landlords, to a decrease in the amount of land owned by actual tillers, and to an increasing number of poor tenant and tenant owner farmers.[67] As we have seen, there are a number of problems with this mode of analysis. Nakamura exaggerates the extent of differentiation in the nineteenth century, overlooks the cessation and then reversal of the trend toward tenancy in the twentieth century, explains away too easily the significance of the growth of middle farming at the expense of both large landowners and "minute farming" (*reisainō*), sees only downward mobility for non-landlord villagers when there was both upward and downward movement, and overplays area of land owned and underplays area of land cultivated as determinants of rural class.

Kurihara Hakujū presented just after World War II and Nishida Yoshiaki advanced again more recently data which show a steady movement toward middle-sized farms between 1908 and 1939. The percentage of *landowners* and *cultivators* at the extremes (over 3 *chō* and under 5 *tan*) decreased significantly, and the number of middle-sized *landowners* and *cultivators*, who, according to Nishida, took small-businessman-like entrepreneurial approaches to farming, increased. Nakamura counters in his reply to Nishida that the cause of the growth of middle-sized farms was landlord failure, not tenant success, but, either way, non-landlord farmers benefited.[68] And, as the evidence for Kubo Nakajima shows, not only was there this trend toward the middle, but also, al-

[67] Nakamura Masanori, *Jinushiseishi kenkyū*, pp. 1-117.

[68] Kurihara Hakujū, *Nihon nōgyō no kiso kōzō*, pp. 27-28; Nishida Yoshiaki, "Nōmin undō," pp. 161-162; Nakamura, *Jinushiseishi kenkyū*, pp. 269-270.

though farmers lost land and even left the hamlet between 1870 and the 1940s, many added to their landholdings, and almost all who remained in the hamlet tilled larger farms after World War I than they had in the late Tokugawa period. Thus, although the *nōminsō bunkai* approach may fit to some extent for the nineteenth century, it is not apt in the twentieth, when, after Finance Minister Matsukata's policies had set a sound foundation for Japan's economic growth, the value of production improved for rich and poor farmers alike. Kubo Nakajima's patterns of landownership and cultivation underline these changes.

The data in Table 4-14 indicate that the number of landless or nearly landless cultivators increased between 1685 and 1887, but decreased between 1887 and 1942. In fact, Professor Nishida's entrepreneurial, middle farmers, owner tenants (5-10 *tan* owned), and tenant owners (1-5 *tan* owned), whom he sees as the motive force of twentieth-century agricultural improvement, increased sharply from one-third in 1887 to over one-half of the hamlet's households in 1942.

TABLE 4-14
Landownership in Kubo Nakajima,
1685, 1870, 1887, and 1942,
by Household

	1685	*1870*	*1887*	*1942*
10 *tan* or more	8	8	7	6
5-10 *tan*	4	6	2	7
3-5 *tan*	5	4	5	7
1-3 *tan*	7	4	6	6
0.1-1 *tan*	13	17	3	3
No Land			16	10
Total	37	39	39	39

Source: *KNJ*, pp. 11, 13, 156, 159, 165 (1685 and 1870, 1 *koku* = 1 *tan*).[69]

[69] My data give actual areas of land owned for 1887 and 1942, but taxable yields (*kokudaka*) for 1685 and 1870. Thus, I have had to transpose *koku* of yield into *tan* of land and have done so on the basis of 1 *tan* producing 1

One should not think, however, that all households waned and waxed equally, or even that all the same people lived in Kubo Nakajima in 1887 and 1942. A comparison of the hamlet at the two times, household by household rather than cumulatively, indicates that some families left to be replaced by other newly created ones, and that some families lost land while others gained. The comparison also shows that the new farmers owned more land than the departed, and that the gainers slightly outnumbered the losers. Twelve households gained land over the 55 years, ten lost land, and eight owned the same amount; of the eight whose holdings remained unchanged, four owned no land in either 1887 or 1942. Nine households in the 1887 sample either left the village or died out before 1942; six of the nine had little or no land (five were landless and one had less than one *tan* in 1887), and with two exceptions, all moved or ceased to exist before 1912. The most well-to-do departing farmer, Tanaka Ginzaemon, held 9.5 *tan* when at the beginning of World War I he moved out of Kubo Nakajima, according to other villagers, "for health reasons."[70] One of the poor families left the hamlet in the 1920s. Thus, it seems that only one household moved away from Kubo Nakajima for economic reasons after it recovered from the Matsukata Deflation and the late Meiji floods.[71]

---

koku of rice. As we have seen in footnotes 47 and 62, above, actual rice yields, at least in 1870, seem to have reached levels considerably higher than 1 *koku*, as much as 1.18 to 1.50 *koku*, per *tan*. Nevertheless, I have calculated on the basis of 1 *koku* = 1 *tan* for a very simple reason. My data on taxable yields for 1685 and 1870 give ranges of several *koku*—1-3 *koku*, 3-5 *koku*, etc.—rather than exact amounts per household. Since I do not know where each household falls within these ranges, to simplify calculations I have chosen to turn each *koku* into a *tan*. If actual yields were higher in 1870, then holdings in that year were smaller than those shown in Table 4-14; thus it is likely that 1887 holdings were not as much smaller than 1870 ones as the table indicates.

[70] *KNJ*, pp. 13, 28, 159, 165; Amemiya, footnote 47, p. 155.

[71] In fact, there was one other family that left Kubo Nakajima after the Taishō period which has not been included here. The Hagiwara departed in

Eight branch families (*bunke*) of existing hamlet house-holds and one new family replaced these nine (each moved into a residence vacated by a departing family) and kept the hamlet's number of households at thirty-nine. All but one of the branches owned more land in 1942 than the households they replaced had owned in 1887, although only two of the new families were offshoots of well-to-do main households (*honke*) and only one received land from its founding family. Ishihara Kanji (5), an owner farmer who had as a *honke* the Ishihara landlord with the smallest holding, received over 7 *tan*. Each of the others, including the other landlord branch, was given no land, and at best received the parent house-hold's right of tenancy to a few of its fields. In spite of these humble origins, four of the seven branches which had received no land from their *honke* had become tenant owner farmers and held from 3 to 5 *tan* in 1942. Although five of the nine families which had died or moved out owned no land in 1887, only the one new household and one of the branch households was landless in 1942.

Among the households present in Kubo Nakajima both in the early Meiji period and during World War II, three lost good-sized landholdings, five rose to replace them, and one fell from owner tenant to landless farmer and then rose again to owner tenant status. Two of the four downwardly mobile farmers lost most of their land between 1870 and 1887 and were not large landowners at the beginning of our compar-ison; the other two, including the one who later rebuilt his estate, dissipated their holdings between 1887 and the end of the Meiji period. The Kurosawa (19) and the Komiyama (17) held the hamlet's fifth and sixth largest assessments in 1870 and served in leadership posts; both had become tenant own-ers by 1887. In 1942, the Kurosawa, renamed the Amemiya

---

1937 for Manchuria. I have excluded this household from my discussion because they moved into the village during World War I, and thus are not included in the 1887 data. *KNJ*, p. 125.

(19), had no land, and the Komiyama (17) had but 2 *tan*.[72] Ishihara Akifusa, who owned 1.1 *chō* of land in 1887, lost all his land by 1912. The father of Ishihara Kōichi (8) managed to squander a full *chō* of land between 1887 and 1900, but Kōichi owned 1.8 *tan* in 1925, and owned 7-10 *tan* and tilled 16 *tan* in 1942. Although landless in 1913, Kōichi had become the hamlet's sixth largest taxpayer by 1936. Not only did some families fall and others rise between 1887 and 1942; it appears that a few managed to do both.[73]

Several families rose to replace the faltering households and the departed Tanaka. The most dramatic success story in modern Kubo Nakajima was that of Ishihara Taizō (4), whose family owned no land in 1887, but who was an owner tenant who owned 12.2 *tan*, rented in 9 *tan*, cultivated 16.8 *tan* (an average size farm in the hamlet was 11.8 *tan*), and rented out 4.4 *tan* in 1925, and who rivaled the three "landlord" Ishiharas as a taxpayer in 1940.[74] Although Taizō helped found the Kubo Nakajima tenant union in 1921 and served as one of its original directors, he fell out with the rest of the union's leadership in 1924 over the construction of an irrigation canal for the union's collective field which impeded his own water supply. Taizō brought court charges against his fellow union leaders over the issue and was punished with the hamlet's ultimate weapon, ostracism (*mura hachibu*), a sanction which remained in effect until 1945. But in spite of being cut off from virtually all communication with his union neighbors, being expelled from the labor cooperative and thus being excluded from receiving any communal assistance even at the time of weddings and funerals, Taizō and his son Yūzō flourished. After the land reform in

[72] The Kurosawa were the ancestors of Amemiya Yuzuru, the author of the thesis which is one of the primary sources for this chapter.

[73] One other among the eighteen households for whom we have data in 1887, 1925, and 1942 managed to regain lost land. Thus, there may have been three or four such households in Kubo Nakajima.

[74] *KNJ*, p. 207.

1948, he was one of Kubo Nakajima's five largest landowners, its greatest taxpayer, its first farmer to own a power tiller (in 1958), and, surprisingly, in spite of his twenty-one years of isolation and his prickly personality, one of the hamlet's ten most respected people.[75]

The household of Ishihara Eizō (6) was another success story, but, unlike Taizō (4), Eizō had outside help in his rise as a large-scale owner tenant farmer. Eizō's household was created in 1878 when his father Otokichi, the youngest uncle of the resident landlord Ishihara Toshiharu (2), was set up in a branch household. Otokichi received no land from the main household at the time of his branch's establishment, and in 1887 he headed a landless household. But in 1912, thirty-four years after the creation of Otokichi's branch, he received a paltry 0.73 *tan* from the *honke*, but, more significantly, 4.5 *tan* from the family of his wife, a tenant owner family in the hamlet. This 5.2 *tan* of land, together with purchases of 3.5 *tan* in the Taishō period, made Otokichi and Eizō owner tenants who cultivated 16 *tan*. Additional purchases allowed Eizō to own over a *chō* of land by 1942, and after the land reform to rank second only to Taizō (4) as a hamlet taxpayer. He too ranked among the hamlet's ten most respected men in the 1950s.[76]

The other two upwardly mobile farmers were Takizawa Sadayoshi (7) and Ishihara Kōtarō (9). Sadayoshi's family owned only 2 *tan* in 1887, but had 6 *tan* and cultivated 15 *tan* in 1925 and 1942. After the land reform, he ranked among the hamlet's eight largest taxpayers, and also among the most respected villagers. Kōtarō's family owned no land in 1887, but held 6 *tan* and cultivated 14 *tan* in 1942. He ranked among Kubo Nakajima's ten top taxpayers in 1936, 1940, and 1953. The households of the owner tenant farmers Oto-

---

[75] *KNJ*, pp. 106-107, 167, 223, 243-249.

[76] Otokichi's and Eizō's branch is not included in the eight discussed above or along with the one branch which received land from its main household, because their branch was formed in 1878, before the starting point of our 1887-1942 comparison.

kichi and Eizō (6), Sadayoshi (7), and Kōtarō (9), and for three years even Taizō, served the hamlet's tenant farmer union well. Only two other families held more leadership posts between 1921 and 1945 than the first two families, Kōtarō served a term as union chief, and Taizō was for three years a director.[77]

We must mention once again Ishihara Kanji (5), the head of the 1899 branch of the landlord household of Ishihara Ichitarō (3). Unlike Otokichi (6), Kanji received good treatment at the hands of his *honke*. In 1899, when his branch was established, he was given 7.2 *tan* of land. Between 1913 and 1921, Kanji bought 9 more *tan* and became Kubo Nakajima's only pure owner farmer. He, together with the three landlord Ishiharas and Shimizu Tsugutama, the priest of Fukusenji, did not join the tenant union in 1921. Although he ranked only behind the three landlords and Taizō (4) in tax paying before the land reform, Kanji slipped to tenth place in 1950 and to the middle of the hamlet ranking by 1953, possibly an indication that his prewar wealth had been built as much or more on his main family's help as on his own ability and hard work.[78]

Although both Kurihara Hakujū's and Nishida Yoshiaki's statistics and the Kubo Nakajima evidence raise doubts about a simplistic analysis of change in rural Japan based on the concept of the "differentiation of the rural classes," one still cannot deny the existence of poverty in the prewar countryside. After all, even if we accept that many farmers gained or retained the same area of land after 1900, others lost some or all their holdings and fell on hard times. The market created opportunities for the industrious, intelligent, and providential; it also set traps for the lazy, incautious, and unlucky. For almost every successful Ishihara Taizō (4) and Eizō (6), there was a failure like Hoshino Isokichi (10). He owned no land in 1887, none in 1942, cultivated only 7 *tan* in the 1920s

[77] *KNJ*, pp. 58-60, 88, 197-198, 207, 241-249.
[78] *KNJ*, pp. 58-60, 205, 207.

and 1930s (compared to the 11.8 *tan* hamlet average), 5.2 *tan* in 1947, 3 *tan* in 1953, ranked among the smallest taxpayers in the hamlet in 1923, 1936, 1940, 1950, and 1953, and had become one of the hamlet's two least respected farmers in the mid-1950s. One might blame Isokichi for his problems—when he finally lost his land and left Kubo Nakajima in 1959, his neighbors regarded him as one of the hamlet's three "lazy farmers." Nevertheless, one could also argue that he and his family never had a chance; they were poor in 1959, and had been so from at least the early Meiji period.[79]

But even if one recognizes the existence of such poor households—Nakamura sees many, Nishida and I some—this does not force me to alter my interpretation of the effects of the commercialization of agriculture on the outbreak of tenancy disputes. To begin with, poor as even Isokichi was, he was better off than his father, grandfather, and ancestors before him. Although some may find the self-sufficient village of the communal past (if it actually ever existed in its oft-remembered form), with its authoritarian but theoretically benevolent and secure order, a precapitalistic golden age, we have little evidence to tell us what life was actually like in those days of hierarchical, restrictive, and self-contained farm communities.[80] And what we do know makes

[79] *KNJ*, pp. 159, 165, 173-174, 205-207, 247-249.

[80] Arne Kalland and Jon Pedersen, "Famine and Population in Fukuoka Domain during the Tokugawa Period," *The Journal of Japanese Studies*, 10-1 (1984), p. 33, argue that as village solidarity broke down during the transition from estates worked by servants to tenancy in seventeenth-century northern Kyushu, small peasants faced greater dangers of famine than ever before. I am not in a position to reject their assumption for early Tokugawa villages, although I would have more confidence in it if they could demonstrate that famines did not occur during the estate period. But, even if their assumption is valid for early Tokugawa villages, I do not think it holds up for post-1868 rural Japan, when rapidly growing crop yields, modern transportation, and uniform national government made famine relief faster and surer than ever before. Domenico Sella, in his study of economic change in seventeenth-century Lombardy, has commented that the purely self-sufficient rural community has probably existed nowhere outside the pages of the textbooks. *Crisis and Continuity: The Economy of Spanish Lombardy in the Seventeenth Century* (Cambridge, 1979), p. 7.

them seem less golden. We know, for example, that there were famines which killed thousands in eighteenth- and pre-Meiji nineteenth-century Japan, but none after 1900. Even the Tōhoku "famine" of 1934, which caused severe hardship in rural northern Japan, cannot be called a real famine like the Temmei disaster of the 1780s; farmers in Iwate Prefecture in the mid-1930s ate millet and radish instead of rice, but no one actually starved to death.[81] The tendency to romanticize the communal past and to damn the capitalistic present is not based on reality.

FARM SIZE AND SOCIAL STRATIFICATION

More important, one cannot determine poverty in twentieth-century rural Japan on the basis of landownership alone. That tenancy increased does not necessarily mean that tenants became poor. As a tenant's rent as a percentage of yields fell, and as his surplus after paying rent rose, he often found that greater success came from cultivating a larger farm than from owning a smaller one. Thus, a farmer who wanted to expand production and income, who was fortunate enough to live in a highly commercial area, and who had the necessary labor, might use his capital more effectively by renting additional land and spending his money on seeds, equipment, fertilizer, and chemical weed killers than by purchasing additional land (especially because the army might draft or call up part of his labor force at any time). The surplus after rent, which in Yamanashi and elsewhere in the 1920s and 1930s, as we have seen, grew substantially, made large-scale cultivation even for a tenant farmer who owned no land at all a way to improve his standard of living.

[81] Mikiso Hane, in his polemical book about "the underside of modern Japan," uses the term famine to describe both the Temmei Famine of the 1780s, when tens of thousands died, and the Tōhoku "famine" of 1934 when poor families in Iwate, he writes, ate millet, barnyard grass, rice mixed with white radish, acorns, and chestnuts. While thousands, as he reports, may have been on the "verge of starvation" in 1934, this is distinctly different from the thousands who did starve to death in the Temmei Famine. *Peasants, Rebels, and Outcastes*, pp. 7-8, 114-115.

It is clear from our earlier discussion that extensive land reclamation allowed the Kubo Nakajima cultivator to till a much larger farm in 1942 than he had in the early Meiji period. Thirty-nine households and thirty-eight farm families had an overall assessment of 312 *koku*, indicating an area of cultivation of 8.5 *tan* each in 1870. The same number of households tilled 45 *chō* in 1942, an average of 11.8 *tan* and an increase of almost 40 percent each.[82] Reclamation allowed Kubo Nakajima farmers to operate larger and more profitable farms than ever before.

But there were differences of scale and success within the hamlet as well. By 1925, enterprising men like Ishihara Taizō (4) (17 *tan*), Ishihara Eizō (6) (16 *tan*), Maruyama Yutaka (11) (21 *tan*), Ishihara Toyokichi (12) (20 *tan*), and the owner farmer/landlords Ishihara Ichitarō (3) (22 *tan*) and Ishihara Yasuzō (1) (19.5 *tan*) tilled large farms, and "lazy farmers" like Hoshino Isokichi (10) (7 *tan*) and Komiyama Yasuichi (13) (5-10 *tan*) did not. As Table 4-15 indicates, most hamlet

TABLE 4-15

Scale of Cultivation in Kubo Nakajima, 1942
by Household[83]

Over 20 *tan*	3
15-20 *tan*	13
13-15 *tan*	10
10-13 *tan*	8
5-10 *tan*	4
1-5 *tan*	0
0-1 *tan*	1
Total	39

Source: *KNJ*, pp. 165, 174.

[82] See footnote 47, above. I have excluded Fukusenji from my calculations since the priestly Shimizu family tilled less than one *tan* of land, enough for a small kitchen garden.

[83] The household which cultivated 0-1 *tan* of land was that of Shimizu Tsugutama of Fukusenji. The figures on which Table 4-15 are based seem

cultivators worked 13 *tan* or more, a few struggled along by tilling less than 10 *tan*, and a number of others fell in between.

Although we know that certain large-scale cultivators like the owner tenants Taizō (4) and Eizō (6) and the two owner farmer/landlord Ishiharas prospered, and that certain small-scale ones like Isokichi (10) and Yasuichi (13) floundered, we do not have sufficient evidence to draw a hard-and-fast correlation between farm size and income in Kubo Nakajima. Unfortunately, data on value of production by household in the prewar years do not exist. We do have the voting roll of 1919, tax records for 1923, 1936, 1940, 1950, and 1953, and a list of the tenant union's leaders for its thirty-year history.[84] The roster of eligible voters, which was based on taxes paid, and the pre-land reform tax records do not help us because taxes were assessed on the basis of land owned rather than income earned. Thus, they tell us only what we already know, who Kubo Nakajima's largest resident landowners were; as one might expect, the "three Ishiharas," the priest of Fukusenji, Taizō (4), Eizō (6), the owner farmer Ishihara Kanji (5), and by 1936 the "up-down-up" Ishihara Kōichi (8) headed the lists.[85]

If we compare area of cultivation for 1942 with tax records for 1950, shortly after the land reform, however, we get quite a different picture. All the hamlet's top eight taxpayers in 1950, including only one of the three Ishihara landlords, ranked among those sixteen cultivators who tilled over 15 *tan* of land in 1942; the four households with the smallest

---

to overstate the size of individual Kubo Nakajima farms by at least 8 percent. If one totals all the farms recorded in the table, determining the actual farm size of each farm to be the number of *tan* at the *lower end* of each category, Kubo Nakajima contained 485, not 450 *tan* of arable land. The source, *KNJ*, pp. 165 and 174, provides no explanation for this discrepancy.

[84] Until 1925, only those who paid a certain amount of taxes had the right to vote.

[85] *KNJ*, pp. 197-198, 205-207; *Taishō hachinen Naka Koma-gun kenkai giin senkyo yūkensha meibo*, p. 11.

farms in 1942 were among the eight lowest taxpayers in 1950.[86] If one extends this analysis more deeply, the correlation still holds; of the thirteen top taxpayers in 1950, eleven cultivated 15 *tan* or more in 1942. Twenty-one of twenty-six farmers who cultivated 13 *tan* or more in 1942 fell into the top twenty-six taxpayers in 1950 and of the five who did not, three were just below the cutoff line. In other words, there seems to be a connection between farm size and income.[87]

Obviously one must pursue this line of analysis with caution. In 1950, after the land reform transformed Kubo Nakajima's tenant farmers into owner farmers, cultivators no longer paid rent (although, of course, they did pay higher taxes). Thus, these tax records are not a completely accurate guide to prewar income because the taxpayer's income was higher than his prewar income by that amount which he had remitted to the landlords, minus, of course, the lower prewar tax burden, and adjusted for inflation. As we have seen in Chapter Two, Yamanashi rents in the 1930s ran from about 15 percent of income on mulberry orchards to about 40 percent of yields on single-cropped rice paddies; taxes ran from about 2 percent of income for tenant farmers to 10 percent for owner farmers. Accordingly, the real income of a Maruyama Yutaka (11), who owned 2.4 *tan* but cultivated 21 *tan* in 1942, and who ranked second as a taxpayer in 1950, must have been about 25 percent lower before 1948 than after.[88] Nevertheless, the close correlation between the

---

[86] Ishihara Yasuzō (1), Kubo Nakajima's largest-scale resident landlord, who rented out 4.7 *chō* of land, was its largest taxpayer in 1945; by 1950, he had fallen to the lower middle of the hamlet group, twenty-seventh of forty-one households. *KNJ*, p. 207.

[87] *KNJ*, pp. 174, 207.

[88] Although Maruyama paid about 30 percent of his value of agricultural production in rent before the land reform, he probably remitted no more than 2-3 percent in taxes. Thus, we can estimate that he paid out about one-third of his farm income in rent and taxes. After 1948, he paid no rent, but lost about 10 percent of his value of production in taxes. By these rough calculations, Maruyama's real income (assuming no changes in productivity or real prices) was about 25 percent lower before than after the land reform.

amount of 1950 tax payment and 1942 area of land cultivated hints at least that operating large-scale farms had economic benefits for tenant farmers.[89]

Finally one finds a close correlation between the scale of cultivation and leadership in Kubo Nakajima's tenant farmers' union, and this also indicates the economic success of the large-scale farm managers. Twenty-two of the thirty-three union households provided chairmen and vice-chairmen during its thirty-year history. Twelve of the sixteen large-scale farmers (15 *tan* or more) in the village joined the tenant union, and eleven of the twelve provided at least one chairman or vice-chairman (three of these households provided three top leaders, and were the only ones to do so). The four small-scale farmers provided none. One would expect the non-landlord villagers to choose the men they most trusted and respected, the hardest working and brightest farmers, as their leaders, and to shun the "lazy." In Kubo Nakajima as elsewhere, the most successful cultivators who were not landlords or owner farmers ran the union.[90]

This sparse evidence seems to confirm that we must consider scale of operation as well as scale of ownership when determining successful farm management and when drawing village class and status lines. Since in Kubo Nakajima only four of thirty-eight farm families tilled farms under 10 *tan* in size, the hamlet's lower class seems to have been limited to the "lazy farmers."[91]

[89] Because the land reform permitted tenants to buy out their landlords cheaply, the large-scale farmers profited the most from this reform of the American occupation authorities.

[90] Nishida, "Nōmin undō," p. 175; Kurihara Hakajū, in *Nihon nōmin undōshi*, p. 572; Nishida, "Shōnō keiei," pp. 24–41; *NSSS*, Vol. 3, p. 599; Waswo, "In Search of Equity," p. 371.

[91] Actually, villagers designated only three of the four farmers who tilled 7-10 *tan* in 1942 "lazy farmers." The other, Odagiri Junsaku, was clearly an industrious man. He headed a branch household formed only in 1942. At the time of its establishment, Odagiri's family owned no land. After the land reform, however, he managed to own and till an average size farm of 10-13 *tan* (in 1959, 20 of 38 farm households in the hamlet fell into this category) and went from being one of the four or five smallest taxpayers in

What I have drawn here is a picture of a relatively egalitarian and closely knit hamlet made up of fairly large-scale, relatively successful farmers. Kubo Nakajima's resident landlords rented out little land and cultivated good-sized farms themselves. At least thirty-four of thirty-eight cultivating households operated farms larger than the county-wide average; only four tillers cultivated less than one *chō* of land. Even Kubo Nakajima's religious life, customary communal labor organ (*uma aite*), and 1919 voting role underlined its equality. The villagers had no tutelary (*ujigami*) shrine, which in many villages was dedicated to the patron deity of one of the landlord houses, and worshipped communally at a Buddhist temple of the Rinzai Zen sect and at a hall dedicated to the kitchen god (*kōjin*) within the temple compound.[92] The *uma aite*, although after 1924 without the ostracized Ishihara Taizō (4), became the basis of a tenant union which maintained its solidarity from its formation in 1921 until its dissolution in the 1950s; studies of the tenant movement in other villages suggest that such solidarity was not always the case.[93]

The Ōkamada voting roll, made up for a prefectural election in 1919, six years before universal manhood suffrage

---

1945 to a position safely in the middle of the taxpaying group in 1953. In other words, in contrast to the "lazy farmers," Odagiri improved his economic status in the hamlet. *KNJ*, pp. 165-167, 174-176, 205-207.

[92] Morioka, *Wagakuni*, p. 14.

[93] Fukutake Tadashi, in a study of the tenant-farmer movement in Shiota Village in Ogata County, Nagano Prefecture, demonstrates that pre-tenant-movement hamlet cohesion severely restricted organization along class lines. Some tenants with close ties to landlords did not join the village's tenant union; others joined but left the union when pressured by landlords with whom they had affective relationships. "Buraku no 'heiwa' to kaikyūteki kinchō," *Nihon sonraku no shakai kōzō* (Tokyo, 1959), pp. 459-470. Nishida Yoshiaki, in his analyses of the tenant-farmer movement in Kanazuka Village in Kita Kambara County in Niigata and Hanabusa Village in Yamanashi, has also found that the tenant union disintegrated when some tenant farmers gave in to landlord enticements and pressure and deserted the union. "Shōnō keiei," pp. 24-41; Nagahara, *Nihon jinushisei*, pp. 264-265.

went into effect, and based on the payment of three yen of income tax, listed 53 villagers of whom one-quarter (13) lived in Kubo Nakajima. Since only 16 percent of the village's households (39 of 250) were located in our hamlet, Kubo Nakajima clearly had a larger "middle class" of farmers who met the tax requirement to vote than did the more stratified hamlets. In fact, the Mikami's Futsuka Ichiba enrolled only seven voters (4 Mikamis and 3 others) in 59 households (12 percent).[94]

The only irritants in this relatively egalitarian community were the three semi-absentee landlords, the Mikami, the Gemma, and the Sakurabayashi, and the absentee landlord Mikami Hatsu, who between themselves owned half of the hamlet's farmland. In spite of their significant contributions to village life and in spite of their relatively good treatment of their Kubo Nakajima tenants, it was the semi-absentees who bore the brunt of the hamlet's tenant-farmer movement. To understand why this was so, therefore, we must turn finally in this chapter to a discussion of Kubo Nakajima's landlord-tenant relations.

There are four basic interpretations of the effect of landlord-tenant relations on tenant-farmer attitudes toward landlords, i.e., on the tenant's propensity to involve himself in anti-landlord activity. One, propounded by Nakamura Masanori and many others, sees the parasitical landlord's high rent and oppressive treatment of his tenants as the cause of tenancy disputes. The tenant farmer, unable to make ends meet and under pressure from his capitalistic landlord who wanted to regularize and maximize profits, developed a "wage laborer's mentality" and joined the anti-landlord movement "to demand, together with industrial workers, a day's wage for a day's production" from the rural and industrial capitalists.[95] The tenant especially attacked the absentee landlord because he was the most capitalistic and

---

[94] *Taishō hachinen Naka Koma-gun kenkai giin senkyo yūkensha meibo*, p. 11.
[95] Nakamura, *Jinushiseishi kenkyū*, pp. 243-244.

therefore the most oppressive. We can call this the "capital-ist-proletarian" view of landlord-tenant relations.

Ann Waswo proposes another, differing view of landlord-tenant relations. Although she agrees with Nakamura that the absentee (and she thinks many resident landlords were like absentees in behavior) landlord's capitalistic desire to ra-tionalize his investments and enlarge his profits, of which the return from land was one, led to the disputes, thereafter they part company. While Nakamura's landlord impelled the ten-ant to become a proletarian, Waswo's caused the tenant to try to remain a peasant. As her absentee or resident/absentee landlord became a modern entrepreneur and investor, he abandoned his precapitalist, paternalistic mode of behavior and drove his tenants to join the anti-landlord movement out of discontent with the landlord's businesslike impersonal ap-proach to landlord-tenant relations.[96] Waswo's interpretation can be entitled the "capitalist-peasant" view. Although Na-kamura's and Waswo's approaches differ radically, they share, as we have seen, one important similarity—both be-lieve that the landlord's actions caused the formation of the tenant farmer's attitudes. If landlords had not charged high rents or abandoned paternalism, tenants would not have re-acted in the 1920s.

The third view, that of Nishida Yoshiaki, places the re-sponsibility for the tenant's attitudes and actions much more in his own hands. According to Nishida, the tenant farmer took part in anti-landlord activity because of the "contradic-tion" between the tenant's "small businessman-like farm management" and the restrictions of the landlord system. In the twentieth century, tenant farmers, or at least tenant own-ers and the upper stratum of tenant farmers, prospered, be-came increasingly modern and businesslike in their cultivat-ing and farm managerial techniques, but were forced to pay rents in kind, to receive the landlord's permission before planting new crops, and otherwise to face traditional restric-

[96] Waswo, *Japanese Landlords*, pp. 66-93, 135-139.

tions on their freedom of action. They challenged the land-lords to rid themselves of these impediments to good farm management.[97]

The fourth interpretation, my line of argument, is a two-fold revision of Nishida's "capitalist-capitalist" approach, rather than a totally new one. Although Nishida emphasizes "self-salvation" (jiriki) rather than "salvation from without" (tariki), if I may borrow two Buddhist terms, I think he, like Saint Hōnen does not go far enough. He argues that the contradiction between the landlord's and the tenant's self-interests led to the unrest. I would like to place more emphasis on tenant self-interest, or to avoid a term that some may find pejorative, tenant initiative. The non-landlord farmer, whose income grew from at least 1900 on because of education, new cultivating techniques, more capital, and better farm management, wanted it to expand even more; he joined the tenant movement to increase profits and capital by winning lower rents, standard methods of regulating when and how to determine rent reductions, and the freedom to plant what he liked when and where he wanted.

I also deviate from Nishida's view that one of the major goals of the tenant-farmer movement was a revolutionary one, the overthrow of the landlord system. I think that the movement was almost entirely reformist. If the tenant farmer at one time or another called for the confiscation of the landlord's land, it was not because he really thought it possible (of course he wanted the landlord's land since the tenant's ultimate goal was to become an owner farmer), but only because the radical national tenant union officials, with whom he had minimal contact, demanded it. As Kurihara Hakujū wrote of farmers in Okayama's Kōjō Village, if the national union won land reform, "nobody wanted to be late for the bus."[98]

Finally, I believe as Nishida and Waswo do that the tenant

---

[97] Nishida, "Nōmin undō," pp. 141-181.
[98] Kurihara, Nihon nōmin undōshi, p. 572.

farmer took on his absentee or semi-absentee rather than his resident landlord for a very different reason than does Nakamura. It was not the relative harshness that led tenants to challenge the absentees. It was that the non-resident landlords were softer touches; they made greater concessions more often and more quickly than did the resident landlords. Now let us turn to our discussion of pre-tenant dispute, landlord-tenant relations in Kubo Nakajima as a basis for seeing in subsequent chapters how they changed.

LANDLORD–TENANT RELATIONS IN KUBO NAKAJIMA HAMLET

Early-twentieth-century landlord-tenant relations developed, like common law in Anglo-Saxon countries, out of hundreds of years of customary interaction between the powerful village leaders and their economic, social, and political followers. This web of tradition, whose strands were rarely written down, gave both parties certain rights and obligations which neither could ignore. Even the landlord, who clearly had the upper hand, could not cross mutually recognized boundaries of behavior without paying a stiff price—one has only to read Yoshida Teigo's study of dog-spirit possession in Kōchi Prefecture to understand the costs of excess to the rural wealthy.[99]

As Japan entered the modern world in the Meiji period, landlords and then tenants began to change. Landlords, as Ann Waswo has explained so persuasively, modernized; many tried to escape this complex web and reorganize their relations with their tenants on straight economic lines. And then, in the twentieth century, tenants changed too. Newly literate, better-educated in agricultural techniques, less provincial than their forebears, and possessing more capital from larger profits, they too began to look on their farms and their

---

[99] Yoshida Teigo, "Mystical Retribution, Spirit Possession, and Social Structure," *Ethnology* 6 (1967), pp. 237-262, especially p. 248.

relations with their landlords as small businessmen would: as something to be organized rationally. But in spite of the desire of both sides to modernize their dealings, change came slowly—each side, naturally, wanted its interests to benefit most.

The basic "document" of the landlord-tenant relationship was the contract. Although not often in writing before modern times, it established the facts, rights, and obligations surrounding each piece of rented land: location and size of plot, amount and quality of rent, length of lease, type and size of bale for rent rice, date and place of rent payment, conditions under which the rent could be reduced, limitations on the use of the land, and grounds for termination of the contract. Traditionally, the contract enumerated little else explicitly. But, as the landlord became more businesslike, to make contracts easier to enforce he wanted more and more spelled out. Thus, twentieth-century contracts often specified responsibility for improvements to the fields, for taxes, for compensating the other party if the lease was broken, sanctions for late rent payment, limitations on subleasing and crop types, more precise terms for deciding when and how to break the contract or to reduce rent, the court in which to file suit if litigation were necessary, actions to be taken if the tenant joined an anti-landlord union or sold his crop before paying his rent, and a host of other questions.[100]

The tenant, as he too became more businesslike, also wanted more specific contracts, but only when they benefited him; when the written contract's terms favored the landlord, as was frequently the case, the tenant preferred ambiguity: better to have vague and open-ended contracts than ones with set terms of leasehold if the landlords did not want to renew. Thus, tenants did not universally welcome the trend toward specificity and written contracts either nationwide or in Yamanashi. In 1912, only the large-scale absentee landlords used written contracts, but by 1921, 29 per-

---

[100] *Hompō kosaku kankō*, 1912, pp. 78-80.

cent of the nation's and 50 percent of Yamanashi's were on paper. In 1912, contracts tended to have no fixed term of duration, but by 1921 more and more imposed set limits, in Yamanashi normally five years.[101] When tenants tried to change their contracts in the 1920s and 1930s, they attacked not only traditional restrictions on their freedom to run efficient farms, but also modern, landlord-imposed contracts whose specific terms they found difficult to obfuscate and evade.

We know few details about the content of Kubo Nakajima's contracts; no actual examples remain today. We do know, however, that the resident landlords used oral contracts, but the semi-absentee landlords preferred written ones. Moreover, because a contract was on paper did not mean that it was a modern legal document of the type contemporary apartment dwellers sign. In Kubo Nakajima, the tenants trekked each January (January 11 in the Mikami case) to Futsuka Ichiba, Emmanji, and Miyanohara to the homes of the Mikami, Gemma, and Sakurabayashi to perform a ritual that local farmers called "pressing the stamp" (*hantsuki*). They arrived hat in hand at the landlord's house, stood respectfully in the kitchen to read the following year's contract and pressed it with their seal (*hankō*, the Japanese equivalent of a signature). If they were particularly brave (as tenants often became after 1921), they read the contract through; if they were particularly lucky, they drank a cup of wine. Often they returned home having done neither.[102]

We also know that Kubo Nakajima tenants normally paid their rent by one of two methods: "garden payment" (*niwa osame*) or "come to take payment" (*osametori*). The first type, which Kubo Nakajima resident landlords used (and which the semi-absentee landlords used at home) was the most humiliating. Under this system, the tenant threshed the rice but left it unhulled, wrapped it in a *hyō*-sized bale (1 *hyō* of un-

---

[101] *Ibid.*, 1912, pp. 1-5, 77; 1921, pp. 1-2, 36-44.
[102] *KNJ*, p. 51.

hulled rice or *momi* in Yamanashi equalled 6.6 *tō*, .66 *koku* or 119 liters), and carried it to the landlord's storehouse. On a day determined by the landlord, usually in December or early January, the tenant returned and watched while the landlord inspected the rice, and weighed and measured the bale.[103] Although the three Ishiharas did not have the wealth and power to terrify their tenants, one can imagine a Futsuka Ichiba tenant quaking while Mikami Saburō, or more likely his steward, checked the rent payment's accuracy.

The Mikami, Gemma, and Sakurabayashi practiced, against their will, the other method of payment, *osametori*, in Kubo Nakajima.[104] In December, each dispatched his agent (*sahaijin*) to Kubo Nakajima to collect the rent. Since the landlord usually sent a conscientious tenant from the home hamlet, the agent strove to fulfill the landlord's interests. The Kubo Nakajima tenants, on the other hand, tried to soften up the *sahaijin* with food and drink, but, according to hamlet tradition, they always failed. But then, the old timers also told stories of the days when their only profits were straw (*wara-mōke*) after they paid their rent, or when the landlords even took the rice-cake rice and the tenants had a "New Years without rice cakes" (*mochinashi shōgatsu*), the Japanese equivalent of a Christmas without plum pudding.[105]

There was in fact a third kind of rent payment, one which when used benefited the tenants and which they practiced in Kubo Nakajima even before the union's formation in 1921: "self-payment" (*uchi osame*). In years of bad harvests, and, later, of falling crop prices, the tenant paid only part of his

[103] *KNJ*, p. 42.

[104] The Mikami and the Gemma normally used the garden payment method of collecting rent, and demanded its use in Kubo Nakajima when they bought land there in the nineteenth century. The hamlet's tenants successfully resisted the adoption of this humiliating type of payment, and farmers in Ōkamada's other hamlets believed that Kubo Nakajima's tenants had it easy (*raku da*); it was the least-oppressed hamlet that had the village's most active tenant-farmer movement. *KNJ*, pp. 43–44.

[105] *KNJ*, pp. 41, 45. This must be what Roger Bowen means by "Dickensian . . . poverty." *Rebellion and Democracy in Meiji Japan*, p. 104.

rent and *then* requested a reduction. After successful negotiations, they paid the rest, but when an agreement could not be reached, the tenants often paid no more.[106] One would expect that in such cases the landlords would use the law to force payment or to evict the tenant, and they often did. But the one time that Kubo Nakajima's semi-absentee landlords went to court, in 1930, they went down to abject defeat. Not only did they not get their land back, but in the so-called "Emman Deal" of 1930, which we shall describe more fully in Chapter Six, they gave the tenants a 70 percent reduction.[107] The egalitarian Kubo Nakajima may not have been typical (case studies rarely are, since who can define what typicality is). *Uchiosame* was not practiced elsewhere in Ōkamada before the 1920s, and such utter landlord capitulation was probably rare. Still, there is considerable evidence in the *Tenancy Annual* and other contemporary studies of tenant disputes to demonstrate that landlords failed more often than not in their attempts at evicting their tenants or at using the threat of eviction to force the payment of overdue rent.

Kubo Nakajima, like most Japanese hamlets, had a long tradition of rent reductions in years of bad rice harvests. The method of determining the reduction was known as "harvesting a *tsubo*" (*tsubogari*: one *tsubo* equals 3.31 square meters or 3.95 square yards); the tenant and the landlord (or his agent) met at a set field on a set day shortly before the harvest for a test cutting which then served as a basis for determining whether to allow a reduction and, if so, how much. Intricate negotiations took place over when and where to do the *tsubogari* since flood, drought, insects, and blights affected different fields differently, and each side wanted to choose an advantageous test site; normally, as one might expect, the landlord had the upper hand in the dickering. It is not surprising, therefore, that the Kubo Nakajima (and Kōfu Basin) tenant-farmer movement made the attainment of mutually acceptable methods of deciding when to reduce rent

[106] *KNJ*, p. 46. [107] *KNJ*, p. 113.

and of fixed schedules of reductions for fluctuations in both yields and prices a major goal.

Tenants in Kubo Nakajima seem also to have faced limitations on their freedom to use their rented fields as they wanted, but these restrictions may have been less severe than those in the Mikami's Futsuka Ichiba or the Sakurabayashi's Miyanohara. Kubo Nakajima farmers told Professor Hattori stories of landlord attempts to forbid double cropping of rice paddies because of fears that winter grains would deplete the soil and lessen rice yields, and to force tenants to plant smaller and heavier-grained rice to increase rent income. Villagers also recounted landlord injunctions against remaking rice paddy into mulberry orchard. The storytellers, however, did not inform Hattori when they faced these prohibitions, and, as we have seen earlier, the rapid expansion of mulberry cultivation in Naka Koma and Ōkamada belie the effectiveness of the mulberry interdiction. It would seem that early-twentieth-century tenants in Kubo Nakajima encountered the same kinds of limitations as did their brethren elsewhere in the Kōfu basin; before a farmer could modify the topography of a leased field or plant semi-permanent crops like mulberry, he needed the landlord's permission. Otherwise, so long as the landowner did not object, the tenant could do what he wanted with the land he rented.

Hamlet stories in Futsuka Ichiba and Miyanohara reflected greater restrictions on tenant freedom. According to Amemiya, tenants there could not begin to harvest their rice crops until the Mikami and Sakurabayashi "opened the scythe" (*kama hiraki*).[108] Amemiya does not tell us, however, whether landlords still maintained this convention in the twentieth century, and neither the 1912 nor the 1921 studies of landlord-tenant practices mention it among their lists of normal or exceptional Yamanashi customs. Since we know that the transformation of rice paddy into mulberry orchard

---

[108] Amemiya, footnote 85, p. 162; *KNJ*, p. 53; *Hompō kosaku kankō*, 1912, p. 51; 1921, pp. 253ff.

took place in Futsuka Ichiba and Miyanohara as well as in Kubo Nakajima, it would appear that even Mikami and Sakurabayashi tenants had some leeway in using their fields, even if they had less than farmers in Kubo Nakajima. All in all, Ōkamada tenant farmers in the World War I period seem to have had more independence than ever before, but considerably less than they would win in the 1920s and 1930s.

The final and most important piece of evidence about the nature of Kubo Nakajima's tenancy contracts is an itemized report of the hamlet's rents prepared in 1926 for the Yamanashi headquarters of the Kantō Regional Alliance of the Japan Tenants' Union. This document allows us to compare contract rents, that is, basic rents specified in the contract rather than those actually paid which were lower, landlord by landlord (Table 4-16). We can make three significant inductions from these data.

First, Kubo Nakajima landlords do not appear to have charged particularly high rents. The absentee, three semi-absentee, and two most important resident landlords charged an average contract rent of 2.15 *koku* of unhulled rice per *tan* of paddy land. We know that in 1925 the average Ōkamada rice paddy produced 2.14 *koku* of hulled rice per *tan*. If we follow the Agriculture Ministry's calculations for 1908-1912, that two-and-one-third *koku* of unhulled rice produce one *koku* of hulled rice, then the average rice yield was 5.0 *koku* and the average contract rent was 43 percent of the yield.[109] If we calculate more conservatively that two *koku* of unhulled rice produced one of hulled rice, contract rents reached half of the rice crop. Since we know from Hattori that Kubo Nakajima tenants received a 25 percent reduction in rice-paddy rent in 1925, and from Kawada Shirō that average actual rents in Yamanashi between 1903 and 1912, even before the formation of tenant unions, were 20 percent lower than contract rents, Kubo Nakajima tenants appear to have

[109] Amemiya, p. 65, footnotes 66 and 67, p. 159; *Hompō kosaku kankō*, 1912, p. 16.

TABLE 4-16
Kubo Nakajima Contract Rents by Landlord, 1925

	Paddy			Dry Fields		
Landlord	Area (chō)	Rent (koku)	Rent per tan (koku)	Area (chō)	Rent (yen)	Rent per tan (yen)
Semi-Absentees						
Mikami Saburō	9.35	190	2.03	2.1	252	12
Mikami Hatsu	0.69	18.2	2.64	0	0	0
Gemma Yoshinori	6.5	146	2.24	2.3	460	20
Sakurabayashi Hokaku	2.2	42	1.91	0.4	48	12
Subtotal	18.74	396.2	2.11	4.8	760	15.8
Residents						
Ishihara Yasuzō (1)	3.0	69	2.30	1.2	144	12
Ishihara Toshiharu (2)	1.1	27	2.45	0	0	0
Subtotal	4.1	96	2.34	1.2	144	12
Total	22.84	492.2	2.15	6.0	904	15.1

Source: *KNJ*, pp. 48-49; Amemiya, footnote 66, pp. 159-160.

paid in rent as little as one-third and at most 40 percent of the rice yield; they paid none of the other grain or vegetables harvested in the paddies.[110]

More startling is the evidence for dry-field rents. In 1925, tenants paid an average rent of 15.1 yen per *tan*. If we assume that the Kubo Nakajima allocation of dry fields in 1925 was in the same proportion as that in all Ōkamada—two-thirds mulberry and one-third *mugi*—and assuming that the value of production per *tan* was the same—144 yen for mulberry and 24 yen for *mugi*—rents reached only 14.5 percent of

[110] Kawada Shirō, *Nōgyō rōdō to kosakusei* (Tokyo, 1923), p. 280; *KNJ*, p. 78.

value. Even if some of Kubo Nakajima's mulberry orchards were newly planted and not yet productive, it would appear that the hamlet's dry-field rents were considerably lower than those elsewhere in Yamanashi, which were already quite low. (See Table 2-15.)[111] No wonder that farmers in Kubo Nakajima and all over the Kōfu Basin in the 1920s rebuilt paddy into mulberry orchard and made the removal of restrictions on their use of rented land one of their union's primary goals.

Second, the Kubo Nakajima evidence supports Waswo's view that absentee landlords charged lower rents than did resident landlords.[112] As the subtotals in Table 4-16 indicate, the semi-absentee and absentee landlords' paddy rents averaged 2.11 *koku* of unhulled rice per *tan*, some 10 percent lower than the residents' average rents of 2.34 *koku* per *tan*.

Third, our data tell against the view that landlords collected higher rents from intractable tenants than they did from docile ones. The 1926 report includes a list, complete with area of land rented and contract rent, of all of Mikami Hatsu's and most of Mikami Saburō's paddy-field tenants in Kubo Nakajima. By comparing this list of twenty households with the roster of the tenant union's sixteen officials in the 1920s, we find that the twelve farmers enumerated in both documents (i.e., the leaders who were Mikami tenants) paid slightly less rent (2.15 *koku* per *tan*) than did the eight tenants who did not serve as union officials (2.22 *koku* per *tan*). When we compare rents paid by the three union founders who were Mikami tenants with the four Mikami

---

[111] *Yamanashi tōkeisho.* Rents for dry fields were lower, and possibly much lower, than 14.5 percent of yields. First, since the *Statistical Yearbook* does not give a figure for Ōkamada's value of mulberry production for 1925, I have used the Naka Koma average value, which is undoubtedly lower than the village's. Second, value of production per *tan* is based on mulberry, not on cocoons, as in Table 2-15. If we recalculate dry-field rents using Naka Koma's value of cocoon output per *tan* of mulberry in 1925, 253 yen, rent comes to only 8.5 percent of value of dry-field production.

[112] Waswo, *Japanese Landlords*, pp. 88–89.

tenants least involved in union affairs (each held three or fewer union leadership posts between 1921 and 1945, compared to thirteen each for the three founding households), we find that the activists' rents were 17 percent lower (1.9 *koku* to 2.22 *koku*) than the followers.[113] Although the sample is small and the differences may not be statistically significant, these Mikami data suggest that two of Kubo Nakajima's largest landowners did not punish union leaders, i.e., recalcitrant tenants, by charging them higher rents. Rather, they greased the squeaky wheels. Moreover, the Mikami's two Kubo Nakajima tenant-clients paid 8 percent higher rent (2.22 *koku* to 2.06 *koku*) than did the nine less intimately related, non-client tenants. Although this sample is also tiny, it suggests that a tenant did not benefit economically by forming a close patron-client relationship with Mikami Saburō.

Before leaving the subject of rent, I would like to make one final point. When the Kubo Nakajima tenant farmers formed a union in 1921 "in order to secure our right to live," their actual purpose was to oppose (successfully) an attempt by Mikami to raise their rents to bring them in line with those in Futsuka Ichiba.[114] In 1921, Mikami charged 14 percent lower rent in Kubo Nakajima than in his home hamlet.[115] In other words, tenants in Kubo Nakajima formed a union in March of 1921, took vigorous steps to gain concessions from their landlords from then until the Pacific War,

---

[113] *KNJ*, pp. 48-50, 88, 197-198.

[114] I believe that many of the statements of the tenant movement's leaders are formulaic and cannot be taken at face value. Because the Kubo Nakajima union formed "in order to secure (its members') right to live" does not mean that the members were desperately poor and had to fight to stay above the margin of subsistence. Certain words floated through the atmosphere of the tenant movement in the 1920s, and many local groups tended to use them because they were available. I believe it is a more fruitful approach to try to reconstruct the tenants' motives on the basis of what they did rather than why they said they were doing it. We shall return to this theme in the following chapters.

[115] *KNJ*, pp. 71-73.

remained organized even during the war, and disbanded only after they became owner farmers during the American occupation, although they paid relatively low rents and earned relatively high income. In Kubo Nakajima, economic success bred the desire for more.

As much as Kubo Nakajima's modern landlords might have wished it, their dealings with their tenants were not strictly economic. The hamlet's landlords, particularly the resident ones, and its renters had extensive patron-client (*oyabun-kobun*) social ties. As early as the Tokugawa period, production for the market had begun to dilute the economic content of these relationships in Yamanashi, and by the 1920s Kubo Nakajima patrons rarely protected their clients' livelihoods or received labor service in return. The patrons functioned only as marriage go-betweens and advisers to their clients in time of family crisis.[116] In other words, even if the economic content of Kubo Nakajima's patron-client relationships had drained away, the feelings remained deep. It was because of this affective significance and the reformist nature of the tenant movement that in the 1920s and 1930s the hamlets' clients could maintain social ties with their landlord/patrons and still challenge them economically.

The lessened economic significance of Kubo Nakajima's patron-client relationships is reflected in their distribution. Although, as Table 4-17 reveals, all but one of the hamlet's seven patrons were landlords, there is no correlation between amount of land rented out or number of tenants and number of *kobun*. The large-scale non-resident landlords had the fewest clients, but that is not surprising since they lived elsewhere in Ōkamada. What is unusual is that among the three resident Ishihara landlords there was an inverse relationship between land rented out and number of tenants, on the one hand, and number of clients, on the other. Ishihara Toshiharu (2) and Ichitarō (3), whose landholdings did not really

[116] Two of the poorest Kubo Nakajima households performed labor service of 10 and 15 days respectively for semi-absentee landlords. Hattori tells us neither who the tenants nor who the landlords were.

TABLE 4-17

Kubo Nakajima Patrons (*Oyabun*) and Number of Clients (*Kobun*)
Before and After 1926

Patron	Status	Number of Clients		Number of Tenants	Land Rented Out
		Before 1926	After 1926		
Ishihara Yasuzō (1)	Landlord	7	8	7	4.7 *chō*
Ishihara Toshiharu (2)	Landlord	11	12	5	1.6
Ishihara Ichitarō (3)	Landlord	16	13	2	0.3
Ishihara Kanji (5)	Owner Farmer	2	2	0	0.0
Gemma Yoshinori	Landlord	6	5	2[117]	8.8
Gemma Hideyoshi	Landlord	0	6	0	0.0[118]
Mikami Saburō	Landlord	3	3	19	11.45
Total		45	49		

Source: *KNJ*, pp. 48–50, 134–135, 162.

[117] Since Gemma Yoshinori owned 8.8 *chō* of land in Kubo Nakajima, he must have had more than 2 tenants in the hamlet.

[118] Gemma Hideyoshi became temporary family head of Yoshinori's line in 1930. Thus, at the time of the Emmanji Incident of 1930, Hideyoshi, a cousin, served as the Gemma landlord.

qualify them as landlords, serviced over half of the hamlet's clients. One can only guess why this was so. Both Toshiharu's and Ichitarō's households had had larger assessments than Yasuzō's in 1870, which indicates their status may have been based on a higher premodern economic standing. Toshiharu and Ichitarō may have had warmer and more benevolent personalities than Yasuzō. But, whatever the reason, the data indicate that in Kubo Nakajima greater landholdings did not lead a landlord to play a more important, paternalistic role.

Our grasp of the weak connection between the resident landlords' economic and social functions is further strengthened by the information in Table 4-18, which indicates that the clients of Kubo Nakajima's landlords were often not their tenants. Only 8 of the 3 resident landlords' 39 clients were simultaneously tenants; only 8 of 14 tenants were simultaneously clients. Even the semi-absentee landlord, Mikami Saburō, had 16 tenants in Kubo Nakajima who were not clients and his colleagues Gemma Yoshinori and Hideyoshi apparently had 7 clients who were not tenants (although the source must be in error since the Gemma, with 8.8 *chō* of land in Kubo Nakajima, must have had more than 2 tenants).

If we view these relationships from the tenants' perspec-

TABLE 4-18

Correlation Between Tenant and Client Status

Landlord	Number of Non-Landlord Clients	Number of Tenants	Clients Who Are Tenants	Clients Who Are N Tenants
Ishihara Yasuzō (1)	8	7	3	5
Ishihara Toshiharu (2)	13	5	3	10
Ishihara Ichitarō (3)	18	2	2	16
Mikami Saburō	3	19	3	0
Gemma	9	2(?)	1	8
Total	51	35	12	39

Source: *KNJ*, pp. 134-135.

tive, the evidence is equally compelling. Eight of the 17 tenants whose landlords we can identify were the clients of the landlord; 9 were not. The 17 households had 48 landlords (2.8 per) and 26 patrons (1.5 per); in only 11 cases were the landlords and the patron the same man. (Three of the tenant households had 2 landlord/patrons each.) When Kubo Nakajima's farmers selected ceremonial sponsors, more often than not they turned to those of the village's upper class with whom they had no close economic connection.

Our understanding of the essentially non-economic role of Kubo Nakajima's patron-client system is further clarified by another of its surprising aspects; the rise of the tenant-farmer movement in the 1920s appears to have had little effect on *oyabun-kobun* ties. The number of such relationships between tenants and landlords increased by four after 1926, from 43 to 47, in spite of the union's militancy. All but 2 of the hamlet's tenants entered into at least one such connection; of these 2, 1, Ishihara Taizō (4), the crotchety and industrious farmer whom the union expelled, apparently had shown his independence of mind even before 1924. Eight tenant/clients had at least 2 patrons both before and after 1926, and 1 of the 8, Ishihara Kōichi (8), an important union leader, formed 3 before 1926 and 1 more afterward. Only 2 union members, Maruyama Yutaka (11) (21 *tan* cultivator) and Ishihara Chūji (15), severed relations with their patrons in the 1920s, and neither rented land from his former patron. Even the most militant union leaders like Ishihara Yoshinaga (16), who in 1925 became the first tenant farmer to serve on the Ōkamada village assembly, and Hoshino Kōhei (17), the union's "struggle committee" chief, continued their relationships. Tanaka Masayoshi (18), the tenant union's first chairman, maintained a patron-client tie with Gemma Hideyoshi even after Tanaka's son received a four-month suspended sentence for his role in a drunken attack on Gemma's house in 1930.[119] Thus, although tempers flared and tenant farmers broke off

---

[119] *KNJ*, pp. 88, 112-113, 134-135; *Yamanashi nichinichi shimbun*, July 12, 1930, p. 3.

economic relations with some of their landlords during the period of greatest conflict in the mid-1920s and early 1930s, Kubo Nakajima's clients for the most part continued ceremonial, social affiliations with their "enemies"; because the landlord maintained his economic and social predominances separately, the tenant could attack one without challenging the other.

We cannot end our discussion of Kubo Nakajima before the rise of the tenant movement without mentioning politics, because in this realm, as in that of economic if not social life, changes took place in the 1920s. As we have seen, the three Ishiharas and several other landowning families filled the hamlet's leadership posts in the early Meiji period. After the Kurosawa and Komiyama lost their land, the Ishiharas held every important post: hamlet chief, hamlet deputy chief, village assemblyman, and village public works' committee member, until 1925. In fact, Ishihara Tsunehyoe, who adopted Toshiharu (2) as his heir in 1916, served as mayor of the joint administration of Ōkamada and Futagawa villages from 1916 to 1919.

The formation of the tenant union in 1921 and the establishment of universal manhood suffrage in 1925 changed this dramatically. In the first election under the new law, Kubo Nakajima sent a tenant, Ishihara Yoshinaga (16), to the Ōkamada Village assembly, and four years later, in 1929, the hamlet sent two tenants. Throughout the Kubo Nakajima union's history, at least one member held a seat on the twelve-man village assembly, and in 1929-1933 and 1937-1942 two served. By taking over the assembly seats, Kubo Nakajima's tenants also gained control of the hamlet's government, and this was very important. From 1925 on, every contact between outside officials and Kubo Nakajima came through the tenant union. It controlled the hamlet's agricultural association, its credit union, all of its funds from the Ōkamada village office. From 1925 to 1951 the tenant union ran Kubo Nakajima.[120]

[120] *KNJ*, pp. 102, 117-122, 178-192.

This tenant-farmer success in politics after 1925 raises a fascinating question: why did Kubo Nakajima's tenants not elect an assembly member or try to gain control of the hamlet before 1925? As we have already seen, 13 household heads in the hamlet met the taxpaying requirement to vote and hold office in 1919. Of these, 3 were landlords and 1 an owner farmer. But, even if one ranked Ishihara Taizō (4), the owner tenant who left the union in 1925, on the landlord side (which he was not when the union was formed in 1921), union members still outnumbered non-union members, 8 to 5. Moreover, 6 of the 8 and Taizō helped found and lead the union in 1921.[121] The answer is probably twofold. One, given the range of possible landlord pressures, three or four votes were not a wide-enough margin, especially when one considers that three of the nine tenants headed branches or sub-branches of landlord households (although this did not stop some of them from leading the union after 1921), and one was the declining old-elite Komiyama. Two, the tenants probably did not think of challenging the landlords' predominance before the 1920s. Only a combination of growing tenant prosperity, the creation of tenant unions in 1920-1921, their success, and the right to vote in 1925 made tenants aware for the first time that they had power. After 1920, relatively prosperous tenants in relatively egalitarian Kubo Nakajima usurped the landlords' political control of the hamlet because it brought concrete economic rewards; tenants left social relationships largely unchanged because their patron-client ties with the hamlet's landlords brought concrete emotional rewards.

[121] *Taishō hachinen Naka Koma-gun kenkai giin senkyo yūkensha meibo*, p. 11.

FIVE

Tenant Disputes in Japan,
1917–1941

IN THE twenty-two years from 1920 to 1941, 72,027 anti-landlord tenant disputes, involving (statistically) 488,737 landlords, 1,859,377 tenant farmers, and 1,234,958 *chō* of land, occurred.[1] As the data in Table 5-1 indicate, every hamlet and almost half of the non-cultivating landlords, tenant farmers, and tenanted land in Japan seem to have been involved at some time during the interwar years. The tenant movement appears to have disrupted the countryside greatly.[2]

INTERPRETING THE DATA ON TENANT DISPUTES

Although the disputes signify a unique attempt before the land reform by poorer farmers to better their conditions of tenancy and improve their economic situation, for two reasons the incidents were not as disruptive as the data in Table 5-1 might have us believe. First, tenant farmers in some hamlets demanded lower rents or the continuation of their rental contracts almost on an annual basis. In Kubo Naka-

---

[1] The 1925 *Kosaku chōtei nempō* reports that 669 tenant disputes took place in 1917-1919; since it gives no data on the number of landlords and tenants or area of land involved in these disputes, I have excluded them from the 72,027 total presented here.

[2] The Agriculture Ministry published its initial annual report on tenancy disputes in 1926 under the title *Tenancy Mediation Annual—1925* (Kosaku chōtei nempō—1925); this first volume contained data on disputes from 1917 through 1925. The ministry renamed the series *Tenancy Annual* (Kosaku nempō) with the 1927 edition, and *Farm Land Annual* (Nōchi nempō) for the 1940 and 1941 issues.

TABLE 5-1
Scale of Tenancy Disputes Compared to Landlord and Tenant Farmer Population and Area of Tenanted Land, 1920-1941

	Disputes		*Rural Society*
Incidents	72,027	Hamlets	76,000[3]
Landlords	488,737	Non-Cultivating Landlords	1,000,000 approx.
Tenants	1,859,377	Tenants	3,856,677
Land Area	1,234,958 *chō*	Tenant Land	2,824,295 *chō*

Calculated from *Kosaku chōtei nempō*, 1925-1926; *Kosaku nempō*, 1927-1939; *Nōchi nempō*, 1940-1941; Waswo, *Japanese Landlords*, pp. 7, 9; Kurt Steiner, "Popular Political Participation and Political Development in Japan: the Rural Level," in Robert E. Ward, ed., *Political Development in Modern Japan* (Princeton, 1968), p. 236.

jima, for example, the local tenant union requested rent reductions every year from 1921 through 1931, and in 1932 and 1934 asked for permanent methods of lowering rents in years of bad harvests or falling rents. Kubo Nakajima, therefore, represents at least thirteen disputes, 91 landlords, and 429 tenants in Table 5-1. Although the hamlet may be an extreme example, its case and many other similar ones suggest that the data in Table 5-1 overstate the number of hamlets, landlords, tenants, and *chō* of land involved in disputation.

Second, most tenant disputes lasted only short periods of time and occurred in the agricultural slack season. Thirty-five percent of all disputes between 1925 and 1940 lasted one month or less; 65 percent, almost two-thirds, were over within three months. Seventy percent of the total, almost 50,000 disputes, began between November and April, the slack months of the agricultural year. The tenant-farmer

[3] Kurt Steiner reports 76,000 hamlets in 1910; Waswo reports 79,000; Fukutake Tadashi, in *Japanese Rural Society*, p. 11, assumes 150,000. If we use Fukutake's figure, tenant disputes disturbed a smaller percentage of hamlets than reported here.

movement was certainly significant—it brought lower rents and better tenancy conditions to both participants and non-disputants alike—but one should not let the aggregate statistics lead one to believe that the interwar countryside was in constant turmoil.

There are also other dangers in uncritical reliance on the Agriculture Ministry's copious data on tenant disputes. Let me cite two examples to demonstrate how this was so. To many students of the tenant movement, the 1917-1921 period stands as a watershed. Before this time, few tenant farmers challenged their landlords; afterward, many did. What makes this view particularly attractive is that Japan's rural economy boomed in 1917-1919, but contracted in 1920-1922—albeit only to a level 4 percent above 1915-1917. Thus, it is convenient to interpret retrenchment after the euphoria of expansion as the primary immediate cause of the outbreak of disputes.[4] The problem here is this: to what extent did the gradual increase in disputes from 1920 to 1926 indicate the actual spread of anti-landlord disputation rather than an improvement in the government's methods of collecting information? Were there actually four times as many disputes in 1921 as in 1920, or did the researchers only count more? This question is impossible to answer conclusively. We know from other sources that many disputes occurred before the end of World War I; on the other hand, they seem to have been fewer than after 1920-1921.[5] What we can con-

---

[4] Ushiyama Keiji, *Nōminsō bunkai no kōzō*, p. 96.

[5] Takegawa Yoshinori, *Yamanashi nōmin undōshi* (Kōfu, 1934), p. 3, writes that tenant farmers formed their first union in Yamanashi in 1892; 30 unions had been established by 1917 (395 by 1931). Agriculture Ministry officials reported a dispute in Nawa Hamlet in Ueno Village, Chita County, Aichi, which had recurred annually from 1897 to the year of the report, 1929. *Kosaku sōgi oyobi chōtei jirei*, 1929, pp. 92-98. Aoki Keiichirō, in his multi-volume collection of data on agrarian movements from the late Edo period to the 1950s, copiously documents pre-1917 disputes. *Nihon nōmin undōshi*, 6 vols. (Tokyo, 1958-1962). Nakamura Hideo in *Saikin no shakai undō* (Tokyo, 1929), gives a brief overview of the pre-1917 tenant movement. One must be careful to distinguish between the "peasant uprisings" (*hyakushō*

clude tentatively, I think, is that disputes did increase and intensify after 1920, but that they did not erupt for the first time in the postwar years, and were not accurately counted before 1923, when the Agriculture Ministry took over responsibility for gathering data on disputes from the Home Ministry.[6]

The other example deals with one of the basic areas of agreement among all scholars of the tenancy movement, no matter what their approach, that the Agriculture Ministry's data show that the nature of the disputes changed from the 1920s to the 1930s. These statistics indicate clearly that the number of disputes increased (in 1934, almost four times the number of disputes as in 1924), that their scale decreased (about one-fourth of the number of tenant participants per dispute in 1934 as in 1924), and that continuation of tenancy contract replaced reduction of rent as the primary tenant demand. Scholars like Nakamura Masanori and Waswo use these data to conclude that tenants in the depression years of the 1930s joined in small-scale, defensive disputes to protect their rights of cultivation and thus their livelihoods rather than, as in the more "prosperous" 1920s, in large, multi-hamlet, aggressive disputes to reduce rents and improve tenancy conditions. I agree that defensive disputes increased in number (I do not think they became the primary type of tenant disputation, however), but I also think that part of the difference in the number and scale of disputes between the two decades may reflect the increasingly accurate and detailed reporting and the changing categories of the Agriculture Ministry's statistics. Although the prefectural Tenancy

---

ikki) of the late Tokugawa and early Meiji periods, which are discussed by Roger Bowen, *Rebellion and Democracy in Meiji Japan*, and Stephen Vlastos, *Peasant Protests and Uprisings*, and the tenant-farmer movement (*kosaku sōgi*) of the 1920s and 1930s. During the late Tokugawa, Meiji and Taishō eras, at speeds differing from region to region, peasants became farmers, and reformist tenant disputes replaced indignant, anti-government, anti-usury, millenarian uprisings.

[6] *Kosaku chōtei nempō*, 1925, Section II, Appendix 2-6.

Officers had responsibility for gathering information on disputes, they, never more than two or three per prefecture, could not themselves form a close picture of every one of the hundreds of hamlets in their prefectures. Thus, they distributed forms with predetermined categories and depended on village officials over whom the officers had increasingly firm powers of supervision to fill out and return the questionnaires. The village office became more and more accurate in performing this task. And, more importantly, the Agriculture Ministry, which nowhere in the *Tenancy Annual* defines the term "tenancy dispute," seems in the 1930s to have broadened its conception of what constituted a dispute. In the early 1920s, it tended to emphasize confrontations replete with violence, threats of violence, or harsh words; afterward, the definition became increasingly broad to include simple requests for the lessening of rent or the continuation of contract. Since we know from descriptions of individual disputes reported in the Agriculture Ministry's *Examples of Tenant Disputes and Mediation* that the confrontations tended to take place on a larger scale than did the milder requests, the difference in number and scale of disputes in the 1920s and 1930s might reflect changes in Ministry definition as well as differing economic conditions and tenant-farmer goals. Still, the *Tenancy Annual* provides our only comprehensive material for studying the tenant-farmer movement in the interwar years. Thus, keeping its weaknesses in mind, we, like all other scholars of the tenant-farmer movement, shall use the yearbook as the basis for our macroscopic analysis.

Table 5-2 presents the Agriculture Ministry's data on the number of disputes, landlord and tenant participants, and arable land involved per year from 1920 to 1941. As is readily apparent, disputes increased from 1920 to a high point in 1926, fell off shortly before the depression set in at the end of the decade, increased again through 1936, and declined once more until they stopped (or the counting stopped) when war broke out with the ABD powers in 1941. These trends have led Nakamura Masanori to divide the two tenant

320

TABLE 5-2
Number of Disputes and Landlords, Tenants and Land Involved,
1920-1941

Year	Disputes	Landlords	Tenants	Land (Chō)
1920	408	5,236	34,605	27,390
1921	1,680	33,985	145,898	88,681
1922	1,578	29,077	125,750	90,253
1923	1,917	31,712	134,503	89,080
1924	1,532	27,223	110,920	70,387
1925	2,206	33,001	134,646	95,940
1926	2,751	39,705	151,061	95,652
1927	2,052	24,136	91,336	59,168
1928	1,866	19,474	75,136	48,694
1929	2,434	23,505	81,998	56,831
1930	2,478	14,159	58,565	39,799
1931	3,419	23,768	81,135	60,365
1932	3,414	16,706	61,499	39,028
1933	4,000	14,312	48,073	30,596
1934	5,828	34,035	121,031	85,838
1935	6,824	28,574	113,164	70,745
1936	6,804	23,293	77,187	46,420
1937	6,170	20,230	63,246	39,582
1938	4,615	15,422	52,817	34,359
1939	3,578	9,065	25,904	16,623
1940	3,165	11,082	38,614	27,625
1941	3,308	11,037	32,289	21,898
Total	72,027	488,737	1,859,377	1,234,954

Sources: *Kosaku chōtei nempō*, 1925-1926; *Kosaku nempō*, 1927-1939; *Nōchi nempō*, 1940-1941.

dispute decades into four periods: seven or eight years until the government crushed the Communist Party in 1927-1928, during which tenants, revealing the "wage earner consciousness" side of their dual nature, joined with urban workers under the leadership of the left to attack the oppressive emperor system with its malignant capitalist-landlord-military-civil bureaucratic cabal; 1928-1930, when the many tenants, having won rent reductions and without the rallying leadership of the suppressed communists, allowed the other, "petty bourgeois consciousness" side of their character to dominate and retreated from the anti-emperor system, anti-landlord struggle; 1930-1936, when all tenants, either upper, middle or marginal, joined together during the depression in a desperate fight to protect their tenanted land from landlord confiscation and to protect their precarious existence—what one can call the "depression-poverty-eviction" explanation; and 1937-1941, when the tenant movement succumbed to the government's repressive fascism.[7] In making this analysis, Nakamura overlooks one major aspect of these data; as Matao Miyamoto and Kozo Yamamura point out for the depression years, one gains a better understanding of the rise and fall of the tenant movement from studying the number of participants and the amount of land involved than by looking at the number of disputes themselves.[8] Why is this so?

As one can see from even a cursory scanning of Table 5-3, the scale of disputes decreased in a steady, almost unbroken decline from 1920 to 1941. Although many have used this trend to underscore the difference in the nature of pre-depression and depression disputes, its steadiness even within the various sub-periods suggests what we discussed above: transformations took place in the method of counting and the definition of what constituted a tenancy dispute. It may well be that what village officials reported as village-wide disputes in 1925, they counted as 3-4 hamlet-level disputes in 1935. This line of speculation, and admittedly it is only

[7] Nakamura, *Jinushiseishi kenkyū*, pp. 233, 247, 256-257, 261-288, 296; "Nisshin sengo keieiron," pp. 138-170; "Shihonshugi kakuritsuki no kokka kenryoku," *Rekishigaku kenkyū*, 1970 special supplement.

[8] Kozo Yamamura and Matao Miyamoto, "Toward a Quantitative Economic Analysis of the Tenancy Disputes of Interwar Japan: A Preliminary Report," unpublished paper, p. 8.

TABLE 5-3

Number of Disputes and Landlords, Tenants, and Area of Land
Involved per Dispute, 1920-1941

Year	Disputes	Landlords per	Tenants per	Area per	Tan per Tenant
1920	408	13	85	67 chō	7.9
1921	1,680	20	87	53	6.1
1922	1,578	18	80	57	7.2
1923	1,917	17	70	46	6.6
1924	1,532	18	72	46	6.3
1925	2,206	15	61	43	7.1
1926	2,751	14	55	35	6.3
1927	2,052	12	45	29	6.5
1928	1,866	10	40	26	6.5
1929	2,434	10	34	23	6.9
1930	2,478	6	24	16	6.8
1931	3,419	7	24	18	7.4
1932	3,414	5	18	11	6.3
1933	4,000	4	12	8	6.4
1934	5,828	6	21	15	7.1
1935	6,824	4	17	10	6.3
1936	6,804	3	11	7	6.0
1937	6,170	3	10	6	6.3
1938	4,615	3	11	7	6.5
1939	3,578	3	7	5	6.4
1940	3,165	4	12	9	7.2
1941	3,308	3	10	7	6.8

Calculated from Table 5-2, above.

speculation, is supported by two pieces of evidence hidden
within Tables 5-1 and 5-3. Although the number of disputes
generally increased and their scale gradually decreased from
the 1920s to the 1930s, the amount of land involved per tenant fluctuated very little after 1920, from a low of 6.0 *tan* in
1936 to a high of 7.4 *tan* in 1931 (as seen in Table 5-3), and

in its variations showed no clear trends.[9] Since the average Japanese tenant farmer rented 7.3 *tan* of land in 1930 (Table 5-1), when a tenant participated in a dispute, whether in the 1920s *or* 1930s, he seems to have involved almost all his land and, therefore, almost all his landlords. In other words, although the scale of a dispute qua dispute apparently changed from 1920 to 1941, the scale from the perspective of the tenants involved did not change at all. What this suggests to me is that to better understand the changing scale and nature of the tenant movement, rather than looking at the number of disputes per se, we should begin by looking at the number of tenants or the area of tenanted land involved each year. Since the latter two tended to rise and fall in similar patterns, I shall look at the number of tenant participants involved.

Tenant participation followed a similar, but slightly and I think significantly different, pattern from that of the number of disputes. Tenants took part in disputes in larger numbers from 1921 through 1926, and then in somewhat smaller, but still substantial, numbers from 1927 through 1929. Thus far, the degree of participation followed the flow and ebb of disputes fairly closely. But, while disputes rose in number sharply from the onset of the depression in 1929-1930, the number of tenants involved fell even further until the last year of the depression in 1934. Two years of fairly high tenant engagement followed in 1934-1935, and then a gradual downward trend, one which set in during the peak years in number of tenancy disputes, continued until 1941. This overall pattern can be seen more clearly if we set up multiyear averages for the five periods identified. (See Table 5-4.)

How do we interpret these variations in tenant participation in disputes? Waswo's approach, which, like Nakamura's, is based on the number of disputes, divides the

[9] Contrary to expectations, given Nakamura's and Waswo's view, area of land involved per tenant disputant decreased only 3 percent between the 1920s and the 1930s. Using Waswo's periodization (*Japanese Landlords*, p. 100), one finds an involvement of 6.71 *tan* per tenant in 1920-1931, and 6.51 *tan* per tenant in 1932-1941.

TABLE 5-4
Annual Average Tenant Participation in
Tenancy Disputes by Period, 1921-1941

Period	Average Annual Participation	Index
1921-26	133,796	100
1927-29	82,823	62
1930-33	62,318	47
1934-35	117,098	88
1936-41	48,343	36

Calculated from Table 5-2, above.

twenty-five years of tenant farmer activism into two periods, 1917-1931, when tenants challenged landlords aggressively, and 1932-1941, when they reacted defensively.[10] This
view, because of its broadness, buries more complex trends.
How does it explain the low points in participation during
the relatively prosperous late 1920s and late 1930s, *and* the
depression of 1930-1933? Even Nakamura's more complex
periodization does not answer the question of causation completely since, according to his mode of analysis, participation
should have been highest in the depression years, when all
classes of tenant farmer struggled to subsist. In fact, one is
hard put to find consistent correlations between economic
indicators like annual fluctuations in rural income or filature
workers' wages and dispute participation.[11]

Table 5-5 presents indices of real value of farm production

[10] Waswo, "The Origins of Tenant Unrest," in Bernard S. Silberman and
H. D. Harootunian, eds., *Japan in Crisis: Essays on Taishō Democracy* (Princeton, 1974), pp. 381-382.

[11] I compared statistically the annual indices of real value of agricultural
production per farm worker and of number of dispute participants presented
in Table 5-5 and found no correlation whatsoever. The same comparison
was made with a one-year time lag (hypothesizing that last year's lower
income caused this year's disputes); again there was no correlation
whatsoever.

TABLE 5-5

Indices of Real Value of Agricultural Production per Agricultural
Worker, Real Wages per Female Filature Worker, and Tenant
Participation in Disputes, 1921-1939 (1915-1917 = 100 for value
and wages)

Year	Real Value of Agricultural Production	Real Filature Wages	Dispute Participation
1918-19	136	86	
1920	107	121	
1921	106	138	100
1922	100	154	86
1923	110	141	92
1924	120	144	76
1925	130	144	92
1926	119	153	104
1927	112	147	63
1928	114	151	51
1929	116	165	56
1930	89	161	40
1931	85	159	56
1932	100	140	42
1933	116	136	33
1934	105	124	83
1935	120	121	78
1936	134	122	53
1937	141	115	43
1938	136	110	36
1939	186	120	18

Calculated from *Kosaku chōtei nempō*, 1925-1926; *Kosaku nempō*, 1927-1938; *Nōchi nempō*, 1939; *Chōki keizai tōkei*, Vol. 8, pp. 135-136, 243; Vol. 9, pp. 146-147, 218-219; Ohkawa and Shinohara, *Patterns of Japanese Economic Development*, pp. 294-295, 388.

per agricultural worker, real wages per female filature worker, and dispute participation from 1921 to 1939. If one attempts to analyze participation in disputes on the basis of fluctuations in value of production alone, one comes face to face with the following difficulties. If the high level of participation in 1921-1923 can be attributed to the 1920-1923 "recession" after the 1918-1919 boom, how does one explain the continued high level of tenant-farmer involvement in disputes in 1924-1926, when the rural economy reached its highest levels of prosperity in the decade? If Nakamura is correct in regarding the tenant farmers' success in achieving lower rents as the reason for reduced participation in the continuing good years of the late 1920s, to what does one attribute the very low participation during the depression, when rural real income per worker fell sharply? If the need to protect their small rented holdings against confiscation led tenants to join in a desperate anti-landlord struggle during the 1930-1933 years, why did tenant participation in disputes increase as the Japanese countryside began to recover from the depression in 1933-1935?[12] In other words, if one chooses the poverty of tenant farmers as the primary cause of disputation, the low level of activism during the depression years and the high level of activism in the recovery years do not make sense.

Given these data, a modified version of Nishida Yoshiaki's eclectic approach, which emphasizes for the sake of analysis two groups of tenant farmers—the prosperous upper and middle "small businessman" farmers and the poorer marginal tenants who tilled only small holdings—seems more satisfactory than Nakamura's or Waswo's.[13] Following and

[12] One possible explanation is that three successive bad years in 1930-1932 caused the 1934-1935 upsurge in participation. This explanation would be in keeping with Ushiyama's that the recession of the early 1920s led to the original outbreak of tenant disputes. (See footnote 4 above.) One problem with this approach, however, is that a good year, 1933, intervened before the increase in dispute activity.

[13] Nishida believes (as do I) that there were more than two categories of tenants, but limits himself to two for the sake of analysis. "Nōmin undō," pp. 165-167, 175.

extending Nishida's line, we can attribute high participation in 1920-1926 to an upper-middle tenant-poor tenant alliance to lower rents and to better tenancy conditions in general. In the late 1920s, some tenants, having won lower rents, dropped out of the movement, but others, motivated by the same reformist desire to further rationalize their businesslike farm management, continued. During the depression years, marginal tenants, hard hit by falling rice and cocoon prices and threatened with eviction, became the motive force behind a smaller-scale anti-landlord movement; many of the upper and middle tenants, who were more secure economically, tended not to participate during these years, although some continued to do so.[14] In the mid-1930s, as conditions began to improve, other upper and middle tenants saw renewed opportunities to extend their profits, and a new upsurge of participation took place. Finally, a combination of the highest real-farm incomes before the 1950s, the successful attainment through the tenant-farmer movement of lower rents and better conditions of tenancy, government policies to encourage production which favored tenants, and the "consensus" environment of immediate prewar and early wartime Japan led to a waning of the tenant movement.

This mode of interpretation is partly reinforced by wages earned by female raw-silk spinners, one of the main sources of non-agricultural income for prewar farm households. Real filature wages climbed dramatically from 1918 to 1922, and then remained at extraordinarily high levels—almost double 1918—until 1931, the second year of the depression. Tenant farmers in the 1920s had a solid source of outside income and high farm returns, and yet participated in disputes, un-

---

[14] Even Nishida realizes that poor tenants were not the exclusive motive force for disputes during the depression, however. In his study of the San-jōmai Incident in Kanazuka Village, Kita Kambara County, Niigata, he found that it was the village's poorest tenants who knuckled under to landlord pressure and deserted the movement in 1928. The most prosperous tenants who tilled the largest farms continued to fight the landlords during the depression years. "Shōnō keiei," pp. 34-35.

derlining the reformist, businesslike nature of the disputes. But, in 1932, real filature wages began to fall as real farm income had two years earlier, and, unlike the latter, wages never recovered. Japan's silk industry in the 1930s confronted not only the world depression, but also rayon and nylon, and by 1939 real filature wages fell to a level 27 percent below 1929 (but still 40 percent above 1918-1919). It seems possible that reductions in this major source of outside income for tenant households, already sharp in 1934, could have played a role in the upsurge of tenant participation in disputes in 1934-1935. Nevertheless, even this revision of Nishida's interpretation, as we shall see, is not completely persuasive.

The *Tenancy Annual* provides other data on disputes in addition to number, participants, and area of land involved, and these have been used by students of the tenant-farmer movement to demonstrate how the nature of the disputes changed over time. They also show the difficulties of arriving at consistent conclusions. Both Nishida and Waswo use statistics on immediate causes, principal tenant demands, and regional variations to contrast the disputes of the 1930s, in which poor tenants, especially in the less commercial northeast, joined the movement to protect their rented holdings from confiscation, with the more entrepreneurial disputes of the 1920s in the more developed west.[15] And yet, when one analyzes the data closely, one finds that the shifts from west to east and from reduction of rent to protection of tenure as the cause of disputes are much less certain than Nakamura, Nishida, and Waswo would have us believe. In whichever period in whatever periodization schema we use, immediate causation is complex.

Table 5-6 presents data on the immediate causes of disputes, gleaned from the *Tenancy Annual*. Because these statistics are enumerated by dispute rather than number of par-

---

[15] Nishida, "Nōmin undō," pp. 173-174; Waswo, "Origins of Tenant Unrest," pp. 381-397; *Japanese Landlords*, pp. 96-99.

TABLE 5-6
Annual Average of Disputes Caused by Rent and Contract
Problems Compared, by Period, 1921-1941[16]

Year	Average per Year	Rent Related	Contract Related	Other
1921-26	1,944	76%	5%	20%
1927-29	2,117	62	25	13
1930-33	3,328	40	46	14
1934-35	6,326	48	45	7
1936-41	4,607	38	52	10
21 Year Avg.	3,411	48%	40%	12%

Calculated from *Kosaku chōtei nempō*, 1925-1926; *Kosaku nempō*, 1927-1939; *Nōchi nempō*, 1940-1941.

ticipants or area of land involved, and because the local officials who filled out the data collection forms could designate only one cause, no matter how complex the actual causation, these statistics exaggerate the changes which took place in the nature of disputes. Those incited by problems of landlord-tenant contracts were few when they were first counted in 1923 (less than 1 percent), but were a majority by 1936-1941. Problems of rent caused 76 percent of the disputes in 1921-1926, but only 38 percent in 1936-1941. It is these trends which have led to the "depression-poverty-evic-

[16] The *Tenancy Annual* reports many categories of cause of disputes and does not list one called "rent-related." Thus, I have arbitrarily decided that disputes defined as occurring because of "crop failure or poor harvest," "rent raised," "high rent," and "non-payment of rent" are rent-related disputes. I have excluded "decline in farm prices" from either category although it might best be entered in the rent column. Waswo translates the contract-related category, "kosakuken kankei matawa kosakuchi hikiage" in Japanese, as "attempted eviction of tenants" (*Japanese Landlords*, p. 98) although it literally reads "related to the tenant contract and the withdrawal of rented land." Thus, although other evidence shows that this category usually referred to the landlords' eviction attempts, it did not necessarily do so. I have called such disputes "contract-related."

tion" mode of interpretation. And yet, although it is to some extent correct—the depression surely brought economic hard times and more scrambling for land compared to the 1920s—for a number of reasons, these changes have been overstated.

The data on immediate causes and on tenant demands do not always follow the overall economic trends in ways that one would expect. Table 5-7 compares the disputing tenant farmers' demands (again enumerated by dispute) with the real value of agricultural production per agricultural worker and indicates that the "depression-poverty-eviction" approach does not consistently mesh with economic reality. Although problems of contracts supplanted rent as the focus of tenant demands for the first time during the depression, how does one explain the sharp upward trend in the number of disputes over contracts before the depression and its continuation afterward, when the rural economy climbed to its loftiest prewar heights? As we have seen in Chapter One, even pure tenant farmers earned profits before 1929 and of 8 percent or more from 1935-1937 on.

TABLE 5-7

Tenant Demands in Disputes Compared to the Index of Real Value of Agricultural Production per Agricultural Worker by Period, 1923-1938

Year	Avg. Number of Disputes per Year	Rent Related	Contract Related	Index of Value
1923-26	2,102	88%	6%	120
1927-29	2,117	65	26	114
1930-33	3,328	42	45	98
1934-35	6,326	40	45	113
1936-38	5,863	26	55	136

Calculated from *Kosaku chōtei nempō*, 1925-1926; *Kosaku nempō*, 1927-1938; *Chōki keizai tōkei*, Vol. 8; Ohkawa and Shinohara, *Patterns of Japanese Economic Development*, pp. 294-295.

Nishida's approach, with its two types of tenant farmers, seems to handle this apparent enigma. Although tenant farmers who owned some land or tilled large holdings and thus sought lower rents may have gained their objectives and gradually dropped out of the tenant-farmer movement from the late 1920s, marginal ones with small farms and without the safety net of the high filature wages which they had had in the 1920s may have continued to fight for land. They needed every bit of land they tilled or could till to feed their families. But even this explanation is not adequate. The contract disputes occurred primarily in the northeast (in 1930-1939, 68 percent of all Tōhoku disputes compared to 24 percent of all disputes in Kinki), a region which provided few filature workers. In the west, with its greater number of lost industrial jobs, tenant disputants continued to fight for lower rents—in 1930-1939, 63 percent of all disputes in Kinki had as their primary cause the desire for rent reductions, compared to only 23 percent in Tōhoku. But, although Tōhoku with its predominance of contract disputes had a greater number of disputes than Kinki in the 1930s, 14,546 to 8,412, far more tenants participated in the west than in the east. From 1930 to 1939, 275,374 tenants took part in Kinki, where rent disputes predominated, compared to only 57,154 in Tōhoku, where contract disputes held sway; since Kinki had only 52 percent as many farm households as Tōhoku, the incidence of participation in disputes was over nine times greater in the western than in the eastern region in the 1930s. That is to say, Kinki, not Tōhoku, remained the primary locus of the tenant movement, and rent reduction, not maintenance of land tenure, remained the primary cause of disputes even in the 1930s.[17]

[17] *Kosaku nempō*, 1930-1939. Kozo Yamamura and Matao Miyamoto have made the point ("Quantitative Analysis," p. 8) that many observers overstate the shift in center of disputational gravity from Kinki to Tōhoku because they concentrate on the number of disputes rather than on the number of participants. In my calculations I have followed Nishida Yoshiaki and included Aomori, Iwate, Akita, Miyagi, Yamagata, Fukushima, Ibaragi,

Although it is clear that farmers in Tōhoku suffered more from the depression than did tillers in the west—in 1932, for example, a middle-level rice paddy in Akita Prefecture produced a surplus after rent of 9.63 yen compared to 24.5 yen in Hyōgo Prefecture—in the east even more than in the west the flood tide of tenant participation in disputes and of disputes over contracts came at the end or after, not during, the depression.[18] As Table 5-8 shows, post-1920s participation reached its peak in 1935-1936 in Iwate, 1936-1937 in Yamagata, and 1934-1936 in Niigata. Conversely, in the west, where disputes over rent continued to dominate, the greatest tenant activity took place during or right after the depression: 1931 and 1934 in Hyōgo and Kyoto, and 1934-1935 in Aichi. And the percentage of disputes over contracts in Tōhoku reached its peak, 79 percent of all disputes, in the immediate post-depression years of 1935-1937. Thus, even Nishida's interpretation does not tell us why Tōhoku farmers, who had little outside industrial income and therefore did not suffer as much from falling filature wages, fought for their land in increasing numbers *after the depression*, when their farm economies were improving. Could it be that the desire to raise their expanding farm incomes even more provided part of the motive force?

The immediate causes and demands, moreover, do not correlate with increases in the size of the rural work force as they should following the poverty-eviction approach. According to this view, disputes over the continuation of contract increased in the depression years, partly because small landlord cultivators needed to till more land to support families enlarged by unemployed workers who had returned

---

and Tochigi prefectures in Tōhoku and Mie, Shiga, Kyoto, Nara, Wakayama, Osaka, Hyōgo, and Okayama prefectures in Kinki. If I were to follow tradition and exclude Ibaragi and Tochigi, among the "Tōhoku" prefectures with the most disputants, from my calculations, the predominance of Kinki in the disputes of the 1930s would be even more one-sided than the nine-plus times reported above.

[18] Nishida, "Nōchi kaikaku no rekishiteki seikaku," p. 164.

TABLE 5-8
Tenant Participation in Tenancy Disputes by Prefecture (in 100s)

Year	Iwate	Yamagata	Niigata	Aichi	Kyoto	Hyōgo
1920	0	0	3.4	25	2.1	33
1921	0	0	16	277	0.1	246
1922	0.8	4	37	137	13	242
1923	0	5.5	26	114	25	258
1924	0	5.7	17	69	49	156
1925	2.3	9	35	95	58	115
1926	0.5	1.5	98	34	99	179
1927	0.01	1.9	65	73	31	69
1928	0.2	11	32	17	37	38
1929	0.8	6.1	32	29	36	42
1930	0	7.4	28	25	38	32
1931	0.3	4.9	37	34	89	53
1932	0.1	4.8	33	46	18	16
1933	0.2	5.5	26	20	32	18
1934	1.5	5.8	36	47	72	71
1935	3	4.3	39	97	25	41
1936	2.6	8.4	34	25	30	36
1937	0.9	8	23	41	32	44
1938	0.6	5.4	12	5.4	16	28
1939	1.4	4.3	5.3	20	3.4	14
1940	2	3.6	3.2	23	5.2	18

Sources: *Kosaku chōtei nempō*, 1925-1926; *Kosaku nempō*, 1927-1939; *Nōchi nempō*, 1940.

from the cities; if one adds to this tenants who for the same reason needed more land to feed larger families, one can see the potential for increased conflict.[19] But, in fact, the size of the agricultural work force dropped steadily from 1874 until 1940, with a slight increase only between 1926 and 1932; although the agricultural work force grew by 3.2 percent between 1925-1929 and 1930-1934, the non-agricultural

[19] Waswo, *Japanese Landlords*, pp. 128-129.

work force increased even more, by 8 percent.[20] Could it be that in some cases higher output per worker, based on improved technology, led to the desire for larger farms, and thus to disputes over land?

Finally, disputes for lower rents continued in unreduced numbers, especially in the west, even as those over contracts trebled. (See Table 5-6 and 5-7.)[21] All in all, one can only conclude that even during the harsh depression years tenant farmers challenged their landlords for complex reasons. While the fear of eviction undoubtedly motivated many of the poorest tenants to demand renewed contracts from their landlords, many of the others continued to fight for lower rents. And even many of the eviction disputes, especially before 1929 and after economic recovery began in 1934-1935, must have grown from seeds other than abject poverty.

In fact, the dramatic increase in the number of disputes over landlord-tenant contracts may be related to landlord tactics as well as to economic conditions, and this would help explain their unbroken upward trend in spite of economic fluctuations. When tenants demanded rent reductions, they usually withheld part or all of their rent during negotiations. When the dispute continued over several years without agreement or was renewed year after year in spite of annual solutions, landlords often went to court to force payment of rent, and failing in that, to evict their tenants. The landlord threatened to oust his tenants, not because he needed or even wanted his land back, but as a bargaining tactic. Thus, officials might classify a new dispute in the 1920s as a rent dispute, but several years later, in the late 1920s or 1930s, call a

[20] Ohkawa and Shinohara, *Patterns of Japanese Economic Development*, pp. 295, 392-393.

[21] Although Tōhoku disputes decreased in scale from 33 tenant participants per dispute in the 1920s to 3.9 in the 1930s, the size of Kinki disputes decreased only from 56 to 33 tenants per dispute. Since Kinki disputes even in the 1930s took place primarily over problems of rent, we can probably assume that rent-related disputes were considerably larger than contract-related ones.

continuation of the same conflict a contract dispute, even though the original cause was the tenants' demand for lower rent. One of Nishida's own case studies, the Hanabusa Village dispute in Yamanashi, is such an example. The dispute began when tenants demanded rent reductions of 50 percent to 90 percent, but ended after the landlords went to court to evict some of their tenants to force them to pay their overdue rent.[22]

This discussion of the problems of interpreting the *Tenancy Annual*'s statistics is not meant to depreciate the adverse effect that the world depression had on rural Japan; certainly it, like the Matsukata Deflation a half century earlier, damaged the livelihoods of many Japanese farmers; certainly it impelled many of them to join the tenant movement to protect their small rented holdings. Still, it is surprising that so few did so. Only 2 percent of all Japanese owner tenant, tenant owner, and tenant farmers took part in disputes in 1931, the depression year with the greatest involvement, and a majority of them still did so, as they had in the 1920s, over questions of rent, not of contract.

The difficulty in making correlations between income fluctuations and the causes of tenancy disputes suggests to me that the basis for the outbreak of the tenant-farmer movement lay on foundations far deeper than the annual rise and fall of rice and cocoon prices or factory wages. Rather, the long, upward economic trend which began at the turn of the century and continued unbroken except for the early 1930s until almost the end of World War II seems to me more important causatively. Cultivators from long experience handle the rise and fall of prices, yields, and income better than most of us do, and are unlikely to be goaded into antilandlord activism by annual fluctuations of the scale of those in the recession of 1920-1921. I am more persuaded that disputes took place in the 1920s because tenant farmer/small

[22] Nagahara, *Nihon jinushisei*, p. 317; Masumi Junnosuke, *Nihon seitōshiron*, Vol. 5, pp. 340-341.

businessmen wanted to increase their profits by paying lower rents and negotiating better contract terms, and that success in the early going led others to try disputes later. This view is not uniquely mine. Nishida Yoshiaki has made it repeatedly in his oeuvre during the past two decades. But my interpretation does differ from his in two important ways. By seeing the tenant-farmer movement as reformist, as seeking incremental change, rather than as a radical attempt to destroy landlord ownership of land, I, unlike Nishida, view compromise as an indication of tenant victory. I think the "petit bourgeois" approach continued in the 1930s, especially in western Japan and especially after rural Japan began to recover from the world depression in 1934.

NON-ECONOMIC CAUSES OF TENANT DISPUTES

The attempt to find a close correlation between income fluctuations and disputation not only deemphasizes long-term economic trends, but also attenuates the role of social, educational, and political causes in the rise of the tenant-farmer movement. And yet these forces, difficult as they are to quantify or link to the disputes precisely, also played some part. Take education and cosmopolitanism, for example. By the 1920s, almost all rural Japanese men under the age of forty and most under sixty had attended elementary school and had learned to read and write. This literacy allowed tenants to keep records and account books and to exchange information with their peers in neighboring hamlets and villages and with the national and regional liaison offices of their tenant unions.[23] It also helped to instill in tenants the belief that they should have greater independence and control over their own lives.

[23] The data presented in Table 4-16, on Kubo Nakajima's rents in 1925, which are drawn from a hamlet tenant union report to its prefectural liaison office, are indicative of the effects of literacy. If Kubo Nakajima's tenant union officials had not been able to read and write, they could not have compiled this report.

Waswo argues that education played only a limited role in changing the attitudes of tenant farmers because the schools emphasized in their curriculum "the official orthodoxy of the Japanese state—the divine origin of the nation and the throne, the value of harmony and cooperation, the virtue of filial piety . . ." and "did not introduce material which conflicted with the existing social order."[24] She is certainly correct in her description of the content of Japanese elementary education, but this does not necessarily negate the importance of education in the upsurge of tenant activism in the 1920s. Could one not be an orthodox Japanese who believed in the divinity of the emperor, obedience to political authority, the invincibility of the imperial army, and even the social superiority of the landlord, and still take part in anti-landlord disputes? Although present-day scholars like Nakamura and Inoue Kiyoshi equate landlords with the "emperor system," we have little reason to believe that tenants in the 1920s viewed their society in this way.[25]

It was not, I think, the content of education, but the basic skills learned and the *idea* of an education which were crucial to tenant activism. Mori Eikichi, whom Waswo quotes to document that farmers were too tired from their hard physical work in the daytime to read newspapers in the evening, may well be correct, but this did not seem to stop them from reading apolitical materials like sericultural and agricultural periodicals which were closely tied to their livelihoods.[26] Literacy, whether learned in Japan's nationalistic school system

---

[24] Waswo, "Origins of Tenant Unrest," pp. 378-379.

[25] See footnote 7 above; see also, Inoue Kiyoshi, *Tennōsei* (Tokyo, 1953), pp. 51-53.

[26] Waswo, "Origins of Tenant Unrest," p. 379. The survey conducted in April 1924 of members of tenant unions in four Okayama counties indicates that 30.5 percent (343 of 1,124) of the households surveyed subscribed to newspapers, however. Ōta Toshie, "Kosakunō kaikyū no keizaiteki shakaiteki jōtai," p. 103. If, as some scholars suggest, rural people circulated newspapers and magazines within their neighborhoods, at the very least, one-third of Okayama tenant union households had members who read newspapers.

or not, allowed tenants to adopt new farming techniques from sources other than their landlord. And education not only weakened the landlord's hold on his tenants but also gave the tenant a greater feeling of self-worth. One of the landlord's advantages over his tenants, literacy, was gone. Thus, if one views the tenant movement as a reformist attempt to better conditions of tenancy rather than as a revolutionary challenge to landlord predominance, one can view education as an underlying cause of the disputes.

Cosmopolitanism had a similar effect. Before the 1870s, few farmers had left their home districts or in many cases even their villages. But, after 1900, the army, factories, trains, and bicycles drew villagers to other parts of their region and country. Wider literacy strengthened the new cosmopolitanism because it allowed at least some farmers to read newspapers, magazines, and books, many of which were written in a form of Japanese easily understood by elementary-school graduates. After all, even the technical *Yamanashi Silkworm and Mulberry News*, with its reports of sericultural developments elsewhere in Japan and the world, and the reservists' *Comrades in Arms*, with its grossly patriotic view of the world, helped broaden their readers' narrow perspective. One did not have to read radical newspapers like the Communist Party's *Red Flag* for education, literacy, and cosmopolitanism to influence one's participation in a reformist tenant-farmer movement.

The results of Education Ministry tests given in 1930 to 20-year-olds when they took the army's physical examination for conscripts attest to the knowledge and broadened world view of twentieth-century Japanese.[27] Over 60 percent of the 8,561 respondents correctly identified such people, terms, events, and organizations as strike, Japan's primary

---

[27] Mombushō, *Sōtei shisō chōsa* (Tokyo, 1931). This volume presents the results of a test given to 8,561 young men in 11 communities at the time of the conscription physical examination in May-July 1930. The testees represented 1.4 percent of the 619,825 youths who took the physical examination in 1930.

export, unemployment, London Naval Disarmament Conference, mortgage, League of Nations, *Chronicle of Ancient Matters*, Ninomiya Sontoku, secondary employment, land tax, parliament, and Army Day. Over half successfully answered questions about Motoori Norinaga, the Kamakura period government, Mussolini, the national budget, opposition parties, the dissolution of parliament, the age at which one becomes an adult, the nation's primary product, the country which produced most of Japan's imported raw cotton, the organization which issued the one-yen note and the Charter Oath of 1868.[28] Urban test scores were higher than rural ones, 56 percent for all forty questions in four city areas tested, compared to 45 percent for seven rural regions. Nevertheless, young men in more highly commercialized rural districts, like Niigata's Minami Kambara County, a focal point of tenant union organization, and Kanagawa's Naka County, near Yokohama and Tokyo, achieved grades close to those in Tokyo's Nihombashi Ward and Kure and Kobe cities, and higher than those in Tokyo's Fukagawa Ward. Testees in only one of the eleven districts involved, Nishi Tsugaru County in Aomori in the far north, had extremely bad results in the examination. Young men there managed to answer only 30 percent of the questions correctly, compared to 53 percent in Minami Kambara County and 60 percent in Nihombashi.[29] Although we have no comparative test data for the early Meiji period, it seems safe to assume that the widespread illiteracy at the time bespoke a narrower understanding of the larger world: even the modest test scores of 1930 indicate that young men, and especially those in urban and commercialized rural areas, had a broader knowledge than had their grandparents and great grandparents in the 1870s.[30]

[28] *Sōtei shisō chōsa*, pp. 105-107.

[29] *Ibid.*, pp. 112-134.

[30] Only slightly more than half of the Japanese high-school students tested in 1982 could identify Tōjō Hideki as Japan's wartime prime minister or Chiang Kai-shek as China's Nationalist leader during the Sino-Japanese

The Education Ministry examiners also asked questions about attitudes toward work, reasons for voting for members of parliament and paying taxes, local government, and the solution to labor and tenancy disputes, and these results also reveal the comparative modernity of the young men's attitudes. Over 60 percent of those surveyed, for example, stated that their families remitted taxes to pay for essential government services, a modern attitude, while only 17-18 percent said that they paid to fulfill a debt which they owed to their country (*ongaeshi*). There was no significant difference between commercialized rural and urban districts, but a higher percentage of respondents from remote Aomori, 29 percent, stated that their households paid taxes out of a sense of obligation to their country, compared to only 15 percent in Nihombashi and Minami Kambara.[31]

The respondents also answered overwhelmingly—73 percent, to 27 percent combined for the other five answers—that they believed the best way to solve labor and tenancy disputes was through compromise. (See Table 5-9.) Very few—14 percent in agriculture and 18 percent in manufacturing—saw government intercession as the solution to disputation, even if the government did not take sides. In other words, the young men surveyed rejected the traditional role of strong government in solving disputes for solutions achieved locally and peacefully by factory owners and laborers, and by landlords and tenants themselves. If these twenty-year-olds, who because of their youth one would expect to be more hotheaded than their fathers who led the tenant movement, viewed compromise as the best solution to tenancy disputes, no wonder so many ended through peaceful negotiations.[32] But more important to our understanding of the role of literacy, knowledge, and cosmopoli-

---

War. *Chronicle of Higher Education*, December 1982. Thus, the 1930 results may not be as modest as they appear.

[31] *Sōtei shisō chōsa*, pp. 65-81.

[32] For an example of the hotheadedness of youth, see the description of the Emman Affair of 1930 in Chapter 6, below.

TABLE 5-9

Attitudes toward the Settlement of Labor and
Tenancy Disputes, by Profession

	Total Sample	Agriculture	Manufacturing
Number Surveyed	7,703	1,898	2,038
Compromise	73.0%	71.5%	70.7%
Equitable Government Intervention	9.1%	8.5%	10.3%
Worker and Tenant Farmer Surrender	6.8%	9.2%	7.1%
Factory Owner and Landlord Surrender	4.4%	4.9%	4.1%
Government Sides with Tenants and Workers	5.8%	4.4%	7.1%
Government Sides with Owners and Landlords	0.9%	1.4%	0.7%

Source: Mombushō shakai kyōikukyoku, *Sōtei shisō chōsa* (Tokyo, 1931), pp. 30, 142-143.

tanism in the anti-landlord movement, the belief in compromise shows that tenant farmers had pragmatic, reformist views of what they could achieve through disputation. The relatively illiterate and provincial peasants of the Tempō, *bakumatsu*, and early Meiji periods took part in spontaneous, violent outbursts which often ended with little gain and harsh punishments for the participants; the comparatively literate and cosmopolitan farmers of the 1920s participated in planned, generally non-violent disputes which ended when they had achieved, without penalty, clear-cut, limited, and attainable programs—and they could demand them anew the following year.[33]

[33] Often writers who claim to sympathize deeply with the plight of the Japanese peasant (or farmer) see his mentality as unchanging and him as unable to improve his condition from the late Tokugawa to the early

Tenant farmers had become better educated between 1870 and 1930, and also the nature of government and their role in it had changed—this too influenced the tenant-farmer movement. Without trying to answer the sticky question of how democratic "Taishō democracy" was, I think it safe to say that the Japanese public played a greater role in politics in the 1920s than ever before. No one voted and few commoners participated in government in the late feudal or early Meiji period; even after the establishment of local representative assemblies and a national parliament in the 1870s and 1880s, only substantial taxpayers cast votes or held office. But in the twentieth century the government extended suffrage to more and more people until, from 1925 on, all men over the age of twenty-five, regardless of tax payments, gained the right to vote. Even in 1921, when men needed to pay three yen in direct taxes to vote, tenants won 2,311 seats on town and village assemblies, but in 1925 tenant farmers broke the landlords' grip on local political power. In the election for village and town assemblies in 1925, the first in which all men could vote, tenant and owner tenant farmers won 9,061 of the 42,738 seats contested (21.2 percent) in 3,142 (27.3 percent) of Japan's villages and towns and took control of 340 assemblies. Eight years later they expanded their strength to 14,514 (26.3 percent) seats on 3,632 assemblies (31.9 percent) of which they controlled 634. It is in part this dramatic increase in tenant power which has led the political scientist Masumi Junnosuke to view the interwar decades as an era in which those owner, owner tenant, and tenant farmers who had proved their ability as leaders of tenant unions and productive association branches took charge of hamlet and village government. When the tenant unions weakened the landlords' economic position, the unions' leaders began to inherit the landlords' political power.[34]

Shōwa period. As an example, see E. H. Norman, *Japan's Emergence as a Modern State*, pp. 156-157.

[34] *NSSS*, Vol. 3, pp. 64-65; *Shōwa hachinendo chōson kaigi ni okeru kosakuningawa tōsen no gaikyō*, pp. 18-27; Masumi, *Nihon seitōshiron*, Vol. 5, pp. 342, 344-351.

In this political realm, however, it was not participation qua participation in local government or power qua power that was of primary importance in stimulating the tenant-farmers' movement. As Kimbara Samon has pointed out, poor farmers and workers provided a major driving force for Taishō democracy; that is to say, commoners were not given the vote but won it themselves by dint of their own cumulative power.[35] It is rather the new awareness of potency, born of political success, literacy, knowledge, and cosmopolitanism which is central, and it influenced tenant farmers to take a more instrumental view of life and disputes. A small taste of power made them hungry for more; success bred success. Two of the reasons that more and more tenants joined the movement after its small beginnings in 1917-1920 must have been their increased realization that they gained from disputation, and their growing sense of power.

A number of scholars have emphasized the impact on the tenant movement of various exogenous, "proletarian" influences like the Russian Revolution of 1917, the urban Rice Riots of 1918, labor unions, and radical activists, and these too, although difficult to link specifically to the tenant movement, cannot be ignored.[36] Stories of the October Revolution, the Rice Riots and industrial strikes, and direct contact with members of one's own or neighboring families who had taken part in urban labor disputes could well have spread the idea of direct action against one's economic betters. Democracy was in the air in Japan as elsewhere after World War I, and even farmers probably learned a little about it.

One must be careful, however, not to make too much of some of these influences.[37] In the multiple-choice questions

---

[35] Eguchi Keiichi et al., *Shinpojium Nihon rekishi 20: Taishō demokurashii* (Tokyo, 1969), p. 46.

[36] See, for example, George O. Totten, *The Social Democratic Movement in Prewar Japan* (New Haven, 1966), pp. 336-358, and Nakamura, *Jinushiseishi kenkyū*, pp. 244-245.

[37] Waswo makes this point in "Origins of Tenant Unrest," pp. 379-380.

of the 1930 examination of draft-age young men, for example, only 25.5 percent of the testees identified the Soviet Union as the post-revolutionary name for Russia; 8.8 percent thought it was Czechoslovakia, 6.3 percent Australia, 3.2 percent the United States, and over half had no idea. Only. 20.9 percent chose the correct Chinese characters (*minshū-shugi*) for the English loan word *demokurashii*; 15.7 percent selected egoism (*rikoshugi*), 10.9 percent radicalism (*kageki shisō*), 6.7 percent mob psychology (*gunshū shinri*), and the rest left the question unanswered. As one might expect, young men from Tokyo's Nihombashi Ward had the highest rate of correct answers (51.5 percent and 32.7 percent) for both questions, Aomori young men (10.2 percent and 8.2 percent) the lowest, with Niigata's Minami Kambara County (19.8 percent and 27.9 percent) and Tokyo's Fukagawa Ward (29.3 percent and 18.8 percent) in between.[38] While we might not expect young men with only six or eight years of elementary education to define correctly an abstract foreign concept or to know the location of a remote country, one would expect them to have a better idea than their less-well-educated fathers, who led the local tenant and labor unions. Given these test scores, one can only wonder how strong an influence foreign ideas had on tenant farmers—or, for that matter, on industrial workers.

The examination indicates a greater knowledge of the Japanese labor movement. Sixty-nine-and-nine-tenths percent of the testees correctly defined an unemployed person (*shitsugyōsha*) as a "person who lost his job and was badly off," 68.5 percent a strike (*sutoraiki*) as a "league to walk off the job," and 48.9 percent a proletarian (*puroretaria*) as a "person without property." Young men in every region tested got these three questions correct far more often than they did the questions on the Soviet Union and democracy. It would appear that even farmers' sons, and thus probably their fathers as well, had more knowledge of the urban labor movement than they did of foreign events and concepts.[39]

---

[38] *Sōtei shisō chōsa*, pp. 107-109; 135-138.   [39] *Ibid.*

This awareness of the workers' movement was probably relatively widespread because it came to the countryside directly, through family members who worked in factories and labor organizers like Suzuki Bunji, Kagawa Toyohiko, Sugiyama Motojirō, Hirano Rikizō, and Asanuma Inejirō, who organized nationwide tenant union headquarters in the 1920s, rather than secondhand through newspapers and hearsay. These organizers founded the Japan Farmers' Union (*Nichinō*) on April 22, 1922, and by the end of 1925 it enrolled 72,794 members in 957 branches. Other national or regional unions sprung up or split off from *Nichinō*, and in 1927, the peak year of tenant union membership, the regional or national unions organized 135,690 members. The national tenant-farmers' movement, led largely by labor leaders and socialist intellectuals, was not an insignificant force.[40]

And yet, one must be wary of attributing too much rural influence to the urban socialist/labor leaders. To begin with, *Nichinō*, even in 1925-1927, before its unity was weakened by internal squabbling, enlisted fewer than 25 percent of all *organized* tenant farmers, and 2 percent of all tenant farmers. In 1927, 68,710 of 365,332 tenant union members (19 percent) belonged to *Nichinō*. Another 66,980 (18 percent) had joined other national, regional or prefectural unions. The remaining 229,632 (63 percent) had enlisted in local unions, usually organized at the hamlet or village level.[41] In fact, although tenant unions attracted about 5-10 percent of all tenants from the mid-1920s to the late 1930s (Table 5-10), enrollment in nationally organized unions fell off after 1925-1927. *Nichinō* had 72,794 members (24 percent of total union

---

[40] *Kosaku nempō*, 1927; Totten, *Social Democratic Movement*, p. 337; *Nōmin kumiai gojūnenshi*, p. 14.

[41] *Kosaku nempō*, 1927. Masumi Junnosuke, *Nihon seitōshiron*, Vol. 5, pp. 339, 438, points out that the centrally organized labor and tenant unions enlisted an "extremely small number" of members when viewed in the context of the whole society. See Smethurst, *A Social Basis for Prewar Japanese Militarism*, p. 146, for a similar view.

TABLE 5-10
Tenant Union Membership, 1923-1941

Year	Members	Year	Members
1923	163,931	1933	302,736
1924	232,125	1934	276,246
1925	307,106	1935	242,422
1926	346,693	1936	229,209
1927	365,332	1937	226,919
1928	330,406	1938	217,883
1929	315,771	1939	210,208
1930	301,436	1940	75,930
1931	306,301	1941	23,595
1932	296,839		

Source: *Kosaku chōtei nempō*, 1925-1926; *Kosaku nempō*, 1927-1939; *Nōchi nempō*, 1940-1941.

membership) in 1925, and 68,710 members (19 percent) in 1927, but its successor, the National Farmers' Union (*Zennō*), enlisted only 53,814 (18 percent) farmers in 1930 and 32,273 (13 percent) in 1935.[42] The inability of national and regional unions to attract widespread support or to dominate the tenant movement is reflected in politics as well as in membership. Of 9,061 tenant farmers elected to local assemblies in 1925, only 1,312 (14 percent) belonged to unions, local, regional, or national, and only 609 of these (7 percent of the total 9,061) represented Nichinō; in 1933, only 1,454 (10 percent) of the tenants who won seats on assemblies belonged to tenant unions.[43]

The question one might ask, therefore, is not why labor's influence was so deep, but, conversely, why it was so shallow. Why did the labor movement and its university-educated socialist leaders make so weak an impression on the

[42] *Kosaku chōtei nempō*, 1927; *Nōmin kumiai gojūnenshi*, p. 14.
[43] *NSSS*, Vol. 3, p. 65; *Shōwa hachinendo chōson kaigi ni okeru kosakuningawa tōsen no gaikyō*, pp. 18-27.

countryside that at the peak of their influence they could recruit only 2 percent of the nation's tenants and elect only 609 of *Nichinō*'s members to local office? One answer, put forward by George Totten, draws on the putative dual character of the farmer, what he quotes E. H. Norman as calling the "Janus head of the Japanese peasant." The benighted peasant was either "the picture of feudal subservience to authority and privilege" or a participant in "angry, indignant revolt." The peasant took part in organized political movements like the proletarian one of the 1920s only when its intellectual leaders led him "by the hand."[44] This patronizing approach overlooks two basic characteristics of Japanese society in the 1920s. On the one hand, the farmer of the late Taishō era was not a peasant. By the time of *Nichinō*'s founding in 1922, rational farmers had long since outgrown this passivity-explosion syndrome and searched for moderate, reformist ways to improve their living standards. On the other hand, Japanese socialist intellectuals tended not to be pragmatists. The national union's leaders, especially as *Nichinō* moved to the left in the mid-1920s, often advocated "land for the tiller," class struggle, and sometimes even revolution, but the actual cultivators wanted lower rents and better tenancy conditions.[45] The national unions seemed to have played a significant role in the rare and extensively studied violent tenant disputes like the famous ones at Kisaki Village in Niigata, Fujita Village in Okayama, Odajima Village in Yamagata, Gōdō Village in Gumma, and Maeda Village in Akita.[46]

[44] Norman, *Japan's Emergence*, p. 156; Totten, *Social Democratic Movement*, pp. 341-342.

[45] *Nōmin kumiai gojūnenshi*, p. 7; Shiota Shōbē, *Nihon shakai undōshi* (Tokyo, 1982), p. 113; Masumi, *Nihon seitōshiron*, Vol. 5, pp. 449-450.

[46] A survey of the literature shows that these atypical cases appear over and over. The Kisaki and Odajima disputes appear in Hane, *Peasants, Rebels, and Outcastes*, and Nakamura, *Rōdōsha to nōmin*; the Maeda dispute in Hane and the *Asahi Journal*'s *Shōwashi no shunkan*, Vol. 1 (Tokyo, 1966); and the Kisaki, Fujita, and Gōdō disputes in *Nōmin kumiai gojūnenshi*, for example. The editors of *Nihon nōmin undōshi* (Tokyo, 1961), one of the major sources for the study of the tenant movement, present the Kisaki, Gōdō, Maeda,

But normally, tenant and owner tenant farmers organized hamlet or village-level unions and called on regional or national organizations only when they needed large-scale cooperation or legal aid. Otherwise, farmers avoided the urban intellectual labor organizers (and especially the radical ones whose presence invited police repression), with whom they had little in common.[47]

Although tenants generally did not join or participate actively in national tenant organizations, the formation of unions during disputes was one of their primary tactics. Like urban trade unionists, tenants realized that they could not deal with "management" successfully without unity; thus, normally all of a hamlet's tenants, whether rich or poor, formed a league to provide mutual economic security and to confront their landlords collectively during negotiations. Tenants formed unions, otherwise acted jointly, or called on regional or national unions for assistance as their first tactic in at least three-quarters of all disputes in the late 1920s and early 1930s.[48]

That tenants tended to see the formation of unions as a pragmatic way to build a base to negotiate with their land-

---

and Odajima disputes among the eight case studies described in detail. See also Shiota, *Nihon shakai undōshi*, pp. 68, 113.

[47] Nakamura describes in some detail and with sympathy the Odajima Incident of March 7, 1931, in which intellectuals, former industrial workers, owner farmers, and some tenant farmers led impoverished and landless local tenants in an effort to gain farms of a size adequate to support their families. These actions led to the arrest of the leadership from the national union's Yamagata Prefecture regional headquarters en masse, the eventual indictment and conviction of 84 (86 according to *Nihon nōmin undōshi*, p. 1,052) union leaders, and the death by torture of three of those arrested. *Rōdōsha to nōmin*, pp. 326-329. One must chastise such police brutality. Nevertheless, Nakamura does not tell us how many of those involved were actual tenant farmers, and how many were urban intellectuals and labor leaders. Given the absence of police repression in most tenant disputes, I find it likely that the actions of the non-farmer outside leaders, not the tenant dispute per se, attracted the attention of the authorities.

[48] *NSSS*, Vol. 2, pp. 324-327; *Kosaku chōtei nempō*, 1925; *Kosaku nempō*, 1928, 1929, 1931.

lords rather than as a reactive, aggressive, revolutionary step which permanently endangered hamlet social and economic harmony is shown by the type of men they chose as their leaders. If the tenants' primary motivation for disputation and unionization had been born of intense stratification and class struggle, one would expect the poorest, most desperate tenants to guide the unions. But, as a number of Japanese investigators have found, the relatively well-to-do owner tenants and upper tenants, not the economically marginal poor farmers, organized and led the local tenant organizations. Studies of disputes by Nishida Yoshiaki for Hanabusa Village in Yamanashi and Kanazuka Village in Niigata, by Kurihara Hakujū for Kōjō Village in Okayama, by Takahashi Iichirō and Shirakawa Kiyoshi for Asahi Village in Aichi, and by Fukutake Tadashi for Shiota Village in Nagano—all indicate that the economically secure, mainstay (chūken) farmers, those just below the small landlords and owner farmers in status and income, took charge of their villages' unions. As we shall see in Chapter Six, this was also true in Kubo Nakajima.[49]

The evidence from the Tenancy Annual on "first tenant tactic per dispute" (see Table 6-6) shows that tenants took many other moderate steps aimed at gaining immediate pragmatic goals besides the forming of unions. Most frequently the tenants sought mediation (24 percent of reported first tactics excluding unionization), and occasionally they held public meetings, called in speakers or otherwise demonstrated (8 percent), withheld rent payments to force landlord concessions (8 percent), contacted defense attorneys (5 percent), or petitioned for lower rents (5 percent). In only 343 of 9,109 cases reported for 1925, 1926, 1928, 1929, and 1931 did the tenants take first measures which disrupted the

---

[49] Nagahara, Nihon jinushisei, pp. 219-318; Nishida, "Shōnō keiei," pp. 24-41; Kurihara Hakujū, Nihon nōmin undōshi, pp. 557-587; Takahashi Iichirō and Shirakawa Kiyoshi, Nōchi kaikaku to jinushisei (Tokyo, 1955), pp. 99-102; Fukutake Tadashi, "Buraku no 'heiwa' to kaikyūteki kinchō," p. 459.

local order: threats of violence, 156; destruction of the land-lord's crops, 55; the introduction of outside agitators, 48; withdrawal of children from school, 30; withdrawal from the credit union, youth association, or fire department, 27; breaking off all ties with landlords, 12; formation of a league not to return foreclosed farm land, 12; ostracism, 2; and ar-son, 1.[50]

Records of criminal charges and the dearth of policemen in the Japanese countryside further reinforce this interpreta-tion, which emphasizes the pursual of moderate, pragmatic, and reformist rather than extremist, revolutionary, and working-class-based goals. As Table 5-11 shows, the police brought criminal charges against *at most* 8,538 of 1,275,412 (0.7 percent) tenants participating in disputes between 1925 and 1940.[51] Ronald Dore and Tsutomu Ouchi point out that in both 1920 and 1930 the density of policemen in three rural areas, Aomori, Nagano, and Kagoshima prefectures, was under 6 per 10,000 populace, only slightly more than half the police density of the English countryside.[52] Prefectural statistics show something similar for Yamanashi. If the po-lice feared rural class struggle and violence in the 1920s and 1930s, one would expect a higher concentration of policemen to handle the potential unrest.

Tenants did not resort to violence and thus compel a higher concentration of police in the countryside because

[50] *NSSS*, Vol. 2, pp. 324-327; *Kosaku chōtei nempō*, 1925; *Kosaku nempō*, 1928, 1929, 1931.

[51] If the procurator indicted a person for more than one crime, the records count him more than once. In 1931, a year for which we have evidence about multiple charges, 603 of 1,027 indictments represent second, third, or fourth, etc., crimes, and only 424 or 41 percent of the total represent sepa-rate individuals. If the same ratio held for all of 1925-1940, only 3,500 per-sons were indicted for crimes committed during tenant disputes in these years. Moreover, we have no evidence to prove that the authorities charged only tenants; they may have indicted landlords and the tenants' outside sup-porters as well. *Kosaku nempō*, 1931.

[52] R. P. Dore and Tsutomu Ouchi, "Rural Origins of Japanese Fascism," in Morley, *Dilemmas of Growth*, p. 187.

TABLE 5-11

Number of Criminal Charges Made in Tenancy Disputes,
and Tenant Participants in Disputes, 1925-1940

Charge	Number Charged
Violation of Violence	
Control Law	3,477
Riot	1,027
Assault and Injury	891
Impeding the Police in the	
Performance of Public Duty	653
Property Damage	516
Fraud and Corruption	336
Use of Threatening Language	287
Extortion	236
Violation of Police Crime	
Penalty Regulation	235
Impeding Business	188
Violation of Peace	
Preservation Law	154
Theft	152
Slander	27
Attempted Murder	13
Arson	10
Other	336
Total Charges	8,538
Total Tenant Participants	1,275,412

Calculated from Naimushō keihōkyoku, *Shakai undō no jōkyō,* 4 (1932), pp. 1,258-1,259; 5 (1933), pp. 1,237-1,238; 14 (1942), pp. 727-729.

they did not need to; tenants were neither desperately poor participants in "angry, indignant revolt" nor rural proletarians involved in attempting to win land or even more radical goals from implacable landlords. Rather, tenants consistently won concessions which brought down their rent, assured their long-term rights of tenancy, or otherwise enabled them to improve their livelihood.

COMPROMISE AND THE SUCCESS OF THE
TENANT-FARMER MOVEMENT

Table 5-12 presents data on the outcome of tenancy disputes by period between 1920 and 1941. As is apparent, the percentage which ended in compromise or tenant victory remained consistently above 96 percent of all disputes settled throughout the interwar decades. The percentage which landlords won outright never exceeded the 3.7 percent of the early 1920s. This combination of the rarity of landlord victory and the infrequency of police intervention leads one to wonder how scholars could interpret the tenant-farmers' movement as an effort doomed to failure in the face of landlord intransigence and governmental repression. Rather, it would appear that tenants consistently held the upper hand.

Evidence for rent reductions requested and actually received also supports the conclusion that tenants gained concrete advantages from disputation. In 1926 and 1928, two reasonably good years for farmers, disputing tenants asked for average rent reductions of 35 percent and 34 percent and received an average of 24 percent each year. In 1931 and 1933, depression years, tenant disputants requested average

TABLE 5-12
Outcome of Tenancy Disputes, 1920-1941

Years	Number of Disputes Settled	Percentage Settled by Compromise	Percentage Won by Tenants	Percentage Won by Landlords
1920-24	5,626	89.0%	7.3%	3.7%
1925-29	8,522	92.7%	5.1%	2.2%
1930-34	14,998	78.3%	18.4%	3.3%
1935-37	16,503	91.6%	5.8%	2.6%
1938-41	12,906	84.7%	11.8%	3.5%

Calculated from *Kosaku chōtei nempō*, 1925-1926; *Kosaku nempō*, 1927-1939; *Nōchi nempō*, 1940-1941.

reductions of 37 percent and 40 percent lower rents and received 29 percent and 31 percent.[53] It would appear that
when landlords and tenants compromised, they did not split
the difference; negotiated settlements favored the tenants.

Compromise benefited tenants rather than landlords in
disputes over the continuation of tenancy as well as over
rent. Landlords demanded that tenants turn back rented land
22,523 times between 1925 and 1940, but tenants actually
returned the landlord's land unconditionally in only 5.3 percent of these cases. In another 39 percent of eviction disputes,
tenants gave back part of the disputed land or received another piece of land or monetary compensation for returning
it. But, in another 48 percent of the cases, the tenant's right
of cultivation was upheld and he returned nothing, and in 4
percent of the cases he was able to purchase from the landlord the land under contention. Although, as one might expect, landlords had more success during the depression years
in their attempts to use their private property as they
wanted, even then landlords managed to regain their land in
fewer than half of their attempts.[54] (See Table 5-13.) And
tenants won a higher percentage of land tenure disputes than
ever before during the "fascist" years after the outbreak of
the war in China, when, according to Nakamura, the tenant
movement waned because of government repression. Given
his view, that tenants in 1938-1940 managed to keep their
right of cultivation unconditionally in 57 percent of all landlord attempts to force its return comes as something of a
shock.

What allowed relatively poor tenant farmers to gain lower
rents, maintain their rights of cultivation, and otherwise improve tenancy conditions in the face of the opposition of the

---

[53] *NSSS*, Vol. 2, pp. 312-315; *Kosaku nempō*, 1928, 1933. The *Tenancy
Annual* does not report information on rent reductions demanded and received after 1933.

[54] Since those disputes in which tenants received another equal plot of land
when required to return a piece of land, 3-4 percent of the total, are included
under "other return," tenants suffered in eviction disputes to a lesser extent
than these data demonstrate.

TABLE 5-13

Disputes over Landlord Attempts to Evict Tenants from Rented Land,
1925-1940

Year	Average Number of Disputes per Year	Percentage of Unconditional Return	Percentage of Other Return	Percentage of Contract Continuation	Percentage of Tenant Purchase
1925-29	312	5.4%	41%	44%	6%
1930-34	1,438	6.9%	42%	45%	4%
1935-37	2,888	4.6%	40%	48%	4%
1938-40	1,702	3.8%	34%	52%	5%
Total	1,408	5.3%	39%	48%	4%

Calculated from *Kosaki chōtei nempō*, 1925-26; *Kosaku nempō*, 1927-1939; *Nōchi nempō*, 1940.

richer and more powerful landlords in the 1920s and the 1930s? Partly the relative scarcity of labor, which we discussed in Chapter One, made it difficult for landlords to find tenants to replace those whom they evicted. But, equally important, the government provided a mechanism for compromise by its passage of the dispute mediation law in 1924. According to this law, either landlords or tenants could submit their differences to non-binding arbitration by local representatives of the prefectural Tenancy Officers (*kosakukan*). Between 1925 and 1941, 62.5 percent of all tenancy disputes, 40,589 of 64,913, were submitted to arbitration under the law; the arbitrators successfully resolved 27,404 of these cases. When one adds 3,739 disputes which "men of local influence" mediated outside the law's framework, 48 percent of all tenancy disputes between 1925 and 1941 were settled through arbitration. Although Nakamura views this farm dispute mediation law as part of the government's efforts to bolster landlord power and "emperor system authority," tenants must have seen it differently.[55] Tenants requested arbitration in 62 percent of all mediated disputes, and landlords

---

[55] Nakamura, *Jinushiseishi kenkyū*, pp. 256-257.

did so in only 34 percent; both parties applied jointly in the other 4 percent.[56] The success of conciliation in resolving disputes, the propensity for tenants to be the ones who requested it, the compromise settlements that tended to favor the tenants over the landlords, and the absence of forceful government intervention on the landlord's side—all allowed the tenant farmers to improve their livelihoods without upsetting permanently hamlet harmony. Even to call most of the disputes "disputes" is clearly a misnomer.

Given what social scientists like John Embree, Chie Nakane, Richard Beardsley, Harumi Befu, Robert Smith, and many, many others have written about the importance of harmony and cooperation in Japanese rural society, it should come as no surprise that most disputes ended in compromise.[57] In fact, it is more astonishing that so many scholars can see class struggle pervading the interwar countryside.[58] That tenant farmers used collective action effectively to advance through largely peaceful means their personal (household) fortunes reveals a pragmatism which I find admirable. Rational farmers diversified their crops, spread commercial fertilizer and weed killers, used new cultivating techniques, and participated in tenancy disputes, all as a way of improving their livelihoods.

The success of the tenant movement was not limited to its

[56] *Kosaku chōtei nempō*, 1925-1926; *Kosaku nempō*, 1927-1939; *Nōchi nempō*, 1940-1941.

[57] John Embree, *Suyemura: A Japanese Village* (Chicago, 1939), pp. 112-157; Chie Nakane, *Japanese Society* (Berkeley, 1970); Richard K. Beardsley et al., *Village Japan*; Harumi Befu, *Japan: An Anthropological Introduction* (San Francisco, 1971); Robert Smith, "The Japanese Rural Community: Norms, Sanctions and Ostracism," Jack M. Potter et al., ed., *Peasant Society: A Reader* (Berkeley, 1967), pp. 246-255.

[58] A good example of this is the popular article by Shiota Shōbē in the *Asahi Journal's Shōwashi no shunkan*. Professor Shiota discusses one dispute, the violent one which took place at Maeda Village in Akita Prefecture, at some length. He then presents data on the number of disputes and tenant participants per year, and thus implies that the interwar countryside was in chaos. *Shōwashi no shunkan*, Vol. 1, pp. 114-122.

members; non-participating members of rural society benefited as well. A study of 518 villages conducted by the Imperial Agricultural Society (*Teikoku nōkai*) for 1926 (Table 5-
14) demonstrates that tenants living in communities adjacent
to disputing villages received rent reductions of about two-
thirds the size of those received by disputants themselves.
Average paddy field rents nationwide fell by 11 percent from
1.17 *koku* of rice per *tan* in 1921 to 1.04 *koku* in 1937; over the
same period, yields increased by 6-7 percent.[59] Tenant farmers who joined in the disputes adopted a tactic which worked
not only for themselves but also for their non-participating
fellow tenants.

TABLE 5-14

Rent Reductions for Rice Paddies in Disputing and
Neighboring Villages, May–December 1926

	Disputing Villages	Neighboring Villages
A. Rent Before Disputes	1.22 *koku*	1.26 *koku*
B. Rent After Disputes	1.03	1.13
A—B	0.19	0.13
Percentage of Reduction	15.6%	10.3%
Number of Villages Surveyed	352	166

Calculated from Teikoku nōkai chōsabu, *Kosaku sōgichi oyobi sono rinsetsuchi ni okeru kosakuryō narabini tochi baibai kakaku no hendō ni kansuru chōsa*
(Tokyo, 1927), mimeographed, no page numbers.

[59] *Kosaku nempō*, 1938, pp. 6-8; *Chōki keizai tōkei*, Vol. 9, pp. 168, 217.

SIX

Tenant Disputes in the
Kōfu Basin

NISHIDA YOSHIAKI, in his richly detailed study of Hanabusa, a Yamanashi village several miles to the northeast of Ōkamada, states that "although the commercial tenant farmers became the leaders of the local tenant movement, they, because of their petit bourgeois (*puchiburu*) attitudes, had to weaken at the crucial moment" of the dispute.[1] In the 1920s, he writes, these owner tenants and upper tenants joined with their poorer "subsistence farmer" brethren, the rural proletariat, to fight the landlords because they both wanted lower rents, the commercial stratum to increase profits and gain greater control over the land they tilled, the marginal stratum to keep the wolf a bit farther from the door. But once the upper tenants successfully obtained lower rents and were given the opportunity to own more land, they abandoned their poorer and weaker compeers. Attitudes determined by their *puchiburu* class membership, particularly their desire to possess their own farms, no matter how tiny, compelled them to desert. The subsistence tenants in the 1930s found themselves forced to stand alone, fighting a defensive action to protect the fragile tenure of their fields from landlord confiscation.[2] Thus, Nishida, who has presented a compelling revision of the orthodox interpretation of the tenant-farmer movement in the 1920s by demonstrating that most tenants participated for reformist goals—to gain lower rent, better terms of tenancy, and if possible more land—concludes in-

---

[1] Nagahara, *Nihon jinushisei*, p. 271.
[2] *Ibid.*, pp. 251, 269, 273, 498.

consistently that these disputes were a revolutionary attack to overthrow the landlord system which failed at least partly because upper tenants had petit bourgeois, not working class attitudes.[3]

The tenant movement, like any broad social movement, was complex, and some of its members, largely its urban intellectual sympathizers, joined out of the desire to create a new economically and socially egalitarian order. But I think, as Nishida *demonstrates*, that most tenant farmers fought for reformist goals. The newly literate tenant farmer raised his standard of living between 1900 and 1919 (in Naka Koma, real farm income per household doubled between 1909 and 1919 alone), and he saw tenant disputes, as well as new and better fertilizer, seed types, tools, techniques, and farm management, as a way of increasing income even more. When viewed in this light, the commercial tenant, who, as Nishida's Hanabusa and Shōnai and my Kubo Nakajima data indicate, was one of the vast majority of rural society, did not desert a revolution; rather, he rationally pursued his own interests.[4]

One might better compare the tenant-farmers' movement of the 1920s and 1930s with the postwar labor movement rather than with a revolutionary one. Tenants in a given hamlet, to pursue their households' goals, banded together in unions because they found success came through collective action. Their landlords, although fewer in number, had many advantages: more money, better education, readier access to political authority, and greater experience with the legal system. But the tenants discovered that if they pooled their resources to act collectively, developed tactics based on their own strengths (and their landlords' weaknesses), and called on national organizations to provide lawyers and other specialists when needed, they could battle successfully their

---

[3] Nishida, "Nōmin undō," pp. 172-173; "Nōchi kaikaku no rekishiteki seikaku," p. 160.

[4] Nagahara, *Nihon jinushisei*, p. 240; Nishida, "Nōmin undō," pp. 165-166; Chapter Four above, pp. 283-296.

customary superiors and gain major concessions. Although the American occupation's land reform killed the landlord system once and for all in the late 1940s, it began to die with the rise of the tenant movement after World War I.[5] The matador who killed the bull may have been General Mac-Arthur, but tens of thousands of petit bourgeois picadors made his job easy. The purpose of this chapter, therefore, is to look closely at tenant disputes in the Kōfu Basin and Kubo Nakajima hamlet to demonstrate the broadening success of what I admire as a sanguine and pragmatic reformist movement.

Yamanashi was a hotbed of tenant-farmer disputes throughout the 1920s and 1930s. In the succinct words of Takegawa Yoshinori, chronicler of the prefecture's movement, "Yamanashi had as many tenant disputes as it has cormorant droppings," and as the reader of the nō play Ukai, set near Hanabusa, recognizes, the prefecture is famous for that big bird. Between 1920 and 1940, 54,252 tenant farmers participated in 3,514 tenant disputes involving 20,981 chō of tenanted land. Since Yamanashi had 51,332 full-time and 10,080 part-time tenant households and 27,706 chō of tenanted land, its rate of involvement almost doubled the national average. (See Table 5-1.)[6]

One characteristic of tenant-farmer disputes which has been widely noted is the shift of their geographical center of gravity from the Kinki and Chūbu regions in the west in the 1920s to the northeast in the 1930s.[7] Few prefectures man-

---

[5] Of all the Japanese scholars who write on tenant disputes, Nishida Yo-shiaki comes closest to viewing the two decades of tenant disputes as a period in which landlord power was broken. But even he equivocates. On page 272 of his contribution to the Nagahara volume on the Japanese landlord system, Nishida writes that landlords regained the upper hand over tenants in the 1930s—he calls this the reintegration (saihensei) of the landlord system; on page 317, he writes that the late 1930s brought the end of the landlord system.

[6] Kosaku chōtei nempō, 1925-1926; Kosaku nempō, 1927-1939; Nōchi nempō, 1940; Yamanashi tōkeisho, 1930.

[7] Waswo, Japanese Landlords, pp. 96-99; Nishida, "Nōmin undō," pp. 173-174; Nakamura, Jinushiseishi kenkyū, pp. 278-279.

TABLE 6-1

Number of Disputes and Index of Disputes per Farm Household
in Fifteen Leading Prefectures, 1920-1929 and 1930-1941

| | 1920-1929 | | | 1930-1941 | |
Prefecture	Disputes	Index	Prefecture	Disputes	Index
Osaka	2,229	510	Yamanashi	3,303	100
Hyōgo	2,587	287	Akita	3,391	73
Nara	564	175	Yamagata	3,155	68
Kyoto	606	147	Tokushima	1,566	51
Gifu	922	133	Aomori	2,119	48
Wakayama	487	128	Osaka	1,323	39
Tottori	357	122	Miyagi	1,853	39
Fukuoka	918	122	Nara	970	39
Mie	687	112	Fukushima	2,511	37
Kanagawa	418	105	Tochigi	1,899	37
Aichi	983	100.5	Fukuoka	2,165	37
Yamanashi	424	100	Mie	1,673	35
Kagawa	415	98	Toyama	1,106	34
Tokushima	353	90	Kagawa	1,069	33
Shimane	351	74	Hokkaidō	2,959	32

Calculated from *NSSS*, Vol. 2, pp. 278-279 and *Kokusei chōsa*, 1950.

aged to rank among the leaders in density of disputation in
both periods. But, as the data in Table 6-1, which compares
number of disputes with number of farm households per
prefecture, indicate, Yamanashi stood near or at the top of
the list in both decades. It ranked with Aichi and Kagawa at
the top of the second ten of forty-seven prefectures between
1920 and 1929, and ranked first between 1930 and 1941.
Only Osaka, Hyōgo, Nara, and Kyoto prefectures in the
west ranked significantly above Yamanashi in the 1920s; only
Akita and Yamagata in the northeast came close in the 1930s.
Over the total twenty-two years, Yamanashi's 3,727 disputes
ranked third only to Hyōgo (4,126) and Akita (3,771). When
adjusted for number of agricultural households, Yamanashi
led, outranking its closest contender, Osaka, by 11 percent.

In short, Yamanashi, a small prefecture located halfway between the western stronghold of the 1920s and the northeastern bastion of the 1930s, stood as a citadel of tenancy disputation throughout the interwar years.[8]

Yamanashi's tenancy disputes were not evenly distributed across the prefecture; the overwhelming majority—90.4 percent in the years we have data for—took place in the five counties which form the relatively prosperous sericultural Kōfu Basin (Table 6-2). Because only 60 percent of Yamanashi's farmers lived in these counties, the Kōfu Basin, when separated from the less central parts of the region, ranked in frequency of disputes in the 1920s with Nara, Kyoto, and Gifu, and significantly below only the top two prefectures, Osaka and Hyōgo; in the 1930s, the basin's frequency of dispute doubled that of Akita, its nearest competitor.[9] The correlation between the basin and disputes was so close that when one compares the number of disputes with the number of agricultural households per county, one finds Higashi Yatsushiro, tiny Nishi Yamanashi, Naka Koma, and Higashi Yamanashi, the principal basin counties, leading the way. Kita Koma, the Yamanashi county with the largest agricultural population, had many upland, non-sericultural villages

[8] The writer of the introduction and conclusion to the Nagahara volume (Nagahara himself?) agrees that Yamanashi topped the nation in tenant disputes in the 1930s, but states that in the 1920s "among all of the prefectures, it was in the middle or even lower ranks." He thinks that Yamanashi had few disputes in the 1920s because it had a less highly developed market economy and a less mature landlord system than Gifu, Aichi, Osaka, and Hyōgo prefectures. Since the author sees a correlation between maturity of the landlord system and the rise of tenant disputes, he concludes that the tenant movement was a "concrete criticism of the landlord system" (pp. 6, 495). The weakness in the author's argument is that he does not index the number of tenant disputes for the number of farm households or tenants in the various prefectures. When one does so, areas like Nara Prefecture and the Kōfu Basin move to the top of the list in the 1920s.

[9] Because 90.4 percent of Yamanashi's disputes took place in the five counties which had 60 percent of the prefecture's rural population, the Kōfu Basin's index rises from 100 to 150, behind only Osaka, Hyōgo, and Nara in the 1920s.

362

TABLE 6-2

Tenancy Disputes by County in the Kōfu Basin,
1919-1924, 1926, and 1931-1935

Year	Prefecture	Kita Koma	Naka Koma	Higashi Yatsushiro	Higashi Yamanashi	Nishi Yamanashi
1919-24	165	46	57	12	19	14
1926	28	7	8	5	5	1
1931	166	38	51	33	23	10
1932	126	24	24	32	25	6
1933	150	19	46	38	21	6
1934	143	29	33	51	18	5
1935	445	26	96	124	112	42
Total	1,223	189	315	295	223	84
Index		59	100	136	93	117

Calculated from *Chihōbetsu kosaku sōgi gaiyō* (1926), p. 66; (1932), p. 75; (1934), p. 278; Nagahara, *Nihon jinushisei*, p. 14; *Kosaku sōgichi ni okeru nōson jijō* (1934), p. 67.

outside the basin, and trailed a distant fifth.[10] In short, Kōfu Basin tenant farmers, who lived near filatures and railroads, produced cocoons and rice for the market, supplemented their households' budgets with non-agricultural income and had the prefecture's highest rural standards of living, dominated efforts in Yamanashi to seek lower rents and greater profits through disputation. In the absence of detailed statistics of the disputes' participants, causes and demands by county, it seems safe to analyze the Yamanashi data as infor-

[10] If one eliminates Kita Koma County from the calculations, 75 percent of Yamanashi's disputes took place in four counties with 44 percent of the prefecture's farm population. The basin's index rises to 170, alongside Nara and below only Osaka and Hyōgo. It is probably safe to assume that most of the Kita Koma County disputes took place in the areas of the county near or in the basin. To judge from his descriptions in Chapter One, Ronald Dore's Shinohata seems to be in Yamanashi in the upland, non-basin areas of Kita Koma, and he reports that in spite of an active tenant movement elsewhere in Japan, little class tension and no tenant union appeared in Shinohata. *Shinohata*, Chapter One and p. 48.

mation about the tenant movement in the Kōfu Basin only.

Both Nishida and Nakamura, in explaining the causes of tenant disputes in Yamanashi Prefecture, adopt the lines of interpretation they follow in analyzing nationwide disputes. Both write that tenants in the 1920s were on the attack, seeking lower rents, land, and a new social and economic order, but that tenants in the 1930s were on the defensive, attempting desperately to protect their small plots from landlord confiscation. Differing economic conditions, to Nishida the comparative prosperity, to Nakamura the less extreme poverty of the 1920s, and the indigency of the depression years in the 1930s, underlay this transformation. At this point, Nishida and Nakamura part company, however. Nishida, as we discussed above, sees commercial and subsistence tenants cooperating in the 1920s, but the latter fighting alone in the 1930s. Nakamura, who rejects this division of the tenant class, believes each and every tenant had both a petit bourgeois commercial and a proletarian subsistence side to his nature. In the slightly less poverty-stricken 1920s, the former held sway; in the desperate 1930s, the latter. Worsening economic conditions in the depression years, to Nakamura, caused an upsurge in anti-landlord activity which explains the increase in number of disputes both nationally and in Yamanashi after 1930. Thus, for Nishida's analysis to stand up to scrutiny, one would expect a decrease in tenant unrest in the depression years; for Nakamura's to pass muster one would expect an increase.[11]

When we compare data on real household income with statistics on tenancy disputes, as we do in Table 6-3, we find that the evidence fits Nishida's mode of analysis (excepting his conclusion about the revolutionary nature of the disputes) more closely than it does Nakamura's. The first column of Table 6-3 lists the number of tenant disputes which took place in Yamanashi, that is, with a few exceptions, in the

[11] Nishida, "Nōmin undō," pp. 173-174; Nakamura, *Jinushiseishi kenkyū*, pp. 247, 261-264; Nagahara, *Nihon jinushisei*, pp. 314-315.

Kōfu Basin, between 1920 and 1940. The single unequivocal assertion one can make about the data is that the number of disputes increased in a steady, upward trend from 1920 until 1936, after which it tapered off. One can find no correlations between number of disputes and real income, either in Yamanashi or in Naka Koma, which I use here to represent the Kōfu Basin, the highly commercial nexus of Yamanashi's tenant unrest.[12] A superficial look at column one might lead a reader to conclude that its trend supports Nakamura's approach since disputes do increase in frequency during the depression, but it does not. The peak years of tenant disputes in the Kōfu Basin were not the depression years, but the recovery years of 1935-1937, during which tenant disputes expanded by almost four times over 1930-1934 as real income per farm household increased by one-third.

When one looks at the number of tenant-farmer participants, a more significant factor than the number of disputes, one observes the trends which support Nishida's approach more than they do Nakamura's. Tenant involvement increased to a high level in 1922-1926, when farm income in the basin was relatively high (132); fell off in 1927-1928, when farm income dipped (123); and recovered in 1929-1930, the first a remarkably good year, the latter the first depression year. Tenant participation fell to a relatively low level during the depression (114), increased sharply in 1935-1937 as Kōfu Basin farmers recovered sharply from the depression (152), tapered off in the increasing prosperity of 1938-1939 (213), and finally rebounded dramatically in 1940. Although one is hard pressed to discover a correlation between the number of tenant disputants and farm income in

---

[12] I ran statistical tests to see if I could find correlations between rice and cocoon prices, income per farm household, cocoon income per sericultural household, and real income per farm household, on the one hand, and number of disputes, number of participants, and participants per dispute, on the other, for Yamanashi between 1920 and 1939, but found no correlations whatsoever. The only identifiable trend is the fairly steady annual increase in disputes from 1920 to 1936.

TABLE 6-3

Indices of Real Income per Farm Household in
Yamanashi and Naka Koma, Number of Tenant Disputes,
Tenant Participation, and Amount of Land Involved, 1920-1940
(Yamanashi 1915-1917 = 100)

Year	Number of Disputes[13]	Tenant Participants	Land Involved	Yamanashi Index	Naka Koma Index
1918-19				125	162
1920	12	1,902	787 chō	67	77
1921	18	1,577	885	83	103
1922	41	3,638	1,853	91	(110)[14]
1923	45	3,006	978	108	(130)
1924	49	3,476	2,032	102	(125)
1925	43	3,124	1,436	119	162
1926	39	2,988	1,157	102	133
1927	38	2,025	961	91	114
1928	53	838	317	101	131
1929	86	1,736	726	117	158
1930	144	2,300	642	74	98
1931	150	1,456	875	72	97
1932	139	1,274	379	76	110
1933	133	1,696	489	111	161
1934	126	1,876	511	74	104
1935	460	3,372	821	95	137
1936	613	5,390	2,151	113	157
1937	503	3,513	1,075	115	161
1938	373	2,250	567	91	141
1939	271	2,625	789	191	285
1940	178	4,190	1,550	—	—

Calculated from *Kosaku chōtei nempō*, 1925-1926; *Kosaku nempō*, 1927-1939; *Nōchi nempō*, 1940; *Yamanashi tōkeisho; Chōki keizai tōkei*, Vol. 8, pp. 135-136.

[13] The total numbers of disputes shown in Table 6-3 vary slightly from those reported in Table 6-2 because the tables are based on different sources.

[14] In the absence of Naka Koma data, I have estimated real income for 1922-1924 on the basis of annual differences between Yamanashi and Naka Koma for 1915-1921 and 1925-1929. The figures in parentheses therefore may be incorrect by 4 or 5 points up or down, but give the reader a general idea of Naka Koma real household income for 1922-1924.

the Kōfu Basin, if one finds any pattern it is between partic-ipation and *high*, not low, farm income. What these data seem to indicate is that there is only a very loose correlation between tenant disputes and short-term fluctuations in the rural economy; the transition from the 1920s to the 1930s which Nakamura and Nishida describe, especially following Nakamura's line of interpretation, may not be so apparent as it seems to them. Analysts might better look for long-term trends like literacy, education, commercialization, rising liv-ing standards, and increasingly rational and modern farm management, which Nishida does to a large extent, not to the annual ebb and flow of the rural economy, to understand the causes of the tenant-farmer movement in Yamanashi and elsewhere.

I have reintroduced Nishida's and Nakamura's view of 1930 as a dividing line between two kinds of disputes, a ten-ant farmer Sekigahara (the decisive battle which brought the Tokugawa to power in 1600), as Nishida calls it, because I believe, unlike even him, that tenant disputes were largely commercial and entrepreneurial in causation both in the 1920s *and* the 1930s.[15] I agree with these two scholars that some characteristics of the disputes after 1930 were different from before—the later disputes were often on a smaller scale and were more concerned with land tenure and contract problems—but I do not agree that they were all *ipso facto* less commercial and more directed toward protecting subsistence tenants' land tenure and livelihoods. I hold my view for a number of reasons. As we have seen in Chapter Five, when one looks at the number of tenants involved, one finds many more tenant participants in disputes over rent, i.e., for entre-preneurial reasons, than over contracts, even during the depression. Although there were more disputes in Tōhoku than in Kinki in the 1930s, the greatest number of tenant participants in disputes were still in the highly commercial re-gions in the west, where rent reduction disputes continued to hold sway. Even in disputes over land tenure, landlord

---

[15] Nagahara, *Nihon jinushisei*, p. 253.

efforts to take back land seem to have been as much a tactic to force tenants to remit unpaid rent as they were to allow landlords to till the land themselves, sell it, or rent it to other tenants. The great upsurge of tenant disputes in Yamanashi in the mid-1930s took place in the Kōfu Basin, the highly commercial central region, not in the remote mountainous areas.[16] The high point of tenant-farmer participation in disputes nationally and in Yamanashi in the 1930s came at the end and after, not during the depths of the depression. And in spite of the landlords' efforts to "confiscate" their own private property in the 1930s, in Yamanashi their success was even more paltry than it was nationwide.

One should not think that, because I question the predominant role of the need to protect poor tenants' livelihoods as a cause of disputes in the 1930s, I underestimate the adverse impact of the world depression on farmers' livelihoods. As a glance at Table 6-3 indicates, real income per farm household in Naka Koma fell by 38 percent in 1930, a drastic decrease in income; it was 1933, and more permanently, 1935, before farm income returned to the high level of the late 1920s. One would have to be blind to underrate the consequences that four very bad years in five must have had on the standard of living of highly commercial Kōfu Basin households, landlords included. But one cannot posit "poverty," à la Nakamura, and continue as if it needs no explanation; thus, I feel compelled to make several interpretive remarks. First, to call 1930 a "Sekigahara" between the 1920s and 1930s is hyperbole. Nineteen-thirty was not the dividing line between prosperous and poverty-stricken decades; rather, it was the beginning of a five-year interregnum in a long-term, upward

[16] In 1935, 84 percent of all Yamanashi tenant disputes took place in Naka Koma, Higashi Yatsushiro, Nishi Yamanashi, and Higashi Yamanashi counties, the basin counties which contained 44 percent of the prefecture's farm population. In that year, therefore, those four counties had a dispute index of 191. The other five counties, Kita Tsuru, Minami Tsuru, Nishi Yatsushiro, Kita Koma, and Minami Koma had 16 percent of the disputes and 56 percent of the agricultural population, for an index of 29.

trend for Kōfu Basin farmers, one which began in the 1890s and ended only with the collapse of the national economy at the end of World War II. The years between 1935 and 1943 were the best economically that farmers in Naka Koma and its neighboring counties had ever known. Second, the areas which were hardest hit by the depression were the least, not the most, commercial—Tōhoku, and in Yamanashi, the areas outside of the basin. This runs counter to Nakamura's contention that the more commercial, i.e., the more capitalistic a region, the more market fluctuations will affect its farmers' livelihoods. Third, the greatest concentration of tenant participation in disputes in the 1930s came, not in Tōhoku and Yamanashi's peripheral regions, the relatively noncommercial areas where the depression hit the hardest, but in the "capitalistic" regions where the tenants had greater protection from recession. And, fourth, therefore, even during the depression many tenants continued to maintain satisfactory livelihoods and challenge landlords for commercial reasons. This was particularly true in commercial areas like Naka Koma, where average household incomes in 1930-1931 maintained levels higher than average Yamanashi ones in 1922 and 1927.

CAUSES AND NATURE OF KŌFU BASIN TENANT DISPUTES

The Agriculture Ministry's statistics on immediate causes of tenant disputes and tenant-farmer demands during disputes, in Yamanashi as nationally, seem to support Nishida's and Nakamura's interpretation of the changing nature of the tenant movement from the 1920s to the 1930s. The data in Table 6-4 on causes show that disputes over contracts increased steadily between the early 1920s and the mid-1930s, and surpassed problems of rent as the primary cause of disputes during the late depression years. We have already discussed at length the problems of using national data to support the "depression-poverty-eviction" mode of analysis for the dis-

TABLE 6-4
Immediate Causes of Tenant Disputes in Yamanashi and Index of
Real Farm Income per Farm Household in Naka Koma, 1921-1940

Year	Index of Income	Causes	
		Rent-Related	Contract-Related
1921-26	127	33 (85%)	2 (5%)
1927-29	134	34 (58%)	15 (25%)
1930-34	114	61 (44%)	60 (43%)
1935-37	152	193 (37%)	285 (54%)
1938-40	209	91 (33%)	152 (55%)

Calculated from *Kosaku chōtei nempō*, 1925-1926; *Kosaku nempō*, 1927-1939; *Nōchi nempō*, 1940; *Yamanashi tōkeisho; Chōki keizai tōkei*, Vol. 8, pp. 135-136.

putes of the 1930s compared to the 1920s; these arguments hold for Yamanashi as well. Thus, I shall not reintroduce my views except to reiterate one important point: landlords often tried to confiscate their land, not to cultivate it themselves, sell it, or change tenants, but as a tactic, usually unsuccessful, to force tenants to pay their delinquent rent. For a qualitative grasp of the causation of disputes in Yamanashi, let us look in detail at the example of Kubo Nakajima hamlet.

Tenant farmers in Kubo Nakajima first formed a union to negotiate collectively with their landlords on March 5, 1921. The original stimulus to activism, which fits the data presented in Table 6-4, was an attempt by Mikami Saburō, the hamlet's leading semi-absentee landlord, to raise his rents. Mikami charged rents in Kubo Nakajima which were 14 percent lower than the rents he received in his home hamlet of Futsuka Ichiba; in 1920 he moved to bring them into balance. His action could not have been timed more poorly; not only did Ōkamada rice yields fall to unprecedented lows in 1920-1921, but rice and cocoon prices slumped in the recession which followed the 1917-1919 boom. This galvanized Kubo

Nakajima's tenants to action. They formed their tenant union, made up of all the hamlet's thirty-four owner tenant, tenant owner, and tenant households, prevented Mikami's higher levy, and, more strikingly, won a 17 percent rent reduction from their resident and non-resident landlords (i.e., 1921 rent was 83 percent, not 114 percent, of 1920 rent).[17]

These Kubo Nakajima tenant farmers, and others like them in neighboring Kōfu Basin villages, introduced several new elements into landlord-tenant relations. They adopted new tactics which we shall discuss later; they also formed collective unions and demanded rent reductions because of falling crop prices, something which they had rarely done in the past. Nevertheless, the behavior of Kubo Nakajima's tenants in 1921 could be interpreted as broadly customary; tradition certainly allowed tenant farmers to ask for rent reductions and to resist rent increases in years of bad harvests.

If their 1921 actions were more or less within the realm of the acceptable, their subsequent steps were unprecedented and must have worried the landlords considerably. Kubo Nakajima's tenant farmers did not disband their collective association after the 1921 victory; instead, they organized for the future by collecting membership fees and dues and cultivating a field jointly to raise money, by coercing internal solidarity through the use of rewards for loyal behavior and threats of punishment for those who dragged their feet, and in 1925 by taking over the hamlet's government.[18] The tenants demanded annual rent reductions and better terms of tenancy even as yields and prices recovered and more or less stabilized until the end of the decade.

Kubo Nakajima tenants demanded and received throughout the 1920s increasingly large rent reductions. In 1921, the year of their decision to act collectively, tenants paid only 83 percent of their contract rent; by the end of the decade they

[17] Amemiya, p. 152; *KNJ*, pp. 71-73, 78.
[18] Nakamura, in *Rōdōsha to nōmin*, p. 64, calls the use of rewards and punishments a "premodern" (*zenkindaiteki*) method of motivating people.

371

paid only half. And they did this, as Table 6-5 indicates, in spite of generally good economic conditions. Both rice and cocoon income in Kubo Nakajima remained at fairly steady levels or even grew slightly between 1926 and 1929. If we can extrapolate from countywide data, it would appear that real household income in Kubo Nakajima rose from 1920 through 1925, then fell somewhat in 1926 and 1927, after which it recovered in 1928 and 1929. When one compares the rent reductions with these economic data, one can find no customary basis for such sharp rent reductions, at least

TABLE 6-5

Reductions from Contract Rent and Indices of Real Rice and Cocoon Income per Household for Kubo Nakajima, and Index of Real Income per Household for Naka Koma, 1921-1930

Year	Rent Reduction	Real Rice Income	Real Cocoon Income	Naka Koma Real Income
1921	17%	—	—	103
1922	18%	—	—	(110)
1923	25%	—	—	(130)
1924	22%	—	—	(125)
1925	25%	100	—	162
1926	50%	88	100	133
1927	50%	98	102	114
1928	50%	92	99	131
1929	100%[19]	91	115	158
1930	70%	68	62	98

Calculated from Amemiya, p. 152; *Yamanashi tōkeisho; Chōki keizai tōkei*, Vol. 8, pp. 135-136.

[19] Landlords and tenants did not actually negotiate a 100 percent rent reduction in rent for 1929. Tenants, in the heat of the dispute in 1929-1930, did not pay. Landlords, after they capitulated at the time of the Emman Deal of 1930 and recognized a 70 percent reduction for 1930, and after the courts declared their rent collection company, the Yamanashi Land Company, illegal in 1931, simply never collected.

until the depression year 1930. Even the reduction of income in 1926, 18 percent countywide and 12 percent for rice in Kubo Nakajima, did not in a customary sense justify a 50 percent reduction in rent.

What happened in Kubo Nakajima in the 1920s that allowed tenant farmers to pay less and less rent in spite of comparatively good economic conditions? To begin with, a combination of the hamlet's labor shortage because of higher labor productivity and the availability of outside jobs, the inability of the semi-absentee landlords to till land themselves, and the comparative inefficiency of the resident landlords as cultivators meant that landlords had lost their primary means to force tenants into line. In the nineteenth century, a landlord could take back his land from a recalcitrant tenant to rent it to someone else; in the 1920s in Kubo Nakajima, such opportunities rarely existed.[20]

More important than the hamlet's changing labor market, however, were the changes taking place in the attitudes of tenant farmers. Kubo Nakajima tenants by 1921 had achieved the highest standards of living in the history of their hamlet. The sale of mulberry and cocoons and the jobs provided by the raw silk filatures allowed tenant farmers to rise well above the level of subsistence. This economic improvement not only gave them the financial security to maintain their tenant union over twenty-eight years, but it also changed their self-perceptions. Growing surpluses allowed tenant farmers to market more and more of their produce after they paid their rent; as the tenants became more and more deeply involved in the commercial market, they began to think more and more like small businessmen. These new attitudes, reinforced by their schooling, literacy, and awareness of the outside world, strengthened their feelings of independence. Tenants in 1921 could provide for themselves many of the services formerly provided by landlords. In

---

[20] See Chapter Four, pp. 256-265 for a discussion of the dearth of farm labor in Ōkamada, a central basin village, in the 1920s.

short, the tenant farmer in Kubo Nakajima in the 1920s did not depend emotionally, economically, and politically on the landlord to the extent that he had in the past.

But if Kubo Nakajima tenants began to stretch their wings of independence after World War I and this led to their resistance to Mikami Saburō's rent increases, their success in 1921 demonstrated something they had little awareness of until then: their power. Tenant farmers in 1921 found that by forming a union, maintaining internal cohesion, adopting militant but accommodating tactics—although they also found that occasional minor violence or its threat helped too—and using their advantages (like their majority in politics and their paucity in the labor market), they could win concessions from their landlords. Although the original immediate cause of this tenant dispute in 1921 had to do with rent, and although the prefectural officials undoubtedly continued to fit Kubo Nakajima into the rent category throughout the 1920s, the actual cause was the tenant farmers' growing awareness of their independence and power, which in turn flowered from the soil of the long-term changes in economic opportunity, farm management, and education discussed above.

Up to this point in my interpretation of the Kubo Nakajima evidence, my analysis matches Nishida's of Hanabusa, with its aggressive, commercial tenant-farmer movement in the 1920s. But what of the 1930s? Did the union's actions fit into the defensive, subsistence view that he and Nakamura propound? The answer, I think, is no, they did not.

Nineteen-thirty was a crucial year in the history of the Kubo Nakajima tenant union, a year in which a dispute over rent turned into a dispute over land tenure, and in which petty violence, arrests, convictions, and consequently landlord capitulation took place. In the spring of 1930, the hamlet's landlords sent certified letters to their tenants, demanding remittance of 1929 rent, none of which had as yet been paid. At the same time, the landowners began court proceedings to force tenants to return their rented land. Although the Agriculture Ministry's officials probably classified this dispute in the 1930 statistics as one over contract rather than over rent, it is clear that the landlords began litigation as a tactic to force tenants to pay their delinquent rent.[21] The tenants reacted by refusing either to pay their 1929 rent or to return the land.

On the night of July 7, while the dispute had not yet been resolved, a number of Kubo Nakajima youths, passing the home of the landlord Gemma Hideyoshi in Emmanji on their way home from a drinking party in Miyanohara (given for the Ōkamada tenant union's youth auxiliary for its role in "helping" a tenant get his land back from a sublessor), decided to "negotiate" with him. Six of the more tipsy young men pushed into Gemma's courtyard and shouted "good evening." Since the Gemmas were asleep, no one answered. The youths, a trifle miffed by this seeming rebuff, threw gravel at the side of the house. When they still got no response, angered, they cut the wire that powered the electric lights and then spread feces from the outhouse all over the garden. The next day, Gemma, a rather proud and pompous gentleman, called the police, who investigated and, when Gemma preferred charges, arrested the six pranksters. On July 25, they went on trial in Kōfu; although dozens of noisy union members crowded the courtroom and Katayama Tetsu, after World War II Japan's one socialist prime minister, came from Tokyo to defend the young men, on August 19 the six received jail sentences of three or four months. The defendants appealed, however, and on October 27 they had their sentences suspended.[22]

In spite of what might appear on the surface a landlord victory in the summer of 1930, the so-called Emman Incident, named after its place of occurrence, the hamlet Emmanji, led to a major *tenant* victory. Kubo Nakajima's other

---

[21] Amemiya, p. 152; *KNJ*, p. 111.

[22] Takegawa, *Yamanashi nōmin undō*, pp. 76-78; *Yamanashi nichinichi shimbun*, July 10, 1930, p. 3; July 11, p. 3; July 12, p. 3; *Yamanashi jiji shimbun*, July 11, 1930, p. 3; July 12, p. 3.

landlords, and thus subsequently Gemma himself, agreed to the Emman Deal (*Emman teuchi*) which authorized a 70 percent rent reduction for 1930, abandoned all proceedings to get land back, and dropped temporarily efforts at collecting 1929 rent. The landlords capitulated in 1930 because they found Gemma's insistent prosecution of the youths for a trivial offense embarrassing and gave in as an apology. As we shall see more clearly when we deal with tactics in disputes, tenants in Kubo Nakajima and elsewhere very cleverly used threats to hamlet harmony, the facade of which at least landlords tried desperately to maintain, as a way of gaining concessions.

In 1931, Mikami Saburō, who by the end of the 1920s was forced to reduce rents even in his home hamlet of Futsuka Ichiba, went to court to get either his 1929 rent or his land back.[23] Again the tenants refused to surrender, kept their land, sought mediation, and eventually signed a permanent compulsory mediation agreement for rice-paddy rent with all of their landlords; in 1935, the union reached a similar agreement with landlords for mulberry orchards and other dry fields. Because of these two agreements, Kubo Nakajima tenant farmers negotiated lower rents throughout the 1930s.[24] Mikami and the other landlords attempted to use the courts in 1930 and 1931 to force tenants to return their rented lands, and thus officials must have designated these Kubo Nakajima disputes as contract-related ones; nevertheless, rent reductions still remained the immediate cause of the conflict. In both years, landlords used the threat of eviction as a tactic to force tenants to pay back rent. And, strikingly, the landlords failed; no Kubo Nakajima tenant either had any land confiscated in the 1930s or paid any 1929 rent.

One should not think of the Kubo Nakajima dispute, which moved from the rent to the contract category without changing in actual causation, as unique; as one read through

---

[23] *Kosaku sōgi oyobi chōtei jirei*, 1929, pp. 557-559.
[24] *KNJ*, pp. 115-116.

the case studies presented in the Agriculture Ministry's annual *Examples of Tenant Disputes and Mediation* and Takegawa Yoshinori's *The History of the Yamanashi Farmers' Movement*, the primary sources for brief descriptions of disputes, one finds that landlords in the late 1920s and 1930s frequently countered demands for lower rent with attempts at the eviction of tenants.[25] Nishida's own study of Hanabusa is a case in point. On January 7, 1930, 26 tenants in Nakagawa hamlet asked for 50 percent to 90 percent reductions in 1929 rents. Their landlords countered immediately by demanding payment of the back rent or return of the land.[26] It would appear that disputes over contracts, in Yamanashi, at any rate, often occurred because of the landlord's use of the threat of eviction as a tactic to force the payment of delinquent rent. Many tenants in the depression years may not have been fighting desperately to maintain their precarious livelihoods by defending their small plots of land from landlord confiscation; rather, they may still have been, as in the 1920s, trying to advance their standards of living by demanding and receiving lower rents. Certainly many poor tenants, particularly in the depression, joined the tenant movement to subsist; but others, probably the majority, in the 1930s as well as the 1920s participated as petty entrepreneurs to extend their improving livelihoods.

Tenant Tactics During Disputes

The commercial causes and reformist goals of the disputes are reflected most clearly in the incremental and pragmatic tactics that tenant farmers used. They normally acted in a way which would not greatly upset the local social order. In fact, it appears that tenants tried to stretch the skin of their

[25] *Kosaku sōgi oyobi chōtei jirei,* 1927, 1929, 1930, 1932, 1933; Takegawa, *Yamanashi nōmin undō;* see also *Kosaku sōgichi* and *Chihōbetsu kosaku sōgi gaiyō,* 1936.

[26] Nagahara, *Nihon jinushisei,* p. 254; *Kosaku sōgi oyobi chōtei jirei,* 1929, pp. 67-70.

hamlets little by little so that it rarely ruptured; nevertheless, when one compared the hamlet in the late 1930s with the early 1920s, one found a different place.

Many tenant tactics were based on hamlet custom. When they formed unions, for example, tenants normally used the existing hamlet cooperative association, the *yui* or *uma aite*, sans the hamlet upper class, as their base. They persisted. If the landlords gave a temporary rent reduction one year, the tenants asked for the same and a little bit more the next. If the landlords gave a permanent, contract rent reduction, thinking that that would relieve the tenants' siege, the tenants came back for more, either temporarily or permanently, the next year. They were innovative and alert to landlord vulnerability in adopting their tactics. Tenants not only played on the landlords' obvious weakness, their paucity, but also, as soon as they discovered that landlords feared outward displays of hamlet disharmony, tenants deliberately disrupted harmony. Thus, although tenants rarely resorted to violence, they found it or its threat could help them achieve their goals. And, finally, tenants in the 1920s and 1930s, because of their literacy, cosmopolitanism, and tenant organizations, knew what was happening in other villages, counties, and prefectures. Landlords did not face an atomized tenant movement; even if tenants in one hamlet did not think of a certain tactic, they soon heard of its use elsewhere. It is because of their flexible, informed tactics that I have compared the prewar Japanese tenant groups with postwar labor unions.

Table 6-6 presents statistics on the principal first tenant tactics nationwide in the late 1920s and early 1930s, and supports the points outlined above. Although the data here are incomplete since officials were allowed to report only one tactic per dispute and not all disputes are covered, they give us a general idea of what tenants did once a dispute broke out. Tenants normally formed unions and acted collectively to use their superior numbers to counterbalance the landlord's advantages in wealth and power; in Yamanashi, 50 percent of all tenants belonged to unions in 1926 (Table 6-7). Tenants also sought mediation, withheld rent, and organized demonstrations to threaten their landlords symbolically, but generally eschewed violence and other actions which seriously threatened hamlet harmony. With the exception of "threaten violence," which itself was uncommon, all the extreme tactics—withdrawing from local organizations like fire departments and schools, destroying crops, severing relations with or ostracizing landlords, arson, and calling in outside agitators—fall near or at the bottom of the list. The data do show the shift from rent reduction toward contract disputes between 1925 and 1931 since tactics like "cultivate collectively" and "harvest crops in violation of injunctions" increased, and this led to a small but significant augmentation in threats of violence and crop destruction. Although the *Tenancy Annual* does not include tenant tactics after 1931, we know from other sources that the slightly higher level of violence was temporary and that by 1933 violence had disappeared almost completely both in Yamanashi and nationwide. Let us now flesh out this quantitative skeleton with descriptions of tenant actions in Kubo Nakajima and elsewhere in the Kōfu Basin to get a meatier idea of tenant tactics.

The first step taken by Kubo Nakajima's tenant farmers when they confronted Mikami Saburō's proposed rent increase in 1920-1921 was the formation of a union; their primary problems were maintaining union solidarity and raising money in order to achieve their goals, blocking rent increases, and then winning rent reductions and better terms of tenancy. The founders of the Kubo Nakajima tenant union were Ishihara Yoshinaga (16, b. 1879), a pure tenant who tilled a moderately large farm of 14 *tan*; Ishihara Hisashi (14, b. 1880), a tenant owner who cultivated a large farm of 18 *tan*; Ishihara Toyokichi (12, b. 1869), a tenant owner who tilled the second largest farm in the village (20 *tan*); and Tanaka Masayoshi (18, b. 1876), who also cultivated a large farm of 17 *tan*. All four shared a common motivation to

TABLE 6-6
First Tenant Tactic, per Dispute, 1925, 1926, 1928, 1929, 1931

	1925	1926	1928	1929	1931
Form or Affiliate with a Union	696	1,091	849	955	45
Seek Aid from a Union Headquarters	46	60	117	118	463
Seek Mediation under the Mediation Law	191	272	—[27]	34	114
See Mediation outside Mediation Law	116	99	123	48	139
Make a Collective Agreement Not to Pay Rent	121	190	185	71	47
Withhold Part of the Rent Owed	77	103	69	55	62
Hold Demonstration	64	103	59	59	105
Store or Sell Rent Collectively	53	124	115	65	74
Call on a Defense Attorney	45	27	—	61	100
Form a League to Return Landlord Land	44	18	—	5	—
Raise Funds To Finance Dispute	43	48	—	10	11
Threaten Violence	25	32	23	3	73
Petition for Lower Rent	20	56	37	44	70
Submit a List of Farm Expenses	18	28	—	1	—
Call in an Outside Agitator	14	16	3	6	9
Petition Officials	13	30	—	—	—
Cultivate Collectively	12	68	76	40	179
Harvest Crops in Violation of Injunctions	13	28	36	39	149

Withdraw Tenant Children from School	6	12	—	9	3
Withdraw from the Fire Department	5	8	5	4	0
Destroy Landlords' Crops, Seeds, or Seedlings	4	4	16	1	30
Break off Relations with Landlords	4	5	1	2	—
Postpone Tax Payments	4	6	0	3	—
Censure Officials	3	1	0	—	—
Ostracize Landlords	2	—	0	—	—
Withdraw from the Credit Union	2	2	0	—	—
Form a League for Self-Sufficiency	1	2	0	—	—
Form a League Not To Return the Landlord's Land	1	6	0	5	—
Withdraw from the Youth Association	0	1	0	—	0
Arson	—	0	1	0	—
Total (A)	1,643	2,440	1,715	1,638	1,673
Total Disputes (B)	2,206	2,751	1,866	2,434	3,419
A/B	74%	89%	92%	67%	49%

Sources: *NSSS*, Vol. 2, pp. 324-327; *Kosaku chōtei nempō*, 1925; *Kosaku nempō*, 1928, 1929, 1931.

[27] Where there is a dash (–), I indicate that the source, for unknown reasons, gives no data. A dash does not indicate zero.

TABLE 6-7
Tenant Unions and Union Membership in
Yamanashi, 1921–1940

Year	Unions	Members
1921	56	—
1922	87	—
1923	141	13,145
1924	181	16,484
1925	237	19,949
1926	255	31,270
1927	280	24,756
1928	302	24,292
1929	304	21,432
1930	326	21,456
1931	395	23,581
1932	390	25,714
1933	379	27,699
1934	354	23,176
1935	271	19,246
1936	256	17,117
1937	259	17,570
1938	244	15,967
1939	245	16,027
1940	224	14,230

*Owner Tenant, Tenant Owner, and Tenant Farmer
Households in Yamanashi, 1930*

Total	61,412
Full Time	51,332
Part Time	10,080

Sources: *Kosaku chōtei nempō*, 1925–1926; *Kosaku nempō*,
1927–1939; *Nōchi nempō*, 1940; *Yamanashi tōkeisho*, 1930.

action: Mikami Saburō was their primary landlord. Thus, when the parasitologist attempted to raise his rents in 1920, the three Ishiharas and Tanaka, all commercially oriented farmers, reacted quickly and succeeded in organizing the hamlet's tenant farmers, including those who did not rent land from Mikami, into a union.[28]

From the start, the four leaders realized that the hamlet's tenant farmers had overlapping, but different, interests, and did not hold equal commitment to all the union's goals and tactics. Some had kinship ties to landlord households, others were particularly prosperous or poor, others were especially enterprising and diligent and balked at submerging the fruits of their efforts in a collectivity. Thus, the four men devised a remarkable system of maintaining tenant unity, but one which made no effort to force members to share wealth or labor except through regular small donations of money, grain, and labor, and larger donations of land in time of crisis.

Basic to the union's solidarity was the candy and the whip, the Japanese equivalent of the carrot and the stick. To begin with, the union provided very real candy to its members. Not only did it gain large rent reductions, but also the union gave the tenants security during periods of confrontation with the landlords and small loans at any time. The union raised a large strike fund, so large in fact that by 1928, in spite of loans and emergency outlays, the union had almost 4,000 yen, and by 1934 almost 5,000 yen in postal savings, and earned 300–400 yen per year in income. In 1928, the union loaned its 33 members 2,080.5 yen more, about 6–7 percent of their total borrowing, at 8 percent interest. (In that year, the average lending rate for regular bank loans to farmers was 10.2 percent.)[29]

The primary sources of these funds were membership fees and dues. Each member paid the union 1 yen at the time of founding in 1921, 20 and later 30 *sen* dues per month, and 3

---

[28] *KNJ*, pp. 71-78, 88.   [29] Amemiya, pp. 137-138.

kan (about 26 pounds) of unhulled barley per year (this came to about 8-9 percent of the hamlet's total barley production). The union marketed the grain collectively. Since the market price of barley in 1925 was 14.6 yen per *kan*, the union raised over 1,400 yen; even during the depression it earned 700-800 yen.[30]

Another source of union candy as well as a principal method of applying the whip to wavering members was the union's collectively cultivated field. In May 1922, Kubo Nakajima's tenant union rented from a Buddhist temple and a Shinto shrine in Kōfu a "calamity field" (*sainanden*) in Kamijō Arai, a hamlet in neighboring Kokubo Village. The right to cultivate this large 5.5 *tan* paddy belonged to a Kokubo farmer named Kobayashi, who did not till it because of a local superstition that an individual household which farmed it would meet disaster. The legend said nothing about dangers to collective cultivators. The union paid Kobayashi the bargain price of 47 yen for the rights to till the field and rented it for 10.2 *hyō* of unhulled rice; since the paddy's yield in 1927 was 43 *hyō* rent came to only 24 percent of yields, which was only 60 percent of average normal paddy rents. Profits from the field reached 369 yen in 1926 and 255 yen even in 1930, all of which, of course, went into the union's coffers.[31]

The tenant union tilled this field continuously throughout the interwar years, World War II, and the American occupation period. When the union disbanded at the time of the land reform in 1948, Kubo Nakajima hamlet took title to the paddy, and former union members continued collective cultivation. They used the profits to make capital outlays for major hamlet improvements, like a loudspeaker system in 1952 and a sprayer in 1953; even in the 1950s, households which had not been union members could not use these facilities.[32]

[30] Amemiya, p. 165; *KNJ*, p. 81.
[31] Amemiya, pp. 136-137, 164; *KNJ*, pp. 82-85.
[32] Amemiya, pp. 136-137, 164; *KNJ*, pp. 82-85, 129-130.

The leaders of the union, which at the time of its founding enrolled all thirty-four households in the hamlet's cooperative cultivating group (*uma aite*), used physical coercion and its threat, continual reinforcement of union policy at periodic meetings and collective work days at the calamity field, and the hamlet's customary sanctions as the whips which kept union members in line. The principal aide to the union's first two chairmen, Tanaka and Ishihara Yorinaga, and its first two assistant chairmen, Ishihara Toyokichi and Hisashi, in leading the union in its early years was Hoshino Kōhei (17, b. 1865), a tenant owner farmer who cultivated a large 18-*tan* farm. Hoshino, an imposing, physically strong, man, served as "struggle committee chairman," who "used persuasion and even force" to keep "members who showed fear of the landlords" in line.[33] This was solidarity based on the longer whip; "persuasion's force is felt."

The union held a monthly meeting on the fifth at the hall dedicated to the kitchen god (*kōjindo*) and used the opportunity to reinforce solidarity and to bolster the courage of the timid. The union's bylaws obligated each member household to send the same person, usually in practice the household head, to the meeting so it would be clear to the leaders who held the family's responsibility. That person used the opportunity to pay his household's 30 *sen* dues.[34] After universal manhood suffrage was introduced in 1925, the union took control of the hamlet's politics, and non-union households were excluded from any participation in or benefits from local government. Thus, the union meeting on the fifth became the hamlet's official assembly. Conversely, the official monthly gatherings (*yoriai*) held in each of the hamlet's four subdivisions (*kumi*) expelled non-union members and became the union's meetings. The hamlet's four primary officials, the chief, the two representatives to the village council, and the public works' committeeman attended each subdivision *yoriai*; after 1925, they were almost always union lead-

[33] *KNJ*, p. 93.   [34] *KNJ*, pp. 80-81.

ers and used the opportunity of the *kumi* gatherings to strengthen further the union's internal discipline.[35]

The union's leaders also used the occasion of collective cultivation at the calamity paddy in Kamijō Arai to maintain the organization's unity. Each household was required to send workers for the four major functions of the cultivating season, rice transplanting, weeding, harvesting, and threshing. Early in June each family sent one man and one woman to transplant the rice from seedling beds to paddies. The process took half a day, and was followed by a party at lunch. On July 7, the day of the *tanabata* festival, each household sent a member for collective weeding. On two days in the fall, set according to the weather, each household sent two people to harvest and thresh the rice. After the threshing was completed, all the union's member households gathered in the grounds of a local Buddhist temple (not the non-member Fukusenji) for a celebration of collective success known locally as the "bucket-raising festival." The process of mutual farming was "overseen" by a "chief of collective farming," who usually was a union member of *low* commitment and dependability. Thus, mutual work and celebration at the union's field not only reinforced collective solidarity but also allowed the union to keep weak members in line by making them lead.[36]

---

[35] A resident landlord, Ishihara Kumazō (3), the son of Ichitarō, was elected as one of the hamlet's two village assemblymen in 1933 in spite of the tenant union's efforts. Kumazō won because of careful landlord planning. Although in theory all village councilmen were elected at large from the whole village, in practice voters normally cast ballots only for candidates from their own hamlet; thus, Kubo Nakajima held 2 seats, not because they were allocated to the hamlet, but because the whole council had 12 seats and Kubo Nakajima had one-sixth of Ōkamada's voters. In 1933, the 33 union households split their votes among the 2 tenant candidates. All 6 non-union electors voted for Kumazō. He then "borrowed" his other votes from landlords in safe hamlets who could still determine for whom their tenants should vote. Although Kumazō held one of the four key hamlet posts from 1933 to 1937, he attended no hamlet or *kumi* meetings and had no success in wresting control of the hamlet from the tenant union. Kumazō lost his seat in 1937, after serving one term. *KNJ*, pp. 117-122.

[36] *KNJ*, pp. 84-85, 127-128, 174, 197-198.

Finally, the union used hamlet custom to whip wavering members into line. Prewar farm hamlets had an array of punishments ranging from timely gossip to ostracism (*mura hachibu*) to enforce conformity; since the Kubo Nakajima tenant union at the time of its founding enlisted all of the members of the hamlet's work cooperative, it could use these sanctions to enforce union discipline. The cases of Ishihara Otokichi (6), an owner tenant, his son Eizō (b. 1895), and Takizawa Sadayoshi (7, b. 1894), a tenant owner, demonstrate this point. Otokichi, Eizō, and Sadayoshi played central roles in the founding of the union in 1921, and as prosperous, mainstay farmers were considered among the hamlet's and the union's bulwarks. But Otokichi was the younger brother of the landlord Ishihara Ichitarō (3) and Sadayoshi was married to the landlord's daughter. When Ichitarō's wife died in April 1923, although custom dictated that all hamlet families participate in the funeral, the union's leadership decided not to take part and forced the other union members, who had already gathered at Ichitarō's house for the funeral, to leave. Otokichi and Sadayoshi were outraged, stayed at the funeral, and withdrew from the union; at the time, they stated that participation in the tenant movement and fulfillment of one's familial and patron-client obligations were two separate matters. The union-cooperative punished these two households by excluding them from the benefits of both union and hamlet membership. Worst of all, they received no cooperative labor from their neighbors.

Otokichi, Eizō, and Sadayoshi stayed outside the tenant community for two years before they returned to the fold in 1925. Significantly, however, their return reflected, not their capitulation to union demands, but a compromise which led to a moderation of the union's anti-landlord stance. When the two households rejoined the union in 1925, Eizō (6) replaced the more militant Yoshinaga (16) as chairman, and Sadayoshi (7) became vice-chairman. From this time on, the union placed greater emphasis on rent reduction than on causing social upheaval. Patron-client ties between tenants and landlords actually increased from 43 to 47 after 1926; the union patched up its non-economic differences with the landlord Ichitarō (3); and, as we have seen above, large rent reductions began only in 1926.[37] It is probably not chance that in the 1950s the moderates, Eizō and Sadayoshi, were among the most honored men in the hamlet, while the militant Yoshinaga, in spite of his service to his fellow tenants, did not rank in the top 50 percent in earning the respect of his neighbors.[38]

The case of Ishihara Taizō (4) is also worth recounting because it is one where a union member was expelled, placed under a sanction of ostracism, given no cooperative labor, and yet did not yield and rejoin the union. Taizō and his family lived and worked virtually alone from 1924 until after World War II. In the early 1920s, Taizō, one of the village's most successful farmers, who owned 12.2 *tan* of land, rented in 9 *tan*, and even rented out 4.4 *tan*, was a militant union leader. He served on the union's original board of directors and led the funeral boycott in April 1923. Nevertheless, his militance ran thin during a conflict with Mikami Saburō, who owned one-quarter of Kubo Nakajima, in the summer of 1924. Mikami decided to raise his rents, which had been reduced by 25 percent in 1923, to 1921 levels; the union, which had successfully opposed a rent increase in 1921, chose to resist. When by July negotiations had come to naught, the tenant leaders decided to stop cultivating the landlord's fields. Their plan was to support themselves by tilling the collective paddy and by dividing up the other landlords' fields among all the union's members, and to bring Mikami to his knees because of his fear that he would lose all his Kubo Nakajima income. The plan worked, and the tenants blocked the rent increase, but not before the union expelled and ostracized Taizō for refusing to honor the boycott.

Not only did Taizō continue to cultivate his Mikami fields against the will of his tenant peers, but also he challenged the union for threatening his access to water, and this too

---

[37] *Ibid.*, pp. 97-100, 107.　　　　[38] *Ibid.*, p. 248.

increased the wrath of his neighbors. In 1924, the union's leaders decided to build a new waterway for the collective field. The canal impeded Taizō's water supply and he brought charges against the union in the Kōfu Procurator's office. Taizō's expulsion in 1924 was unique in the history of the union. Unlike Nishida's Hanabusa union, which lost key members in 1930 under the pressure of the landlords' divide-and-conquer techniques, all 33 tenant households remained loyal from 1924 until the union disbanded at the time of the land reform. The various candies and whips described above maintained this solidarity.[39]

Tenant farmers in the Kōfu Basin formed unions as their primary tactic during economic disputes with their landlords, and affiliated with, sought aid from, or solicited defense attorneys from national or regional tenant union headquarters in many other cases, as enumerated in Table 6-6. When tenant disputes first erupted and local unions first appeared in Japan and Yamanashi in substantial numbers after World War I, tenant farmers and their labor-intellectual urban sympathizers began to organize national and regional headquarters to coordinate their efforts. The first regional headquarters in Yamanashi was formed in Higashi Yamanashi County in December 1920, and Naka Koma followed suit in April 1923. In February 1924, following the formation of the Kantō Alliance of the Japan Farmers' Union (*Nichinō*) in Tokyo the year before, Furuya Sadao, Hirano Rikizō, Usui Jirō, and other tenant farmer sympathizers founded the alliance's Yamanashi consolidated headquarters. From the mid-1920s through the early 1930s, about half of the basin's organized tenant farmers affiliated with regional or national unions; during the mid-1930s, when Yamanashi disputes reached their greatest number, about one-third of all union members belonged to branches of larger organizations. Kōfu Basin tenant farmers not only formed unions more frequently than their national compeers; they also affiliated with

---

[39] *Ibid.*, pp. 100–107; Nagahara, *Nihon jinushisei*, p. 264.

regional unions more often. In 1931, 49 percent of Yamanashi, but only 32 percent of Japan-wide, tenant union members, belonged to regional or national organizations.[40]

These regional and national headquarters provided many important services for their members in the Kōfu Basin. Tokyo attorneys like Katayama Tetsu traveled to Kōfu to defend indicted tenant farmers. National leaders like Kagawa Toyohiko, Suzuki Bunji, and Asanuma Inejirō came to encourage the farmers with oratory. Regional headquarters gathered and disseminated information to and from the newly literate tenants.[41]

But the principal reason for the success of union organizers in the Kōfu Basin was their understanding of the reformist goals and needs of real farmers. Although the Japan Farmers' Union's central leaders opposed both the Mediation Law (1924) and the Law to Establish Owner Farmers (1926), two pieces of legislation which subsequently helped lighten the financial burdens of tenant farmers, the most successful leaders of the Kōfu Basin's consolidated headquarters did not.[42] Tension between the reformist ideas of the Kōfu Basin leaders and the more revolutionary ideas of some of the national officials led to a clash at *Nichinō*'s annual convention in Kyoto in March 1926. Hirano Rikizō criticized the mainstream leaders for emphasizing ideology and revolution at the expense of the real concerns of tenant farmers and for attacking the government for policies which had nothing to do with agriculture—foreign policy, for example. He was expelled from the national union for his "right-wing" position, and returned to Kōfu to found a tenant union which advocated his pragmatic views. The new organization em-

---

[40] *Kosaku sōgichi*, p. 64; *Chihōbetsu*, 1932, p. 279; 1934, p. 285; Nōmin undōshi kenkyūkai, *Shōwaki nōmin undō ni tsuite no jakkan no kentō* (1956), pp. 70-71; Takegawa, *Yamanashi nōmin undō*, pp. 5-10, 17; *Kosaku nempō*, 1931.

[41] Takegawa, *Yamanashi nōmin undō*, pp. 10, 17-19, 67, 72-74, 76, 78, 99.

[42] Takegawa, *Yamanashi nōmin undō*, p. 18; *Chihōbetsu*, 1932, p. 285; Nishida, "Nōchi kaikaku no rekishiteki seikaku," p. 164.

phasized economic progress and eschewed confrontation, class struggle, and attacks on the "emperor system."[43] That part of the Yamanashi tenant movement which was organized into regional organizations eventually divided into three parts: Hirano Rikizō's reformist All Japan Alliance, Usui Jirō's moderate and reformist Yamanashi Tenant Union, and the Communist Party's revolutionary All Japan Conference Faction. Hirano's "right wing" union consistently enrolled 50-75 percent of all Yamanashi tenants organized into regional associations; his and Usui's groups enlisted about 90 percent, leaving the non-reformist conference faction with about 10 percent of the affiliated tenant union membership in Yamanashi.[44] And, more important, the conference faction enrolled only 3-5 percent of the total tenant union membership in the region; more than 95 percent of organized tenant farmers in the Kōfu Basin belonged to unions which sought evolutionary, not revolutionary, change.

The national and regional headquarters functioned only as service centers to provide information, advice, speakers, lawyers, and coordination. They had no command authority over their member unions, which acted independently of the center except when in need of the assistance of specialists. In fact, tenant farmers tended to suspect the urban intellectuals who often represented headquarters, especially those who advocated direct action, and found excessive central aid dangerous because it attracted the attention of the police.[45] Takano Morizō, a tenant farmer from Saijō Village near Ōkamada, reported, for example, that after Asanuma and Katayama visited his village to speak in the mid-1920s, agents of the Special Higher Police arrived to investigate the visitors' activities. The police showed no other interest in the village's tenant movement either before or after this event.[46]

[43] Takegawa, *Yamanashi nōmin undō*, pp. 18-27; Nagahara, *Nihon jinushisei*, p. 274; Masumi, *Nihon seitōshiron*, Vol. 5, pp. 449-450.

[44] *Shōwaki nōmin undō*, pp. 70-71; Shiota, *Nihon shakai undōshi*, p. 112.

[45] *Chihōbetsu*, 1932, pp. 282-283.

[46] Interview with Takano in his home, June 14, 1977.

The Kubo Nakajima union, although officially a branch of the Yamanashi consolidated headquarters of the Kantō Alliance of Nichinō, had almost no contact with the Tokyo leaders. The union maintained closer ties with the Yamanashi headquarters, and particularly with one of its founders, Usui Jirō, a prefectural assemblyman and mayor of Jōei Village. When Usui and Hirano fell out in 1927-1928 over the latter's support for one of Usui's opponents in the prefectural election, Kubo Nakajima affiliated with Usui's smaller, moderate Yamanashi Tenant Union. But even Usui, although he received political support in Kubo Nakajima, had little influence on the direction and tactics of the hamlet's tenant union. The leaders prepared for the regional headquarters information such as that on 1925 rents presented in Chapter Four; went in the early 1920s to neighboring villages to hear speakers like Suzuki, Katayama, and Asanuma; requested legal aid at times of crisis like the 1930 Emman Incident; and sent members to prefectural and national meetings to learn about tactics used elsewhere (and have outings in Tokyo and Kyoto courtesy of the hamlet union), but made all of their decisions locally. As Amemiya Yuzuru, basing his view on talks with union leaders like his father Ishizō and Ishihara Yoshinaga (16), writes, "in the end (Kubo Nakajima) had its own union and there were no outside leaders. The hamlet's tenant movement arose from local conditions, not exogenous forces. Outside ideology had very little influence in Kubo Nakajima at all." Other villagers told Hattori Harunori, speaking of the union's founder and most militant leader, Ishihara Yoshinaga, that "he received no ideological influences from outside the village, nor any kind of organizational leadership from socialist organizations. Yoshinaga seems only to have been concerned with lower rents."[47] Tenant farmers frequently formed unions and often affiliated with regional unions, but were clearly chary of depending on outsiders, on non-farmers, when treating with their landlords.

[47] Amemiya, pp. 10-11, 151; *KNJ*, pp. 93, 108-110, 113; Nagahara, *Nihon jinushisei*, p. 274.

The tenant farmers' main purpose in creating unions was to negotiate from positions of collective strength with their landlords for lower rents and better and more secure terms of tenancy. In the early and mid-1920s, tenants dealt with their landlords directly. After the government enacted its mediation system in 1924, tenants and landlords increasingly resorted to arbitration by its committees, which usually led to compromise, as a way of resolving disputes. This law had a spectacular impact in the Kōfu Basin; from 1927 through 1940, almost all Yamanashi disputes were mediated, with an 82 percent success rate.[48] But, whether tenants negotiated directly or used go-betweens, they often adopted aggressive tactics, like the holding of demonstrations, to pressure the landlords, who in turn developed counter-tactics, like threatening eviction, to weaken the tenants' resolve.

Tenants held demonstrations to soften up the landlords through harassment and shows of strength during negotiations. National police data show that 154,843 tenants took part in 3,594 demonstrations during the depression years.[49] Although each demonstration and demonstrator does not represent a separate dispute or tenant farmer among the 19,139 disputes and 370,303 participants in 1930-1934, since many unions demonstrated several times during any given dispute, demonstrations occurred fairly frequently. And, as the example of Manzai hamlet in Ryūō Village near Ōkamada shows, they had their effect.

On April 3, 1931, the Manzai tenant union requested a 50 percent reduction in 1930's rent for all its members. When the landlords rejected the demand, replying that the 1930 harvest was excellent (which it was), and filed suit in the Kōfu District Court to evict the tenants from the land if they did not pay their rent, the tenants organized for a long dispute and made plans to demonstrate. They decided not to cultivate any of the fields, tilled their remaining fields collec-

---

[48] *Kosaku nempō*, 1927-1939; *Nōchi nempō*, 1940.

[49] *Shakai undō no jōkyō*, 4(1932), p. 1,248; 5(1933), p. 1,226; 14(1942), pp. 721-722.

tively to support everyone, set up a dispute headquarters on a vacant lot next to the house of Fujikawa Ryūichi, one of the primary landlords, and carried out their continual demonstrations, day and night, while negotiating with him at his house. These activities included prayers for a legendary ghost to come out from a well near the landlord's house to pester him, a song about his attack turning to clay, the banging of pots and pans at night, and finally the gathering of all the tenants' children to sing a version written for the occasion of the Japanese children's song about the race between the tortoise and the hare. The standard version began:

> Hello, hello, turtle, Mr. Turtle,
> There is no one in the world
> As slow of foot as you.

The tenant version ran:

> Hello, hello, Mr. Fujikawa Ryūichi
> There is no one in the world
> As greedy and immoral as you.

It is reported that even the landlord's children, caught up in the excitement, joined in the singing. The tenants, who had a large advantage in numbers over the landlords, demonstrated in shifts while the union's leaders carried out frequent and long negotiations with Fujikawa at his house. The union put powerful psychic pressure on the embattled Fujikawas, none of whom left their home during the week of demonstrating and negotiating. It must have been as Takano Morizō explained about a similar event in Saijō: "when we demonstrated, the landlords became small (*chiisaku natchatta*)."[50] In late April Fujikawa and his fellow landlords agreed to lower rent by 2 *to* per *hyō* (6.6 *to*), 30 percent. Although this reduction was less than the 50 percent demanded by the union for 1930, the landlords agreed to the same 30 percent reduction for 1931 and 1932 *in advance* although they had no

---

[50] Interview with Takano.

knowledge of future yields and prices. Moreover, the agreement made this 30 percent the base reduction and did not preclude further union efforts to lower rent in 1931 or 1932.[51] Thus, the settlement which the week-long demonstration helped bring about must be seen as a tenant victory.

Another tactic which tenant farmers employed to force concessions from their landlords during negotiations, one which unions in Kubo Nakajima and Manzai used successfully in periods of scarce labor, like the 1920s and even the 1930s, was the non-cultivation of the landlords' fields during disputes. If the tenants could prevent the landlord from finding other tenants to replace the boycotters, he faced a choice between reduced or no rents and was likely to capitulate quickly. Essential to the tenants' success, therefore, was the union's solidarity and its sufficiency of funds and other fields to support its members during the dispute. In Kubo Nakajima, dues, the collective field, and landlord disunity provided this base; the hamlet's tenants, opposing Mikami Saburō's attempt to raise rent in 1924, supported themselves partly by tilling the other landlord's fields while they boycotted Mikami's. No wonder Mikami quickly abandoned his rent increase in 1924 (actually he won a bit of it since 1924 rents were only 22 percent lower than 1921 although 1923 rents had been 25 percent lower; in 1926, however, rents fell to only half of 1921 levels); no wonder Manzai's landlords compromised in 1931. When a landlord could not find other tenants, he must have preferred receiving part of his rent rather than nothing at all.

Another common tactic which tenants in Kubo Nakajima and elsewhere used to sway their landlords during negotiations, one which was often tied to the non-cultivation of a landlord's fields, was not paying rent. As we can see in Table 6-6, tenants frequently made a mutual agreement not to pay any rent or withheld that part of their rent which they demanded as a reduction and then stored or sold the unpaid

---

[51] Takegawa, *Yamanashi nōmin undō*, pp. 132-136.

rent collectively. When they did not pay any of their rent, as in Kubo Nakajima, tenants forced their landlords either to negotiate a compromised settlement or to go to court to get the rent or their land back. Because landlords had limited success in using the legal system during disputes, they tended to come to terms with the tenants, especially when the latter refused to till the landlord's fields. Again, the landlord faced a choice between losing part or all of his income from a field.[52]

The tenants also profited from selling the rent grain they withheld. Before the dispute era, tenants normally paid their rent in kind in December, not long after the harvest and threshing, when prices were low. The landlord, who was wealthier than his tenants, could hold the rent grain until rice prices rose in the spring and make a nice profit. Tenants, who had less economic security and who individually marketed only small amounts of grain, usually could not wait for rising prices and sold at the most inopportune time; moreover, they had to pay 10–15 percent interest on late rent. But when in the 1920s and 1930s the union guaranteed its members' livelihoods, sold large amounts of unpaid rent rice (and non-rent rice) at one time, and won freedom from interest payments on overdue rent, it too could maximize its profits. What made this tactic especially useful was that when the tenants finally came to terms with the landlords and paid in cash whatever rent they negotiated, they often paid at December's low prices. Thus, the tenants could gain a profit on the market as well as a rent reduction. No wonder that Nishida, in analyzing the records of the Sekimoto, a landlord family in Hanabusa hamlet, concludes that the rise of the payment of paddy rents in money rather than in kind between World Wars I and II marked the decline of the landlord system. Before 1920, Sekimoto received all his rent in kind, in much the same manner as we have described for Kubo Nakajima in Chapter Four, but by 1943 he received all his paddy rent in money, which allowed the tenants rather than

[52] *KNJ*, p. 46.

the landlords to profit from rising market prices for rice after 1934. A dramatic shift in the balance of power between tenants and landlords had taken place.[53]

Tenants also used, albeit rarely, a series of tactics which seriously endangered the harmony of the hamlet order: collective withdrawal from local organizations like the fire department, youth association and primary schools, ostracism against landlords, and violence or threats of violence. (See Table 6-6.) One should not think of most of these incidents, however, as examples of outbursts of intense "rural proletarian" anger. Although violence erupted sometimes because of the strong feelings of the tenant participants, occasionally released by drink, many other incidents took place because of the tenants' realization that landlords tended to honor highly village harmony, or at least its facade to the outside world. By disrupting that harmony, tenants might force intransigent landlords to bend.

Membership in some hamlet organizations, like the farm cooperative, the volunteer fire department, the youth association, and the youth training center, was voluntary, but universal, enforced by the long-standing cohesiveness, cooperative spirit, and sanctions of the community. Participation in other local functions, like attendance of one's children at school or payment of one's taxes, was the legal obligation of each household, but even it was reinforced by the hamlet's customary need for harmony, and its concomitant enforcement. The hamlet would be embarrassed if villagers dropped out of school or did not pay taxes. Thus, even in times of internal hamlet economic conflict rural Japanese normally continued to serve, attend, and pay; only those who either invited or had received the sanction of ostracism, like Ishihara Taizō in Kubo Nakajima, did not or could not participate.[54]

Landlords, who had held the lion's share of power in the

[53] Nagahara, *Nihon jinushisei*, pp. 314-315; *Kosaku jijō chōsa*, pp. 101, 111-113.

[54] Robert J. Smith, "The Japanese Rural Community," pp. 246-255; Smethurst, *A Social Basis for Prewar Japanese Militarism*, pp. 53-55.

Japanese countryside from the misty past until the 1920s, took pride in their role as strict, but fair and paternalistic, leaders. The symbol of their benevolent rule, à la the Confucian mandate of heaven, was the harmony of the community. Because until the formation of tenant unions in the 1920s landlords had had greater contact than tenants with outside government and society, many of this rural elite felt that a breakdown in the facade of harmony reflected badly on them. Thus, landlords often compromised in tenant disputes rather than allow tenants to dirty this face. As we can see from the data in Table 6-8, on a few rare occasions (0.28 percent of disputes), tenants challenged this harmony collectively by withdrawing their children from school, dropping out of the fire department (although they continued to fight fires at tenant union homes), not paying local taxes, and leaving a number of hamlet organizations. As Kōfu Basin examples show, the tactic worked.

Tenants in Yoshizawa in Naka Koma demanded 60 percent rent reductions in 1925, withdrew their children from school, and received 70 percent reductions for both 1925 and 1926. Tenants demanded 40-50 percent in Tamahata in Naka Koma in 1926 and received it after they withdrew their children from school. Tenants in Ochiai in Naka Koma asked for 30 percent in 1929, left the school, and received 48-50 percent rent reductions. Tenants in Ono in Higashi Yamanashi in 1930 left the school, fire department, sericultural cooperative, and Buddhist temple worship organization and had their rents reduced by 50 percent. Tenants in Manzai in 1930 asked for 50 percent, dropped out of the school and fire department, and, as we have seen, received 30 percent rent reductions for three years. In fact, the only report I have seen of a case where this tactic failed was in Hanabusa, the hamlet analyzed by Nishida, where in 1930 tenants asked for 50-90 percent, withdrew their children from school, and in the end accepted the landlords' original offer of a 20 percent rent reduction. But Nishida writes that the landlords were embarrassed by the school withdrawal, which received wide pub-

TABLE 6-8
Collective Withdrawals from Community Organizations, Nationwide, 1925-1937

Year	Total Disputes	Total Withdrawals	School	Fire Dept.	Youth Association	Youth Center	Committees	Tax
1925	2,206	11	6	5	0	0	0	0
1926	2,751	21	12	8	1	0	0	0
1930	2,478	15	6	4	0	0	1	4
1931	3,419	24	14	6	4	0	0	0
1932	3,414	19	9	2	1	0	1	6
1933	4,000	9	5	1	0	1	1	1
1934	5,828	11	2	4	1	0	4	0
1935	6,824	9	2	6	0	0	1	0
1936	6,804	3	3	0	0	0	0	0
1937	6,170	2	2	0	0	0	0	0
Total	43,894	124	61	36	7	1	8	11

Sources: Naimushō keihōkyoku, *Shakai undō no jōkyō*, 6 (1934), p. 1,252; *NSSS*, Vol. 2, pp. 324-327; *Kosaku chōtei nempō*, 1925-1926.

licity, and that it was the tenant leaders' mistakes in timing and the breakup of the union's solidarity, not the inefficacy of the tactic, which led to the Hanabusa defeat.[55]

Although the tenant's withdrawal of their children from school worked successfully, largely because of the embarrassment it caused the landlords in the eyes of government officials and fellow landlords elsewhere, resignation from the fire department added a dimension of fear as well. In Shimo Ishimori in Kanōiwa Village in Higashi Yamanashi, for example, when tenants left the fire company they did not actually leave it. Rather, they abandoned the "public" organization by expelling their landlords; then the tenants took possession of the fire-fighting equipment and organized a "private" group to put out fires at tenant union members' homes and to patrol against "crime," i.e., to threaten the landlords with the possibility of group violence. The landlords found themselves both without fire protection and vulnerable to the tenant union's coercion. The landlords appealed to the police to ban "private" fire departments, but the authorities replied that they had no legal basis to do so.[56]

Two of the tenants' strongest weapons, if I may be repetitive, and two which made their tactics work, were their numbers and their solidarity. In the Tokugawa and Meiji eras, the hamlet collective functioned because of the "brains" and money of the few landlords and the "brawn" of the many tenants. When, in the 1920s, tenant farmers had more money through the market and more "brains" through schooling and contact with the outside world, they could maintain their own solidarity, expel the landlords from the collective, and function on their own as the hamlet's cooperative organization.

[55] Nagahara, *Nihon jinushisei*, pp. 257, 279; *Kosaku sōgichi*, pp. 66-67, 75; Takegawa, *Yamanashi nōmin undō*, p. 85; *Kosaku sōgi oyobi chōtei jirei*, 1930, p. 67.

[56] Takegawa, *Yamanashi nōmin undō*, p. 111; Tenants in Shimo Ishimori also used their private fire department to patrol against landlord seizure of their cocoons; their plan was to use the fire bell to sound the warning if the landlords or their agents came to confiscate the tenants' cocoons.

The landlords, on the other hand, in spite of their money and customary status, were few. Thus, when, in a hamlet like Takano Morizō's Katō Nakajima in Saijō Village, tenants ostracized their landlords, negotiations worked to the tenants' advantage. Tenants in Katō Nakajima, according to Takano, maintained a sanction of *mura hachibu* against their landlords for four or five years without ever resorting to violence. In the end, the tenants received permanent rent reductions of 30 percent and much freer contract terms.[57] Even landlords, after all, need to talk to someone.

Although tenants rarely applied such severe pressure as ostracism to landlords, modified versions, as in the case of Kubo Nakajima, often softened up the landlord considerably. Tenants there continued to maintain and even increased social patron-client ties with their landlords in the 1920s and 1930s, but, at the same time, the tenant union took control of the hamlet's government and virtually excluded nonmembers from its political and economic life. The six nonunion households took part in no hamlet or *kumi* meetings, gained no technical aid through the hamlet's agricultural and sericultural associations, and received no information through the hamlet chiefs from higher levels of government. In a sense, one might say that tenants in Kubo Nakajima spoke to their landlords socially, but ostracized them politically and economically. It must have been a strong landlord family that survived this kind of isolation without making a concession.

The final tactic which threatened hamlet harmony was violence and its *explicit* threat. Violence probably should not be called a tactic, because normally it was not planned, but erupted in the heat of divisive disputes (and often in the heat of summer), at times when the tenant farmers' animosity toward landlords ran high. Thus, violence was rare even in Yamanashi, where it or its threat occurred four times more frequently than nationwide.[58] Between 1926 and 1937, police

[57] Interview with Takano.
[58] According to Army and Agriculture Ministry reports, Yamanashi peo-

401

indicted only 512 people (of 7,663 nationally), 1.8 percent of all tenant participants, for crimes of any sort, and many were charged with more than one crime and thus counted two or three times in the records. Police charged 289 with violation of the Violence Control Law, and these offenders may only have threatened, not actually committed, violent acts.[59] Few people, only 23 nationwide between 1925 and 1940, and none in Yamanashi between 1926 and 1931, were arrested for the most serious violent crimes, attempted murder and arson.[60] But, even if violence was rare, petty, and unplanned, it often worked to the tenant/perpetrators' advantage. Kubo Nakajima tenant farmers, as we have seen, received 70 percent rent reductions after the Emman Incident of the summer of 1930. Nothing demonstrated to the outside world the hamlet's disharmony and the landlords' failure like a dipping of feces, police intervention, a trial, and the inevitable newspaper articles in the Kōfu *Daily News*. The unfortunate but almost comical event at the Gemma house on July 7, 1930, led to landlord capitulation and overwhelming tenant victory.

The last tactic, clearly a reformist one, which tenant farmers used in their attempt to lower rents and improve their

ple were aggressive and more prone to violence than other Japanese. The commander of the army's Kōfu Regimental District reported in 1913 that Yamanashians "are aggressively self-centered when moderation and a sense of duty are called for. . . . There is a lamentably thin feeling of national and social responsibility. . . . Pragmatism has spread and destroyed morality. The tendency is to put the profit of one's household before everything else. Yamanashi people are self-assertive and not public-spirited." *Kaku rentaiku kannai minjō fūzoku shisōkai genjō*, reports dated December 1913 from 73 of 74 regimental district commanders to Watanabe Jōtarō, aide de camp to Field Marshal Yamagata Aritomo, Vol. III (handwritten with no pagination). Agriculture Ministry officials reported in 1932 that "Yamanashi people are famous for their short tempers. . . . Because of this, there is a high incidence of arrests . . . and of violent incidents in Yamanashi." *Chihōbetsu*, 1932, pp. 273-274.

[59] Nagahara, *Nihon jinushisei*, p. 257.

[60] *Shakai undō no jōkyō*, 4(1932), pp. 1,258-1,259; 5(1933), pp. 1,237-1,238; 6(1934), pp. 1,216-1,217; 14(1942), pp. 727-729; *Kosaku nempō*, 1926-1931.

economic position, was rural politics. With the implementation of universal manhood suffrage for the local elections of 1925, tenants won many seats and took control of a number of Yamanashi's village assemblies and offices. In the 1925 election, tenants won 729 seats, over one-third of the 1956 openings contested, gained at least one seat in 173 and an absolute majority in 58 of 227 assemblies. In 1929, the tenants increased their seats to 776, but in 1933 they captured only 640 positions in 151 councils and control of 36 assemblies. Even in 1933, tenants in Yamanashi controlled more village assemblies than in any other prefecture in Japan.

What is striking about these election results is that affiliation with a national union did not seem to have been a key to success. Only 88 of the 729 winners in 1925 belonged to Nichinō; in 1933, 93 of 640 assemblymen belonged to Hirano Rikizō's patriotic union, which supported the State Socialist Party and called for the military and economic development of Manchuria, and only 8 were enrolled in the Communist Party's Conference Faction, which advocated direct action. Altogether, 541 tenant councilmen in 1925 and 437 in 1933 had no ties to unions, either local, regional, or national.[61]

In those cases like Usui Jirō's Jōei Village, where tenants controlled the village assembly and the mayorship, they wielded great power. Tenants devised budgets, allocated funds, and determined who should have access to which governmental resources at the level of official local government, the village. Such cases were undoubtedly rare. But even in communities where tenants had less power at the village level, where they controlled only the legislative wing of government, or no wing at all, tenants still could use their political power effectively. Yamanashi in this period contained 227 villages (*mura*), each made up of 5 or 6 hamlets (*buraku*); a *buraku* normally sent one or two men to the vil-

---

[61] *NSSS*, Vol. 3, pp. 64–73; *Shōwa hachinendo chōson kaigi sōsenkyo ni okeru kosakuningawa tōsen no gaikyō*, pp. 18–27.

lage assembly. Chances are, therefore, that 729, 776, and 640 tenant victors meant that about half of Yamanashi's hamlets elected tenants. Thus, although only a small number of village governments were in the hands of tenant farmers, a large minority of hamlets fell, like Kubo Nakajima, under their domination. We have seen how tenants there furthered their own economic purposes by dominating government and agricultural organizations. If many other hamlets which elected tenant assemblymen followed suit, politics played an important role in bringing rural economic change in Yamanashi in the 1920s and 1930s.

Tenants used a series of moderate tactics to pursue their reformist goals. They formed local unions, called on regional and national organizations for specialized legal and organizational help on the few occasions that they needed it, negotiated, used the government's mediation system, demonstrated, boycotted landlord fields, held back rent payments, and sold unpaid rent rice to soften up their landlords, and used local politics, none of which seriously threatened the harmony of the hamlet order. On rare occasions, they also resorted, either by plan or not, to more disruptive tactics; they withdrew from local cooperative organizations, broke off social ties with or ostracized landlords, or resorted to violence. But even when tenants used these extreme tactics, they tended to use them for pragmatic ends, to win immediate concrete goals like rent reductions and better and more secure contract terms. One can only be amazed at the imaginative diversity and effectiveness of the methods tenant farmers used to achieve their pragmatic goals in the years between World War I and II.

LANDLORD TACTICS DURING TENANT DISPUTES

Landlords, needless to say, did not sit back and watch tenant farmers eat into their rent income; in fact, landlords fought back in defense of their interests so vigorously that scholars like Nakamura Masanori believe they won.[62] We shall return later to an evaluation of who gained the most, that is to say, of the effect that the tenant farmer movement had on the economic, political, and social life of the Kōfu Basin. But, before we do that, let us describe the landlords' tactics in resisting the tenants' advance.

Landlords, who had more money and power, but were fewer in number than their tenants, answered the creation of tenant unions in the 1920s by forming organizations of their own. They decided to meet the collective opposition collectively. Although the landlords' first village association in Yamanashi dated from 1908, they began to organize in earnest only after tenants formed unions to demand rent reductions. The number of members in Yamanashi landlord groups rose gradually from 72 in 1923, to over 900 by the end of the decade, to a high of 2,000 in the mid-1930s, before falling off to 600-700 in the early years of the Pacific War.[63]

Landlords formed organizations for reasons not dissimilar from the tenants' in creating unions. If they wanted to protect their incomes by avoiding, or after the early 1920s minimizing, rent reductions, solidarity was essential. Landlords did, as we shall see, try to conquer their tenants by dividing them; but tenants also tried the same tactic, often successfully, as when Kubo Nakajima's tenant union resisted Mikami's rent increase in 1924 by tilling other landlords' fields while boycotting his. It was for this reason that when landlords in Ochiai in 1929 formed an association, they pledged to negotiate collectively, never individually.[64] Landlords by forming associations could also exchange information about how best to combat various tenant tactics, jointly hire lawyers and other specialists, and pool financial resources. One must keep in mind that for each large-scale landlord like Wakao, Nezu, and even Mikami, who could afford to en-

---

[62] Nakamura, *Jinushiseishi kenkyū*, p. 253.
[63] *Kosaku nempō*, 1934, 1939; *Chihōbetsu*, p. 278.
[64] *Kosaku sōgichi*, p. 71.

gage his own legal assistance, there were dozens of small-scale ones like Kubo Nakajima's "three Ishiharas." Landlord associations especially helped these men, who had little more wealth than owner, owner tenant, or even hard-working tenant owner or tenant farmers.

But the landlords, who formed their first prefectural association in January 1927, did not stop at collective negotiations and legal help. In 1929 they founded the Yamanashi Land Company to handle their disputes. The idea was to turn business contacts with tenants over to agents, specialized negotiators, who would dun the tenants for back rents. Tenants, who obviously preferred dealing collectively with individual landlords, disliked this landlord attempt to fight fire with fire, and the Kōfu Basin's most divisive disputes broke out in 1930. But, while some tenants clashed with landlords, others took them to court. In May 1931, the Supreme Court (*Daishin'in*) in Tokyo found the landlords' use of the land company to collect unpaid rent in violation of the Credit Law. After only two years of relying on agents, landlords once again had to negotiate individually, or at best collectively at the hamlet level.[65] It seems that landlord associations did not provide landlords with the same leverage in disputes that tenant unions gave tenants.

Landlords, like their tenants, negotiated. Although in the early 1920s, landlords believed they could block rent reductions and preserve the hamlet's status quo, they soon realized they would have to compromise with their tenants. Of the 2,871 disputes solved in Yamanashi between 1920 and 1940, landlord demands were met in only 44 (1.5 percent).[66] Thus, while tenants came to the table to advance their interests as far as possible, landlords bargained to minimize their losses.

Unfortunately, we have no Yamanashi-wide statistics to compare tenant demands and landlord concessions, and the examples introduced above are not necessarily typical dis-

[65] *Chihōbetsu*, 1934, p. 286; Nagahara, *Nihon jinushisei*, p. 499.

[66] *Kosaku chōtei nempō*, 1925-1926; *Kosaku nempō*, 1927-1939; *Nōchi nempō*, 1940.

putes. True, Kubo Nakajima's landlords gave 70-100 percent reductions in 1929-1930, Manzai landlords 30 percent in 1930-1932, Yoshizawa landlords 70 percent in 1925-1926, Tamahata landlords 40-50 percent in 1926, Ochiai landlords 48-50 percent in 1929, and Ono landlords 50 percent in 1930, but these examples are all disputes in which tenants adopted unusually strong measures to pressure landlords to make concessions.[67] However, if we juxtapose the national data presented in Chapter Five—that disputing tenants in 1926 and 1928 asked for 35 percent and 34 percent rent reductions and received 24 percent, and in 1931 and 1933, depression years, asked for 37 percent and 40 percent and gained 29 percent and 31 percent, with the comparatively high degree of disputation and tenant union organization in Yamanashi—we can surmise, I think, that landlords there made even greater concessions. The Nezu, Yamanashi's largest landlord house after the collapse of the Wakao empire in the 1920s, collected 91 percent of its contract rents in 1900, but only 47 percent and 28 percent of its paddy and dry-field contract rents, respectively, in 1933; Nezu real rent income fell by 65 percent over this third of a century.[68] Clearly, landlords negotiated in a retrograde action against the tenant offensive, to salvage what they could of their diminishing rent income.

Landlords, like the tenants, used various tactics to pressure their adversaries to make concessions during negotiation, but theirs had less effect than the tenants'. Since landlords bargained over rent and contract tenure for fields which they themselves owned, they employed the court system, which they expected would uphold their rights of private property, as their principal bargaining lever. Thus, when tenants refused to pay rent as a tactic to force landlords to lower rent, landlords countered by suing for payment of the rent or return of the fields involved. Much to the amazement of the landlords, and, one suspects, of modern scholars who write

[67] See footnote 55, above.
[68] Nagahara, *Nihon jinushisei*, pp. 56, 128-129.

that the courts and the landlords were both part of the "emperor-system state authority" which oppressed tenants, this tactic did not work very well.

As Table 6-9 indicates, the courts between 1925 and 1940 forced tenants in the Kōfu Basin to return their rented land unconditionally in only 4.7 percent of landlord attempts to get it back (68 of 1,442 cases); the courts required tenants to return part of the land, to return it with landlord compensation or to exchange it for another plot of land in only 24 percent more. In fully 60 percent of all landlord attempts to evict tenants, the courts upheld the right of tenancy over the right of ownership, and in 9 percent the tenants were allowed to buy the contested land. In short, the tenant/defendants won two-and-one-half times more often than the landlord/plaintiffs in these cases. In 44 percent of the tenant victories (and 30 percent of all cases) the courts awarded the tenants permanent rights of tenancy. Although the threat of eviction strengthened some landlords in their negotiations with tenants, it seems hardly to have stood as one of the foundation stones of an authoritarian emperor system.

TABLE 6-9

Disputes over Landlord Attempts to Evict Tenants from Rented Land in Yamanashi, 1925-1940 (Average per Year)

Year	Land Disputes per Year	Uncondi- tional Return	Conditional Return	Not Returned	Permanent Tenancy
1925-29	8	2.6%	40%	53%	(16%)
1930-34	45	9.8	37	51	(25%)
1935-37	255	4.6	22	70	(28%)
1938-40	138	2.4	20	72	(37%)
Total	90	4.7%	24%	69%	(30%)

Calculated from *Kosaku chōtei nempō*, 1925-1926; *Kosaku nempō*, 1927-1939; *Nōchi nempō*, 1940.

Not unexpectedly, evictions increased in percentage during the depression years, when hard economic conditions beset landlords and tenants both; in 1930-1934, the courts evicted tenants unconditionally in 9.8 percent and conditionally in 37 percent of disputes. But even in those difficult years, the actual number of disputes and evictions were small (only 225 cases and 22 evictions in five years), and tenants still maintained their rights to farm the landlords' fields in more cases than they lost them. By 1935-1937, the peak years in number of disputes in the Kōfu Basin when landlords had the "initiative," tenants continued to till the land unconditionally after 70 percent of landlord attempts at eviction.

fields and to seize crops and other property of tenants who withheld rent payments. The landlords hoped that by seizing the crops in the fields or, better yet, by seizing them after the harvest and saving themselves work or expense, they could force tenants to capitulate to avoid losing the fruits of their labor. Although this weapon was a powerful one and sometimes even forced tenants to organize to protect their crops, it was rarely used. As Table 6-10 indicates, the courts allowed landlords in all Japan to block tenant access to fields or to seize crops from only 246 *chō* of land per year between 1925 and 1940; this came to less than one-half of one percent of all farmland involved in tenant disputes. Courts allowed landlords to attach a little less than 64,000 yen of movable property, usually cocoons, per year; this was equivalent to the agricultural income of tenants in two or three hamlets in a nation of 76,000 farm communities.

Yamanashi data on such injunctions is limited to 1932-1940. During those years, which included the second half of the depression in 1932-1934, and the peak years of Yamanashi disputation in 1935-1937, courts ordered no trespassing injunctions for 3.82 *chō* and permitted seizure of crops for 3.6 *chō* of 8,332 *chō* of land involved in disputes (0.08 percent); courts allowed landlords to seize 6,281 yen worth of property, about the income of 5-10 tenant families in a prefecture of about 60,000 tenant households. Clearly this weapon, though a puissant one when used, had limited application.

Another landlord tactic which seems to have had some effect, although how much is difficult to assess in the absence of quantitative evidence, is the technique of "divide and conquer." Landlords such as those in the villages Nishida Yoshiaki studied, Hanabusa in Yamanashi, and Kanazuka in Niigata, offered their own candy and whips to tenant union members to wean them from the movement. Landlords appealed to some tenants through kinship or patron-client ties. Landlords cajoled others, particularly poor tenants, with threats of eviction or offers of rent compromises which were less generous, but more sure, than the ones the tenants might get if they remained firm. Landlords attracted the more well-to-do tenants, whose goal was to establish their own farms, with offers of the sale of land through the government's program to establish owner farmers. The latter program was particularly effective in Hanabusa because the local union's leaders were mostly from among the upper tenants. When

TABLE 6-10

Court Orders Banning Tenants from Entering Their Fields, and Seizing Crops or Movable Property, Nationwide, Average per Year, 1925-1940

Year	Total Area of Land In Disputes	No Trespassing	Seizing Crops	Seizure of Property
1925–29	71,257 chō	219 chō	200 chō	132,671 yen
1930–34	51,125	134	114	37,291
1935–40	39,226	77	24	28,000
Average per Year	52,954	139	107	63,613

Calculated from *Shakai undō no jōkyō*, 4 (1932), 5 (1933), 6 (1942).

they left the union in 1930, the landlords negotiated with a leaderless organization and forced it to accept their original offer of a 20 percent reduction in rent.[69]

As we saw when we described tenant tactics during disputes, group unity was one of the keys to victory, whether it be the landlords' or the tenants'. Where the tenants' solidarity crumbled, as in Hanabusa, the landlords gained the upper hand; where the landlords' solidarity weakened, as in Kubo Nakajima, the tenants won out. One might view the tenant disputes of the interwar years as something akin to a series of chess games on a giant board. Each side used its pieces to probe and weaken its opponent. When one player exploited an opening, it could go on to win the game; when it was forced to retreat, it lost. But, whichever side won, it rarely did so without losing some of its pieces. Few disputes ended in complete victory for either side; although, as we have seen, the landlords in Yamanashi won outright only 44 disputes between 1920 and 1940, the tenants won outright but four-and-one-half-times more, 194.[70] Still, over all, this chess game of solidarity and divide and conquer favored the tenants, who lowered their rents, bettered their tenancy conditions, and cut sharply into landlord income between 1920 and 1942. The landlords won some games, but in the long run their victories only slowed and did not stop their steady retreat. One should remember that when tenants compromised, they gave up only demands; when landlords compromised, they surrendered actual income.

Landlords, like tenants, occasionally threatened violence to counter the tenants' use of force or their refusal to pay rent or return leased land. Because all our evidence for landlords' physical coercion comes from accounts of individual disputes, we do not know how widespread it was. Still, the following accounts from Inazumi, Nango, Tamahata, and

[69] *Ibid.*, pp. 264-274.

[70] *Kosaku chōtei nempō*, 1925-1926; *Kosaku nempō*, 1927-1939; *Nōchi nempō*, 1940.

411

Ochiai villages in the central part of the Kōfu Basin give us an idea of some of its varieties. On March 8, 1923, when Suzuki Bunji lectured at Inazumi during a tour of eastern Naka Koma County, members of the Kokusuikai, a right-wing organization, appeared (whether they came by landlord invitation or on their own initiative is unclear) and shouted epithets at him as he spoke. The police tried, but did not have sufficient strength, to eject the young rightists. Thus, the tenants took matters into their own hands and quickly dispersed the counter-demonstrators. On November 18, 1925, just before the rice harvest, eight Koreans appeared in Nango village to place no-trespassing signs on paddies for which rent had not been paid and to confiscate the property of the tenant union's leader. Before the outsiders could begin their duties, the tenant union mobilized, chased the Koreans from the village, and harvested the crops in the disputed fields. In the summer of 1926, after Tamahata tenants had resigned from the village fire department to form their own "public safety" organization, the landlords hired Tokyo thugs for "protection" from the tenant group. The threat and counter-threat speeded negotiations, and in October the landlords met the tenants' demands for 40 percent and 50 percent rent reductions for single- and double-cropped paddies and dismissal of the bullies in return for the tenants' agreement to rejoin the landlord-led fire department. In the summer of 1930, Ochiai landlords organized a vigilante group made up mostly of their younger male family members to protect themselves from the tenants' paramilitary organization. Both sides disbanded their groups when ordered to do so by the police.[71] Thus, we see here right-wing ideologues, mercenaries, and landlords themselves serving as the landlords' threats of force, but we see no actual landlord violence, and, even more striking, no landlord victories in any of these cases.

[71] Takegawa, *Yamanashi nōmin undō*, pp. 74, 81-96, 129-131.

THE ROLE OF THE GOVERNMENT IN TENANT DISPUTES

Scholars like Nakamura Masanori and Shiota Shōbē might argue that one reason landlords did not resort to violence as often as tenant farmers is that they did not need to do so; landlords had the protection of the government. Nakamura, as we know, argues that the tenant movement, like all progressive forces in the interwar years, faced a formidable foe, the "emperor-system state authority." The civil and military wings of government, "monopoly capitalists," and "parasitical landlords" joined together under the aegis of the emperor, or more accurately, under the symbol of the emperor as a semi-divine national father, to crush social or political movements which did not build national wealth and power.[72] Even Nishida Yoshiaki, who shuns such dramatic depictions of the government's maleficent role in fighting the "proletarian movement," writes that the government sided with the landlords against the tenants.[73] To Nakamura, Shiota, and Nishida, landlords could avoid the use of violence because they did not need it.

The main weapons in the government's repressive arsenal were, according to Nakamura, the police, the courts, the mediation law, and politics. But when one analyzes the workings of the four institutions in the Kōfu Basin, the evidence seems to indicate a system which was relatively even-handed. Thus, let us look at them to evaluate to what extent one can fairly conclude that the government did not take sides.

We have already reiterated in Chapter Five Dore's and Ōuchi's point that if the interwar Japanese government had feared rural unrest, they would have assigned many more policemen to rural districts. If we look at data for the internal distribution of policemen within Yamanashi, we find evi-

---

[72] Nakamura, *Jinushiseishi kenkyū*, pp. 253, 256-257; Shiota, *Nihon shakai undōshi*, p. 68.

[73] Nagahara, *Nihon jinushisei*, p. 274.

dence which reinforces their view that the government believed the countryside was safe. Yamanashi had twelve police stations in the prewar decades, one in Kōfu; four in upland districts, where there was little tenant unrest; and seven in the Kōfu Basin, where tenant disputes were rife. As Table 6-11 indicates, the government assigned more policemen to upland than to basin stations. Even when one combines basin and Kōfu policemen, on the grounds that the government could dispatch the urban officers as reinforcements to suppress disputes in nearby villages, to calculate the density of law enforcement, one finds not only that the Kōfu Basin had fewer policemen per 10,000 population than rural England à la Dore and Ōuchi, but also that the basin had fewer officers than the dispute-free periphery. Two hundred and eighty-three men, including headquarters personnel, supervisors, inspectors, and constables, served in the police force in Kōfu and the basin in 1925, hardly a force sufficient to suppress a tenant movement of 25,000-30,000 union members committed to violent change in the social order. So much for the police as the landlords' agent of repression.

Another sign of government/police/court suppression of the tenant movement would be frequent indictments of tenant disputants on various trumped-up charges like disturbing the peace, star chamber proceedings in trial, and harsh punishments for those (all?) found guilty. And yet, as we have

TABLE 6-11
Policemen in Yamanashi (per 10,000 population)

	1920	1925	1930
Kōfu	11.0	9.9	9.1
Basin	5.6	5.5	5.7
Upland	7.1	6.6	7.0
Basin/Kōfu	6.5	6.3	6.4

Calculated from *Yamanashi tōkeisho.*

414

seen earlier in the chapter, the courts made only 512 indictments in tenant disputes in 12 years (and let me reiterate that we have no reason to believe that the 512 indictments represent 512 different people or that all those indicted were tenant farmers), the tenant defendants were allowed counsel and given public trials, and the penalties were mild, usually three or four months' imprisonment, with the sentences often suspended. The longest sentence meted out in Yamanashi for an offense committed during a tenant dispute was 18 months, given to a man who knocked a policeman unconscious. Those arrested during peasant uprisings in the Tokugawa and early Meiji periods, if they had been alive to do so, would have looked with disbelief at the leniency of the Taishō-Shōwa courts.

The only people who seem to have received harsh treatment at the hands of the authorities were members of what the government considered subversive organizations like the Japan Communist Party. Both Nakamura and Nishida use the government's mass arrests of radicals in the late 1920s and early 1930s as examples of its repression of the tenant movement.[74] But if I can repeat my earlier points, that the left established itself at the "head" of the tenant movement by *self-appointment* and that actual tenant farmers had little to do with and minimal sympathy for these non-farmer "leaders," the mass arrests of early Shōwa Japan had only marginal effect on the pragmatic, reformist tenant movement. The government clearly disliked the radical left far more than it feared tenant farmers.

Not only did this small police force make few arrests of

[74] Nakamura, *Jinushiseishi kenkyū*, p. 247; Nagahara, *Nihon jinushisei*, p. 274. Japanese scholars of the tenant-farmer movement tend to use the terms "tenant dispute" and "farmers' movement," which refer largely to the activities of the national tenant union organizations, synonymously. See Shiota, *Nihon shakai undōshi*, p. 67. This view has permeated Western scholarship as well. For a capsule presentation of this interpretation, see T.R.H. Havens, "farmers' movement," in *Kodansha Encyclopedia of Japan*, Vol. 2, p. 249.

tenant farmers, but its actions when it did intervene in disputes were largely non-violent ones aimed at protecting property and maintaining harmony and order rather than at abetting the landlords' cause. Reading through Takegawa Yoshinori's descriptions of the Kōfu Basin's ten most contentious tenant disputes, where a scholar of the Nakamura school would expect the strongest government reaction, one finds nine cases where the police intruded, but only two where they adopted anything resembling repressive action.[75] In Inazumi in 1923, the police intervened to avoid a clash between the tenants and the Kokusuikai. In Tamahata in January 1926, they arrived on the scene when a tenant demonstration with 700 participants was underway, but took no steps to disperse the crowd, even though the speakers made venomous anti-landlord speeches. In Jōei in May 1925 and Kubo Nakajima in July 1930, the police arrived the day *after* incidents of tenant violence to investigate and make arrests. In Shimo Ishimori in 1930, the police took no steps to interfere with the tenants' "private" fire department in spite of a landlord request that they do so.[76] The police in these cases took what one can only call a defensive position. So long as tenants did not damage property or attack others, they could do what they wanted: demonstrate, create private fire departments, withdraw children from school, withhold rents, and even till fields which the landlords owned and demanded back. In fact, when the Nango tenant union chased the eight Koreans out of town and harvested crops in violation of a court injunction in 1925, the police did not intrude at all.[77]

The only two cases of forceful police intervention thus stand out as exceptional. One took place after tenants attacked and badly injured a policeman; the other may have been much less forceful than the tenant union, to embarrass the police, made it seem. The first incident occurred in Oku-

---

[75] These examples come from Chapter Two, entitled "Extreme Disputes," of Takegawa's *Yamanashi nōmin undō shi*. Eight of the disputes took place in Naka Koma County.

[76] Takegawa, *Yamanashi nōmin undō*, pp. 74, 76-78, 88, 98, 112.

noda Village in Higashi Yamanashi on the evening of July 2, 1930. An overly enthusiastic police officer named Furuya attempted to investigate a gathering of 150 members of the Okunoda tenant union's youth auxiliary who were encamped illegally in a Shinto shrine in a neighboring village. As he approached, the young men bombarded him with stones. Furuya, covered with blood, continued to advance and arrested one of his tormentors; they in turn counterattacked to save their captured comrade. In the melee which followed, Furuya passed out and had to be rushed to the hospital. Later that evening, policemen arrived in Okunoda, arrested many of the youths and a number of union leaders who had not participated in the attack, searched the homes of tenant farmer activists in Okunoda and surrounding villages, and confiscated a variety of tenant union documents. In the end, the procurator indicted 17 of the participants; the court sentenced the leader to 18 months in jail, and the others to 3 to 8 months.[78]

The other incident took place in Manzai, the hamlet of the week-long demonstration. On the afternoon of April 10, 1931, while tenants and landlords, serenaded by children singing in the vacant lot next door, negotiated, 30 union members barged into the landlord's garden to intimidate him by shouting raucously. Police officers sped to Manzai from their Ryūō headquarters nearby, grabbed the trespassing farmers' weapons, their hoes and sickles, and chased the intruders away. During the scuffle, one of the tenants, a man named Ōsugi, was knocked unconscious. On the 13th, three days after the incident, a union doctor examined Ōsugi and reported that he "hurts everywhere and his left collar bone is in intense pain because he was hit in the breast with a blunt instrument. Both his hands are severely bruised, he cannot use his right hand at all, and he has severe headaches. It may be difficult to save Ōsugi's life."[79]

After hearing Doctor Nishi's report, the tenant headquar-

[77] *Ibid.*, pp. 178-184.   [78] *Ibid.*, pp. 115-128.   [79] *Ibid.*, p. 134.

ters of eastern Naka Koma mobilized 100 members, who placed the injured man on a stretcher and carried him to the Kōfu District Court five miles away to charge the police with brutality. Two weeks later the tenants won 30 percent rent reductions in advance for 1931 and 1932.[80]

Okunoda is the single most striking case of police intervention in a tenant dispute recorded for the Kōfu Basin. The authorities detained not only the young men who attacked Officer Furuya, but other Okunoda tenant union leaders as well; they also used the opportunity to search homes and seize documents. The police authorities here used the pretext of one violent incident to cast their net more widely to gather information about the tenant movement in general; they did so because they believed that activists who were neither local people nor tenant farmers had participated in the incident.[81] We see in this isolated incident two of the classic occasions for strong police action, an attack on one of their number and intervention by outsiders. And yet, in spite of what the police must have considered strong provocation, they committed no violent acts, quickly released those dé tenus not directly involved in the attack, and the court's sentences do not seem grossly excessive, given the severity of the defendants' offenses. One does not see in the police reaction to the Okunoda incident the workings of a repressive police state.

In the Manzai case, we come upon the only case of police assault in Yamanashi that I have found. And, even here, the attack took place while tenants resisted a police order to disband, and, more importantly, the degree of police violence is almost impossible to assess accurately. Although Dr. Nishi's report reads as if the victim was at death's door and possibly was the victim of police overreaction, one wonders how so seriously injured a victim withstood the five-mile stretcher trip to the Kōfu courthouse. It may be that the

[80] *Ibid.*, pp. 133-136.
[81] *Yamanashi nichinichi shimbun*, July 6, 1930, p. 3.

union exaggerated the extent of Ōsugi's injuries to discomfit the police. The degree of police intervention in these 10 disputes, the most violent of all 3,000 Yamanashi disputes, does not seem to support Nakamura's conclusion that the police sided with the landlords to forcibly suppress the tenant movement.

The courts do not seem to have favored the landlords any more than the police did. They sentenced those few tenants arrested during disputes to short terms of servitude and, more frequently than not, suspended their sentences. Take the case of Shinohara hamlet in 1930, for example. On May 9, 100 tenants armed with clubs attacked a landlord's house front and back, broke down his gate, and threw rocks at his walls. The police arrived after the tenants had broken off the engagement and arrested only 7 of the 100 participants. Later in the month, a trial was held in Kōfu, and the judge sentenced one defendant to 4 months' imprisonment and awarded the other six suspended sentences. It is hard to believe that these sentences reflect the government's employ of the legal system to destroy the tenant movement.

The courts did not uphold the landlords' rights of private property either, to the extent that one would expect in a democratic, much less an allegedly authoritarian, society. Yamanashi landlords, as we have seen, went to court hundreds of times to force tenants to pay rent or relinquish their rights of cultivation. The courts, as we have also seen, upheld the landlords' position even partly in only 29 percent of all cases, and completely in only 4.7 percent. The courts allowed Yamanashi landlords to seize property as recompense for unpaid rent on only one-seventh of one percent of all land involved in disputes, and for only 6,281 yen worth of property in a decade. The courts do not seem to have favored the landlords over the tenants in civil cases any more than they did in criminal ones.

Possibly the most striking example of the government's even-handed treatment of landlord-tenant conflict is the system for mediating disputes which the government established in 1924. Professor Nakamura writes that the mediation system favored the landlords because it encouraged compromise and emasculated the tenant movement.[82] But if one views the tenant movement as an evolutionary rather than a revolutionary attempt to change rural society, compromise became tenant victory. Mediation, as a tool which aided in compromise, functioned as an important tenant, not landlord, weapon. When tenants and landlords compromised, tenants gave up demands, but landlords gave up income.

Virtually all Kōfu Basin tenant disputes after 1925 (over 90 percent) were submitted to arbitration under the terms of the mediation law. As Table 6-12 indicates, landlords and tenants reached agreement in 82 percent of all attempts at mediation. The success rate reached its peak, 95 percent, in the mid-1930s, the years of greatest landlord-tenant contention. And tenants requested arbitration more often than landlords, except in the mid-1930s. Nevertheless, one should not, à la Nishida Yoshiaki, interpret this shift to "landlord initiative" in 1935-1938 as an indication of the "reintegration of the landlord system"; during these years, as we can see from Table 6-9, landlords, in spite of their efforts, had less success than ever before in using their own land as they wanted by evicting their tenants.[83] Tenants clung to their land in 70 percent of landlord efforts to take it away. It is hard to believe from this evidence that the government's mediation system, through which tenants received substantial rent reductions, albeit smaller ones than they demanded, and through which landlords saw their rent income and power to use freely their own private property melt away, functioned as a government weapon to reinforce landlord power.

There is one other area, politics, where the government made reforms which actually favored the tenants. In 1925, the government promulgated universal manhood suffrage,

---

[82] Nakamura, *Jinushiseishi kenkyū*, pp. 256-257.
[83] Nagahara, *Nihon jinushisei*, p. 253.

TABLE 6-12
Mediated Disputes in Yamanashi (per year)

Year	Mediated Disputes	Landlord Request	Tenant Request	Mutual Request	Success	Percent of Success
1926–29	60	15	43	2	35	58%
1930–34	200	61	91	48	152	76
1935–37	399	195	128	75	377	95
1938–40	255	96	110	49	201	79
Total	213	83 (39%)	89 (41%)	41 (19%)	175	82%

Calculated from *Kosaku chōtei nempō*, 1926; *Kosaku nempō*, 1927–1939; *Nōchi nempō*, 1940.

which permitted tenants to play a larger role in local government. Although it is true, as Nakamura Masanori points out, that the authorities also proclaimed a number of repressive ordinances like the Peace Preservation Law when they established universal manhood suffrage in 1925, for two reasons tenants clearly benefited from their new political opportunities in the Shōwa era.[84] The new repressive laws had little impact on tenants. Between 1925 and 1940, only 3,866 people, less than one-third of one percent of all tenant participants in disputes nationwide (again assuming only tenants were arrested and we count no one more than once) were arrested under the terms of the six laws Nakamura singles out; the police charged only 154 of them, 4 percent of the ⅓ percent, under the terms of the infamous Peace Preservation Law. In contentious Yamanashi between 1925 and 1937, the authorities arrested 295 people, 1 percent of tenant participants, under these laws, but none whatsoever under the terms of the Peace Preservation Law. In both jurisdictions, police charged over three-quarters of those arrested with violating the Violence Control Law, an ordinance adopted, not to repress social movements, but to achieve a primary police purpose, the maintenance of public order.[85] These six laws, therefore, do not seem to have been used extensively to crush the tenant movement.

Although these regulations had only a marginal effect on the tenant movement, new political opportunities helped tenants immensely. They sent their representatives to 26-32 percent of all village councils in Japan in 1925-1933; about one-quarter of all rural assemblymen nationwide were tenants; they took control of 340 villages in 1925, 496 in 1929, and 634 in 1933. In Yamanashi, as we have seen, tenants did even better, winning seats on two-thirds or more of all councils, holding about one-third of all seats, and winning in 1925

[84] *Ibid.*

[85] Nagahara, *Nihon jinushisei*, p. 257; *Kosaku chōtei nempō*, 1926; *Kosaku nempō*, 1927-1931; *Shakai undō no jōkyō* 4(1932), pp. 1,258-1,259; 5(1933), pp. 1,237-1,238; 14(1942), pp. 727-729.

a majority of seats on one-quarter of the prefecture's assemblies. And, equally important, electoral success allowed tenants to take control of many hamlets, as in Kubo Nakajima. There is no evidence to indicate that "emperor-system state authority" made any attempt to reverse these election results, force tenant assemblymen to resign, or hinder in any way tenant efforts at local governance. In fact, one bureaucrat wrote in the Home Ministry's magazine, *Shimin*, in 1927, that the increase in tenant assemblymen "stimulated self-awareness and attentiveness among the so-called propertied council members, helped to eliminate past abuses, and gave the tenant farmers increased self-confidence. Thus, we think village government should proceed more smoothly in the future."[86] The tenant's success in using their newly won votes to influence local government far outweighed the limitations placed on their actions by Nakamura's six laws.

Tenants also had some success at electing their representatives to higher legislative levels. In October 1927, Yamanashi voters sent two tenant union candidates, one of whom was eastern Naka Koma's Usui Jirō, to the prefectural assembly. In 1937, Hirano Rikizō, a leader of the large reformist wing of the Kōfu Basin's tenant movement, was elected to the national parliament in Tokyo.[87] The prefectural assemblymen, however, lost their re-election bids in 1931, partly at least because the regional and national union headquarters, by emphasizing radical change rather than short-term benefits for members, alienated tenants. In the words of the Agriculture Ministry's researchers, "the unions have antagonized tenants by preferring to increase the number of victims (to speed a revolution) rather than to work for attainable goals."[88] On the other hand, Hirano was elected in 1937, after several near misses, at least partly because he was a "right-wing" union leader who advocated evolution not rev-

[86] *Shōwa hachinendo*, pp. 18-27; Masumi, *Nihon seitōshiron*, Vol. 5, p. 343.
[87] *Shakai undō no jōkyō*, 9(1937), pp. 863-864; Amemiya, p. 151; *Kosaku nempō*, 1928, p. 357.
[88] *Chihōbetsu*, 1932, p. 279.

olution, and supported the monarchy and the governmental policies likely to be popular with conservative and patriotic farmers. Although the tenants' voice in the Kōfu and Tokyo legislative chambers was small, it was heard for the first time in the early Shōwa era because of the Universal Manhood Suffrage Law of 1925. Neither the police, nor the courts, nor the mediation law, nor the political system, helped the landlords crush the tenant movement; rather, all seem to have helped tenants extend their power vis-à-vis the landlords.

CONCLUSION: THE EFFECT OF TENANT DISPUTES ON KŌFU BASIN VILLAGES

I believe that the tenant movement in Yamanashi succeeded in both the 1920s and 1930s for the very reasons Professor Nishida thinks it succeeded in the 1920s but failed in the 1930s—tenant farmers held petit bourgeois entrepreneurial attitudes. Many of these small businessmen joined tenant unions to improve their living standards by lowering rents and improving contract terms. The tenant unionists sought evolutionary, not revolutionary, change and succeeded in transforming the face of the countryside between 1920 and the early 1940s. As Nishida himself has written, "after 1935, the landlord ownership of land ended its historical life."[89] The tenants' key tactic in bringing this change, as we have seen, was to negotiate collectively with their landlords, often through the government's effective mediation system.

The success of negotiation as a tactic is attested by the outcome of the Kōfu Basin's disputes. As Table 6-13 shows, 98.5 percent of all tenant disputes in Yamanashi ended in either complete tenant victory or compromise. Even during the depression years of 1930-1934, landlords won only 3.2 percent of all disputes (3 per year), their highest percentage of victory in any of the periods reported, but hardly a dramatic level of victory for a class of men who in hard eco-

[89] Nagahara, *Nihon jinushisei*, p. 317.

nomic times allegedly used the powers of government and monopoly capital to squeeze their tenants.

Table 6-13 indicates that in almost all disputes in the Kōfu Basin tenants gained something and landlords lost something. No wonder that the Nezu household's real rent income fell by 65 percent between 1900 and 1933. No wonder that the paddy rent income of Okuyama Genzō, the leading landlord of Kasugai Village in Higashi Yamanashi, fell from 178 *hyō* in 1918-1921 to 123 *hyō* in 1938-1939, a drop of 31 percent, although contract rent remained unchanged at 200.4 *hyō*. No wonder that the Sekimoto, a landlord house in Nishida's Hanabusa Village, collected the same rent from its mulberry orchards in 1940 as in 1931 although sericultural income per unit of land had increased by 6⅔ times.[90] Where did this lost rent income go if not to their tenants?

We have presented in this and earlier chapters considerable evidence supporting the contention that it was tenants who

TABLE 6-13
Outcome of Tenant Disputes in Yamanashi, 1921-1940

Year	Solved Disputes per Year	Tenant Victory	Landlord Victory	Compromise
1921-26	27	4 (14.8%)	0.5 (1.9%)	23 (85%)
1927-29	33	2 (6.1%)	0.3 (0.9%)	31 (94%)
1930-34	95	14 (14.7%)	3 (3.2%)	78 (82%)
1935-37	468	21 (4.5%)	6 (1.3%)	441 (94%)
1938-40	240	10 (4.2%)	2 (0.8%)	228 (95%)
Total	2,871	194 (6.8%)	44 (1.5%)	2,633 (91.7%)

Calculated from *Kosaku chōtei nempō*, 1925-1926; *Kosaku nempō*, 1927-1939; *Nōchi nempō*, 1940.

[90] *Ibid.*, pp. 59, 130, 216, 314. Nishida writes in Nagahara, p. 314, that Sekimoto rent remained the same while the unit price of cocoons increased by 3½ times. In doing so, he overlooks increases in productivity in the 1930s; from 1931 to 1940, the output of cocoons per *tan* of mulberry land increased by 90 percent.

won what landlords lost. We have seen in this chapter cases in which Kōfu Basin tenants received rent reductions varying from 20 percent in the defeat at Hanabusa to 70-100 percent in the victory at Kubo Nakajima. We have also seen how tenants in all disputes nationwide in 1926, 1928, 1931, and 1933 had their rent lessened in compromise by 24 percent, 24 percent, 29 percent, and 31 percent respectively, two-thirds to four-fifths of what they demanded. We have seen in the preceding chapter how tenants in villages adjacent to disputing villages in all Japan received rent abatements two-thirds the size of those received by disputers. The same source indicates that tenants in 8 villages without disputes in Yamanashi in the mid-1920s gained rent reductions of 13.7 percent, 74 percent of the reductions of 18.4 percent won by tenants in 8 disputing villages.[91] And, finally, we have seen in Chapter Two that between 1916-1920 and 1933-1935, average Yamanashi rice rents for all tenant farmers fell by 17 percent for single-crop paddies and 23 percent for double-crop paddies, and that real mulberry money rents sank by 41 percent.

Tenants won not only reductions in rent; they also won permanent methods of determining rent reductions for bad harvests and for falling crop prices. Landlords throughout the Kōfu Basin agreed that if cocoon prices fell below 7 yen per *kan*, tenants would automatically receive a 10 percent reduction in rent for each yen of price lost. If the price dropped under 4 yen, the rent would be reduced by 50 percent, and if under 3 yen, by 60 percent. Landlords in the Kōfu Basin also agreed in the 1930s to give automatically 10-30 percent reductions for slumping rice prices and landlords in grape growing villages allowed 20 percent lower rent when the price of grapes per *kan* fell under 70 *sen*, 30 percent for prices under 60 *sen*, 50 percent under 50 *sen*, and 60 percent under 40 *sen*.[92] Kubo Nakajima farmers, as we have

[91] *Kosaku sōgichi oyobi sono rinsetsuchi ni okeru kosakuryō narabini tochi baibai kakaku no hendō ni kansuru chōsa.*

[92] *Kosaku jijō chōsa*, p. 96.

seen, negotiated with their landlords permanent agreements for rent reductions for bad harvests and falling prices in 1931 for rice paddies and in 1935 for mulberry orchards. Clearly one reason that contract problems replaced rent reductions as a major cause of tenancy disputes in the 1930s is that rent reductions had become routine.

Tenants also won better contract terms during the tenant disputes of the interwar years. We have seen earlier in the chapter that landlords lost far more often than they won when they brought suit to use their own land as they wanted by forcing tenants to return rented land. In fact, in such cases the courts awarded tenants permanent tenancy more often than they allowed landlords to take even part of their land back. Although tenant contracts usually had a clause which read "if the tenant fails to pay his rent at the appointed time, he cannot object if the landlord takes his land back," in practice in Yamanashi in the 1930s a tenant had to default for at least three consecutive years before the courts upheld the landlord's right of private property.[93] By the outbreak of World War II, tenants had more security on their rented land than ever before in modern history.

Tenants demanded and received other important concessions from their landlords in the 1920s and 1930s. Landlords agreed not to charge interest rates for late rent payments. Before the 1920s, they had regarded overdue rent as loans and received 10-15 percent interest per year. Landlords increasingly allowed tenants to change dry and even paddy fields into mulberry orchards, although this alteration led to reductions in rent incomes and endangered the fertility of the fields. Landlords who wanted to sell their land agreed to give tenants first option to buy it under the terms of the Law to Establish Owner Farmers. Tenants could often afford to buy the land not only because the government's program offered low interest loans (3.5 percent before 1937, 3.2 percent after), but also because land values had fallen under the pressure of

---

[93] *Ibid.*, pp. 114-115.

the tenant movement. Investors in the 1930s correctly regarded land as an unstable source of income.[94]

As a result of the disputes, Yamanashi tenants won a longer time period in which to pay their rents. Before World War I, tenants were required to pay by the end of the year; increasingly in the 1920s and 1930s, the payment period was extended to late January, although, since they faced no penalties for late payments, the tenants often did not pay at all. Tenants in Kubo Nakajima paid no paddy rent in 1929; tenants in Ochiai, a village on the plateau of western Naka Koma near Zaikezuka, did not pay mulberry orchard rents for 1928-1930 even after their landlords agreed to a 48 percent reduction in rent.[95]

Tenants also won the freedom to sublet their rented land without seeking landlord permission, to sell their rights of tenancy, and in some places in Yamanashi to use their tenancy rights as loan security. When tenants sublet, they encountered the same problem that landlords faced: how to evict the sublessee when his contract expired. In Ōkamada, a Miyanohara tenant called on the tenant union's youth group to "encourage" a recalcitrant subtenant into giving up a piece of land, and it was after the sublessor's party of thanks in July 1930 that the Emman Incident occurred. When tenants sold their rights of tenancy they received 40-50 percent of the land's value for mulberry and fruit orchards, 30-35 percent for rice paddies, and 15-20 percent for *mugi* fields; these prices reflect the relative profitability of the four types of fields, and demonstrate why tenants wanted to grow mulberry in dry and even paddy fields.[96]

Finally, the nature of contracts changed. Most land contracts in the Kōfu Basin before the tenant dispute decades

[94] Nagahara, *Nihon jinushisei*, p. 473; *Kosaku jijō chōsa*; p. 6. Nishida, "Nōchi kaikaku no rekishiteki seikaku," p. 163; The average real price of arable land was 33 percent lower in Yamanashi and 23 percent lower nationwide in 1934 than in 1919. *Yamanashi nōson jijō chōsasho* (Kōfu, 1935), pp. 27-28.

[95] *Kosaku sōgichi*, pp. 76-92; *Kosaku jijō chōsa*, pp. 101, 110-111.

[96] *Kosaku jijō chōsa*, pp. 141, 149, 153, 164.

had been oral, or written ones of the kind described in Chapter Four; the landlord held the contract and gave the tenant the option of reading it (if he had the nerve or ability) when he came around to "press the stamp" in January. Increasingly in the 1920s and 1930s, when tenants and landlords reached mediation agreements, they signed modern written contracts with copies held by both signatories and by the prefectural Tenancy Officer. The agreements, which established future rents, contract terms, and rent reduction schedules, became a legal part of the landlord-tenant contract.[97]

The establishment of a more equal contract regulated by outside authority, the privilege to sublease, sell the right of tenancy or use that right as loan security, the increase in permanent tenancy, the tenants' prerogative to plant whatever crops they wanted where they wanted, and lower rents—all indicated that a change was taking place in the rural balance of power. By the mid-1930s, landlords and governmental authorities, under the tenants' pressure, recognized what tenants had long averred, that the fields they cultivated were theirs *and* the landlords'. The tenants' improved economic position, together with their new political power won through their use of universal manhood suffrage, made them more nearly the equals of their customary masters, the landlords, than ever before. Contemporary recognition of this new power balance is revealed by the actions of the Yamanashi Electric Railroad Company, which in 1929-1931 paid tenants 35-45 percent of what it paid landlowners when purchasing the railroad's right-of-way in western Naka Koma.[98] One should not, therefore, view the dispute years of 1920-1940, as does Nakamura, or even their second decade, in the 1930s, as does Nishida, as periods of tenant retreat before the combined forces of landlord-monopoly capital-government repression. Rather, one should view the interwar years as a period of tenant advance brought about by the tenants' own petit bourgeois reformist efforts. This epoch stands as a tran-

[97] *Kosaku sōgichi*, p. 76.   [98] *Kosaku sōgichi*, p. 77.

sitional period between the pre-World War I years of tenant subservience and the post-land-reform years of owner farming. "The growing good of the world is partly dependent on unhistoric acts; and that things are not so ill with you and me as they might have been, is half owing to the number who lived faithfully a hidden life, and rest in unvisited tombs"—except in Japan, unlike Middlemarch, the tombs are visited.

CODA

BETWEEN 1870 and 1940, Japanese farmers, building on a foundation of agricultural growth in the Tokugawa era and aided by the Meiji government's stimulative programs, adopted new cultivating and sericultural techniques and steadily increased their profits and thus their capital, which in turn allowed them to invest in even more fruitful techniques. During the nineteenth century, landlords had led the way in these efforts, to the benefit of themselves and their tenants; in the twentieth century, owner tenant, tenant owner, and even tenant farmers joined in. By the 1920s, most tenant cultivators operated as farmers not peasants—like small businessmen they approached farm management with a view to maximizing profits and minimizing risks and no longer needed to concern themselves with the problems of somehow staying above the bare margin of subsistence.

Farmers were able to expand productivity and profits not only because the government created an economic milieu conducive to experimentation and growth, but also because of expanding demand for agricultural products, increasing opportunities for secondary employment, and non-economic developments. European and American demand for raw silk helped sericultural regions like Yamanashi to prosper. Growing domestic demand for food to sustain an increasingly larger non-agricultural urban work force brought higher standards of living to areas like Kinki, which benefited from their proximity to markets and transportation. By providing part-time and full-time jobs for members of farm households, modern industry allowed them to increase their non-agricultural income. Railroads hauled farmers' produce to market and their new tools and commercial fertilizer to their farms, and also carried the farmers themselves to their urban jobs. And the trains, like busses, bicycles, newspapers, urban jobs, and even the army, brought cultivators in contact with the larger world outside their hamlets. The central authorities' gradual liberalization and eventual elimination of tax payment requirements for voting extended the political power of the tenant farmers and after 1925 even allowed them to take control of hamlet and village politics in many parts of Japan. Compulsory education in a new public school system bred literacy and positive attitudes which allowed the rural poor to take advantage of these new opportunities.

In 1870, the typical tenant farmer worked almost entirely at farming and at best found by-employment in proto-industrial handicraft industries. He knew only his own and maybe a few nearby hamlets and walked when he took his products to market. He depended on his literate landlords for information about farming techniques and the outside world, deferred to them in politics, and was left in the dark until the sun would rise. By the 1930s, the tenant took or sent his goods to market by train and truck. He traveled to the city himself to serve in the army, attend regional tenant union meetings, benefit from the services of a hospital, or seek entertainment. At home he could sit under his own electric light at night to read about the new farming techniques he employed during the day. In many hamlets, he and his fellow tenants collectively ran the community and informed the landlords about local governmental policies. Over the three-quarters of a century from the Meiji Restoration to World War II, members of the lower economic strata of rural society increased their wealth and power vis-à-vis their landlords so that they no longer merely reacted to landlord initiatives and hamlet custom. Tenants had become small-scale entrepreneurs who considered their landlords' demands as only one of a number of ingredients to be considered when making decisions about how best to manage their farms and run their lives.

As part of the long process by which peasants became farmers, owner tenant, tenant owner, and tenant farmers between 1917 and 1941 negotiated for and won from their landlords lower rents and better, longer, and freer contract terms. The tenants, like members of labor unions throughout the industrialized world, achieved their goals by using a wide variety of moderate, pragmatic techniques, e.g., unionization, negotiation, compromise, strikes (non-cultivation of the landlord's fields), picketing (demonstrations near the landlord's house), and rare but effective threats to hamlet harmony. Of violence or threats of violence there was almost no sign. The government also helped the tenants by its restraint in using the courts and police to support the landlords and its establishing methods of mediating disputes and helping tenants to buy land inexpensively. At the beginning of these two decades, landlords still held the upper hand in rural Japan; by the outbreak of World War II, their position had deteriorated to the extent that buyers of agricultural land had to reimburse tenants as well as pay the actual landowners. The two interwar decades marked a transitional period from a countryside that had been dominated by landlords to one that, in the wake of the 1948 land reform, was controlled by owner farmers, and it was the tenants' entrepreneurship, hard work, and moderate and pragmatic tactics in confronting their landlords that helped bring about this change.

APPENDIX

Kubo Nakajima Households Mentioned in the Text

1. Ishihara Yasuzō
2. Ishihara Toshiharu
3. Ishihara Ichitarō
4. Ishihara Taizō
5. Ishihara Kanji
6. Ishihara Otokichi and Eizō
7. Takizawa Sadayoshi
8. Ishihara Kōichi
9. Ishihara Kōtarō
10. Hoshino Isokichi
11. Maruyama Yutaka
12. Ishihara Toyokichi
13. Komiyama Yasuichi
14. Ishihara Hisashi
15. Ishihara Chūji
16. Ishihara Yoshinaga
17. Hoshino Kōhei
18. Tanaka Masayoshi
19. Kurosawa—Amemiya Ishizō

BIBLIOGRAPHY OF WORKS CITED

G. C. Allen, *A Short Economic History of Modern Japan* (London: 1972).

Amemiya Yuzuru, *Yamanashi-ken Kubo Nakajima buraku ni okeru nōmin undō no kisoteki kaimei* (A Basic Explication of the Farmers' Movement in Yamanashi Prefecture's Kubo Nakajima Hamlet), Chūō University graduation thesis, mid-1950s.

Andō Seiji, ed., *Yamanashi kan* (The Yamanashi Outlook) (Kōfu: 1894).

Aoki Keiichirō, *Nihon nōmin undōshi* (A History of the Japanese Farmers' Movement), Vol. 4 (Tokyo: 1959).

Araki Moriaki, ed., *Kizokuin tagaku nōzeisha giin gosen jimmeibo* (A Register of Large Taxpayers Eligible to Vote for Members of the House of Peers) (Tokyo: 1970).

Asakura Kōkichi and Tobata Seiichi, *Nōgyō kinyūron* (Treatise on Agricultural Finance) (Tokyo: 1949).

Paul Bairoch, "Agriculture and the Industrial Revolution 1700-1914," Carlo M. Cipolla, ed., *The Fontana Economic History of Europe*, Vol. 3 (Glasgow: 1973).

Richard K. Beardsley et al., *Village Japan* (Chicago: 1959).

Harumi Befu, *Japan: An Anthropological Introduction* (San Francisco: 1971).

R. Albert Berry and William R. Cline, *Agrarian Structure and Productivity in Developing Countries* (Baltimore: 1979).

Ester Boserup, *The Conditions of Agricultural Growth* (Chicago: 1965).

Roger W. Bowen, *Rebellion and Democracy in Meiji Japan: A Study of Commoners in the Popular Rights Movement* (Berkeley: 1980).

L. Keith Brown, *Shinjō: The Chronicle of a Japanese Village* (Pittsburgh: 1979).

Robert E. Cole and Ken'ichi Tominaga, "Japan's Changing Occupational Structure and Its Significance," in Hugh Patrick, ed., *Japanese Industrialization and Its Social Consequences* (Berkeley: 1976).

E. Sidney Crawcour, "The Tokugawa Heritage," in William W.

Lockwood, ed., *The State and Economic Enterprise in Japan* (Princeton: 1965).

Ronald P. Dore, "Agricultural Improvement in Japan: 1870-1900," *Economic Development and Cultural Change*, 9 (1960).

————, *Education in Tokugawa Japan* (London: 1965).

————, "Land Reform and Japan's Economic Development—A Reactionary Thesis," in Teodor Shanin, ed., *Peasants and Peasant Societies* (New York: 1971).

————, "The Legacy of Tokugawa Education," in Marius B. Jansen, ed., *Changing Japanese Attitudes toward Modernization* (Princeton: 1965).

————, *Shinohata* (New York: 1978).

R. P. Dore and Ōuchi Tsutomu, "Rural Origins of Japanese Fascism," in James William Morley, ed., *Dilemmas of Growth in Prewar Japan* (Princeton: 1971).

Eguchi Keiichi et al., *Shimpojium Nihon rekishi: Taishō demokurashii* (Japanese History Symposium: Taishō Democracy) (Tokyo: 1969).

John Embree, *Suyemura: A Japanese Village* (Chicago: 1939).

Penelope Francks, "The Development of New Techniques in Agriculture: The Case of Mechanization of Irrigation in the Saga Plain Area of Japan," *World Development*, 7 (1979).

————, *Technology and Agricultural Development in Pre-war Japan* (New Haven: 1984).

Fujino Shōzaburō et al., *Sen'i kōgyō* (Textiles), *Chōki keizai tōkei* (Long-Term Economic Statistics), Vol. 11 (Tokyo: 1979).

Fujiwara Akira, Imai Seiichi, and Ōe Shinobu, eds., *Kindai Nihonshi no kiso chishiki* (Basic Knowledge of Modern Japanese History) (Tokyo: 1974).

Fukada Hiroshi: Interviews conducted July 3, 1969 and June 17, 1977. Questionnaire completed July 1969.

Fukutake Tadashi, *Japanese Rural Society* (London: 1967).

————, *Nihon nōson no shakaiteki seikaku* (The Social Characteristics of Japanese Farm Villages) (Tokyo: 1949).

————, "Buraku no 'heiwa' to kaikyūteki kinchō" (Village "Peace" and Class Tensions) in *Nihon sonraku no shakai kōzō* (The Social Structure of Japanese Villages) (Tokyo: 1959).

Furushima Toshio, *Kazoku keitai to nōgyō no hattatsu* (The Morphology of Family and Agricultural Development) (Tokyo: 1947).

————, *Kinsei Nihon nōgyō no kōzō* (The Structure of Early Modern Japanese Agriculture) in *Furushima Toshio chosakushū* (A Collection of the Writings of Furushima Toshio), Vol. 3 (Tokyo: 1974).

Peter Gay, *The Dilemma of Democratic Socialism: Eduard Bernstein's Challenge to Marx* (New York: 1952).

Alan H. Gleason, "Economic Growth and Consumption in Japan," in William W. Lockwood, ed., *The State and Economic Enterprise in Japan* (Princeton: 1965).

Gōtō Shin'ichi, *Nihon no kin'yū tōkei* (Japanese Monetary Statistics) (Tokyo: 1970).

Hagiwara Tametsugu, *Suhadaka ni shita Kōshū zaibatsu* (The Kai Province Financial Clique Laid Bare) (Tokyo: 1932).

Hagiwara Yoshihira, ed., *Kai shiryō shūsei* (A Collection of Kai Province Materials), Vol. 11 (Kōfu: 1934).

Mikiso Hane, *Peasants, Rebels, and Outcastes: The Underside of Modern Japan* (New York: 1982).

Susan B. Hanley, "A High Standard of Living in Nineteenth Century Japan: Fact or Fantasy?" *Journal of Economic History*, 43-1 (1983).

Susan B. Hanley and Kozo Yamamura, *Economic and Demographic Change in Preindustrial Japan, 1600-1868* (Princeton: 1977).

R. M. Hartwell, ed., *The Causes of the Industrial Revolution* (London: 1967).

————, "The Rising Standard of Living in England, 1800-1850," *The Economic History Review*, Second Series, 13 (1961).

Hattori Harunori, *Kubo Nakajima buraku ni okeru shakai kōzō to kaisō* (Social Structure and Class in Kubo Nakajima Hamlet), unpublished manuscript from late 1950s.

William B. Hauser, "Some Misconceptions about the Economic History of Tokugawa Japan," *The History Teacher*, 16-4 (1983).

Hayami Akira, "Can Stagnation Create Growth? A Comment," paper presented at Princeton University, May 14, 1982.

Hayami Yūjirō, *A Century of Agricultural Growth in Japan: Its Relevance to Asian Development* (Minneapolis and Tokyo: 1975).

Hayami Yūjirō and Yamada Saburō, "Agricultural Productivity at the Beginning of Industrialization," in Ohkawa Kazushi et al., *Agricultural and Economic Growth: Japan's Experience* (Princeton and Tokyo: 1969-1970).

439

Hirano Yoshitarō, *Nihon shihonshugi shakai no kikō* (The Structure of Capitalistic Society in Japan) (Tokyo: 1934).

E. J. Hobsbawm, "The British Standard of Living, 1790-1850," *The Economic History Review*, Second Series, 10 (1957).

———, "The Standard of Living during the Industrial Revolution: A Discussion," *The Economic History Review*, Second Series, 16 (1963).

Horie Yasuzō, "Entrepreneurship in Meiji Japan," in William W. Lockwood, ed., *The State and Economic Enterprise in Japan* (Princeton: 1965).

Hoshino Atsushi, *Nihon nōgyō hatten no ronri* (The Logic of Japanese Agricultural Development) (Tokyo: 1960).

Inoue Kiyoshi, *Nihon no rekishi* (A History of Japan), Vol. 3 (Tokyo: 1966).

———, *Tennōsei* (The Emperor System) (Tokyo: 1953).

Ishii Kanji, *Nihon sanshigyōshi bunseki* (An Analysis of Japanese Sericultural History) (Tokyo: 1972).

Isogai Masayoshi and Iida Ban'ya, *Yamanashi-ken no rekishi* (The History of Yamanashi Prefecture) (Tokyo: 1973).

Bruce F. Johnston, "The Japanese 'Model' of Agricultural Development: Its Relevance to Developing Nations," in Ohkawa Kazushi et al., *Agricultural and Economic Growth: Japan's Experience* (Princeton and Tokyo: 1969-1970).

Kaku rentaiku kannai minjō fūzoku shisōkai genjō (The Present Situation in People's Living Conditions, Morals and Ideology in Each Regimental District), reports dated December 1913 from 73 of 74 regimental district commanders to Watanabe Jōtarō, aide de camp to Field Marshal Yamagata Aritomo.

Arne Kalland and Jon Pedersen, "Famine and Population in Fukuoka Domain during the Tokugawa Period," *The Journal of Japanese Studies*, 10-1 (1984).

Kase Kazuyoshi, Review Essay of Nakamura, *Kindai Nihon jinushiseishi kenkyū*, *Rekishigaku kenkyū*, 486 (1980).

Katō Yuzuru, "Development of Long-Term Agricultural Credit," in Ohkawa Kazushi et al., *Agricultural and Economic Growth: Japan's Experience* (Princeton and Tokyo: 1969-1970).

———, "Sources of Loanable Funds of Agricultural Credit Institutions in Asia," *Developing Economies*, 10 (1972).

Kawada Shirō, *Nihon shakai seisaku* (Japanese Social Policy) (Tokyo: 1937).

————, *Nōgyō rōdō to kosakusei* (Agricultural Labor and the Tenancy System) (Tokyo: 1923).

Albert Keidel, "Incentive Farming," *China Business Review* (November/December 1983).

Kimbara Samon, "Taishō demokurashii jōkyōka no nōmin kumiai undō no kōzō" (The Structure of the Tenant Union Movement under the Conditions of Taishō Democracy), *Nihon rekishi*, 210, 211.

Kiyokawa Yukihiko, "The Diffusion of New Technologies in the Japanese Sericulture Industry: the Case of the Hybrid Silkworm," *Hitotsubashi Journal of Economics*, 25-1 (1984).

Kōfu kōshinsho, *Yamanashi jinji kōshinroku* (A Directory of Yamanashi People) (Kōfu: 1918, 1928, 1940).

Kokusei chōsa hōkoku (National Census Report), Yamanashi Volume, 1920, 1925, 1930, 1935, 1950.

Kurihara Hakujū, *Gendai Nihon nōgyōron* (A Theory of Contemporary Japanese Agriculture), 2 vols. (Tokyo: 1961).

————, *Nihon nōgyō no kiso kōzō* (The Basic Structure of Japanese Agriculture) (Tokyo: 1948).

————, "Wagakuni ni okeru antei nōkasō no kenkyū" (Studies of the Stable Farm Stratum in Our Country) (Tokyo: 1942).

Kyōchōkai, *Kosaku sōgichi ni okeru nōson jijō no henka* (Changes in Farm Village Conditions in Areas Where Tenant Disputes Occur) (Tokyo: 1934).

————, *Nōka rōdō chōsa hōkoku: Izumi-mura nōka keizai chōsa* (A Report on a Survey of Farm Household Labor: An Economic Survey of Farm Households in Izumi Village) (Tokyo: 1934).

Kyoto daigaku bungakubu, *Nihon kindaishi jiten* (A Dictionary of Japanese Modern History) (Kyoto: 1958).

Lillian M. Li, *China's Silk Trade: Traditional Industry in the Modern World, 1842-1937* (Cambridge: 1981).

Peter H. Lindert and Jeffrey G. Williamson, "English Workers' Living Standards during the Industrial Revolution: A New Look," *The Economic History Review*, Second Series, 36 (1983).

Jung-Chao Liu and Daniel B. Suits, "An Econometric Model of a Rice Market," *Tunghai Journal* (1962).

William W. Lockwood, *The Economic Development of Japan* (Princeton: 1968).

Jesse W. Markham, *Competition in the Rayon Industry* (Cambridge, Massachusetts: 1952).

Masumi Junnosuke, *Nihon seitōshiron* (A Theory of the History of Japanese Political Parties), Vol. 5 (Tokyo: 1979).

Paul Mayet, *Agricultural Insurance* (London: 1893).

———, *Nihon nōmin no hihei oyobi sono kyūjisaku* (The Exhaustion of Japanese Farmers and Policies to Relieve Them in Sakurai Takeo, *Meiji nōgyō ronshū* (A Collection of Essays on Meiji Agriculture) (Tokyo: 1955).

Minami Ryōshin, *Nihon keizai no tenkanten* (The Turning Point of the Japanese Economy) (Tokyo: 1970).

———, ed., *Tetsudō to denryoku* (Railroads and Electric Power), *Chōki keizai tōkei* (Long-Term Economic Statistics), Vol. 12 (Tokyo: 1975).

Mizoguchi Tsunetoshi, "Midaigawa senjōchi hatasaku nōson ni okeru gyōshō katsudō" (Itinerant Merchant Activity in Dry Field Villages of the Midai River Alluvial Delta), *Jimbun chiri*, 28 (1976).

Mochida Keizō, *Beikoku ichiba no tenkai katei* (The Development Process of the Rice Market) (Tokyo: 1970).

Mombudaijin kambō, *Mombushō nempō* (The Education Ministry Yearbook), 1905, 1912.

Mombushō shakai kyōikukyoku, *Sōtei shisō chōsa* (A Survey into the Ideology of Draft Age Young Men) (Tokyo: 1931).

Morioka Kiyomi, *Wagakuni ni okeru shakaiteki seisō oyobi shakaiteki idō to shakai kōzō to no kanren ni tsuite* (Concerning the Relationship between Social Stratification and Mobility and Social Structure in Japan), unpublished manuscript from the late 1950s.

Nagahara Keiji et al., *Nihon jinushisei no kōsei to dankai* (The Structure and Stages of the Japanese Landlord System) (Tokyo: 1972).

Nagai Isaburō, *Japonica Rice: Its Breeding and Culture* (Tokyo: 1959).

Naimushō keihōkyoku, *Shōwa nannenchū ni okeru shakai undō no jōkyō* (The Circumstances of Social Movements in the Shōwa Era), 2 (1930), 4 (1932)-9 (1937), 14 (1942).

Naitō Bunji, *Wakao Ippei den* (A Biography of Wakao Ippei) (Yokohama: 1972).

Naka Koma-gunchi (The Government of Naka Koma County) (Kōfu: 1926).

Naka Koma-gunshi (A History of Naka Koma County), 2 vols. (Kōfu: 1928).

Nakamura Hideo, *Saikin no shakai undō* (Recent Social Movements) (Tokyo: 1929).

James I. Nakamura, *Agricultural Production and the Economic Development of Japan 1873-1922* (Princeton: 1966).

————, "Growth of Japanese Agriculture, 1875-1920," in William W. Lockwood, ed., *The State and Economic Enterprise in Japan* (Princeton: 1965).

Nakamura Masanori, *Kindai Nihon jinushiseishi kenkyū* (Studies in the History of the Modern Japanese Landlord System) (Tokyo: 1979).

————, "Nisshin sengo keieiron" (A Managerial Theory of the Post Sino-Japanese War Period), *Hitotsubashi ronsō*, 64-11 (1970).

————, *Rōdōsha to nōmin* (Laborers and Farmers) (Tokyo: 1976).

————, "Shihonshugi kakuritsuki no kokka kenryoku" (National Authority during the Period of the Establishment of Capitalism), *Rekishigaku kenkyū*, 1970 special supplement.

Nakamura Takafusa, *Economic Growth in the Prewar Period* (New Haven: 1983).

Nakane Chie, *Kinship and Economic Organization in Rural Japan* (New York: 1967).

Ron Napier, "The Transformation of the Japanese Labor Market, 1894-1937," in Tetsuo Najita and J. Victor Koschmann, eds., *Conflict in Modern Japanese History: The Neglected Tradition* (Princeton: 1982).

Nihon sangyōshi taikei (An Outline of the History of Japanese Industry), Vol. 5 (Tokyo: 1961).

Ninomiya Masato and Ishikawa Jinzō, *Meijiki ni okeru Yamanashi-ken nōgyō hattatsushi shiryōshū* (A Collection of Materials on Agricultural Development in Yamanashi Prefecture in the Meiji Period) (Kōfu: 1952).

Nishida Yoshiaki, "Jisakunō sōsetsu iji seisaku no rekishiteki seikaku—nōchi kaikaku no igi to no kanren de" (The Historical Characteristics of the Policy to Establish and Maintain Owner Farming—Its Relationship to the Meaning of the Land Reform) in Hayama Teisaku et al., *Dentōteki keizai shakai no rekishiteki tenkai* (The Historical Development of the Traditional Economic Society) (Tokyo: 1983).

————, "Kosaku sōgi no tenkai to jisakunō sōsetsu iji seisaku" (The Development of Tenant Disputes and the Policy to Establish and Maintain Owner Farming), *Hitotsubashi ronsō*, 60–5 (1967).

———, "Nōchi kaikaku no rekishiteki seikaku" (The Historical Character of the Land Reform), *Rekishigaku kenkyū*, 1973 special supplement.

———, "Nōmin tōsō no tenkai to jinushisei no kōtai" (The Development of Farmer Struggles and the Retreat of the Landlord System), *Rekishigaku kenkyū*, 343 (1968).

———, "Nōmin undō no hatten to jinushisei" (The Development of the Farmers' Movement and the Landlord System) in *Iwanami kōza Nihon rekishi*, Vol. 18 (Tokyo: 1975).

———, "Reisainō kōsei to jinushiteki tochi shoyū" (The Organization of Small Scale Agriculture and the Landlord Ownership of Land), *Hitotsubashi ronsō*, 63–5 (1970).

———, "Shōnō keiei no hatten to kosaku sōgi" (The Development of Petty Farming and Tenant Disputes), *Tochi seido shigaku*, 38 (1968).

———, *Shōwa kyōfuka no nōson shakai undō* (Rural Social Movements during the Shōwa Panic) (Tokyo: 1978).

———, "Shōwa kyōkōki ni okeru nōmin undō no tokushitsu" (The Special Characteristics of the Farmers' Movement during the Shōwa Depression) in Tokyo daigaku shakai kagaku kenkyūjo, *Shōwa kyōkō*, Vol. 1 of *Fashizumuki no kokka to shakai* (State and Society Under Fascism) (Tokyo: 1978).

Nōchi kaikaku kiroku iinkai, *Nōchi kaikaku temmatsu gaiyō* (A Detailed Summary of the Land Reform) (Tokyo: 1951).

Nōchi seido shiryō shūsei hensan iinkai, *Nōchi seido shiryō shūsei* (A Collection of Materials on the Agricultural Land System), Vols. 2 and 3 (Tokyo: 1969).

Nōgyō hattatsushi chōsakai, *Nihon nōgyō hattatsushi* (A History of the Development of Japanese Agriculture), Vol. 4 (Tokyo: 1954); Vol. 7 (Tokyo: 1956).

Nōmin kumiai sōritsu gojūshūnen kinensai jikkō iinkai, *Nōmin kumiai gojūnenshi* (A Fifty Year History of Farmers' Unions) (Tokyo: 1972).

Nōmin undōshi kenkyūkai, *Nihon nōmin undōshi* (A History of the Japanese Farmers' Movement) (Tokyo: 1961, reprinted 1977).

———, *Shōwaki nōmin undō ni tsuite no jakkan no kentō* (Some Studies Concerning the Farmers' Movement in the Shōwa Era) (Tokyo: 1956).

Edward Norbeck, "Common-Interest Associations in Rural Japan," in Robert Smith and Richard K. Beardsley, eds., *Japanese Culture: Its Development and Characteristics* (Chicago: 1972).

Nōrindaijin kambō tōkeika, *Nōrinshō tōkeihyō* (Tokyo: 1925-1940).

Nōrinshō keizai kōseibu, *Nōka keizai chōsa* (Survey of Farm Household Economies) (Tokyo: 1930-1935).

————, *Nōka keizai chōsa hōkoku* (Report of a Survey of Farm Household Economies) (Tokyo: 1936-1938).

Nōrinshō naimukyoku, *Chihōbetsu kosaku sōgi gaiyō* (A Summary of Tenant Disputes by Region) (Tokyo: 1926, 1932, 1934, 1936).

————, *Hiryō yōran* (Fertilizer Handbook) (Tokyo: 1925, 1927, 1929, 1936).

————, *Hompō kosaku kankō* (Tenancy Practices in Japan) (Tokyo: 1926).

————, *Kosaku chōtei nempō* (Tenancy Mediation Annual) (Tokyo: 1925-1926).

————, *Kosaku jijō chōsa* (A Survey of Tenancy Conditions) (Tokyo: 1938).

————, *Kosaku nempō* (Tenancy Annual) (Tokyo: 1927-1939).

————, *Kosaku sōgi oyobi chōtei jirei* (Tenant Disputes and Examples of Mediation) (Tokyo: 1927, 1929, 1930, 1932, 1933, 1934).

————, *Nōchi nempō* (Agricultural Land Annual) (Tokyo: 1940-1941).

————, *Nōka keizai chōsa* (Survey of Farm Household Economies) (Tokyo: 1922-1929)

————, *Shōwa hachinendo chōson kaigi sōsenkyo ni okeru kosakuningawa tōsen no gaikyō* (The General Situation of Those Elected from the Tenant Farmer Side in the 1933 Elections for Village and Town Assemblies) (Tokyo: 1934).

Nōrinshō nōseikyoku, *Nōka keizai chōsa hōkoku* (Report of a Survey of Farm Household Economies) (Tokyo: 1939-1940).

E. Herbert Norman, *Japan's Emergence as a Modern State: Political and Economic Problems of the Meiji Period* (New York: 1940).

Nōshōmushō nōmukyoku, *Nōka keizai chōsa* (Survey of Farm Household Economies) (Tokyo: 1921).

Nōshōmushō sōmukyoku hōkokuka, *Nōshōmu tōkeihyō* (Agriculture and Commerce Statistical Tables) (Tokyo: 1883-1924).

Ogura Sōichi, "Niigata-ken beikoku keizaishi no isshaku—beikoku kensa seido kakuritsu katei o chūshin to shite" (One Scene in the History of Niigata Prefecture's Rice Economy—Focusing on the Process of Establishing the Rice Inspection

System), in *Nihon nōgyō hattatsushi*, Supplementary Volume 2 (Tokyo: 1959).

Ohkawa Kazushi et al., *Bukka* (Prices), *Chōki keizai tōkei* (Long-Term Economic Statistics), Vol. 8 (Tokyo: 1967).

————, "Phases of Agricultural Development and Economic Growth," in Ohkawa Kazushi et al., *Agriculture and Economic Growth: Japan's Experience* (Princeton and Tokyo: 1969-1970).

Ohkawa Kazushi and Shinohara Miyohei with Larry Meissner, *Patterns of Japanese Economic Development: A Quantitative Appraisal* (New Haven: 1979).

Omiyayama Kan'roku, ed., *Yamanashi-ken sanshigyō gaishi* (A History of Yamanashi Prefecture Sericulture) (Kōfu: 1959).

Ono Motobē, *Jikken Onoshiki rosō saibaihō* (The Ono Method of Cultivating Rosō Mulberry) (Yamanashi Prefecture: 1880s).

————, *Kazaana aki sanshi ikuhō* (A Method for Raising Fall Silkworms, the Eggs of which were Stored in Caves) (Yamanashi: 1890s).

Harry T. Oshima, "Meiji Fiscal Policy and Agricultural Progress," in William W. Lockwood, ed., *The State and Economic Enterprise in Japan* (Princeton: 1965).

Ōta Toshie, "Kosakunō kaikyū no keizaiteki shakaiteki jōtai" (The Economic and Social Situation of the Tenant Farmer Class), *Sangyō kumiai*, 261 (1927).

Ōtsuka shigakkai, *Shimpan kyōdoshi jiten* (Revised Dictionary of Local History) (Tokyo: 1969).

Ōuchi Tsutomu, *Nihon ni okeru nōminsō no bunkai* (Differentiation of the Rural Classes in Japan) (Tokyo: 1969).

————, *Nōgyō mondai* (Agricultural Problems) (Tokyo: 1961).

————, *Nōgyōshi* (History of Agriculture) (Tokyo: 1965).

Hugh T. Patrick, "The Economic Muddle of the 1920s," in James William Morley, ed., *Dilemmas of Growth in Prewar Japan* (Princeton: 1971).

Samuel L. Popkin, *The Rational Peasant* (Berkeley: 1979).

Kenneth B. Pyle, *The Making of Modern Japan* (Lexington, Massachusetts: 1978).

Rikugunshō, *Rikugunshō tōkei nenkan* (The Army Ministry Statistical Yearbook) (Tokyo: 1934-1935).

William Roseberry, "Rent, Differentiation, and the Development of Capitalism among Peasants," *American Anthropologist*, 78-1 (1976).

James A. Roumasset, *Rice and Risk: Decision Making among Low-Income Farmers* (Oxford: 1976).

Henry Rosovsky, "Rumbles in the Ricefields: Professor Nakamura vs. the Official Statistics," *Journal of Asian Studies*, 27-2 (1968).

Saitō Toshiaya, ed., *Kyōdoshi ni kagayaku hitobito* (People Who Shine in Local History), Vol. 2 (Kōfu: 1969).

Saitō Yoshihiro, *Kōshū zaibatsu monogatari* (The Story of the Kai Province Financial Clique), Vol. 2 (Kōfu: 1976).

Sakisaka Itsurō, *Nihon shihonshugi no shomondai* (Various Problems of Japanese Capitalism) (Tokyo: 1937, revised in 1947, 1958 and 1976).

James C. Scott, *The Moral Economy of the Peasant: Rebellion and Subsistence in Southeast Asia* (New Haven: 1976).

Domenico Sella, *Crisis and Continuity: The Economy of Spanish Lombardy in the Seventeenth Century* (Cambridge, Massachusetts: 1979).

Shihōshō chōsabu, *Setai chōsa shiryō* (Materials on Household Surveys), Vol. 9 (Tokyo: 1939).

Shimazaki Hironori, *Yamanashi-ken shigunsonshi* (A History of Yamanashi Prefecture Cities, Counties and Villages) (Kōfu: reprint, 1977).

Shinohara Miyohei, "Economic Development and Foreign Trade in Prewar Japan," in C. D. Cowan, ed., *The Economic Development of China and Japan* (Tokyo: 1964).

——— et al., *Kōjin shōhi shishutsu* (Personal Consumption Expenses), *Chōki keizai tōkei* (Long-Term Economic Statistics), Vol. 6 (Tokyo: 1967).

Shiota Shōbē, *Nihon shakai undōshi* (A History of Japanese Social Movements) (Tokyo: 1982).

———, "Tochi to jiyū o motomete: kosaku sōgi" (In Search of Land and Freedom: Tenant Disputes) in *Shōwashi no shunkan* (Moments in Shōwa History), Vol. 1 (Tokyo: 1966).

Shōji Kichinosuke, *Kinsei yōsangyō hattatsushi* (History of the Development of Early Modern Sericulture) (Tokyo: 1964).

Richard J. Smethurst, *A Social Basis for Prewar Japanese Militarism: The Army and the Rural Community* (Berkeley: 1974).

Robert Smith, "The Japanese Rural Community: Norms, Sanctions and Ostracism," in Jack M. Potter, ed., *Peasant Society: A Reader* (Berkeley: 1967).

Thomas C. Smith, *The Agrarian Origins of Modern Japan* (Stanford: 1959).

————, "Farm Family By-employment in Preindustrial Japan," *The Journal of Economic History*, 29-4 (1969).

————, *Political Change and Industrial Development in Japan: Government Enterprise, 1868-1880* (Stanford: 1955).

Kurt Steiner, "Popular Political Participation and Political Development in Japan: the Rural Level," in Robert E. Ward, ed., *Political Development in Modern Japan* (Princeton: 1968).

Suzuki Kunio, "Nōmin undō no hatten to jisakunō sōsetsu" (The Unfolding of the Farmers' Movement and the Establishment of Owner Farmers), *Tochi seido shigaku*, 85 (1979).

Taishō hachinen Naka Koma-gun kenkai giin senkyo yūkensha meibo (A Roster of Eligible Voters in Naka Koma County for the 1919 Prefectural Assembly Election) (n.p., n.d.).

Takahashi Iichirō and Shirakawa Kiyoshi, *Nōchi kaikaku to jinushisei* (The Land Reform and the Landlord System) (Tokyo: 1955).

Takano Gikyō, *Yamanashi sanshi yōkan* (The Essentials of Yamanashi Sericulture) (Kōfu: 1934).

Takano Morizō, Interview in Saijō Village on July 14, 1977.

Takegawa Yoshinori, *Yamanashi nōmin undōshi* (A History of the Yamanashi Farmers' Movement) (Kōfu: 1934).

Teikoku nōkai chōsabu, *Kosaku sōgichi oyobi sono rinsetsuchi ni okeru kosakuryō narabi tochi baibai kakaku no hendō ni kansuru chōsa* (A Survey Concerning Changes in Rent and Land Prices in Areas Where Tenant Disputes Take Place and in Their Neighboring Areas), mimeographed (Tokyo: 1927).

George O. Totten, *The Social Democratic Movement in Prewar Japan* (New Haven: 1966).

Tōyō keizai shimpōsha, *Nihon bōeki seiran* (A Guide to Japanese Trade) (Tokyo: 1935).

Tsuchihashi Riki and Ōmori Yoshinori, *Nihon no minzoku: Yamanashi* (Japanese Folk Customs: Yamanashi) (Tokyo: 1974).

Tsumoyuki chihō nōrin keizai chōsasho, *Shōnai chihō beisaku nōson chōsa* (A Survey of Rice Growing Farm Villages in the Shōnai Region) (Tokyo: 1937).

Arlon Tussing, "The Labor Force in Meiji Economic Growth: A Quantitative Study of Yamanashi Prefecture," in Ohkawa Kazushi et al., *Agriculture and Economic Growth: Japan's Experience* (Princeton and Tokyo: 1969-1970).

Umemura Mataji, *Nōringyō* (Agriculture and Forestry), *Chōki keizai tōkei* (Long-Term Economic Statistics). Vol. 9 (Tokyo: 1966).

Ushiyama Keiji, *Nōminsō bunkai no kōzō, senzenki: Niigata-ken Kambara nōson no bunseki* (The Structure of the Differentiation of the Rural Classes, Prewar: An Analysis of Farm Villages in Niigata Prefecture's Kambara) (Tokyo: 1975).

Stephen Vlastos, *Peasant Protests and Uprisings in Tokugawa Japan* (Berkeley, 1986).

Ann Waswo, "In Search of Equity: Japanese Tenant Unions in the 1920s," in Tetsuo Najita and J. Victor Koschmann, eds., *Conflict in Modern Japanese History: The Neglected Tradition* (Princeton: 1982).

———, *Japanese Landlords: The Decline of a Rural Elite* (Berkeley: 1977).

———, "The Origins of Tenant Unrest," in Bernard S. Silberman and H. D. Harootunian, eds., *Japan in Crisis: Essays on Taishō Democracy* (Princeton: 1974).

———, "The Transformation of Rural Society, 1900-1950," in *Cambridge History of Japan: The Twentieth Century*, Vol 6, forthcoming.

Eric Wolf, *Peasants* (New York: 1966).

Yamada Moritarō, *Nihon nōgyō seisanryoku kōzō* (The Structure of Japanese Agricultural Productive Power) (Tokyo: reprint 1960).

———, *Nihon shihonshugi bunseki* (An Analysis of Japanese Capitalism) (Tokyo: 1934).

Yamamura Kozo, "The Agricultural and Commercial Revolution in Japan," in Paul Uselding, ed., *Research in Economic History*, Vol. 5 (Greenwich, Connecticut: 1980).

———, "The Meiji Land Tax Reform and Its Effects," in Marius B. Jansen and Gilbert Rozman, *eds., Japan in Transition from Tokugawa to Meiji* (Princeton, 1986).

Yamamura Kozo and Miyamoto Matao, "Toward a Quantitative Economic Analysis of the Tenancy Disputes of Interwar Japan: A Preliminary Report," unpublished paper.

Yamanashi jiji shimbun, July 11-12, 1930.

Yamanashi-ken, *Yamanashi kensei gojūnenshi* (A Fifty Year History of Yamanashi Constitutional Government) (Kōfu: 1942).

Yamanashi-ken ishikai, *Yamanashi-ken ishikaishi* (A History of the Yamanashi Prefectural Medical Association) (Kōfu: 1969).

Yamanashi-ken kōseibu, *Yamanashi-ken ni okeru chihōbyō no jittai* (The Actual Conditions of Chihō Disease in Yamanashi Prefecture) (Kōfu: 1974).

"Yamanashi-ken ni okeru jijō" (Tenancy Conditions in Yamanashi

Prefecture), Vol. 11, *Nōsei shiryō* (Materials about the Agricultural System), unpublished materials located in the library of Tokyo University's Social Science Research Institute.

Yamanashi-ken nōson jijō chōsasho (Report of a Survey of the Yamanashi Prefecture Farm Village Situation) (Kōfu: 1935).

Yamanashi-ken shihan gakkō, *Sōgō kyōdo kenkyū* (Comprehensive Local Research) (Kōfu: 1936).

"Yamanashi-kenshi iji eisei shiryō" (Materials on Medicine and Hygiene for the Yamanashi Prefectural History), Vol. 11 (Naka Koma), unpublished materials located in the Local History Room of the Yamanashi Prefectural Library.

Yamanashi meikan (Yamanashi Directory) (Kōfu: 1926).

Yamanashi nichinichi shimbun (Yamanashi Daily Newspaper), July 10-12, 1930.

Yamanashi nichinichi shimbunsha, *Yamanashi hyakka jiten* (The Yamanashi Encyclopedia) (Kōfu: 1972).

Yamanashi sansō jihō (Yamanashi Silkworm and Mulberry News), 149 issues from January 1908 to March 1944, located in the Local History Room of the Yamanashi Prefectural Library.

Yamanashi tōkeisho (Yamanashi Statistical Yearbook), 1883-1940.

Yanagida Kunio, *Nihon nōminshi* (A History of Japanese Farmers), in *Teihon Yanagida Kunioshū* (The Authentic Yanagida Kunio Collection), Vol. 16 (Tokyo: 1962).

Yasuba Yasukichi, "Anatomy of the Debate on Japanese Capitalism," *The Journal of Japanese Studies*, 2 (1975).

————, "Another Look at the Tokugawa Heritage with Special Reference to Social Conditions," Discussion Paper #104, The Center for Southeast Asian Studies, Kyoto University.

Yoshida Teigo, "Mystical Retribution, Spirit Possession, and Social Structure," *Ethnology*, 6 (1967).

INDEX

451

Library of Congress Cataloging-in-Publication Data

Smethurst, Richard J.
Agricultural development and tenancy disputes in
Japan, 1870-1940.

Bibliography: p.
Includes index.
1. Agriculture—Economic aspects—Japan—History.
2. Land tenure—Japan—History.   I. Title.
HD2092.S63 1986   338.1′0952   85-43313
ISBN 0-691-05468-1